Research Foundations for Psychology and the Behavioral Sciences

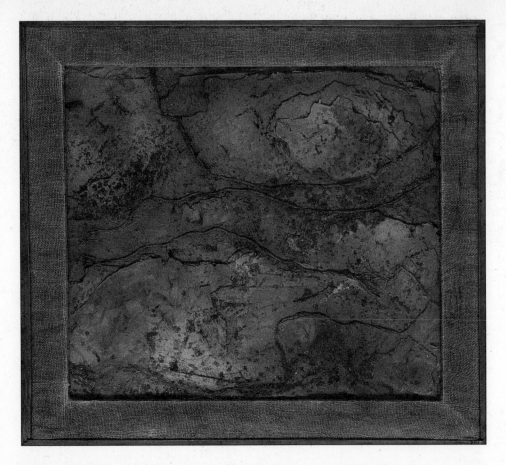

The cover painting, entitled Cavecon I, was created by the author using acrylic paint on corrugated cardboard accented with shredded string and sawdust.

Research Foundations for Psychology and the Behavioral Sciences

FRANK M. LOOS

Northeastern Illinois University

HarperCollins*College*Publishers

Acquisitions Editor/Executive Editor: Catherine Woods
Project Coordination, Text and Cover Design: York Production Services
Cover Photograph: Frank M. Loos
Art Coordination: York Production Services
Electronic Production Manager: Christine Pearson
Electronic Page Makeup: Interactive Composition Corporation
Printer and Binder: R.R. Donnelley & Sons Company
Cover Printer: R.R. Donnelley & Sons Company

For permission to use copyrighted material, grateful acknowledgment is made to the following:

"Sex, Death, and Red Riding Hood." Copyright 1984 Time Inc. Reprinted by permission.

"A Short Course on APA Style for Psychology Students" by John H. Hummel and B. Christiana Birchak. Copyright 1989 by the American Psychological Society. Reprinted with permission from the *APS Observer* newsletter, Sept. 1989.

"Marathon Group: Facilitator of Personal Growth?" by James F. Guinan and Melvin L. Foulds, Bowling Green State University. Copyright 1970 by the American Psychological Association. Reprinted by permission.

Research Foundations for Psychology and the Behavioral Sciences

Library of Congress Cataloging-in-Publication Data

Loos, Frank M.
      Research foundations for psychology and the behavioral sciences / Frank M. Loos.
             p.   cm.
      Includes bibliographical references and index.
      ISBN 0-673-99481-3
      1. Psychology—Research—Methodology.   I. Title.
BF76.5.L68 1995
150'.72—dc20   94-31484
                                                CIP

94 95 96 97 9 8 7 6 5 4 3 2 1

To Mary, who was there in the beginning of the Sunflower heat, through the Brixton winters, and has stuck it out till now.

And special bones for two pals, little Coquette and little Bentley, who slept through many dull and walkless hours of typing.

Contents

Preface

Leaving for a vacation, the first date with a new friend, starting a new job, the initial class meeting in a tough course, or reading the preface in a new text—all produce mixed feelings. The beginning session of a required research methods course is not an event everyone looks forward to with happy anticipation. This book was written with those students in mind who feel a little uneasy about what they might be getting into. I hope this text will help every reader to discover what a great many people have known for a long time. The study of research methods is actually quite interesting, and the material is not nearly so difficult as tradition suggests.

Psychology and other behavioral sciences emphasize research, so statistics and experimental techniques are often required in their disciplines. No one, I think, expects to turn a nonscientist into a scientist in one term, but there are more limited objectives which I believe can be achieved.

We can learn the vocabulary and procedures of scientific investigation, how to do research, and why it is done in certain prescribed ways. By the end of this text readers will understand how to design and carry out good research that will lead to solid conclusions we can depend on. This understanding will be of value to those who go on for advanced degrees.

Even those who have no plans for research will find the material useful. As they learn to interpret research findings they will become more critical judges of the quality of research done by others. We are so overwhelmed with research findings these days, every educated person should be able to figure out "what is rot and what is not."

I have tried to present material in a way that will help to make it meaningful to students who approach it with any of three different levels of skills. Students who have already had a course in elementary statistics will have an opportunity to put that information to good use. I have integrated many statistical ideas in the material where it is appropriate, so students who are studying statistics concurrently with the research methods course will appreciate the synthesis. Readers who have not studied any statistics will nevertheless be able to understand the logic of research methods and the rationale for a statistical evaluation of data. Computing information for several useful statistics is given in detail. A working knowledge of algebra is all that is required.

If I were a professor of English literature who had to choose whether to study 15 of Shakespeare's plays superficially or to study 5 of his plays thoroughly, I would chose the 5-play approach. I believe a beginning course should teach *how to study a subject*. Method is more important than content. People who have learned to enjoy Shakespeare's plays and how to read them will go on to read many of his other plays on their own. I think the function of education is to train people to become lifetime learners.

Instead of an inadequate overview of a large number of topics, I have chosen to provide a fuller coverage of subjects I consider to be foundation material of the discipline. As an example of this, I will devote a great deal more attention to measurement than is common in beginning texts. I think that what we measure and how we measure it are very important in behavioral science research. Although the research material does not lend itself to structure, I have done what I can to organize it into a logical sequence that makes it easier to follow.

I want to call particular attention to several features that make this research methods text different from the many available alternatives.

Meaningful examples and illustrations are important for highlighting concepts and ideas. Although that might be done in a sentence or two, I have expanded a number of stories well beyond that limit, simply because I think they are interesting and I believe many readers will agree with me. I must be true to the complexity of the content, but I have worked very hard to emphasize the *reasons* rather than just presenting facts.

Although I enjoy science and take it seriously, I see no contradiction between humor and science. I have tried to write a science book that is not too stuffy. Any humorous-sounding bits that readers run across were probably intentional. I have even gone so far as to express a personal opinion occasionally, as a person talking with another might.

Several forms of teaching aids are important to my presentation. Many study questions are given at the end of most chapters. Some of the questions help to review the material and are specific to it. Anyone who can fully answer all relevant study questions will almost certainly get high test grades. Other questions are included to stimulate discussion. Some questions might not even be answerable, but that is what makes them interesting. Where the material is appropriate, certain chapters have special projects or assignments that implement the material just studied.

Endnotes introduce additional material that I think illustrates the subject matter in the chapters, but which could not be included directly in the text without markedly interfering with the flow of the discussion. My objective has been to broaden and expand the study of psychology by hinting at the diversity of its topics.

I have brought one other feature to this text that will not long go unnoticed. In the Small Talk diversions, I have created a new type of joke/cartoon combination. These range rather widely in content from comments on legitimate topics relevant to psychology to conversations that might have occurred among college people. College students and faculty will quickly identify familiar themes in some of them. As with all humorous materials, if they have to be explained they will not be funny. Readers who recognize themselves in a particular situation should get a smile. Several technical ideas about I.Q. or cross-modality scaling, for example, are meant for readers with a broader background in psychology. And the several with the Latin phrases—well, why not stretch a little! Every class has someone who remembers these stock phrases from high school Latin class.

Many versions of various chapters have been examined by more than two dozen very critical reviewers. Their numerous comments, suggestions, and corrections—with occasional praise and encouragement—have made the text much better than it could possibly have been without their help. As they read this text they will see their contributions and note how often I have used their ideas. I am especially grateful to the half-dozen reviewers who sent lengthy and detailed evaluations. The reviewers include:

Mary Anne Baker, Indiana University Southeast
W. Robert Batsell, Jr., Southern Methodist University
Gail Bruder, State University of New York, Buffalo
Mark K. Covey, Concordia College
George M. Diekhoff, Midwestern State University
William F. Ford, Bucks County Community College
Paula Goolkasian, University of North Carolina, Charlotte
Robert J. Grissom, San Francisco State University
Richard Haude, University of Akron
Maria McLean, Thomas More College
Linda Mealey, St. John's University
Carol Perrino, Morgan State University
John Pfister, Dartmouth College
Patricia Phillips, Illinois State University
Sylvia von Kluge, Eastern Michigan University
Benjamin Wallace, Cleveland State University
Allen Wallach, Illinois Institute of Technology
Patrick S. Williams, University of Houston.

In addition, I would like to express my appreciation for the fine Smalltalk cartoon artwork done by the illustration team at Dartmouth Publishing, Inc. The Smalltalk creations are one of the unusual features of this text. I gave them the script and some general ideas, which they turned into cartoons that carry the tone of whimsy that I wanted, while maintaining the character of the message. I am delighted that they several times worked in original and creative ideas of their own that I am sure will add to the reader's enjoyment. The pun in the title of a book carried by a spectral manifestation (*Ghost Writing*) in one of the Smalltalk cartoons is strictly theirs—but I wish I had thought of it.

I also want to recognize the significant contributions by Suzanne Ivester, my copyeditor. Her practiced pen picked up the participles that I had unknowingly left dangling. She put in commas that I had left out, took out commas that I had put in—and showed me that dashes can be useful. She questioned ambiguities and then rewrote passages to clarify and simplify them. In a myriad of ways, many of which I do not even understand, she respelled and regrammared until the manuscript finally obtained her imprimatur. Everyone who studies this text should be grateful to her, as I am, for her work in making it better and more readable.

The work of Tracey Topper at York Production Services will be evident throughout the book. As Production Coordinator on this project, she used her personal psychological skills to make suggestions or to achieve a consensus among sometimes disparate points of view. Her experience and technical knowledge brought the work of many people together to transform my typescript into a printed book, that, like the clothing of a well-dressed person, will be appreciated without being obvious.

For inspiration, Benton J. Underwood has more than earned my thanks and the appreciation of several generations of psychologists with his *Experimental Psychology*. His text stands out as the definitive scholarly work on this topic. Readers of my text will see how often I have turned to Underwood for important ideas.

I want particularly to thank Hans J. Eysenck for his instructive guidance during my Ph.D. work at the University of London. He set the example and gave me the opportunity to learn about research in psychology—by doing it.

SMALL TALK

PART ONE

Psychology as a Science

Chapter
1

Research Procedures
From a Beginner's Point
of View

Some difficulties we face in determining the laws of behavior.

He was born with a gift for laughter and a sense that the world was mad.

Opening sentence from Rafael Sabatini. (1921). *Scaramouche.*
New York: Houghton-Mifflin.

Nearly everyone seems to have an interest in psychology. Many of you who are beginning this text might admit that your chemistry, biology, or calculus is not as good as it should be. Not all readers will have a solid background in literature or the arts—but psychology is different. Readers of this text have probably already had several courses in psychology, and they are certainly interested in the subject, but that interest does not necessarily extend to its scientific study.

Early in our lives we became aware of the creatures around us, and we soon discovered many differences among them. All of us have wondered why people behave in different ways. Our attempts to accommodate the complex and sometimes conflicting demands of our family, friends, and "society" force us to study psychology to better understand ourselves and other people.

Unfortunately, our nonscientific ways of studying psychology are not likely to produce results that are useful over the long term. This statement is not meant to suggest that untrained people can never make observations and draw good conclusions from them. There are many examples in the history of psychology, in literature, and in our own experience to show that solid psychological judgments are sometimes obtained in nonscientific ways, but generally the odds are against this happening. Unsystematic, anecdotal evidence is by its very nature imprecise and undependable.

People who approach the study of psychology purely out of personal interest sometimes do not understand why psychologists place so much importance on what is popularly called the "scientific method" as a source of psychological information. These casual observers point out that people who act as if they know what they are talking about provide reasonable information that seems to work. Why is that not good enough? The answer is, we cannot rely on conclusions from nonscientific investigations being right. We cannot always rely on scientific investigations either, but the procedures of science are designed to recommend conclusions that are as close to an accurate understanding of psychological processes as we can get. Even the best scientific endeavors will not guarantee that a particular result is exactly right, but it should be closer than if other methods had been used.

Scientific explanations are always subject to change, reevaluation, and sometimes outright rejection as new information is discovered or new interpretations are formulated. Science is a continuing process. New findings can and often do cause a total reconsideration of ideas previously accepted as true. Nothing in science is fixed and unchanging. A thoughtful person will rarely, and then only with great caution, use an expression such as, "Science has proved that. . . ."

Listing ways in which mistakes happen in our everyday reasoning processes is as easy, and as difficult, as cataloging the ways in which we can go wrong in other areas of our lives. It is easy because examples are so numerous and difficult because selections must be made from an abundance of examples that are interesting. This chapter will take a cursory look at a few of the many nonscientific ways we all use for obtaining psychological information. Research methods applicable to psychology will be more meaningful and more interesting when they are studied against the background of what people are already doing. By starting from where we are, we will be better able to appreciate where we are going.

Newspaper, magazines articles, and books of the sort identified as "popular psychology" provide many examples of faulty reasoning. The professional literature should be, and usually is, much less prone to error than the mistakes we see in popular presentations. The very large number of people who write in the professional journals, their diverse interests and orientations, and their varying skills as scientific investigators do not necessarily produce dependable scientific conclusions. Psychologists who are interested in discovering the general laws of behavior will tend toward the rigorously scientific end of a continuum, whereas those who are trying to explain behavior of a single person in a particular situation will tend to gravitate toward the less scientifically demanding end. In the next chapter we will identify these different perspectives as *nomothetic* and *idiographic* orientations.

College teachers are usually careful in their professional writing, so we will not find many examples of the following logical errors there. But in conversation (sad to say!) our human failings will become obvious. Listen carefully to our unguarded discussions and you will discover that we make the same sorts of mistakes as everyone else makes—although perhaps (we would like to think) not so often. If there were greater agreement among professional psychologists about what is right, or even what is best, we would not fight so much among ourselves. Psychology is a still a young and developing area. Study topics are so numerous that no one person is going to know very much except in his or her own area of specialization.

This book was written to help beginners learn methods and procedures that we can generally depend on to provide useful results, although the complex nature of psychology will often make it difficult to obtain solid conclusions. Despite the limitations of research methods, investigators have made a great deal of progress in helping us to understand behavior. If we keep on with what we have been doing and possibly get a little better at it, we will no doubt learn a great deal more.

SOME DIFFICULTIES WE FACE IN DETERMINING THE LAWS OF BEHAVIOR

Behavior Is Complex

Popular psychology operates on the assumption that behavior can be explained easily, often in a sentence or two. Our acceptance of simple explanations for complex behavior is exemplified by our lack of surprise at statements such as the following, "You want to know why John behaves that way? I'll tell you why he behaves that way." And 15 seconds later we have an explanation.

In one of her columns Ann Landers described a dream about a naked man who went into a stylish restaurant on Wilshire Boulevard. The hostess offered the naked man a necktie because she couldn't seat a man without one in the fashionable restaurant. Ann Landers asked her readers for an explanation of the dream and received more than 11,000 responses. She published 11 of them, each of which contrasted markedly with the others. If any one of the interpretations were true, the others could not also be true. The many explanations did have one characteristic in common—each of the writers seemed to think that his or hers was the correct one!

Our quick and easy explanations often would be shown to be inaccurate if anyone took the time or trouble to check them. One way to get around the difficulty is to qualify our statements. Many people who are in need of psychological guidance and help have turned to books such as one written by Robin Norwood, *Women Who Love Too Much* (1986). This is just one book among dozens (possibly hundreds) that are available to help people understand practical psychology. In various ways Norwood's popular book makes a point that some women are too attracted to men; they cannot stop going after them even when they get hurt. Norwood has concluded that these women probably came from dysfunctional homes in which their own early needs were not met. They might have been subject to actual abuse or perhaps just to constant quiet tension of the sort that children keenly feel. Perhaps parents actively competed for the child's affection. The parents themselves might have been so emotionally disturbed that they had very little loving energy left for the children. Whatever the specific problem was for a particular child, it is clear that her own fundamental emotional needs probably were not satisfied.

Two points should be noted. First, observe the large number of "some," "probably," "might," or "perhaps" words that are typical in popular explanations. Other words having a similar function would include "usually," "often," "typically," or "generally," and these in no way complete the list. Second, most popular explanations (rightly or wrongly—and this is a topic for study in itself) attempt to explain adult behavior in terms of childhood experiences. More on that point later.

The tenuous nature of psychological explanations results in part from the fact that even an apparently simple act is likely to be the result of many interacting conditions: how a person judges the situation, learned reactions to it, the individual's personality (with all of the attributes that this term includes), the biochemical state of the organism at the time, and many other things. It is not just the number of possibly relevant conditions that causes the difficulty, although this is certainly a concern. Not only is any single act of behavior the result of many factors, only a few of which are known or understood, but they can interact with each other in complex ways that are not necessarily the same for all individuals.

A good reason for research is to help us understand how the world works. Given a set of circumstances, we would like to be able to predict, with reasonable accuracy, a particular outcome. We want to be able to measure characteristics that will help us to say what will happen in a specified situation. That is not generally possible now.

Psychology's "Past" Obsession

Most, perhaps all, explanations of behavior are "after the fact." This means that after we have made a behavioral observation we try to explain why it happened.

Beginners, following the tradition in popular writing, try to explain behavior in terms of historical antecedents. A person behaves this way now because of something that happened to him or her at some past time, often in childhood. We should consider several reasons why historical explanations of present behavior are of little value for helping us fully understand it.

A person might state that an adolescent is having trouble learning to read "because he was hit on the head with a baseball bat when he was 7 years old." This "explanation" is no explanation at all. *The science of psychology requires that present behavior be explained by forces and conditions in effect at the present time.* Many people who have been hit on the head with bats do not have reading problems. Destruction of tissue in certain areas of the brain is one, but only one, of many possible explanations for difficulties with reading. Scientific explanations, if they are to have any value, should identify *present* characteristics that are operating *now*.

Explanations of behavior that include reference to early childhood experience are so common in popular writing that one might think they are required. A book reviewer once commented on the large number of books about movie stars that were written to relate shocking, previously untold tales about the personal behavior of people who have quite a different public image. In one example he called attention to the posthumous biography of Grace Kelly, ". . . that revealed her to have been a troubled, alcoholic and compulsively promiscuous woman who sought in the beds of older men the love denied her by her father." One must question whether the complexities of a lifetime of human experience can be summarized satisfactorily and fully explained in a single phrase. As a scientist, I do not know of any way that I can show the statement to be false; and because I cannot show that it is wrong, I have no way to determine whether or not it is true. This idea will be developed fully in a later chapter.

In regard to the huge number of behavioral explanations drawn from early experience (as opposed to later learning, the biological nature of the person, trauma, disease, illness, or other causes), it should be noted that some psychologists question whether adult behavior is forever fixed by childhood experiences. Readers interested in a different point of view may want to read *Early Experience: Myth and Evidence* by Clarke and Clarke (1976), or a more readily available source of information in "The Myth of the Vulnerable Child" (Skolnick 1978).

Fischhoff's (1975) consideration of after-the-fact explanations led to a series of experiments that demonstrated "Hindsight ≠ Foresight." "Making sense out of what one is told about the past seems so natural and effortless a response that one may be unaware that outcome knowledge has had an effect at all on him." Persons who have knowledge of an outcome tend to select prior events that aim in the expected direction, but they are "largely unaware of the effect that outcome knowledge had on their perceptions." Readers of a mystery story who are told at the beginning who committed the murder will study the clues differently from the way in which they would have done it if they had no knowledge of the ending and had to evaluate clues as the story developed. A progressive analysis of evidence will make a previously known outcome seem inevitable. When we do not know what to expect—which is the situation when we make predictions—the logical unfolding of events will not be nearly so clear.

Inappropriate Selection of Evidence

Our own observations are often our primary source of information about behavior. We have little else to go on, so statements such as, "It seems to me...,"

"Based on my experience. . . ," and "I have always found. . . ," are common in conversation. Professionals and nonprofessionals alike often rely on personal experience or unsupported statements from others as the sole source of evidence for their ideas. Anecdotal examples are not a strong foundation for the development of psychological truths.

Any reader can discover easily how readily we see and remember examples of behavior that support our preconceived ideas. Start with an idea like this one: "Heavily bearded men drive clunker cars." A typical person making informal observations with this idea firmly in mind will probably have his or her attention directed to, and will more readily recall examples of, old cars and bearded drivers. Bearded men driving nice cars will tend to be overlooked, as will women who drive old, beat-up cars. Without counting the type of driver and car condition of *every* driver, male and female, in many different locations and at different times, there is no way to know whether the supposition has the support of evidence. Doubtless we would observe different patterns in other parts of the country, urban or rural dissimilarities, and even distinctions between neighborhoods of the same city.

The point is, personal experience will be at best a limited source of information. What we observe in a situation is in part determined by what we are looking for, as guided by our interests, what is familiar, our attitudes, how we felt at the time, and even our subconscious motivations.

Observers are not always objective in what they see or remember. When we are faced with a large number of stimuli we are forced to be selective in our attention. The psychological states listed above, and others, selectively direct attention toward observations that strengthen already established notions, whereas sizable amounts of negative evidence can be disregarded or forgotten. Casual observation is likely to emphasize *affirming instances*—i.e., those that confirm our already established point of view. The human predilection for remembering supporting evidence while overlooking contradictory examples is so pervasive that few of us can avoid the influence.

Personal experience imposes another restriction on the use of our own observations to bolster psychological ideas. In all but the rarest cases, our sample of the world's population is very small indeed. We have family, friends, worshippers at the religious institution of our choice, associates at work or school, neighbors, sports or hobby co-enthusiasts, and who else?

The practice of using limited observations to draw general conclusions has long been identified in logic as "hasty generalization." Although the word *hasty* suggests speed, that is not the issue. Statements made about a large group based on evidence from a small, possibly highly selected sample, are examples of this error in reasoning.

Whenever someone says something to the effect that, "All men are the same. . . " or "Women are like this. . . ," ask the speaker if the intention is to include "all men" or "all women." When it has been established that only "some" is intended, clarify whether "some" means "most," "nearly all," or only "a few." This unrelenting pursuit of accuracy will result in feeble and sterile expressions such as these, "A couple of the men I have observed. . . " or "This woman I once knew. . ."—hardly the significant assertions necessary for identifying laws of behavior. Be warned: The rigorous application of the scientific method ruins conversations, and it is not an effective way to win friends!

This tendency for people to draw general conclusions when only a small sample from the whole has been examined is very widespread indeed. Little, Wilson, and Moore (1955) suggested reasons why this propensity to hasty generalization is so common.

1. Our sense of the dramatic makes us prefer sweeping statements to cautious ones.
2. Our prejudices encourage us to choose or accept instances that are not typical.
3. It is more convenient and involves less effort to examine a few instances rather than many.

We study samples to learn what we can about a population because it is usually impossible to study populations directly. If a sample is to be of any value it must accurately represent its parent population. Incorrect conclusions that result from inappropriate sampling procedures have rarely been better illustrated than in the following example.

At one time the general effect of menopause on women was summarized in this way:

> It can cause depression, fatigue, and decreased interest in sex; and sometimes even an alteration in personality occurs. These physical changes identify the end of a woman's reproductive life. We might also observe serious psychological difficulties at this time.

The preceding symptoms have characterized a common understanding of what happens to many, though certainly not all, menopausal women. The description sounds so authoritative that hardly anyone has questioned it. Reasonable-sounding conclusions from presumably reliable sources are likely to go unchallenged, even by those of us who ought to know better. In this example the conclusions were obtained from a very biased sample of women. The description came from physicians who dealt mainly with women suffering from physical and psychological difficulties such as those described above, and the health picture of menopausal women was thereby badly distorted.

Had a large population of women been randomly selected in an appropriate manner and studied systematically, a different picture would have emerged. When Sonja M. McKinlay, whose research was discussed in an article by Eastman (1988) in the AARP News Bulletin, studied a representative sample of 2,300 middle-aged women, she found that "less than 17 percent expressed any strongly negative feelings toward menopause. . . . The overwhelming message is that biological events of menopause have almost no effect on health—physical or mental."

In many instances, as in the above example, faulty sampling that led to erroneous conclusions was unintentional. In conversation, two words typically signal the selection of evidence: "for example." The presentation of examples is perhaps the most widely employed of all the ways we have of justifying our conclusions. The technique is not exactly cheating, but it is very close.

"Students today can't read at all. Take Abcde for example. . . ." This type of introduction usually leads to a description and analysis of Abcde's reading difficulties. The point is, the student selected is rarely a typical student. The example is chosen to show the extremes of behavior the speaker wants to emphasize. The speaker wants an unthinking listener to make the transition from, "Here is a student who can't read well," to "There aren't any students who read well." The appropriate response is to ask for additional information. What proportion of all the students are like this one?

A colleague once published a short article in our college paper to illustrate the effects that names can have on people. He selected examples to show the influence of names on: (1) character and behavior, (2) the choice of a profession, and (3) the choice of a love object. The evidence consisted entirely of highly selected examples. A certain Mr. Freeze was "extremely cold and unemotional in behavior." Bird is the name of a person who keeps a pet shop. Ezra, which the author states means "virgin," is the name of a lady who "emphatically denounces marriage and avows to remain a virgin."

This is a game anyone can play. In a small town where I once lived I recall that Lenz and Lenz were optometrists, Klink was the state's attorney, and Mr. Fire was a—well, you guess.

By a careful selection of evidence a person can demonstrate almost any proposition. A magazine article in *Time* (1978, November 13, p. 112) discussed the thinking of Alan Dundes, an anthropologist on the faculty of the University of California at Berkeley. Dundes was making a case for football as a homosexual ceremony. "Football is a ritualized form of homosexual rape. The winners feminize the losers by getting into their end zone." As evidence, he showed that the football jargon is erotic: "score," "down," "piling on" (gang rape), "sacking" the quarterback (plunder and rape). "Players try to knock opponents down, putting them in the 'supine, feminine position.'" The three-point stance of football players was seen as a form of sexual presentation. The article contains many other observations of a similar nature.

How should a scientist respond to this? It is not good enough to say the idea is ridiculous and obviously not true, because it might be true. We cannot determine truth by whether we like it or not. Errors in reasoning or research must be identified if the conclusions are to be rejected. Note how football terms that do not fit the hypothesis were not mentioned, and the meanings of the words selected were highly distorted to make them fit the idea being studied. The potential of words to have different meanings does not afford us the Alice-in-Wonderland freedom to alter definitions until words come to mean anything we like.[1]

---

[1] Although *Alice in Wonderland* is the more familiar source of Lewis Carroll quotations, the one that would fit best here is *Through the Looking Glass*. "The question is," said Alice, "whether you *can* make words mean so many different things." "The question is," said Humpty Dumpty, "which is to be master—that's all."

Familiar Sayings, Reasoning by Analogy, and Cliché Thinking

Proverbs, slogans, quotations, and familiar expressions add color to everyday speech and impart the authority of tradition in support of commonly accepted ideas. Concise statements sound convincing in their easily remembered, often rhyming, simplicity. They can, however, be an obstacle in the search for truth because they are already accepted to be true. They are so much a part of our foundation of beliefs that it requires a special effort to question them. Proverbs can be a very useful way to enliven our writing; particularly so because they are often available in alternate forms. We can pick whichever one better suits our purpose.

A penny saved is a penny earned; or, penny wise and dollar foolish.

Fools rush in where angels fear to tread; or, he who hesitates is lost.

Out of sight, out of mind; or, absence makes the heart grow fonder.

The less-well-known alternative to the last one should be, "Absence does to love what wind does to a fire. It extinguishes the small ones, but it makes the big ones burn the brighter."

Anyone who thinks a consideration of proverbs reduces the study of psychology to a trivial level should read how Wright (in Barker, Konnin, & Wright, 1943, chap. 22, p. 379) dealt with the subject. His research is interesting in the history of psychology because it tried to develop ideas of "Topological" psychology that had been proposed by Lewin (1935) and Leeper (1943). Wright explained that "A barrier is defined here as a part of the *region* of the life space that resists locomotion through it in the direction of the goal. According to this definition a barrier and a goal are inseparably related."

> The point of departure for the investigation was a notion met frequently in nonscientific literature. A familiar version of it is the proverb: "grass is always greener on the other side of the fence." The following restatement of this proposition is the central hypothesis of the study. *An obstructed goal has a stronger positive valence than an alternative accessible goal.*

The hypothesis was studied in a simple but ingenious way. Wright created a situation in which he was able to draw conclusions about why people tend to take an object, a piece of pie in his study, from the back of the counter rather than a more easily accessible piece near the front. No, the idea that pieces at the back are the freshest was not an appropriate explanation in the situation he arranged.

The conclusions of this project are much too complicated for a full discussion here, but for interested readers I will identify one of them.

> A comparison of the results for (the second set of conditions) and the (original conditions) points to the conclusion that, within limits, at least, the degree in which the valence of an obstructed goal exceeds the valence of an accessible goal increases with

an increase in the strength of the barrier. . . . The outcome (of the second series) suggests that the hypothesis is not demonstrable when the strength of the barrier is increased beyond a certain point.

In simple terms, and with reference to the grass in the other field being greener, this was the conclusion: The desirability of the grass in the other field will increase approximately in proportion to the height of the fence separating the two fields, until the fence gets too tall, at which point interest in the other field will drop off markedly.[2]

Analogous reasoning is another technique people sometimes use instead of evidence to support a point of view. Reasoning by analogy wants us to accept the idea that if two sets of observations are alike in some ways, they will be alike in others. This process also presumes that inferences drawn from one example will be equally valid when applied to another.

Evidence supplied in the form of analogy can sometimes be useful for improving understanding of a difficult theoretical concept, but reasoning by analogy has a serious fault. The logic rests on the notion that examples that are alike in some respects are *necessarily* alike in others. "If the similarities are merely apparent and not real, if they are real but superficial, or if they are real but sharply limited in number, we have little ground for insisting that similarities exist" (Little, Wilson, and Moore, 1955).

Not so much reasoning by analogy, but thinking by analogy is probably more widespread than one might suppose. "I was so angry I could burst," is an example. "I was so uptight I had to do something to release the pressure." Psychology often uses behavior to characterize aspects of personality or psychological states. A down-sloping line in handwriting is considered indicative of depression; an upward sloping line means elation. The study of body positions and their psychological meaning—body language—makes much of the presumed relationship. One must be constantly on the alert to be sure that proposed relationships between observations are not just fortuitous.

Cliché thinking is reasoning by slogans, and it does not involve much thinking. When ideas have popular support it is difficult to argue against them, because people with strongly held opinions are not willing to listen to alternative ideas. The use of simple, catchy phrases has become very important in presidential campaigns. Picture images that show a few seconds of activity selected to make an impression are a major component in the process of electing people for political offices. The group that can best manage the images and slogans is the one more likely to win.

---

[2] For my part, I wonder if the proverb is not meant to point out that many things look better at a distance than they do up close, or possibly that something we do not know well will seem to have fewer undesirable characteristics than something with which we have had a long familiarity.

Appeal to Authorities

Appealing to authorities for final answers in psychology is a little like trying to guess the correct time from several clocks, each of which shows a different time. For a humorous example of what happens when "experts" get together to discuss their opinions, read the article by John Leo on "Fairy Tales and Society," which follows. When so-called experts disagree so strongly, it is impossible for them all to be right, so we must keep the possibility in mind that they might all be wrong.

BEHAVIOR
Sex, Death and Red Riding Hood[3]
By: John Leo (Time, 1984, March 19, "Behavior," p. 68)

Academics Squabble Amid a Clash of Symbols

Once upon a time, a little girl was told by her mother to take some bread and milk to her grandmother. The child was wearing a small red cap, given to her in the 17th century, when she was already hundreds of years old. The cap could have been a symbol of menstruation or a sign of witchcraft and evil. Or maybe it was just a plain hat.

In the forest, she met a wolf and told him her destination. Big mistake. The wolf got to grandmother's first, devoured or killed the old woman, and either did or did not serve pieces of the body to the girl. The wolf ordered the girl to strip and throw her clothes on the fire, to the clear displeasure of the Brothers Grimm, who were not about to put a striptease into one of their uplifting 19th century tales. The wolf then ate the girl, which is the end of the story, unless a hunter shot the wolf with an arrow, or cut its belly open, allowing the girl and her granny to escape.

Nearly everyone agrees that the story *Little Red Riding Hood* is an evocative tale of sex and violence, but exactly what it evokes is a matter of dispute among folklorists, anthropologists, Freudians, feminists and literary critics. The wolf, for instance, has been variously interpreted as the id, the pleasure principle, the predatory male, the phallus, an outlaw, a demon, the animal in all of us, and the inherent dangerousness of a cruel world.

Such theories were bandied about by 100 zealous intellectuals at a conference on "Fairy Tales and Society" held earlier this month at Princeton University. They considered everything from the role of the simpleton to the psychological makeup of Scheherazade. *Red Riding Hood* drew a good deal of attention; the feminist version of the story seemed ascendant, and the Freudian view in decline. Jack Zipes, a Marxist professor of German at the University of Wisconsin, Milwaukee, charged that male writers had taken an oral tale of a "shrewd, brave, tough and independent" girl and turned it into "a narrative about rape in which the heroine is obliged to bear the responsibility for sexual violation."

Specialists have agreed that French Author Charles Perrault in 1697, and later Germany's Grimm brothers, touched up the gory peasant narrative to make it more appealing to upper-class readers. Perrault, Zipes charged, portrayed the girl as negligent and naive, and added the hood, or red hat, during his time a symbol of sin and the devil. Zipes, author of the book *The Trials and Tribulations of Little Red Riding Hood*, said the Grimms made matters worse by having the mother warn the girl not to stray from the path, thus setting up the subsequent rape as the girl's own fault. The transformed story, said Zipes, carries a sexist message: sex is dangerous for women, women deserve what they get, and only a strong male (the hunter) can rescue foolish girls from their lustful desires.

Other experts took a different view. Princeton Historian Robert Darnton, who was not at the conference, challenged Zipes on a key point. Zipes had asserted that the girl got away from the wolf in the oral tale by saying she had to go outside and relieve herself. That version does exist, said Darnton, but the mainstream one, told for many hundreds of years, ends with the wolf eating the girl. It is, he said, a nonsexist and terrifying tale with a simple message: don't wander outside the village because both life and strangers are cruel.

Zipes and Darnton believe that the Freudians are woefully wrong, that they somberly analyze symbols that never existed in the original story. Psychoanalyst Erich Fromm, for example, in his 1951 book *The Forgotten Language*, says the story's symbolism can be understood "without difficulty": the red cap represents menstruation, the mother's warning to Riding Hood not to drop a bottle refers to the danger of losing her virginity, and the view of sex as a cannibalistic act performed by ruthless males is "an expression of hate and prejudice against men." Psychoanalyst Bruno Bettleheim offers a more sophisticated interpretation in his 1976 book *The Uses of Enchantment*. He says the wolf, who talks the girl into frittering away her time picking flowers, represents both id and pleasure principle. The tale concerns budding sexuality and oedipal longings to overthrow the mother (the devoured granny) and marry a father figure (the hunter).

Princeton English Professor Ulrich Knoepflmacher attacked Zipes, saying, "He brings out a lot, but somehow throws it all into the same pot: Marxism, sociology, Freudianism." Anthony Vidler, a professor of architecture at Princeton, attempted a small joke, saying that the real problem in the tale was a design flaw: the weak lock on grandmother's door.

Gerhard Mueller, of the Rutgers school of criminal justice, made his expected point that *Little Red Riding Hood*, like most fairy tales, is a story about law. "In preliterate society, this is a means of letting people know what's right and wrong, and how to fall in line," Mueller said. The first bishop of the Goths in the 4th century, he said, could find no term in his language for an offender who had committed a capital crime and so used the words "declare to be a wolf." Thus the wolf became the outlaw who had to die.

All the emphasis on sex and death proved too much for some in the audience at Princeton's McCormick Hall. Said a grandmother: "I'm startled. I read these stories to my grandchildren." She has little cause to worry. Academics will always pick at the tales and hunt for meaning. Some will inevitably impose their own ideologies. But the magic of the stories has withstood the centuries, and will survive analysis too.

An insightful reader of this article thought it was interesting, but he went on to say that it just demonstrated that if one gets a group of academic people together with no data, they will talk a lot of rubbish. To illustrate that point is precisely the reason for including the article here. When authorities are brought together in a group we can easily see the contradictions in what they have to say. But readers do not ordinarily have the opportunity to make comparisons of this sort. We might have material from only one or two people. The research traditions in psychology do not require that we submit information in opposition to our ideas, so often the only evidence provided is that which has been selected to support our propositions.

Suppose we checked our college library for information on psychological interpretation of fairy tales. Unless the library were a large one, the only book we would be likely to find on the subject would be Bettleheim's *The Uses of Enchantment*. Bettleheim is widely published, with 15 books to his credit, and his work is often quoted. Our college library has two copies of *The Uses of Enchantment*, both of which appear to have been well used. The marked passages in different inks and pencils suggest the book has been the source of quotable material for many term papers. If not for the contradictions so clearly discussed in the above article, we would likely accept that Bettleheim knew what he was talking about.

Everyone must, from time to time, refer to authorities for ideas and information. We all have difficulty adequately evaluating the competence of the various experts we might have to consult in our work, so it is particularly important in the beginning to recognize that not all authorities are created equal. The most widely published one is not always the best, anymore than a widely advertised product is necessarily the best product. The following discussion lists a few ideas that might be of help in making a wise judgment.

A competent authority will always present *evidence* in support of conclusions. The implicit suggestion to "trust me" should drive away a reasonable reader. The credible authority will demonstrate that he or she has considered different and contradictory information and will give reasons for accepting or rejecting it.

It is sometimes suggested that we can be confident our ideas are firmly based if several "authorities" or "experts" agree on the findings or interpretations. The history of science provides no hope for this easy solution. Many examples are available from all fields of study that show large numbers of experts can be wrong.

It is important for a science to have a means of externally validating its basic concepts and propositions. Physicians usually can determine if their diagnoses and treatments of illnesses were correct. Attorneys can evaluate their competence and judgments by the number of cases they win. Economists can evaluate the accuracy of their predictions. If a psychologist explains a type of behavior by referring to an antecedent cause, how do we know for certain that she or he picked the right one among many that could have been proposed? When a psychologist tells a parent, "This is why your teenaged daughter is acting that way. . . ," how do we know the explanation is *the* correct one and not just *an* explanation that seems to fit?

Psychological explanations of behavior have been called "Just So Stories" after the title of Rudyard Kipling's delightful children's book (first published in

1902). The book tells a number of short, simple, fanciful tales about the beginnings of things: how the whale got his throat, how the camel got his hump, how the leopard got his spots, and many others. In each instance the explanation could be true but of course is not. The title was taken to label a very important and very basic idea: *An explanation of behavior is not necessarily **the correct** explanation.* Just so stories emphasize the importance of a critical and constantly questioning attitude toward scientific explanations. How should we set about to determine for sure which psychological explanations are right and which are wrong? What should we do with explanations that seem to be right some of the time but not all of the time? These are questions that much of the remainder of this book will try to answer.

Several other ways for making mistakes in reasoning will be discussed in different parts of the text as the material becomes relevant to the research method being considered.

SUMMARY OF COMMON FALLACIES IN PSYCHOLOGICAL INVESTIGATION

The following list presents a few of the many errors untrained observers sometimes make as they try to identify causes of behavior.

Behavior is complex. Simplistic explanations are not likely to be sufficient.

Present behavior is inadequately explained by sole reliance on past events. Explanations based entirely on identification of historical antecedents do not identify relevant conditions in effect at the present time. After-the-fact explanations are difficult to test.

Personal observations are usually not random, and they are generally limited in size. What we look for and what we remember tend to be guided by our hypotheses, interests, prejudices, and prior experience. Any evidence collected in a nonsystematic way will be selective and unlikely to represent adequately all possible examples. Limiting the selection of evidence to affirming instances permits support of almost any hypothesis. Few of us, as individuals, have access to large samples that are characteristic of the population of interest.

Familiar sayings, reasoning by analogy, and cliché thinking are misleading. These are all assertions that assume that generally accepted observations are right and can therefore be used as evidence to support a point of view.

Reliance on opinion of authorities does not guarantee accuracy. Authoritative judgments should be evaluated with the same level of critical analysis applied to any other evidence.

*A cause is not necessarily **the** cause.* Identification of one possible cause does not preclude the possibility that there are others. The same behavior can result from many different causes, and alternately, the same cause might produce different effects. Essentially similar causes can produce different types of behavior.

LOOKING AHEAD

The text has been divided into five parts to formally distinguish its structure.

Part 1: Psychology as a Science

Part 2: Measurement

Part 3: Nonexperimental Research Techniques

Part 4: Experiments in Psychology

Part 5: Putting Research to Work

These sections can be even more broadly organized into:

Foundation Material (parts 1 and 2)

Application (parts 3 and 4)

Interpretation (part 5).

Chapter 2 develops ideas that will lead to an understanding of how the so-called scientific method is applied to research in the behavioral sciences. It will also introduce topics on how to begin the collection of references that will be used in research projects. Readers who will do a research project as part of their course requirements should begin a literature search right away. The information given here will help them get started. Others who do not have this requirement can skip this material.

Chapter 3, on the logic of research, is an important chapter, and it is possibly the most difficult. The study of logic is never easy, especially when limited space precludes a complete exposition of the ideas.

Chapter 3 also introduces the "hypothetico-deductive" method. This is expanded into an outline of a standard research sequence from the development of a suitable hypothesis through the analysis of resulting data. A discussion of hypothetical syllogisms explains why the best research is organized to demonstrate that the ideas being tested are *not* true. Science is not good at proving ideas are right, but it can, if properly used, show that they are wrong. Note how this line of reasoning is opposite in direction to the way we would normally expect.

Hypotheses, the poured-concrete foundation of research, are fully discussed, just as their importance to science requires. We need to learn what they are, how they are used, and how to make good ones.

How we define terms and concepts in the behavioral sciences is an important area also discussed in chapter 3. Operational definitions are for me one of the most interesting ideas in the logic of science. They are developed to help answer questions of this sort: "How do I know that (this test) really does measure what the author says it does?" "How do I know that my idea of anxiety is the same as John's?" The common, everyday dictionary definitions of concepts studied in science are of no use in research. This discussion shows how science gets around the difficulty.

Even though I presented only a summary of fundamental measurement ideas, they produced so much material it was necessary to spread the discussions of it over two chapters. This is a much greater body of material on measurement than is typically found in a beginning text and results from my belief that without good measurement we cannot achieve good science.

The remainder of the text develops applications for scientific investigation using two basic, but quite different, research techniques: correlations and experiments.

When it comes time for a statistical evaluation of data, I have always felt it is useful to have a formula and a review of computational procedures available in the text I am using. A reader who has had a course in statistics should find my presentation a handy reference, but I have tried to provide enough information so that even a person who has not had a statistics course can use it.

I evaluated several variations of experimental designs in terms of their advantages and disadvantages. Simple factorial designs are studied, even though they are complicated for a beginning text. Research people are identifying more situations in which this interesting statistic might be applicable.

Within-subjects (sometimes just "within-S") designs are briefly discussed in a separate chapter. This is a technique that has special applications to particular types of research. Several unique difficulties are studied in relation to this method, and their consideration offers an opportunity to expand understanding of psychological variables into different areas. This chapter is short, so it provides a reasonable location for inclusion of material involving naturalistic observation as a research technique.

A final chapter, titled "Getting Professional," mentions many topics that a person needs to know when undertaking research. People who are planning to do advanced-level work in psychology will find information on professional organizations they might like to join. A discussion of ethical principles in research will identify restrictions on the use of human subjects and the care and treatment of animals used in research. As far as we know, fraud is not a major concern in psychological research, but the topic is discussed briefly to call attention to it.

I have included study questions for chapters where I think they might be useful. The questions partly summarize the material of the chapter and in that way outline it for review. Most of the questions relate to factual ideas, but a few "thought" or "discussion" questions have been included. These do not necessarily have answers that will be found in the text, but they may call attention to controversial points and stimulate thinking about a particular subject.

I have put a "D" by questions that are primarily for discussion. Questions that are not identified will generally—although not necessarily always—have answers given in the text. The ambiguity arises partly from the fact that some questions will be answered by instructors in lectures rather than in the text. Certain topics were identified for discussion because they are controversial, or because, for other reasons, they cannot be easily answered. Although I might have answered a question one way in the text, this certainly does not preclude the possibility that other, better answers may be given.

ENDNOTE

Following is a brief excerpt from a very well-known author. The inclusion is to illustrate ways in which interesting ideas can be developed from everyday observations. But it also shows that without subjecting them to a research analysis we cannot be sure the conclusions are justified.

> At a certain time twice a day for six years, I was accustomed to wait for admission before a door in the second story of the same house, and during this long period of time, it happened twice (within a short interval) that I climbed a story higher. On the first of these occasions, I was in an ambitious day-dream, which allowed me to "mount always higher and higher." In fact, at that time, I heard the door in question open as I put my foot on the first step of the third flight. On the other occasion, I again went too far, "engrossed in thought." As soon as I became aware of it, I turned back and sought to snatch the dominating phantasy; I found that I was irritated over a criticism of my works, in which the reproach was made that I "always went too far," which I replaced by the less respectful expression, "climbed too high."

The psychological interpretation of physical acts, to explain them and to give them meaning, is such a common form of explanation in psychology that the practice is scarcely noticed. It is, however, an ongoing task for psychologists to demonstrate, over and over again as each new situation requires, that external behavioral displays are indeed directly related in predictable ways to internal states.

Second, note how the excerpt *explained observations which had already taken place*. First the behavior, then the explanation of it. One purpose of science is to discover the fundamental bases for behavior in order to make predictions. How valuable are explanations after the fact? A valid psychological analysis of this example should demonstrate a consistent relationship between physical directions, such as up or down, and psychological states, such as "irritation" resulting from "going too far" in a publication.

Could we predict that a person, preoccupied with an "ambitious day-dream" that encourages him to "mount always higher and higher," would fail to stop at the second floor, where he meant to stop? It should be noted that according to the author, the same behavior resulted from two quite different causes. In this example, they even appear to entail contradictory feelings; the first instance involved an "ambitious day-dream," which might reasonably be considered a pleasant feeling, and the second instance appeared to result from an unpleasant feeling identified as an irritation resulting from criticism. The fact that the same behavior can be explained in several, often contradictory ways, emphasizes our difficulty in trying to understand it.

This excerpt is from Sigmund Freud's second book, *Zur Psychopathologie des Alltagslebens* (*The Psychopathology of Everyday Life*) originally published in 1904. Over three-quarters of a century has elapsed, but the tone of the explanation sounds modern. In addition to the example used here, from the chapter on "Erroneously carried-out actions," the book includes many other topics of interest: forgetting proper names, childhood and concealed memories, mistakes in reading and writing, and of course there is the chapter concerned with "mistakes in speech," which has enriched the English language with the "Freudian slip" expression.

Everyone has experienced those seemingly accidental twists of the tongue that let words trip out when they were close to, but not quite, what was intended. Occasionally the shifts of meaning can be amusing. I once worked at a college which, for a hundred years, had been connected with a religious organization. As time passed it became an affiliation in name only, but the college president regularly mentioned it at commencement. One year the pro forma message became something special as the president stated, "There has always been a warm blond between the College and the Presbyterian Church."

Freud called attention to these speech aberrations and explained them through presumed connections with hidden motives. By listening carefully one will, in time, find a verbal misstatement that seems to have resulted from an unrevealed logical mechanism, but the rest can be explained more easily by other processes without recourse to a hypothetical subconscious. Recently there has been renewed interest in research on this topic at the Department of Rhetoric and Communication of the University of California—Davis, for example. A readily available reference is Motley (1987), who wrote in *Psychology Today*. His conclusion was that slips in speech are sometimes, but not always, related to predisposing conditions.

STUDY QUESTIONS

1.D When and how did you consciously become aware that you were seriously interested in the study of psychology?

What do you think led you in this direction?

2.D Explain the procedures you have used in deciding why a close friend or relative behaves in a certain way.

What evidence can you propose to demonstrate that your ideas are correct?

What alternate explanations are possible for the same behavior?

3.   What is "pop" psychology?

4.   Why should we turn to the scientific study of psychology rather than using the procedures untrained people typically use?

5.   Why is the study of behavior so difficult?

6.D Assume that many popular explanations of behavior are probably wrong. Why is there not more criticism of the field of psychology?

7.   Why are so many qualifying words used in psychological explanations?

8.D If a car is not working, we look for malfunctioning parts or systems. Explanations of behavior sometimes look for causes in earlier events rather than studying the characteristics of the person at the present time. Why is that?

9.   What is wrong with simple explanations of behavior? They seem to work well enough in a general way.

10.   What was Fischhoff's major objection to the use of historical explanations for present behavior?

11.   What is wrong with personal observation and anecdotes as sources of information?

12.   What does it mean to say that "casual observation is likely to emphasize affirming instances?"

13.   What is the logical fallacy of "hasty generalization," and why is it such a commonly committed one?

14.   How might inappropriate sampling affect conclusions about the larger group the sample was selected to study? (This topic will be discussed later at greater length.)

15.D Give an example from your own experience in which a careful selection of evidence was used to support a particular point of view.

16.D How might proverbs be used as psychological evidence?
Argue the point that any idea that has been around for a long time must have some truth behind it.

17.   What is reasoning by analogy and what is wrong with it?

18.   What is cliché thinking, and how is it used to justify a point of view?

19.   How can we select an authority with reasonable confidence that he or she will provide information we can depend on?

20.   What is a "just so story" as the idea is applied to psychological explanations of behavior?

SMALL TALK

Chapter
2

Introduction to the Scientific Study of Psychology

Alas, alas, this is the fate of almost every single one of us amateur mathematicians almost every single time. Anything we work out that is true is not new; anything that we work out that is new, is not true.

Isaac Asimov. *The Left Hand of the Electron.*

A LITTLE INFORMATION ON THE PHILOSOPHY OF SCIENCE

Much of psychological "knowledge" is based on experience and observation, which chapter 1 has demonstrated is a weak source of reliable information. In order to improve the level of our confidence in the information obtained from observations it has been necessary to establish a set of procedures that are subsumed under the general title, "The Scientific Method." Science cannot prove that propositions are true, but it can suggest reasonable probabilities that they are true. In psychology's rush to become more scientific there seems to have been a movement to begin the study of psychology farther up the trunk of the tree of knowledge and away from its roots in philosophy and the study of logic and epistemology. (Epistemology is a study of various aspects of the nature of knowledge: its origins, methods for studying it, and its limits.) Although we can study research methods and principles without knowing very much about the philosophy of science, I believe it is a mistake to do so. This chapter will try to hint at—*suggest* would be too strong a word—a few of the ideas that I think will add depth to our sometimes too-superficial understanding of how to do research. Good research involves more than a checklist of steps that we can tick off after we have done each item.

A philosophy teacher of my acquaintance who knew of my interest in the philosophy of science passed along a book for my consideration. It is simply named "Human Knowledge: Classical & Contemporary Approaches," (Moser & vander Nat, 1987). The book consists of excerpts from the writings of 32 philosophers who have written about epistemology. The "Classical Sources" part begins with the study of the Greek philosophers Plato, Aristotle, and Sextus Empiricus, and continues through medieval to modern, and various other sources of ideas on epistemology. "Part II: Contemporary Sources," concludes with "Psychological Approaches," a section that considers four authors who have made contributions to the study of epistemology. The two authors most frequently quoted in psychology texts for their writings on the philosophical foundations of modern research methods as they apply to psychology, Popper (1979) and Kuhn (1970), were not included, nor was Newton-Smith (1981), who more recently wrote on the *The Rationality of Science.* Although these authors wrote about the philosophy of science, they were not so much concerned with epistemology.

Moser and vander Nat (1987) posed the following questions as typical ones of interest to epistemologists. "Does all human knowledge originate in sensation or perception, or does some of it originate independently of our sensory experience? In short, *how* do we know anything? *Can* we have knowledge? If so, *does* anyone actually have it? Further, is all human knowledge restricted to what is currently perceived? Can we have knowledge of the past, the future, or the unperceived present?"

Moser and vander Nat carefully explained the difference between knowledge and belief, and in the process they pointed out that, "knowledge requires belief, but belief does not require knowledge." One can know the earth is round without believing it, but "it is also apparent that people sometimes believe things which they do not know to be so, or which are even false."

The first of the two alternate views of beliefs they examined suggests that beliefs are "*dispositions to behave in a certain way*, and nothing more. . . . Our actions are, at least in general terms, fairly predictable. . . . If beliefs are dispositions to act, then one would expect beliefs to be the motivating forces of our actions. And typically they are."

The study of philosophy forces us to go beyond obvious conclusions that appear to work. The preceding paragraph seems reasonable. We might well be inclined to accept it, but Moser and vander Nat continued, "The view that beliefs are dispositions to act faces a serious difficulty. Indeed, it fails precisely on a point that made it seem so attractive, namely, that we can thereby account for our actions." Although beliefs might "account for the *origin* of our actions (we act because we are so disposed), but it does not provide the *reasons* for our actions." The contrast between partial and complete explanations is an important idea that we will have difficulty overlooking.

This discussion of beliefs and other topics of importance to psychological research, such as the distinction between knowledge and truth, would continue for many pages if it were to be brought to a meaningful conclusion. The intent here was to stimulate interest and to encourage readers to look further into epistemology in order to improve awareness of philosophical topics that are fundamental to the understanding of research in psychology.

Before the philosophical foundations of modern research procedures could be developed in their present forms, early philosophers had to reject several sources of knowledge: subjective feelings, intuition, supernatural revelation, authoritarianism, and mysticism are examples. Careful observations repeatedly demonstrated that conclusions from these sources did not agree with characteristics of the physical environment that were known and understood in other ways. Astronomy has provided countless generations of students with a major example. It *feels right* that the sun should move around the earth. It *makes sense* that planets should move in circular orbits. Careful measurements that were not affected by ideas of what should be disclosed that the earth travels around the sun and planets move in elliptical rather than circular orbits.

Chapter 1 discussed some inadequacies of authorities as guides to what is true. Modern science began when people stopped allowing their opinions to be determined by the authority of an institution, ancient writings, or even by a person. If we want to know if an idea is true, we ask for the evidence. "No matter how venerable the teacher may be, it is both the right and the duty of the learner to weigh the evidence for himself, and to come to an independent decision. Truth is to be discovered by reason" (Dotterer, 1924).

Philosophers make a distinction between two different kinds of knowledge, *empirical* (or *a posteriori*) and *a priori*. Empiricism is a point of view that says we should depend on careful observation and measurement to obtain knowledge we can rely on. Empiricism is sometimes compared to and is often confused with *empiricism*, which Wertheimer (1970, p. 19) defines as a "philosophical assumption" that suggests ". . . all human knowledge comes from experience, that no knowledge is innate." If we can by reasoning alone draw valid conclusions from a theory, our knowledge is a priori because it was obtained independent of experience.

Knowledge of physical relationships is an example of empirical knowledge, and knowledge of logical and mathematical truths is a paradigm of a priori knowledge. Seventeenth century developments in mathematics and discoveries about the natural world encouraged philosophers to advance the use of reason, or "rationalism" as the school of thought has come to be called, to be the standard by which knowledge is judged. Mathematics particularly was the best example of clear and correct thinking. The formal structure of mathematics offered many opportunities for proving propositions. An organized system of principles and "truths" should, the philosophers felt, make it possible to obtain accurate information about the world through the logical processes of reason alone.

The concept of pure reasoning, which permits drawing a conclusion without having had previous experience with possible outcomes, is so foreign to thinking in the behavioral and natural sciences that we have to turn to mathematics for an example. This brief diversion into trigonometry is intended to illustrate how the same conclusions can be reached through reason or experience. Mathematical proofs do not depend on evidence derived from experience. They are examples of rationalism in its purest form.

See Figure 2.1 for the following discussion. The figure shows a "right triangle," one that has a right (90°) angle.

I remember wondering as a child how much shorter it was to take a short-cut across a neighbor's vacant corner lot (directly from point A to C) than to stay on the sidewalk and go from A to B, then turn and go from B to C. I had no way to measure the distances on the lot itself, but I thought I could get an idea of what was happening by drawing lines on a sheet of paper. I found that no matter what lengths of lines I chose for the sides, the sum of lines a(AB) and b(BC) was always greater than the length of line c(AC). I had obtained a strictly empirical conclusion which seemed to be dependable. I tried out the basic idea a number of times and I always got the same result. I had no idea whatsoever that there might be a dependable mathematical relationship among the lines that would make it possible to predict the exact length of any one line for given lengths of the other two lines.

The relevant theorem was worked out by Pythagoras, a Greek mathematician who lived about 500 B.C. The illustration is likely to be well known to anyone who has studied trigonometry. The theorem can be easily *demonstrated,* but *proof* is considerably more difficult. Despite the difficulty, many clever and ingenious mathematical proofs of the theorem have been proposed. I have read that the number approaches 200.

The Pythagorean theorem states that the sum of the squares of the lengths of the two shorter sides is equal to the square of the length of the hypotenuse (the longer side opposite the 90° angle). It is usually expressed in this way: $a^2 + b^2 = c^2$.

We could test the theorem by drawing square boxes on lines of various lengths and counting the number of squares we can draw on them. Using lines of 3 inches and 4 inches for the sides, and we would find that exactly 25 squares could be drawn on the 5-inch hypotenuse. After we get the same result from a large number of trials we conclude that we have discovered a basic characteristic regarding how the world works. This form of reasoning is called "empiricism"; experience rather than reason is taken as evidence in support of truth. In this example we can empirically—i.e., by experience—arrive at essentially the same conclusions that mathematicians can reach directly through reason. But keep in mind that *mathematical conclusions (proofs) are more trustworthy and are therefore superior to those obtained from experience only.*

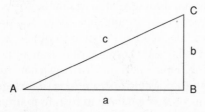

FIGURE 2.1

Rationalism in science in the pure form described above is an almost unattainable goal. Mathematical analyses, given a set of principles, permit conclusions to be drawn a priori, independent of experience. The history of science does not produce many examples in which the development of a theory as a mathematical model preceded observations that would have suggested it, but there is one recent example which is interesting. Hawking's discussion of "black holes" in *A Brief History of Time* (1988) nicely illustrates how theoretical physicists have been able to push speculation beyond their ability to make direct observations that would verify their predictions. Black holes were first "discovered" through reasoning, then the search began for empirical verification. Near the end of May 1994, photographs from the Hubble telescope gave astronomers the information they were looking for. See the Endnote for additional information.

Empiricism involves speculation about the *origins* of knowledge. It does not provide the *standards* for judging knowledge. That is the role of rationalism. A person can be an empiricist when answering one question and a rationalist when answering another. A person who denies "innate ideas" is an empiricist if he or she also maintains that all knowledge should come from experience. As regards the test of knowledge one would be a rationalist when viewing knowledge in terms of the connections, agreements and disagreements, or contradiction among a set of ideas. Modern scientists are generally rationalists in the doctrine they employ for the assessment of truth, and they are empiricists regarding its source.

Readers of beginning texts probably will not want to know more than this about these subtle philosophical distinctions, and I might agree with some readers who think we know too much already! Medawar[1] (1984), a modern philosopher, provides a summarizing comment:

> I am a rationalist—something of a period piece nowadays, I admit—but I am usually reluctant to declare myself to be so because of the widespread misunderstanding or neglect of the distinction that must always be drawn in philosophic discussion between the *sufficient* and the *necessary*.[2] I do not believe—indeed, I deem it a comic blunder to believe—that the exercise of reason is *sufficient* to explain our condition and where necessary to remedy it, but I do believe that the exercise of reason is at all times unconditionally *necessary* and that we disregard it at our peril.

PSYCHOLOGY AND METHODS OF SCIENCE

A person new to the structured study of psychology might suggest that psychology can never be a science because of the intangible nature of many of the attributes psychology studies: feelings, emotion, personality, intelligence, attitudes, memory, and many others. Extrasensory perception and the generally accepted

---

[1] Medawar, with Macfarlane Burnet, won the 1960 Nobel Prize in Physiology and Medicine for research in transplanting human organs.

[2] The use of the words "necessary" and "sufficient" in this way will be fully explained later in this chapter.

phenomenon of the subconscious are areas sometimes identified to illustrate the intangible nature of psychology's subject matter.

The difficulties we face as we consider research in psychology are enough to cause some of us to wish we had become interested in other fields, physics perhaps. But a glance at physics confirms that its topics are about as intangible as those in psychology. Look at a few of them: speed, acceleration, electricity, space, magnetism, gravity, and x-rays. Are these any more solid than attitudes, feelings of affection, or processes of learning? The distinction between what is science and what is not science cannot be made from an analysis of the physical reality of its content. We must not confuse the content of science with its methodology.

One might think that "measurement" is an area in which the physical sciences might have an advantage over psychology, but when we examine measurement examples in physics, we behavioral scientists can note numerous concepts that would require extremes of cleverness to accomplish satisfactory measurement: the speed of light, mass of electrons, time, energy, and the pull of gravity. I hesitate even to mention the measurements required for the quantification of quarks, pions, muons, mesons, and other subatomic particles (whatever they are!). I challenge anyone who thinks that physical science measurement is relatively simple compared to measurement problems in psychology to develop and calibrate three measuring devices, other than with the common glass-tube thermometer, for showing changes in temperature. It is not an easy assignment. Even though current measurement in psychology is not very good, it is workable and it promises to get better. Measurement is an important foundation for any science, so quite a lot of space in this text will be devoted to studying it.

Whether or not psychology is a science depends on the extent to which *psychology uses the methods of science.* It is not what one studies, but how one studies it that defines a science.

Behavioral scientists generally subscribe to a list of principles such as the following. The points will be developed and more fully explained in later discussions.

1. All psychological events can be explained by natural rather than supernatural causes.
2. Only appropriately obtained empirical *evidence* will be used to support or refute points of view. Authoritative opinions based solely on belief cannot be accepted.
3. Research procedures must be repeatable and reproducible by any qualified investigator. Propositions of science must be capable of rejection through appropriate research.
4. The *science* of psychology is concerned with formulating and evaluating general laws rather than with applying its conclusions. (See the following discussion for an explanation.)
5. Quantitative measurement rather than qualitative observations must be emphasized. A tabulation of supporting anecdotal evidence is not adequate.

6. The universality of natural laws is assumed; identical conditions must always produce the same results. Nature is not capricious.

This list includes most but possibly not all of the topics to keep in mind as we study psychology scientifically. Different scientists will almost certainly want to make additions to the list to emphasize the importance of different areas as they see them; outlines of this sort are never finished. The intent here is to illustrate that research work in psychology is based on a foundation of assumptions that all scientists hold in common. If they do not share such assumptions, interpretation and understanding of research findings become difficult.

One might well argue, as Medawar (1984) has done, "There is no such thing as the scientific method." Scientists will use a variety of methods and procedures in attempting to solve their scientific problems. The quality of our scientific procedures will, over time, be judged by the extent to which they produce results we can depend on. Behavioral scientists with good ideas and solid techniques should generally get better results than can be obtained from the "gropings of an amateur."

At this point I should explain the two contrasting ideas mentioned in Item 4 on the list of propositions. Taking the extreme positions we can say that psychology is studied to emphasize two different points of view: *nomothetic* or *idiographic*.

The idiographic orientation attempts to interpret why a *particular* organism acts in a certain way, given a specific set of circumstances. This orientation, when applied to people, is identified with the practice of clinical psychologists and others who are primarily interested in studying and explaining the behavior of individuals.

People who profess a nomothetic orientation will use scientific methods to formulate and verify general or universal laws of behavior that will be applicable to the behavior of all organisms. When working with people, they want to explain people in general rather than individuals.

Like most such dichotomous divisions, this one makes sense only in a general way. No single person is likely to be identified entirely with one or the other group. Probably the largest number of professional psychologists have primary interests in explaining the behavior of individuals, but they also are alert to the possible discovery of general principles. Some psychologists devote most of their time and attention to research, but this does not prevent them from trying to explain why certain people act the way they do.

AN EXAMPLE OF PSEUDO-SCIENCE

It is sometimes easier to learn a procedure by studying how it can go wrong. Psychology does not provide an abundance of examples of absolutely terrible research—or, if it did, we would not want to advertise them! Instead, we can look at an interesting example from another field.

Peter Tompkins and Christopher Bird's book *The Secret Life of Plants* (1973) illustrates what happens when investigators know what they want to find and they are free to select evidence that suits them. All sorts of conclusions are possible to those who ignore ordinary rules of evidence and scoff at the scientific method when it fails to provide support for an already established point of view.

Cleve Backster was a former lie-detection expert for the CIA. In 1966 he taught lie-detection procedures to police and security personnel who came to him for training. Backster used a galvanometer for his measurements. This is a specialized ohmmeter, an instrument that measures resistance by noting tiny changes in the flow of a very small direct current. The amount of original resistance is not important. We want to measure how much resistance *changes*, presumably in reaction to different sorts of stimuli.

Late one night, "on impulse," Backster attached his galvanometer to the leaves of a large plant and found that changes in the instrument readings "were giving him a reaction very similar to that of a human being experiencing an emotional stimulus of short duration." When he got a mental picture in his mind of a match flame burning a leaf of the plant, "there was a dramatic change in the tracing." When he left the room and returned with some matches, "he found another sudden surge had registered on the chart." When he pretended to burn a leaf, as opposed to actually burning one, there was no reaction on the meter. "The plant appeared to be able to differentiate between real and pretended threat." This was essentially the beginning of research into thinking and feeling plants.

Tompkins and Bird propose the following as fact: plants have the ability to reason, they have feelings, and they can react to stimuli in a deliberate manner. They are aware of and respond to their surroundings, they can remember what they observe, they respond to thought and ideas, human speech affects them, they can communicate with each other, and much more.

Backster observed, "If a plant is threatened with overwhelming danger or damage . . . it reacts self-defensively in a way similar to an opossum—or, indeed to a human being—by 'passing out,' or going into a deep faint." His conclusion that plants could be tranquilized led to the idea that plants might in this way protect themselves from the fear of their own death. ". . . plants and succulent fruits might *wish* to be eaten, but only in a sort of loving ritual. . . " Backster suggested that vegetables that believe it is an advantage to "become another form of life" might actually prefer being eaten to being left to rot on the ground.

Marcel Vogel followed Backster's lead and made some discoveries of his own. He accepted that plants might be blind, deaf, and dumb but stated that ". . . there is no doubt in my mind that they are extremely sensitive instruments for measuring man's emotions. They radiate energy forces that are beneficial to man. One can feel these forces! They feed into one's own force field, which in turn feeds back energy to the plant."

As evidence to support the idea that people can affect plants Vogel told a clinical psychologist friend to come and see for himself if there was any truth in his plant research. He was told to ". . . direct a strong emotion to a philodendron 15 feet away." The plant surged into an instantaneous and intense reaction and then, suddenly, "went dead." The psychologist, when asked what he had been thinking, explained that he had been mentally comparing his own much better plant back home with Vogel's inferior specimen. The plant's feelings were so badly hurt that "it refused to respond for the rest of the day; in fact, it sulked for almost two weeks."

Anyone who is thinking about doing psychological research with plants might want to note Vogel's warning, as relayed by Tompkins and Bird: "Experiments with plants can be extremely dangerous to those who do not have the ability properly to alter their states of consciousness. 'Focused thought,' says Vogel, 'can exert a tremendous effect on the body of a person in a higher mental state, if he lets his emotions interfere.'"

How should a hard-headed scientist deal with this material? First we should note that the statements quoted above and a great many more like them are presented with little or no supporting evidence. The book has a bibliography, but no Vogel reference is listed in it even though Tompkins and Bird devoted several pages to a discussion of his work. In science we do not accept research conclusions on faith.

In an early study Vogel divided a class into groups and "challenged them to repeat some of Backster's accomplishments." Vogel himself was the only one successful in the attempts at replication. A critical person might think it odd that the strongest believer is the only one to get positive results. In a general way one can demonstrate almost anything if one ignores the trials that do not work and records only the evidence of the one that fits.

Vogel in part blames investigators themselves for failing to get results similar to his. "If they approach the experimentation in a mechanistic way," says Vogel, "and don't enter into mutual communication with their plants and treat them as friends, they will fail. It is essential to have an open mind that eliminates all preconceptions from beginning experiments."

Perhaps, according to Backster, we should not expect consistency.

> The only problem in this kind of research is that Mother Nature doesn't want to jump through the hoop ten times in a row simply because someone wants her to. It's difficult to structure repeatable experiments. There are some phenomena that occur that make this kind of thing very difficult. For instance, once you are sure something will happen, it very well may not. I suspect that's because you are communicating to the biological material as long as you keep your consciousness involved in the experiment.
>
> (Quoted in the *Christian Science Monitor*, 1973, December 11, 2nd section, p. 9.)

Arthur W. Galston (1974), in a review of the Tompkins and Bird book, replied:

> Isn't that neat? According to that explanation, anyone doing experiments can "prove" anything he wishes simply by getting a result once—or perhaps once in a while. What about the times the experiment doesn't work? Mother Nature is just being a little coy. What about another experimenter who tries to repeat your work and can't? Well, that person may not have the proper mental attitude or may not be properly attuned to the plant being employed.

The approach to research that limits acceptable evidence to a small, highly trained group of believers will probably in time be able to demonstrate "scientific evidence" in support of their beliefs. People who have studied research know that when an investigator is personally involved in an experiment, even random variations can be interpreted as the rare positive finding that "proves" the hypothesis. The alternate belief holds that scientific experiments are repeatable, and the same results will be obtained anywhere in the world when the same conditions have been provided. Although this discussion referred to plants, its overtones can be heard in the literature of parapsychology.

The scientific method helps to reduce erroneous conclusions in several ways, but two of them are of particular importance: (1) findings and information garnered in their support must be made public, and (2) research demonstrations must be repeatable.

This emphasis on the scientific foundation for research may seem to sophisticated readers to be overdone, but it probably does not go far enough. We must not lose sight of the fact that, despite the importance of scientific thinking to modern living, by one report 40 percent of the general population believes in astrology.

The scientific method, with all its variations and ramifications, is the best way we have figured out for the discovery and validation of hypotheses, theories, and ideas. When it is used correctly it produces better results than any other method yet devised.

LOGICAL REQUIREMENTS FOR A CAUSE AND EFFECT RELATIONSHIP

This is not a course in logic, but we must know a little logic in order to appreciate the limitations of research applied to the understanding of behavior. Cause and effect relationships are frequently suggested in daily conversation, even though a little thought will identify the errors in the presumed cause/effect connection. "The ready availability of pornographic information is the cause of. . . ." "Mrs. . . . had a nervous breakdown as a result of worrying about. . . ." "This . . . is just another example of what results from the breakup of the family." The logical requirements of causal relationships are strict and difficult to satisfy in behavioral science research.

In order to say that one thing is **the** cause (not **a** cause, or one of several possible causes) of a particular specified effect we need to satisfy *all* the following four conditions. The "S" and "N" letters in parentheses at the end of each statement identify Sufficient and Necessary conditions. These are important and will be discussed in a later section.

1. When *THE* cause is *present*   *THE* effect would result   (S)ufficient
2. When *THE* cause is *absent*   *THE* effect is absent   (N)ecessary
3. When *THE* effect is *present*   *THE* cause is present   (N)ecessary
4. When *THE* effect is *absent*   *THE* cause is absent   (S)ufficient

We can study the application of these points with reference to this statement: "Graduation from college with a major in psychology will make a person happy." If graduation with a psychology major is *THE* cause, and happiness is *THE* effect we must expect all of the following to be true.

1. Every graduating psychology major will be happy.
2. People who do not graduate with a psychology major will not be happy.
3. All happy people have graduated with a major in psychology.
4. People who are not happy did not graduate with a major in psychology.

Graduating with a major in psychology is clearly not *THE* cause of happiness, but for some people it is probably *A* cause, and for readers of this book it is likely to be a desirable objective. I am sorry that I am unable to think of a good meaningful nontrivial example of a cause-effect relationship in the behavioral sciences. The following discussion will demonstrate.

THE CAUSE AND EFFECT PROBLEM

The identification of causes and their effects is closely related to the complexity of behavior. If a simple cause produces an effect, the task of identification would be easy. When behavior is complex—as it always seems to be in the behavioral sciences—the assignment of a single cause to a single effect becomes impossible.

1. Presumed causes do not consistently produce the same effects.
   Frustration causes. . . .
2. Specified effects do not necessarily result from identified causes.
   Anxiety results from. . . .
3. The same condition can at different times be either a cause or an effect.
   Depression causes. . . .
   . . . causes depression.
4. Both the presumed cause and the presumed effect might be the result of a third variable that has not been identified. Research has shown that older people who are active have better mental health.
   (Good physical health)
   High activity level. . . . good mental health

The following example will illustrate how the above propositions work in an everyday situation.

Henry is having a great deal of difficulty adjusting to college. He has made few friends, he does not enjoy his classes, and as a result he has become very depressed and spends most of his time in his room. Or is it this way: Henry has become very depressed, and as a result, he has stopped trying to make friends and he no longer goes to his classes?

Note first that it is not clear which is the cause and which is effect (Item 3). Is Henry's difficulty in adjusting to college a cause of his depression? A different opinion might reasonably suggest that his depression is the cause of his inability to adjust to college.

Proposition 1 can be illustrated by noting that although some times the inability to adjust to college will produce depression in some people, other people may react to the same difficulty in different ways.

With reference to Proposition 2, we can begin by assuming that depression is an effect and then identify at least several conditions that could cause it. Poor health, worry over an ill parent, an excessive academic load which causes fatigue, money problems, side effects of medication, an unhappy love affair—any of these and others could explain the depression.

Proposition 4 will be apparent if we can find a cause not mentioned in the example that explains both the depression and the inadequate adjustment to college. The student might have come from a rural community where he attended a small high school. Here he was accepted as a popular school leader, who had a greater-than-average number of friends and was active in many school and community activities. When he went to a large, impersonal, urban university he missed the support of his relatives and friends. Competition for grades was stiffer than he was used to, so he was unable to keep up academically.

A reader who wants a little practice can evaluate the following example. Use it to demonstrate each of the four propositions.

> Isabel cannot adjust to her new job. She is tired all the time, she misses a lot of work. She does not like her boss, and she does not get along well with the other people in the unit. She claims that people at work do not like her because she is smarter than they are and she has more friends than they do. Other people in the unit say that she has not been able to learn the simple requirements of her job. She appears to be frustrated by the demands that are placed on her, so she uses every excuse to avoid them.

The topic of cause and effect will be discussed again when we study correlations later in the book. The subject is particularly important there because correlational analyses often suggest causal relationships. The study of correlations must include a full discussion of the idea that just because two sets of observations have been found consistently to go together, we cannot use that as verifying evidence that one of them is necessarily the cause of the other.

NECESSARY AND SUFFICIENT CONDITIONS

The complexity of behavior makes it very nearly impossible to discover true cause and effect relationships. These would require the identification of a single cause that always produces a single effect. We would also look for a single effect that was always produced by the previously identified single cause.

To make sense of relationships in the behavioral sciences we make a distinction between the two sets of conditions mentioned earlier: *necessary* and *sufficient*. A sufficient condition is the one most applicable to psychology.

> A sufficient condition is one that can, by itself, produce an effect, but it does not need to be present for the effect to occur.

If S is a sufficient condition for a particular E effect, whenever S occurs E will result. S, by itself, is sufficient to produce E, but S is only one of numerous sufficient conditions, any one of which is capable of producing the effect. In the behavioral sciences we are generally unable to say that a particular S causes a particular E. Psychological explanations typically include qualifiers such as: "can," "generally," "often," "sometimes," "has been known to," or others like these.

A sufficient condition can be diagrammed this way. Assume that the subscript identifies a possible cause, a particular sufficient condition.

S_P

S_Q

S_R - - - - - - - -> Effect

S_S

S_T

S_U

The diagram illustrates that any one of the conditions subscript P through U is sufficient to produce the effect, but when we have the effect we cannot be sure which *particular* sufficient condition caused it. In a practical way, we might think that X is the cause of Y, but Y might have resulted from something else. When there is reason to suspect that a particular effect has only one cause—in medicine for example—science tries to eliminate all possible causes in order to identify the correct one. Psychology's complexity makes it difficult to identify and list all possible causes (sufficient conditions) for a particular behavior we are studying.

Suppose we ask this question: What is the cause of many students' failure to graduate from college? We know immediately that there is no single cause, so we list possible causes. Following the diagram given above, failure to graduate is the effect, and the S's are possible causes. Poor class attendance, ill health, family problems, lack of money, inadequate background, low motivation, too many hours spent at work, and many other points could be listed. Any one of these possible causes could produce the effect. We can in many instances propose that lack of interest (i.e., low motivation) was a sufficient condition for explaining a person's failure to graduate. We could, for other students, explain the same effect in any of a great many different ways using different sufficient conditions.

We cannot, however, make a very persuasive case by going from the effect to a particular cause. Just because a person failed to graduate does not by itself permit the conclusion the person regularly failed to attend classes.

Unfortunately, many explanations in the behavioral sciences follow that pattern of reasoning from an effect to a presumed cause. We identify a behavior, then we try to explain it. Causes in the behavioral sciences are, in every example I can think of, sufficient conditions. That means that they are sufficient by themselves to have caused the effect, but the mere presence of the effect does not permit us to conclude that a particular sufficient condition was the cause.

As you will see in the following discussion, *necessary conditions* are not of much interest in the behavioral sciences. I like to visualize a necessary condition in the following way:

$$A \textbf{ and } B \textbf{ and } C \textbf{ and } D \textbf{ and } \textit{(whatever)} \qquad \text{cause} \qquad \text{the } \textbf{effect}$$

A necessary condition is one that *must* be present for an effect to occur, but unlike a sufficient condition, a necessary condition cannot by itself produce a particular effect. An effect will not occur unless all the necessary conditions are present.

When the words "necessary" and "sufficient" are combined in a sentence it identifies a true causal relationship. To say that something is both a necessary and a sufficient condition for an effect means that the given entity is *THE* cause of that particular effect. Since there are very few direct cause and effect relationships in the behavioral sciences, we are more likely to see a statement such as this one: "Good intelligence is a necessary but not a sufficient condition for graduating from a major university." This means that a person must have intelligence to satisfactorily complete the required academic work, but intelligence by itself does not guarantee that a person will receive a diploma. Many intelligent people, for a variety of reasons, do not graduate from college.

FUNCTIONAL RELATIONSHIPS

In the behavioral sciences it is important to recognize the distinction between *functional* and *causal relationships*. Earlier discussions have shown that cause and effect relationships are not common. But we also know from repeated observation that certain attributes are often found with certain behaviors. When we have a well-established relationship that we know is not causal in nature, we call it a "functional relationship." Hard work on a project does not necessarily *cause* it to be successful. Hard work and success are obviously not causally related, because it is possible to work very hard on an enterprise that does not succeed. A psychologically healthy childhood does not necessarily cause the development of a well-adjusted adult; but they do often go together, so we can say they are "functionally related."

THE OBJECTIVE OF SCIENCE

In concluding this section I would like to use the best summary I know of. It happens to be from Richard Feynman, a Nobel prize-winning physicist who devoted his life to "The Art of Finding Things Out." As Feynman's collection of autobiographical experiences (1986 and 1988) demonstrates, he was a person with a tremendous breadth of interests. He once applied his critical mind to a project in psychology that he wondered about, he studied music, he became an accomplished artist, and he was by far the most critical witness in trying to get at the truth of the January 28, 1986 Challenger space shuttle accident. As a physicist he was also an excellent psychologist.

In a "Nova" telecast (1983) Feynman used a game analogy to characterize his idea of how we learn about the world. This quotation is in response to the narrator who had noted that Feynman was interested in "trying to figure out more about the world and how it works." (Feynman's conversational response has been altered slightly to make it read better.)

> To get some idea of what we're doing in trying to understand nature, it makes a kind of fun analogy to imagine that the gods are playing some great game and you don't know the rules of the game. You are only allowed to look at the board from time to time. From your observations of what takes place in a little corner of the board you try to figure out what the rules of the game are.

And that will be our objective also as we learn how to study psychology scientifically.

WHERE DO WE BEGIN?

This text will assume that its readers can be divided into two groups. Those readers who do not plan to do research in the future will benefit nevertheless from a careful study of the material to come. From it they will learn how to read, interpret, and draw conclusions from published information. The world seems to need intelligent and critical readers almost as much (perhaps more!) than it needs an increase in the numbers of scientific investigators.

People who will be undertaking research will find a great deal of useful material on developing, setting up, and carrying out research projects and then measuring and analyzing resulting data. As we will see, the whole field of research is in some ways much easier than it was even a few years ago, and in several important ways it has not changed at all.

Of all the sciences psychology is arguably the most difficult. This conclusion is based on two major points. First, the nature of the subject matter of psychology is very diversified. Second, to understand behavior it is often necessary to have a working knowledge of material normally studied in other disciplines: chemistry, biology, physics, mathematics, sociology, and anthropology, to name only a few. The list could also include music, art, and drama as well as history and literature. Possibly more than any other discipline psychology seems to require the creative researcher to know at least a little about countless other fields of study. One must look very hard indeed to find a topic about which a person can honestly say, "I don't need to know that, I'll never need it." In my opinion, good research in psychology requires a lifetime commitment to scholarship.

One of the important things a person learns from the study of general psychology—and it often comes as a surprise—is that the field includes a *very* large number of topics. The older subjects are still with us: learning, perception, personality, motivation, comparative psychology, and physiological psychology. Some areas have been expanded to include different types of material: abnormal psychology, psychotherapy, clinical psychology, measurement, and industrial psychology. Some areas of psychological concern, although certainly not new, have responded to new pressures that have given them a stronger emphasis: developmental processes have been expanded to include material of relevance to older people, and social psychology now looks at social bases of behavior that involve social pathology, cross-cultural differences, and intergroup relations. Psychology has also moved into areas that have become increasingly important in the last decade or so: ecological and environmental psychology. Probably every area of psychology that has ever been of interest to psychologists continues to be of interest to someone today, and an abundance of new topics have been added to the list.

The world's larger population, the greater numbers of people living in urban environments, increased mobility afforded by automobiles and air travel, a quicker and more ready availability of news—these and other things have given a renewed emphasis to human difficulties that have been with us to some extent for a long time. Some areas of concern, such as those that follow, are not much closer to solution today: suicide, particularly among teens and the elderly, abuse of other people (spouses, women, children, elderly); murder, rape, gangs in urban environments, and criminal behavior in general; drug addiction; inadequate academic performance; prejudice and unequal employment opportunities; insanity; poverty; and inadequate health care. Numerous other topics could be added.

Even granting that there is subject-matter overlap among some of these areas, there will still be material in each of them that is relevant to that area alone. The fact that there is so much to learn forces people to become specialists if they are to have more than a superficial understanding of an area and its literature.

The breadth of psychology places special demands on people who work in the discipline. The diversity of psychology is perhaps most clearly indicated by the divisions of the American Psychological Association. The intent here is to indicate only subject areas of current interest to psychologists, so the complete names of the divisions that represent these areas are not listed in Table 2.1. The actual titles usually include variations of the word *psychology* or *psychological*. We should understand that the division for the subject area I have labeled "Teaching" would be "Division on the Teaching of Psychology." The subject area I have identified as "Study of social issues" has the actual title of "The Society for the Psychological Study of Social Issues—A Division of the APA." Divisions that would have been numbered 4 and 11 do not exist.

Looking toward the future it would be interesting to speculate on what new divisions will be added as the study of psychology continues to expand.

The topics of psychological interest are very diverse, as indicated above, but similar skills and procedures are used for doing research in all of them. A background of statistics is required, so enough information on that topic will be supplied in the text to help a beginner get started. The basic pattern for designing a research project, the logic that underlies the collection and interpretation of data—these are fairly standard. A person would need special training and knowl-

Table 2.1

SUBJECT AREAS REPRESENTED IN THE DIVISIONS OF THE
AMERICAN PSYCHOLOGICAL ASSOCIATION

1.	General	24.	Theoretical and philosophical
2.	Teaching	25.	Experimental analysis of behavior
3.	Experimental	26.	History
5.	Evaluation and measurement	27.	Community
6.	Physiological and comparative	28.	Psychopharmacology
7.	Developmental	29.	Psychotherapy
8.	Personality and social	30.	Psychological hypnosis
9.	Study of social issues	31.	State association affairs
10.	Psychology and the arts	32.	Humanistic
12.	Clinical	33.	Mental retardation
13.	Consulting	34.	Population and environmental
14.	Industrial and organizational	35.	Psychology of women
15.	Educational	36.	Religious issues
16.	School	37.	Child, youth, and family services
17.	Counseling	38.	Health
18.	Psychologists in public service	39.	Psychoanalysis
19.	Military	40.	Clinical neuropsychology
20.	Adult development and aging	41.	Psychology and the law
21.	Applied experimental and engineering	42.	Psychologists in independent practice
22.	Rehabilitation	43.	Family psychology
23.	Consumer psychology	44.	Lesbian and gay issues

edge of equipment and appropriate measurement tools, if he or she chooses to work in areas of perception, physiological psychology, and possible learning, to suggest a few.

GETTING STARTED ON A LITERATURE SEARCH

This unit is provided at this point in the text for people who will, as part of their course requirements, have to produce a paper or a research project of some sort. Now is the time to select ideas and get started on the collection of background material. People who will not have to do a literature search have no need to read this section.

The first thing to do is to select an appropriate research topic and have it approved by the person in charge of your project. The topic should be simple enough for research on it to be manageable within the limits of subject availability, equipment, space, time, and research skills. You should check your library to be sure that enough relevant references are available.

I find that I often *begin* my search of the literature with an article I happened to run across while reading something else. Most technical reports, articles, or monographs will contain a list of references that can help the search along. A beginning psychology text is often a good source of ideas and references.

The professional journals in psychology and other fields (anthropology, sociology, social work, biology, medicine, and many supplementary areas) will likely be the major source of research material. The *Social Sciences Index* and *Science Index* are possible sources of references that might provide other ideas, but beginners in psychological research probably will want first to look at and learn to use *Psychological Abstracts* or one of the computer alternatives. I will give instructions on how to use PsycLIT a little later.

Abstracts briefly (in paragraphs of about 100 words) summarize the contents and conclusions of articles and books on psychology published all over the world. These are grouped together according to their dates of publication. The most recent abstracts are published monthly; then they are annually combined into large volumes covering the year. Usually we will find abstracts for topics we want to look at scattered among several volumes.

We can select abstracts by looking up *topics* or *authors*. After a person has worked in a particular field for awhile it will be discovered that certain names keep reappearing. If you know that H. J. Eysenck has written or cooperated in writing several articles on a subject that interests you, you might want to check first to see what he has recently written.

If all you have is a topic or subject, here is how you start: Go to the section of the library where *Psychological Abstracts* is located. In that area you will also find the *Thesaurus of Psychological Index Terms.* You will need a little time to sort out how topics are listed under main and secondary headings. It is sometimes necessary to figure out the closest heading to your chosen topic, as the topic itself might not be listed.

Use the appropriate headings to look up your topic in the "Subject Index." Each publication referenced will have a concise statement of what information is in the article. If a reference sounds promising, copy the *number* of the abstract. Use the number of the abstract (remember, this is not a page number) to find the actual abstract in that volume.

The abstract will begin with a reference citation that lists the author(s), the title, and the article's place of publication. The abstract itself will summarize the article and conclude with an indication of the number of references given, e.g., (17 ref.). If you find a number of references you want to look up, be prepared to spend a lot of time accurately copying the citations.

Only the largest and best-funded libraries will have a comprehensive collection of journals. If your library is not large I would suggest that you first find out what journals it has available on the shelves or on microfilm.

Do not give up if you do not immediately have access to an article you want to read. Some libraries have arrangements for obtaining copies of individual articles, or it is often possible to write to the author and ask for a copy.

Advances in information science have made a search of the psychology literature much easier than it would have been even a few years ago. That is all for the better, because the number of publications is increasing at an enormous rate—probably doubling in 10 years or less.

Any discussion of a literature search using computers almost certainly will be out of date by the time this book is published. This practically guarantees that whatever I tell you will, in many instances, be only partially correct by the time you read it. Only procedures can be given here. The actual procedures you will follow will depend on what system is available at your library. Instructors often can arrange a special visit to the library and a formal discussion by a librarian who has kept up with the annual changes in technology.

A modern library will have computer equipment that will greatly simplify a search of the literature. "PsycLIT" is the name of the system at my university. A computer is used to search a compact disk (CD) for subjects, topics, words, or authors. With a computer system one can get information in a few seconds that previously would have taken many minutes or even hours to find in print and then copy by hand. The PsycLIT system makes it possible to mark important abstracts and have them printed. Gone are the many hours that used to be wasted copying references; gone also are the mistakes made in copying page numbers, years, or volume numbers or in spelling authors' names. Anyone who has learned to use the PsycLIT retrieval system does not willingly go back to the printed volumes of "*Psych Abstracts.*" A computer search will not cover the most recent literature, for which the latest issues of *Psychological Abstracts* will still be required; neither will it list articles and references from many years back.

As with everything else that involves computers, a computer search of the literature works very well indeed, but the procedures tend to be complicated and difficult to learn. There are two reasons for this. First, computers can do a great many different things. The more options we have, the more there is to learn. Second, many beginners have observed that computer instructions usually seem to have been written for people who already know what to do.

Table 2.2 is a copy of the handout used in our library to help guide students into our PsycLIT program. There is, however, a great deal more information a person would need to know in order to efficiently use this system.

The *Thesaurus of Psychological Index Terms* is also used with the PsycLIT system. Here it can be examined in the printed volume or directly in the PsycLIT system itself.

The American Psychological Association has published a set of guides that can be useful for learning the procedures. *Search PsycINFO: Student Workbook* includes information on how to do both a computer search and a manual search in the *Psychological Abstracts.* An inexpensive booklet is available for *Searching PsycLIT on CD-ROM.*[3] This gives a step-by-step sequence for a literature search using that system. Many useful publications on a variety of topics are available from: American Psychological Association, Order Department, 1400 N. Uhle St., Arlington, VA, 22201. Interested readers should write for a copy of the catalog.

The PsycLIT program also provides an on-line tutorial that does well enough to get a beginner started, but a person who has had some computer ex-

---

[3] "ROM" means **R**ead **O**nly **M**emory. One can read the information stored on compact disks but cannot write over it.

Table 2.2

NORTHEASTERN ILLINOIS UNIVERSITY RONALD WILLIAMS LIBRARY: BASIC DIRECTIONS FOR USING PSYCLIT ON CD-ROM
---

1. Select your subject headings using the Thesaurus of Psychological Terms (book) or the **INDEX (F5).**

    READ THE PROMPTS AT THE BOTTOM OF THE SCREEN.

2. When using the **INDEX** to locate subject headings type in your term. Then press **ENTER.** Move the cursor by using the arrow keys to the term(s) you wish to select. Press **ENTER** to **SELECT TERM** then **TAB** over to **FIND.** Then press **ENTER.** The subject headings selected will appear on your search screen.
3. To combine subject headings type the line number(s) separated with the word **AND.** For example: **#2 AND #4 AND #5**
4. When using the Thesaurus type the subject headings you have selected from the Thesaurus of Psychological Terms. Press **ENTER.**

    Example: DEMENTIA AND DRUG-THERAPY ⟨ENTER⟩

The word **AND** is used to connect two or more topics. Also, note that multiword descriptors should be connected with a **hyphen.**

TAKE NOTICE OF MENU OPTIONS WHEN THEY APPEAR ON THE SCREEN.

SELECT AN OPTION BY USING THE TAB KEY TO MOVE THE HIGHLIGHT.

THEN PRESS ENTER.

5. To **SHOW** the records press **F4.**
6. Move through the records by using the **PAGE UP** and **PAGE DOWN** keys. Mark the records you wish to print by pressing **ENTER.**
7. Press **F2** to return to find mode if search was unsuccessful. Select new terms.
8. To **PRINT:** move the highlight with the **TAB** key to **PRINT.** Then press **ENTER.**
9. Use the **TAB** key to highlight **CHANGE OPTIONS.** Then press **ENTER.** (A window will appear in the middle of the screen to alter print options.)
10. At **FIELDS TO PRINT** type the word **ALL.** Then press **ENTER.** Use the **TAB** key to highlight **RECORDS TO PRINT.** If you had marked the records, only those marked will printout. Press **ENTER** to accept options. If you did not mark the records and wish to print all, type **ALL.** Then press **ENTER.** Or type in the numbers of the records to print. For example: **1,2,5-9,12** Then press **ENTER.**
11. **START PRINT** will be highlighted. Press **ENTER** and the printer should begin printing.

    ASK FOR ASSISTANCE AT THE DESK IF YOU NEED HELP.

perience can probably figure out what to do for a simple search from the menu-driven system itself.

Each PsycLIT compact disk covers a time span of several years; the disks in our library cover the period from January 1983 to March 1991, and the earlier disk covers literature for the period January 1974 through December 1982. Upgrades to recent dates are regularly being created.

The PsycLIT procedure permits the use of broad titles which it will then also break into smaller reference units. One search I made on "sense of humor" produced the following:

3,590 sense

467 humor

53 sense of humor

In addition to discovering 53 articles in which the phrase "sense of humor" was used in the title or abstract, we discover that "humor" is mentioned at least 467 times, and "sense," which is a very broad term, has 3,590 listings. By requesting information on "joke" I found 38 references, and 101 mentions of "laughter."

The topic "teen suicide" disclosed 92 references to "teen," 2713 references to "suicide," and only 4 to "teen suicide."

For the time period January 1974 to December 1982 "clinical" was mentioned 11,074 times, and there were 14,736 mentions of the word "experimental." During the January 1983 to December 1989 period there was a change; "clinical" produced a very sizable increase to 21,054 references, whereas "experimental" lost ground to 12,054. The marked shift in the types of articles published in the scientific journals of psychology indicates a reorientation in at least one aspect of the discipline. I will discuss this topic again near the end of the book, when the psychology organizations are discussed. A few minutes spent seeking information on odd subjects can be interesting because it sometimes leads to surprises about what is or is not being written.

After you have found that articles in your area of interest are available, press the appropriate key (F4) to have PsycLit "SHOW" them. You will then see details on the first of the articles: the title, the full reference, and in some cases the abstract of the article. Broad topics that produce many references will not be manageable for a small project, so the list of references can be shortened by making the search words more specific.

The search for books has also been greatly simplified by computers, which in most libraries have entirely replaced the old card catalogs. Computers in many libraries can tap into a library network. If a volume is not available in one's own university library a procedure for interlibrary loans makes it possible to order, through the college library, selected books from any library in the system.

With so much information so readily and so easily available, research should be better than ever—well, perhaps not quite yet. The opening editorial in the first issue of *Psychological Science* (vol.1, no.1 1990, January, p. 1) speaks to this point. "Journals, Journals, Journals" is the title, and not surprisingly it discusses journals as the primary source of information for scientists. William K. Estes, the editor, noted that upwardly spiraling journal prices, together with a continuing growth in the number of journals being published, means that the variety of journals libraries can buy on limited budgets is actually decreasing. There are now too many specialized journals that are directed to groups with relatively narrow interests.

Estes also affirms what everyone already knows: "The problem for users is that limited time and limited reading rates make it impossible to keep up with the literature." There is a great deal more to read and no extra time for reading it. To be of any use, the journal or book still has to be read, evaluated, and incorporated into the scheme of one's own research project. With so much information now available in some areas, what previously had been very difficult is now impossible.

A second impediment often blocks our best research intentions. "Putting a question to nature" is one way to think of research, so it follows that achievements can never be better than the questions the investigator asks and the answers he or she proposes for them. Before we can do good research, we must have good ideas.[4] We then try them out to see if they work. The quality of research is determined by the person who has the best ideas. Good ideas are no more easily found in modern libraries than they were before. The best equipment for literature searches and the ready availability of books and documents are tools to make easier the job of the investigator. Good research still requires imagination and creativity in addition to a knowledge of the subject.

The speed and flexibility of data analysis is another advantage modern researchers have. Computers are readily available to provide analyses of more data and more complex analyses and to provide them more quickly. Interpreting what the results mean becomes a challenging task for investigators who are sometimes swamped with data they do not have time to study.

ENDNOTE

Einstein's theories forced astronomers to develop new ideas about the nature of the universe. If A is true, then B would also have to be true, but in order for B to be true we need to develop a totally different concept from any we have had before. That is the way the reasoning might have gone that culminated in speculation about black holes. John Wheeler, a Princeton University physicist, invented the term in 1967. Even though the concept itself is highly technical, a shadow of the idea has found a place in our everyday speech. A "black hole" is the place where all our things go that become irretrievably lost. You will understand the idea if ever you have once had an object—a particular book, perhaps—but now that you need it, you can't find it no matter how hard you look.

An astronomical black hole is thought to develop from the collapse of a massive star that has exhausted its nuclear energy. The star's density and gravita-

---

[4] We might say, "Good ideas are a necessary but not a sufficient condition for good research."

tional pull increased enormously as it shrunk. Nothing, not even light, escapes the gravitational attraction.

Astronomers found evidence of a black hole in the galaxy M87, in the constellation Virgo. The galaxy is estimated to be 50 million light years away, which means that the light we see now left the galaxy 50 million years ago. It is so far away that its light took 50 million years to get here. We will have to wait another 50 million years to know if it is still there today!

STUDY QUESTIONS

1.D Justify the point of view that the study of history and literature should be required for psychology majors.

What possible relevance could reading something like *The Canterbury Tales* (written 600 years ago) have for a psychology major today? (My answer is that you will never know whether it is relevant until you have read it!)

2. In what area of knowledge does psychology have its roots?

3. What sources of "proof" must be ignored to get at the truth of nature?

4. What is wrong with authority as a source of truth?

5. Distinguish between empirical and a priori knowledge.

6. Define and contrast rationalism and empiricism as sources of knowledge.

Explain the Pythagorean theorem from the point of view of a rationalist and an empiricist.

7. What does it mean to say that "a set of conclusions can be drawn a priori?"

8. Since rationalism and empiricism seem to be contrasting ideas, how is it possible for people to use both in their thinking?

9. What example was given to illustrate that even today it is possible to discover a totally new idea a priori, without any reference to observations from nature?

10.D Discuss whether or not psychology is a science.
What is a science?

11. What are the six principles that in part establish the philosophical foundations of psychology?

12. Contrast the idiographic and nomothetic approach to psychological understanding.

13. What are some reasons why we should not pay much attention to the conclusion given in the Tompkins and Bird book, *The Secret Life of Plants?*

14.D What reasons can you give to explain why so many people believe in astrology?
What evidence is there (or can there be) to "prove" that it works?

15. What are some reasons why it is so difficult to determine causal connections in psychology?

16.   Explain and contrast necessary and sufficient conditions.

What relationship between necessary and sufficient conditions must exist in order for us to say that something is **the** cause of something else?

17.   Contrast a functional and causal relationship.

18.   Why might psychology be considered one of the more demanding sciences?

19.   Name several divisions of the American Psychological Association.

20.   How can a beginner find a good topic for a research paper?

21.   Identify several advantages of computer literature searches over the earlier method.

22.   What are some reasons why research in psychology is no easier today than it ever was, despite the many advantages of modern technology?

23.   Why are some libraries cutting back on their journal purchases?

SMALL TALK

Chapter
3

The Logic of Research

The necessity for logical reasoning

*There are obvious benefits to be gained from the
study of logic: heightened ability to express ideas
clearly and concisely, increased skill in defining
one's terms, and enlarged capacity to formulate arguments rigorously and to analyze them critically.
But perhaps the greatest benefit is the recognition
that reason can be applied in every aspect of human
affairs.*

Copi, I. M., & Cohen, C. (1990). *Introduction to Logic* (8th ed.).
New York: Macmillan, p. *vii*.

Logic is a study of the rules for reasoning. These rules provide the formal
structure that is indispensable for productive thinking.

> Thinking is effective when it is based on adequate evidence, when it follows sound
> procedures and when it produces satisfactory results in the form of problems solved
> or sound decisions made. Occasionally we can make lucky decisions without think-
> ing—by flipping a coin, consulting a fortune teller, or acting on impulse—but the av-
> erage is poor.
>
> (Little et al. 1955, p.1)

Chapter 3 introduces some logical foundations for the research methods applicable to the behavioral sciences. It is true that many people have learned to do

competent research without this background, but even a little logic—which is all this brief introduction will permit—should markedly improve one's understanding of *why* we design our research projects as we do. We will study several different ideas in logic, but there is one idea that tends to be particularly difficult for beginners to understand.

To see the nature of the problem let us look at a couple of texts to see how they treat the statement of theories and hypotheses used in research. One states that, "Causal relationships can never be empirically proved." Later the authors expand on the idea that evidence given in support of a theory "indicates that the theory is useful in making certain kinds of predictions but does not prove the theory." Another text makes the point that hypotheses "must be capable of being established as (probably) true or false." As we examine the *professional* literature of psychology we would have a great deal of difficulty finding experiments that purport to "prove" that the idea being tested is correct.

It is a common, *but false,* supposition that experiments are designed to prove the correctness of the research expectations we are investigating. I think it is important for beginners to understand why experimental proof of hypotheses is impossible. I am sorry that the explanation will be rather involved; that is why it is not regularly discussed in texts similar to this one. Anyone who studies the logical introduction I give in this chapter will have a much better understanding and appreciation of why research is best designed for the negation of research proposals. We are never able to prove our ideas are right; we can only, with confidence, show that they are wrong.

This chapter will make use of a number of technical terms from logic. The words will be familiar, but at various points in the exposition a more detailed definition will be given to ensure that a word's meaning in logic is understood. Take the word "argument" as an example. We all know in a general way that an argument suggests a quarrel, dispute, or disagreement. In logic the term has a more restricted meaning, to suggest only a discussion in which evidence is considered and evaluated. We will take an argument to mean a discussion in which reasons are offered for or against ideas or propositions that have been suggested for consideration.

THE HYPOTHETICO-DEDUCTIVE STRATEGY

In our everyday affairs we collect and analyze information that is available to us, then we frequently go beyond the "facts" to draw conclusions that have been suggested by them. We make an inference. A statement such as "She didn't say that Mike was good-looking, but I inferred it from what she did say about him," is an example. "Inference" is the term used in logic to identify the mental process through which conclusions are obtained from logical reasoning.

The science of psychology would be of little use if all it did was to devise explanations that apply only to a particular group of subjects. In a typical research situation we would probably study a small group of people in order to draw conclusions (make inferences) that will be generally applicable to a much larger group of people who are like them.

The study of logic is important because it helps us to identify the ways in which our reasoning—and the conclusions we draw from evidence—can go wrong. Sometimes, to a person untrained in logic, conclusions appear to be true, and they may be true some of the time. Even though occasionally we may guess an answer that turns out to be correct, we would be better off to follow rules that produce dependable outcomes. Logic has identified some rules for good reasoning. If we violate them we will have made a mistake in our reasoning and our results cannot be guaranteed.

A "fallacy" is an error in reasoning that produces conclusions we cannot depend on. There are a great many of them, so only those relevant to this discussion will be identified. Readers will already be familiar with fallacies of a different sort, which were studied in Chapter 1.

Identification of psychological laws follows from a form of logic called "inductive" reasoning, which permits us to make "inductive inferences." This is a reasoning process that attempts to derive general principles from observation of specific examples. The reasoning progresses from representative cases or observations to general, perhaps universal, conclusions about a much larger number—a population—of similar cases. I have often observed that people who have a good education will get better jobs and earn more money than people who are not well educated. I have observed a number of examples, and from them I have developed a general principle. Thus, I have made an inductive inference.

"Deduction" is a type of reasoning that generally involves "syllogisms." These come in many forms, but only two are relevant to this discussion. I will first define a simple "categorical" syllogism, the sort every one is likely to recognize. Later we will see the relationship between this form and the "hypothetical" syllogism, which is the foundation structure for all research.

A categorical syllogism consists of two premises from which we make a deductive inference. A premise can be a guess, a belief, a supposition, or any idea we use in thinking. The "major" premise, the first one, is the premise that is more universal. The "minor" premise, the second one, is the one that is more specific. A syllogism results when we put these two premises together and draw a conclusion from them deductively.

The following example, learned by every school child, is by far the one most widely known. It evaluates whether or not Socrates is mortal.

Major premise: All human beings are mortal.

Minor Premise: Socrates is a human being.

Conclusion: Therefore, Socrates is mortal.

This is a "categorical" syllogism because it evaluates whether one category (class or group)—Socrates in this example—is or is not validly included in another class (i.e. mortals). Reasoning in a syllogism proceeds from an accepted principle, an inductive inference, to a conclusion about an unknown or specific instance. The premises entail the conclusion, so this type of reasoning is useful for the *evaluation* of information or concepts obtained in other ways.

Induction is the method of *discovery* by observation. Deduction is a method for *using* the information that one has already obtained. Deduction always begins with assumptions, beliefs, or hypotheses which form the premises from which conclusions are derived. We should not exaggerate the differences between the two aspects of the reasoning process these terms represent, because they are interrelated—each depends on the other. They offer two paths along which the inferential process can move.

The testing of hypotheses through the processes of deductive logic explains the name of this section, "The hypothetico-deductive strategy." The following broad outline of the hypothetico-deductive method is not the only way of thinking about the sequential steps. Some experts include additional points and some lists do not include all of these, but the basic ideas are the same.

1. Identify a problem.
2. Develop a hypothesis to explain or solve it.
3. Make the hypothesis the antecedent in a "hypothetical syllogism" (to be discussed later).
4. Deduce certain consequences that would be true if the hypothesis were true.
5. Carry out the research.
6. Evaluate results.
7. Apply conclusions to related and previously unexplained examples.

The power of the method for solving scientific problems is illustrated in the example that follows. As you read it, think about the discovery of the problem, possible explanations of the difficulty, how the explanations were tested, and how they were put to use in explaining quite different observations.

In ancient times, just as now, deep mines often became unworkable because they filled with water. A simple suction pump was developed for pumping the water out of the mines. Modern versions of this pump are still seen today in the long-handled pumps in roadside parks and picnic areas. All such pumps are limited in the heights to which water can be raised, approximately 34 feet. That was a serious problem addressed by scientists 350 years ago. How do these pumps work, and why is there a physical limit to their effectiveness?

One explanation for the fact that a suction pump could suck up a column of water no longer than 34 feet suggested that water has an inherent cohesiveness that is not very strong. It is adequate to hold together a 34-foot column, but beyond that the weight of water itself causes the column to separate. This hypothesis can be illustrated with an analogy. Imagine that a ball of clay has been rolled out into a long thin rope. As the rope is made thinner, there will inevitably come a point at which the weight of the clay is too heavy for its inherent cohesiveness and the clay rope will break. The same idea would apply to a piece of string, a piece of rope, or even a steel cable. If any of these were long enough they would break under their own weight. This explanation for why the water column broke is very narrowly conceived and therefore very limited in the extent to which it can be generalized to other situations.

Galileo noted the 34-foot limitation in 1638 and was unable to explain it. The most popular idea at the time was derived from the "full universe hypothesis" which held that "nature abhors a vacuum." A suction pump works by creating a slight vacuum which is replaced by water that is drawn up the tube. We can see the principle in operation each time we suck a liquid up a soda straw. This hypothesis also explains why a liquid does not run out a bunghole near the bottom of a barrel unless there is also a hole near the top; but it fails to explain why two very smooth, flat pieces of wet glass, microscope slides for example, appear to stick together when one is placed on top of the other. Nor does the hypothesis explain why nature, although very serious about the no-vacuum rule for short lengths—set a 34-foot limit to its enforcement.

Evangelista Torricelli, a pupil and close associate of Galileo near the end of his life, made a series of assumptions that seemed to work very well in explaining all the facts, and they led to others that could be tested. Torricelli accepted the idea that gases had weight and could exert pressure. Second, he assumed that the earth's surface is actually at the bottom of a sea of air that surrounds it. Third, he reasoned that the partial vacuum created by suction did not in fact "suck" the liquid up, but rather it left a space into which a liquid is "pushed" by the pressure of air on the surrounding liquid. The weight of the air, the pressure, was concluded to be the same as the weight of a column of water 34 feet in length.

These conclusions further suggest that the lifting force, the pressure, is independent of the liquid. Torricelli was able to test this hypothesis quite easily. He sealed a long glass tube at one end, then filled it with mercury. He immersed the open end in a dish of mercury. The mercury in the glass tube ran out until it formed a column of mercury about 30 inches in length. This left a vacuum at the sealed top end of the tube. Torricelli's experiment demonstrated that inasmuch as nature had created the vacuum at the top of the tube, obviously a vacuum can exist in nature.

In 1643 Torricelli constructed the prototype for a barometer, a device still used today for measuring the pressure of gases. Mercury is a liquid metal and is much heavier than water. A column of mercury about 30 inches long produces the same pressure at its tip as a column of water about 34 feet tall.

Everyone who swims knows that the pressure of the water increases with its depth. If air is like thin water, and if we are living at the bottom of an ocean of air, the air should get thinner and have less pressure as we move up and away from the bottom. In 1648 the brother-in-law of Blaise Pascal (the famous mathematician) was persuaded to take an inverted tube of mercury to the top of one of the peaks in the Pyrenees Mountains, Pyu-de Dome. At the top he found that the 30-inch column of mercury had fallen to 27 inches, substantial evidence to support the idea that air does indeed get thinner as we move to higher levels. A person watching a similar tube at the bottom of the mountain was able to verify that his tube had not changed. Thus, the hypothesis gained adequate support for acceptance.

The idea that air produces pressure also explains why in our own kitchens a newly washed and still-hot glass will sometimes seem to "stick" to a wet, very smooth surface when the glass is put on it open end down. The same natural law is used to pump toothpaste from a modern pump container. A small amount is discharged by finger pressure, then air pressure pushes a new supply of toothpaste up the tube to replace it.

Note how the steps of discovery and verification in this example follow the hypothetico-deductive sequence outlined above. A problem was identified, and various ideas were formulated to explain it. The first explanation was not a very good one because it was able to explain only a limited set of observations. The best explanations become principles that contribute to a broader understanding of how the world works. The idea that provided the most general explanation of the observations was tested repeatedly. As evidence accumulated to show that the explanation seemed to fit all known facts to which it was relevant, the explanation was accepted—although we should also state that it was not "proved."

HYPOTHETICAL SYLLOGISMS IN RESEARCH

A person cannot have a complete understanding of the foundations of science unless he or she knows the difference between "truth" and "validity." These are terms that some people might think are essentially synonymous, in the sense that a true conclusion must be valid and, certainly, a valid conclusion must be true. It is sometimes difficult to see why we cannot depend on conclusions from invalid arguments, even when we know from independent information that the conclusions are true.

Ideas of truth and validity are primarily relevant for deductive arguments. Conclusions from deductive arguments are valid only if there have been no mistakes in the logical process that has led up to them. A conclusion from a valid argument is inescapable; it is the only possible conclusion based on the evidence presented. Validity applies only to deduction; only deductive inferences can be valid.

"Validity" is an important word for psychology, which uses the term in at least three ways. The definition in the preceding paragraph is applicable to the logical interpretation of syllogisms. "Test validity" and "external validity" of experiments will be discussed in later chapters.

"Truth" is a common, everyday word that in logic refers only to the premises or propositions of an argument. Truth of propositions must be determined by evidence outside the argument, with reference to the real world. A syllogism cannot demonstrate that a conclusion is true unless the premises are known from independent evidence to be true and the argument itself is valid. A little later I will demonstrate that conclusions from invalid arguments can, and sometimes will, be true.

Following is an example of a valid, simple *categorical syllogism* in its familiar form. We will see later in the discussion that even when syllogisms seem reasonable we cannot draw dependable conclusions when the standard rules of logic have been violated.

All who live in Chicago live in Illinois.

Bill lives in Chicago.

Bill lives in Illinois.

Note that the direction of the argument is from a general statement in the major premise about "All who live in Chicago" to a conclusion that identifies where an individual lives. This follows the direction of deductive arguments, from general observations to conclusions.

Logic gives the rules for helping us to determine the difference between valid and invalid arguments. Beginners have trouble understanding that even invalid arguments can have true conclusions. A quick reading of the following syllogism does not disclose a logical error. The premises are true, and the conclusion is true. (See the relevant endnote for an explanation of the logical error in this example. I have also included another syllogism which illustrates another logical error that is even more difficult to figure out.)

All dogs are mammals.

All collies are mammals.

All collies are dogs.

Although the words are different, the *structure* of the following syllogism is identical to the one above, so it includes the same logical error. This time the conclusion does not make sense.

All dogs are thinking creatures.

All college teachers are thinking creatures.

Therefore, all college teachers are dogs.

Scientists accept that we cannot determine whether or not the conclusion to an argument is correct just because it seems to make sense. One must know the rules of logic and apply them correctly in order to arrive at dependable conclusions. The distinction between truth and validity is particularly important for psychology, because we usually do not have an independent means of determining the truth of our propositions.

A few changes in a categorical syllogism produce a *hypothetical syllogism*, which is the type used in research. Its relationship to the categorical syllogism is obvious, but the hypothetical syllogism has its own set of rules for determining validity. The following syllogism is valid.

Major premise: If Bill lives in Chicago (antecedent), *then* he is a resident of Illinois (consequent).

Minor premise: Bill lives in Chicago.

Conclusion: Bill lives in Illinois.

The "if" and "then" italicized in the major premise identify the fundamental terms. The "if" part is the *antecedent,* which is normally the research hypothesis to be tested. The "then" part, the *consequent,* includes the predicted effect, some expected conclusion or result from the action of the antecedent.

The formal structure of good research follows the pattern outlined earlier. First we identify a problem, and then we formulate a tentative hypothesis that solves or explains it. We work out ways for testing the hypothesis. We predict the result we should get if the hypothesis is true.

A testable hypothesis is phrased to form the antecedent of a hypothetical proposition. Consequents are anticipated that would be true *if* the ideas in the antecedent are true.

The general structure of a hypothetical syllogism is given below. We are unlikely to find assertions of this sort so clearly expressed in journal articles, but the general form can usually be worked out. The *if* and *then* are almost never stated, just as *all* in a categorical syllogism is not usually shown.

If my idea about XXXXX (a particular hypothesis)

is correct (antecedent),

then when I do the experiment I have described I should get these yyyyy results (consequent).

Hypothetical syllogisms are evaluated by how the minor premise deals with either the antecedent or consequent of the major premise. The conclusion of a hypothetical syllogism takes the same form as the minor premise, but it refers to the alternate term. If the minor premise affirms the antecedent, the conclusion affirms the consequent. If the consequent is denied in the minor premise, the conclusion denies the antecedent. These are the two valid forms of hypothetical syllogisms. All four variations are given in the following list.

1. A minor premise can "affirm" or agree with the antecedent; it can confirm that the antecedent is true. (Bill does live in Chicago).
   Conclusion: He must therefore live in Illinois. This form is valid.
2. A minor premise can "deny" or disagree with the antecedent; it can confirm that the antecedent is not true. (Bill does not live in Chicago).
   Conclusion: He might, or he might not, live in Illinois. The conclusion is ambiguous, and it is not forced by the premises. This form is not valid.
3. A minor premise can affirm the consequent; it can state that the expected results were obtained. (Bill lives in Illinois).
   Conclusion: He might or he might not live in Chicago. Because we cannot depend on the conclusion, this form is not valid.
4. A minor premise can deny that the statement made in the consequent is true. (Bill does *not* live in Illinois).
   Conclusion: Bill does *not* live in Chicago, Illinois. This form is valid.

Point 4 provides the valid structure for all research. Rejection of the consequent, which means we *did not* get the results we expected, is the only valid form of relevance for research. It follows, of course, that hypotheses must be presented in a way that allows for their rejection.

Point 3 is the one beginners usually find the most difficult to understand:

> If my therapy works, then I should get a statistically significant improvement in the behavior of my patients in 6 weeks.

> I find 6 weeks later that there has been a statistically significant improvement in their behavior.

Doesn't the favorable conclusion prove that my therapy works? The answer is, not necessarily. Common sense, the malingering half-brother of good intentions, is always waiting to make a case for the use of affirming evidence as proof. A careful investigator should not say, "Research proves my therapy works." The therapy might be an excellent one. We did indeed get the results we expected, but affirming the consequent of a hypothetical proposition is not a form of reasoning that guarantees the validity of the conclusion.

Two examples will demonstrate the difficulty of making sense from affirming instances. The premises in the following arguments are almost identical, with the minor premise affirming the consequent in both, but the conclusions are quite different. Invalid arguments are confusing because conclusions from them may be true some of the time, but we cannot depend on them to be true every time.

> If Abraham Lincoln had been assassinated, he would be dead.

> We know that he is dead, and we also know from independent information that he was assassinated.

> If George Washington had been assassinated, he would be dead.

> We know that he is dead, but a conclusion that he was assassinated is false. We know from history that he was not assassinated.

Affirming the second term in propositions presented in this way is not a valid form, therefore we cannot depend on the conclusions derived from them.

It is necessary here to make a distinction between practical applications of research findings and their logical interpretation. Much of what we know about how the world works has come from research that produced the predicted results. When sufficient confirming evidence has been accumulated, research findings should be put to use for solving appropriate problems. The fact that affirming evidence seems to work cannot be used as proof that the research propositions are correct.

> So what does one do with "positive results," that is, an experimental outcome that is consistent with the hypothesis in question? How are these to be interpreted? In a word, cautiously.
>
> (Mahoney, 1978)

HYPOTHESES: CHARACTERISTICS, FORM, AND USE

Good Hypotheses Begin With Good Ideas

Some people believe that the advancement of psychology is held up more by the lack of good hypotheses than by the shortage of observations or "facts."

> It is an utterly superficial view, therefore, that truth is to be found by "studying the facts." It is superficial because no inquiry can even get under way until and unless *some difficulty is felt* in a practical or theoretical situation. It is the difficulty, or problem, which guides our search for some *order among the facts*, in terms of which the difficulty is to be removed.
>
> (Cohen & Nagel, 1934).

A phone book is unquestionably an accumulation of facts. The facts have a practical use, but the phone book can also supply information for interesting research if appropriate questions are asked of it. One might start by comparing the proportion of telephones in various communities. To what extent is this number correlated with income? property values? educational level? How well are communities represented in terms of physicians, restaurants, and businesses of various types? To what extent have there been changes in various "yellow pages" listings over the years? Anyone can develop other and better questions that the phone book can be used to answer. The point is, vigorous research is based on good ideas, not on an accumulation of data or an availability of facts.

My nearly lifelong interest in science has provided me with hundreds of the "I wish I had thought of that" examples. I can be aware of something without being mindful that I have identified a problem that could lead to interesting research. Hundreds of thousands of people must have noticed, as I have, that the moon looks bigger when it is seen rising beyond a clump of trees than it does when it is overhead. I knew this, but the observation certainly never suggested to me a topic for the creative research produced by investigators of the "moon illusion."

Of course, identifying a question is only part of the research procedure. Once one gets the hang of it, asking questions becomes relatively easy. The more difficult part is to provide the answers or explanations. "Moon illusion" is the general topic one would use to search the library and *Psychological Abstracts* to find the surprisingly complex explanations for this interesting phenomenon.

Obtaining Ideas for Research

Consider the task of a person who has been sent to study the people in a village. Where would one begin? A very short list might include: eating practices; education; courting and mating behavior; treatment of the elderly; leadership and government; religion and thoughts of the supernatural; composition of family groups; attitudes toward and treatment of strangers; language; ideas of illness, disease, and treatment. What is the place of women and children in the village? What are the artistic and recreational activities? What is the relationship of the people in this village to people in other villages? One might study the architecture in terms of its utility or its use of applicable materials. Agricultural practices might be interesting, and we could look at types and sources of food, behavior in relation to the climate or geography, clothes, or transportation. Note that I have not given a hint about the type of village I have in mind, so each reader will have formed a mental image of his or her own. Is it one in Africa, South America, Alaska, New England, or the English midlands? At the beginning of a research project it is very difficult to know what to look for, which is no surprise to anyone who has been assigned the task of writing a term paper—on something! There will be more discussion of this topic when we study naturalistic observation as a research technique.

Almost by definition we can say that a person cannot have any good ideas until he or she has chosen a topic and studied it long enough to identify good questions.

Types of Hypotheses

We will eventually study two different types of hypotheses. Before research can begin, the investigator must develop a *research* hypothesis, which provides the reason for doing the research. Statisticians often call this the "alternate hypothesis," and it is usually labeled H_1 or H_A. This important hypothesis will be discussed first. Another type of hypothesis to be studied later is called a "null hypothesis" (H_o). It is used for evaluating statistical conclusions.

The research hypothesis proposes an explanation for the phenomenon being considered. The function of a hypothesis is to give guidance in the collection of data and structure to unrelated ideas.

The following generic definition of a hypothesis is a good one to memorize.

A hypothesis is a tentative (provisional) supposition put forward to explain (relate, summarize, organize) a set of observations (facts).

For a hypothesis to be of any value it must satisfy the requirements listed below.

Criteria for a Good Hypothesis

1. It must summarize and organize observations and be able to explain relationships among them. As it integrates the facts toward the development of a possible law, it should be able to reconcile apparent differences, inconsistencies, and contradictions among them.
2. A good hypothesis *must be testable*. It must be phrased to *permit its rejection*. Denying the consequent in the major premise of a hypothetical syllogism is the only valid interpretation of interest to science. A great many ideas have little value for research because they have not been developed into a form that will permit testing.

    "If no test can be conceived that can prove a proposition wrong, then it is not a proposition of science" (Editorial, *Chicago Tribune*, 1987, January 4,) This statement was from a discussion considering whether or not "creationists'" beliefs on the origin of life constitute a science. A subsequent court ruling established, among other things, that scientific ideas must be testable. There must be a way to demonstrate that hypotheses are wrong. "Beliefs" cannot be tested, therefore they cannot be shown to be wrong.

It might not always be possible to put hypotheses to test in the early stages of their development because suitable conditions are not available, measurement of some variable is not yet possible, or some other restriction prevents it. When a hypothesis is first proposed it is enough for it to be *capable* of rejection. Many of the propositions derived from Einstein's theories could not be tested when they were first developed, and ways for testing some of them still are not available.

The validity of hypotheses that are not directly testable might nevertheless be assessed in one or another of the following ways.

a. They can be checked for internal consistency. Do the parts seem to fit together? Are the concepts mutually consistent?

b. Have they been corroborated by evidence that is already available?

c. Does the hypothesis lead to other predictions that can be tested? What sorts of generalizations are possible from it?

d. Does it work?

e. Do "authorities" consider it reasonable? This is the least satisfactory approach because authorities are notorious for being wrong—and this has been true for many hundreds of years, as history can illustrate. Recall the discussion in Chapter 1.

3. A good hypothesis will encourage predictions into areas that have not yet been directly observed. It is not enough to explain only those observations already in hand; we assume that a good hypothesis can do that, but what else can it explain? It is often said that good research should raise more questions than it answers.

Hypotheses are not eliminated just because they do not work. Psychology subscribes to many different theories of personality. Inherent contradictions make it impossible for all of them to be right, so some of them must be wrong. It does not follow, however, that any of them will be rejected just because they do not work very well. It seems to be a quality of human nature to require explanations for everything; even those explanations that are not adequate are accepted as better than none.

SERENDIPITY IN SCIENCE

People who are not sophisticated in research have been known to argue for a less structured approach. They want an opportunity to try things out, to see what they can discover. If a researcher's vision is restricted by narrow objectives that have to be couched in terms amenable to a statistical evaluation, they argue, some new and wonderful insights that could alter the course of humankind might get overlooked. This is possible, but not likely. Researchers must keep their senses open and remain alert to see and explore any unexpected developments. That point is not arguable. Competent research people who know enough about their fields to have good ideas, who formulate good testable hypotheses, and who design solid experiments for testing them, are not likely to overlook something of importance that pops up along the way. They might, however, be so preoccupied with their own work in a limited time and on a restricted budget that they will be unable to expand on their discoveries.

"Serendipity" is the term used to describe the new and unexpected discoveries that make up the folklore of science. The name comes from the Horace Walpole tale, *The Three Princes of Serendip*, the title characters in which seemed to have an aptitude for making discoveries accidentally. The idea applies to those fortuitous observations, those important and unexpected discoveries that have advanced our knowledge. This is the fun part of research, which produces the stories we enjoy reading about. "Something *blank* was discovered accidentally by *blank* who was working on *blank* in his lab, when *blank*," and the story goes on. The accounts of pure discovery are interesting because there are not very many of them.

Fleming's discovery of penicillin is discussed in many texts as a standard example of how an accidental discovery—or, in his case, a series of them— markedly changed the development of medical science. The discovery was made by a well-trained scientist working in his own field. That is what it takes for the importance of an unusual finding to be identified. Before Fleming's observations could be put to the practical use of saving lives, a great deal more work remained to be done. Fleming's observation of an aberrant mold that killed bacteria growing in a petri dish was only the start. At the time of the initial discovery Fleming was able to show that penicillin was not toxic to animals, and it seemed harmless to body cells. Working in collaboration, Fleming and Rainstrick attempted to isolate and concentrate penicillin but without success. Nearly 10 years elapsed before the project was picked up again, this time by Florey and Chain. The 1945 Nobel Prize in physiology and medicine was shared by Florey, Chain, and Fleming for their joint discovery and development of penicillin. As is often the case in science, the full history of the discovery is much more complex, involves many more people, and is in general more interesting than popular reports disclose. MacFarlane's book (1984) should be consulted to set the record straight on penicillin.

Roberts (1989) in his book *Serendipity* has brought together a number of interesting examples of serendipity at work in science.

"Dans les champs de l'observation, le hasard ne favorise que les esprits prepares." ("In the field of observation, chance favors only the prepared mind.") This is a quotation from one of Pasteur's works, which all beginners should take to heart. The history of science shows that serendipity helps only those people who are knowledgeable about their fields of study. They are the only ones able to recognize and appreciate the surprises that provide the foundation for further research.

Medawar (1984) has reminded us that all scientists have to allow that some of their discoveries have been affected by luck. "Any scientist who is not a hypocrite will admit (this).. . . " But the effect of luck ". . . must always seem to be greater than it really is, because our estimate of its importance is inherently biased: We know when we benefit from luck, but from the nature of things, we cannot assess how often bad luck deprives us of the chance of making what might have been an important discovery—the discoveries we did not make leave no traces."

THE LAW OF PARSIMONY (OCCAM'S RAZOR)

It sometimes happens that two or more hypotheses are available to account for the same observations. How can one choose between (or among) them?

How can we explain mental illness? Is there only one cause or are there several? Any of these ideas might work:

It is just bad luck.

Illness is the result of a curse by an enemy.

Our body is out of harmony with the celestial spheres.

Malevolent gods use illness as punishment for sinful thoughts.

A biochemical imbalance exists in the brain.

Tiny invisible organisms living in the body put out poisons as they grow and multiply.

A psychological dysfunction (whatever that is!) can be the cause of a physiological difficulty.

There is pressure on the nerves, or they just got tired or worn out from too much strain.

A very old rule that gives guidance in choosing among competing hypotheses is *the law of parsimony*, or *Occam's razor*. William of Occam (or Ockham), an English philosopher who lived from 1280 to 1349, wrote the following edict in the classical Latin used by the scholars of his time, "*Entia non multiplicanda sunt praeter necessitatem.*" It means, "Entities are not to be multiplied beyond necessity." Entities can be laws, hypotheses, assumptions, principles, ideas, or suppositions.

The word "parsimony" is not widely used in these times of conspicuous consumption. It describes a case of extreme frugality, a tendency to be overcareful in the spending of money, almost to the point of stinginess. In science, if there is a choice between a hypothesis that involves new, complicated, and untried ideas, in contrast to an explanation that requires only well-understood and readily accepted concepts, the latter hypothesis is the one of choice. Science tries to reduce the variety of principles and laws to the smallest number possible. No new, mysterious, or untested concepts should be admitted to use until all attempts to achieve an adequate explanation with accepted principles and assumptions have failed repeatedly.

It is not quite the idea to say, "Choose the 'simpler' of the two hypotheses if both explain the observations equally well." Trying to define the word simple in this context is the cause of the difficulty. The better of the two hypotheses might not be the simpler, according to the normal meaning of the word. To a person from a primitive society, it might seem simpler to explain illness in terms of a vengeful god than to hypothesize microscopic organisms as the cause of a disease. The one to choose will more fully satisfy the rules listed earlier in the chapter: It is testable, it permits predictions, it fits well with other hypotheses, it explains a larger number of seemingly disconnected observations. And according to the law of parsimony, it will make the fewer new or untested assumptions.

HYPOTHESIS, THEORY, FACT, AND LAW

Because there is so much confusion in the meanings of these words it is necessary to explain the distinctions among them that will apply in this text. The uninitiated use the word "theory" incorrectly, as something opposed to "facts," and even scientific writers often fail to note a logical distinction between the words "hypothesis" and "theory."

A *theory* is generally assumed to be better established than a working hypothesis. Experimental work has accumulated to provide a theory with a solid empirical base. Furthermore, theories are usually broader in their explanations, but in practice they can operate much like hypotheses in attempting to give order and meaning to observations. The amount of supporting evidence assumed is a major distinguishing characteristic that determines our understanding of the differences between hypotheses and theories.

Popular usage endows *facts* with a solid character that is not appropriate in science. Facts are just ideas that are so well supported by evidence, so well established, that no one seriously questions them. Facts are not fixed and unchanging, however. Today's facts might become tomorrow's quaint ideas, as new concepts are developed—or they might be proved wrong. See the Endnote for an example of an important "fact" that changed.

Typically, research begins with a hypothesis. As the hypothesis is strengthened through the accrual of positive findings, it gradually achieves the status of a theory; then as even more supporting evidence accumulates, it becomes a fact.

A fact as a true reality, fixed and unchanging, has no place in the scheme of science. One way that our knowledge advances is by questioning previously accepted "facts." According to Leahey and Harris (1989, p. 22) early behaviorists in the United States were quick to begin work on various projects that used conditioning research methods along the lines developed by Pavlov. The objectives of the American psychologists were quite different. "They were *behavior-theorists*, not physiologists." They sought knowledge of adaptive behavior and were not interested in trying to discover how the brain functions, which was the topic of Pavlov's interest. "They therefore took Pavlovian conditioning as a fact, and Pavlov's technique as a proven method and went on from there, for which Pavlov himself reproved them." Whether a "fact" is or is not a fact obviously depends on who is using it.

There is more scientific prestige in the development of a theory than in a mere hypothesis; anyone discussing his or her own work will therefore want to push it along as far as the evidence can be stretched. A more conservative orientation will permit a hypothesis to become a theory only when there has been a substantial accumulation of positive research to support it. How should ideas of learning be classified—as hypotheses or theories? Should we call them "psychoanalytic theories" or "hypotheses"? Do we have *theories* of personality or just ideas about how to define it?

Each reader will decide for him or herself whether the following is correctly described as a theory, or whether "hypothesis" is the better word. The opening paragraph of an interesting article by Fagan (1992) states in part:

> I have a theory of intelligence. The theory helps me to understand infant intelligence, mental retardation, the determinants of intellectual achievement, and how to search for the neural bases of intelligence. The key point of the theory is that intelligence is not a faculty or trait of the mind. Intelligence is not mental content. *Intelligence is processing.*

If there is a well-established or well-thought out theory available for evaluation, then experiments can be designed to test hypotheses derived from an analysis of the theory. Whether we move from hypotheses to theories or use theories to develop hypotheses is not an important distinction.

A *law* cannot be placed precisely in the sequence given above. It involves a higher level of complexity than will normally be seen in a fact, and it has a higher level of verification than is necessary for a theory. It is more formal and more structured than a theory, but it also functions to show the regularities and relationships among concepts.

Many people hold the belief that scientific laws are "discovered" by scientists. The following quotation from Thurstone (1935) indicates a different point of view.

> A scientific law is not to be thought of as having an independent existence which some scientist is fortunate to stumble on. A scientific law is not a part of nature. It is only a way of comprehending nature . . . The chief object of science is to minimalize mental effort. It is in the nature of science that no scientific law can ever be proved to be right. It can only be shown to be plausible. The laws of science are not immutable. They are only human efforts towards parsimony in the comprehension of nature.

A study of human learning provides examples of how these terms are sometimes applied to psychological information. Leahey and Harris (1989) is a good reference for additional reading on the topic.

In the early days of the 20th century learning was an important area for psychological study to determine the applicable laws. *Contiguity* is one of the fundamental "laws of association." The suggestion here is that ideas held in the mind at the same time will become associated. *Vividness* is a law of association which holds that an observation will more likely become connected with a vivid idea than with a weak one. *Similarity* is a law derived from the observation that similar ideas are easily associated.

Thorndike's famous "law of effect" (1911) attempted to explain the relationship between rewards or punishment on the development of a given response. Remember that laws are just ways of putting thoughts together to explain how we think some process works. They are considered correct explanations of the "facts" only to the extent to which they work. Publications such as those by Tolman, Hall, and Bretnall (1932), and Estes (1972), have shown that Thorndike's "law" only partially explains the processes in that selected area of learning.

SUMMARY

The formal steps in a research proposal can be simply stated.

We begin with the identification of a problem or puzzle we feel we can solve or explain.

We state the explanation as a "hypothesis." Next we identify certain outcomes that we would expect in a research situation if our hypothesis were true. We combine these two statements to form an "If . . . then . . . " proposition, which becomes the major premise of a hypothetical syllogism. We use the major premise to make a deductive inference, which becomes the conclusion of the syllogism.

Next, we test the hypothesis using appropriate research procedures. We apply the principles of formal logic to assess the validity of the outcome.

In science, the only logically valid form of reasoning from a hypothetical syllogism is to "negate the consequent." This would apply if we *did not* get the results we expected. From this we would conclude that the hypothesis is not true.

Affirming research findings, those in the expected direction, cannot be used as proof that the hypothesis is correct. Inability to show that an idea is wrong cannot be taken as direct evidence that it is right. It could be right, it may be right, and certainly we have failed to demonstrate that it is not right—but that is not proof.

ENDNOTES

When Is a Fact a Fact?

Is it not a fact that the normal, average, temperature for a person who is not sick is 98.6°, and you have a fever anytime your temperature goes much over 100°? That is what I have always been taught. Carl Reinhold August Wunderlich is the person generally credited for doing most of the original work on temperature measurement, and he published his conclusions in 1868. Not much has been done since that time to check his conclusions. In the few studies that have been done, samples were small and there were other errors. Therefore, the original figure is still the one we use, but that should change.

According to Mackowiak, Wasserman, and Myron (1992), "98.6°F should be abandoned as a concept relevant to clinical thermometry." Their own work grew out of a complete evaluation of Wunderlich's procedures and data, and their conclusions recommend that 99.2°F should be used as the mean oral temperature of healthy adults. They confirmed Wunderlich's finding of large daily variations, and they also noted that women have a slightly higher temperature than men. They selected 99.9°F to identify the upper limit of the normal temperature range.

The researchers noted that today's thermometers, as compared with Wunderlich's, are smaller, more reliable, and "equilibrate" more quickly. When Wunderlich's axillary temperature measurements were taken the thermometers took 15 to 20 minutes to equilibrate. These variations might account for a portion of the observed difference.

The 98.6°F figure, which is widely accepted in medical practice (e.g, it is the figure given in *Stedman's Medical Dictionary*) "does not fall within the 99.9% confidence limits" in the recent study.

Mackowiak et al. note that modern medicine has difficulty defining the upper limit of the normal oral temperature. They believe the source of the confusion

> derives from individual variability that limits the application of mean values derived from population studies to individual subjects and from the fact that the maximum oral temperature, like the mean temperature, exhibited by any population varies according to time of day. Because of this variability, no single temperature should be regarded as the upper limit of normal.

I hope readers will recognize as I do that if a psychological construct is substituted for temperature in this discussion, we could make an identical statement in regard to many areas of psychology.

Application of the Law of Parsimony

In the British publication *New Scientist*, Humphrey and McManus (1973) raised an interesting question about why artists should have a special preference for painting left or right profiles in their portraits. If one undertakes an examination of a large number of portraits, it is reasonable to expect that half of them would have been painted as viewed from the left side and half from the right. The assumption is that it should be a matter of chance whether an artist decides to paint the left profile or the right profile. Humphrey and McManus examined 1,474 paintings of faces and found that 891 of them were painted showing more of the left cheek and 583 more of the right. The probability of a chance difference as large as 60% more left cheek to 40 percent more right cheek for a sample of this size is very slight indeed.

The first hypothesis put forward to explain this finding suggested that it is easier for right-handed artists to paint a profile toward the left side of the canvas. This hypothesis was rejected when it was discovered that 58 percent of the men had been painted with more of the left cheek visible, compared with a finding that 68% of the women were posed to expose more left cheek. The difference was statistically significant at the .001 level. The authors could not think of any reason why it would be easier to paint women's, rather than men's, faces from the left side. The various preliminary observations did not support the authors' original mechanical explanation, which had to be rejected.

Another idea the researchers examined considered the possibility that left or right profiles have different psychological meanings in their representation of a subject's status. Rembrandt van Rijn painted 57 self-portraits, of which only 16% showed more of the left cheek. He painted his male kin with the same low proportion of portraits showing more of the left cheek. But as paintings of other people were analyzed it was found that the proportion of paintings showing more of the left cheek increased until it reached 52% left-cheek showing to 14% right-cheek showing in representations of female non-kin. The order of change from more right-cheek showing to more left-cheek showing for different subjects is listed in order of their relationship to the painter: male kin, male non-kin, female kin, female non-kin. "Thus whenever Rembrandt painted a portrait he gave some indication of the social distance between himself and the subject."

The evidence from portraits Rembrandt painted, as well as from paintings by other artists of the same period, gave good support for the idea that the left- or right-cheek profiles tended to conform to the perceived relationship, from the artist's point of view, between the artist and the subject. Women who were non-kin were seen as further removed from the male artists than male non-kin.

The publication of Humphrey and McManus's explanations of asymmetry in painting stimulated several responses. One letter writer pointed out a presumed custom in European painting in which the left-hand side of a picture denotes the past and the right-hand side, the future. The fact that there are more right-cheek exposures for men and left-cheek displays for women apparently shows that more men are supposedly more likely to be looking toward the future (toward the right side of the painting). The greater number of left cheeks showing for women suggests that women, at least in paintings, look toward the past. No hypothesis was suggested to explain why this difference would be expected.

Another writer explained the same observations with reference to "social custom and the expectations of the artist. We extend our right hand in friendship on meeting, and the left profile may conversely be taken as the 'cold shoulder', the side of the body which indicates rebuttal."

A third letter writer thought the authors had overlooked a point that could much more easily account for some of the differences between male and female portraits.

> It was common practice in Rembrandt's time for the portraits of a man and a wife to be commissioned at the same time. These were normally painted on separate canvases but in matching styles and designed to be hung side by side. In such circumstances the man would customarily be placed on the woman's right and thus tend to present his right-hand profile to the artist while the woman showed her left-hand profile.

In the course of time many of these portraits, which were originally members of a pair, have become separated and are thus now not always easy to identify as such. But care should clearly be taken before attributing to any notion of 'psychological distance' the result of a rather simpler sociological phenomenon.

Without these additional comments it would have been tempting to accept the psychological explanation given by the original authors as *THE* correct one. Now that alternate ideas are available for consideration it is appropriate to apply the law of parsimony for determining which of them is the one of choice—if indeed the correct one has been mentioned.

We should keep in mind that there might not be a single explanation that covers all the situations. It is possible that the social-distance hypothesis and the husband-right and wife-left explanations are both relevant and correct, as are others we have not yet thought about.

College Teachers Are Not Dogs

Authors of textbooks try in various ways to acknowledge the wide diversity of people who read them. We know in advance that we will frequently fail to satisfy the desires of some readers who want more information, whereas other readers will wonder why we ramble on endlessly to discuss material no one cares about. I will in this instance risk offending this second group of readers by providing a fuller explanation of the logical fallacy in the instructor/dog syllogism. A number of people have asked for a fuller explanation, which I am happy to provide—even though I will not be able to cover the topic thoroughly. I want to furnish enough information so that readers who have had a course in logic will be able to refresh their memories. My point in this illustration was to show that we cannot rely on general appearances to help us determine the validity of logical arguments. We must follow the rules of logic or we will sometimes go wrong.

Following is a valid syllogism for illustration. I have identified the "terms" with letters. Note that each term is used twice; there are two A's, two B's, and two C's. The (d) and (u) symbols show whether the term is "distributed" or "undistributed."

A(d)   B(u)
All (psychologists) are (bright people).

   C(d)   A(u)
(Angelo) is a (psychologist).

   C   B
(Angelo) is a (bright person).

The error in the following syllogism is called the "fallacy of undistributed middle," but first let us look at the valid syllogism given above. The "middle term" is the one that appears in the both premises but never in the conclusion. "Psychologist" is the middle term in the above example. We are dealing with the relationship of classes, and we are trying to determine if a particular class is or is not included in another class. A term is "distributed" if the relationship of the "all" class to the other class is known. The "all" modifier for "psychologists" makes it a distributed term. When the relationship of one term to the other is less than all, the term is said to be "undistributed". We can see that *all psychologists* are *bright people,* but we cannot be sure that all *bright people* are necessarily *psychologists,* so that term is undistributed.

In the second premise, the minor premise, the "Angelo" term is distributed. All of Angelo is a psychologist, but not all psychologists (undistributed) are Angelo. In this syllogism the "psychologist" middle term is distributed in the major premise. The rules of logical reasoning require the middle term to be distributed at least once. As far as that particular rule is concerned, this is a valid syllogism.

The syllogism given earlier in the chapter is reprinted below. Note that "mammals" is the middle term. Although the premise states that *all dogs* are *mammals,* it does not make it clear whether *all mammals* are *dogs,* so the "mammals" term is undistributed.

The minor premise takes the same form. We know that all of the class of *collies* is included in the class of *mammals,* but we cannot conclude that all *mammals* are *collies.* The "mammal" term is again undistributed. This syllogism violates the rule that says the middle term must be distributed at least once.

> A   B
> All dogs are mammals.
>
> C   B
> All collies are mammals.
>
> C   D
> All collies are dogs.

Everyone who has ever studied logic will understand and sympathize if this is not entirely clear! The fallacy cannot be understood from this very simplified presentation. I am not trying to teach logic, but I do want to make the point that an understanding of logic can help us to avoid some of the common mistakes in reasoning.

I think the following syllogism is particularly interesting because we know the conclusion is in fact true, but there is a logical error in the argument that might another time cause us to make a mistake. One of the rules for a valid categorical syllogism states that it must have three "terms," each used twice. Try to find the logical error in the following syllogism.

The Sears Tower (1,450 feet) is taller than the Standard Oil Building (1,136 feet).

The Standard Oil Building is taller than the Hancock Center (1,107 feet).

The Sears Tower (1,450 feet) is taller than the Hancock Center (1,107 ft).

Common sense shows the conclusion to be true, but there is an error in the reasoning which keeps the argument from being valid.

The example has four terms, so the syllogism is not valid because it has committed the "four terms fallacy." Actually, this argument is not even a syllogism because a syllogism, as we saw above, is defined as an argument having three terms, each used twice.

        A   B
The (Sears Tower) is (taller than the Standard Oil Building).

           C   D
The (Standard Oil Building) is (taller than the Hancock Center).

        A   D
The (Sears Tower) is (taller than the Hancock Center).

The fallacy is caused by the two different forms of the terms that apply to the Standard Oil Building, terms B and C. In B there is a class "taller than" the Standard Oil Building, and in C the Standard Oil Building is itself a class.

The following syllogism has a conclusion that might or might not be true. We do not know, because the form of the syllogism is not valid.

      A   B
Tom is Henry's landlord.

      C   D
Henry is Mark's landlord.

      A   D
Tom is Mark's landlord.

In a way, this syllogism summarizes the major ideas of this discussion on logic. Science cannot accept what might be true or what seems to be true. In the real world we can never be absolutely certain, but we strive to get as close to the truth as we can. The purpose of scientific investigation is primarily to obtain the information for the premises of syllogisms so that we can make *valid* deductive inferences from them. Investigation can verify that Tom is Henry's landlord. Further research will disclose that Henry is Mark's landlord. From that information we want to draw a valid conclusion about the landlord/tenant relationship between Tom and Mark. The flaw in the structure of this argument makes it impossible to draw a valid conclusion from it. A similar argument made sense when we talked about heights of buildings. That time it worked, but we cannot depend on the conclusion from a syllogism that does not satisfy all the rules for logical reasoning.

STUDY QUESTIONS

1.   Discuss, comment on, and be prepared to explain the lead paragraph of this chapter.

2.   What is "logic"?

3.   What are two main areas of logical reasoning? Explain and give examples of the differences between them.

4. What is an inference?
   Differentiate between an inductive and deductive inference.

5. What is a fallacy?

6. What is validity?

7. Define "argument," as the term is used in logic.

8. What does it mean to say that an argument is "valid"?

9. Explain the "hypothetico-deductive" research strategy.

10. What are the steps in the hypothetico-deductive method?
    How is it used in psychological research?

11. With reference to research, what is the only valid way for the minor premise to deal with the major premise?

12. Why is "affirming the consequent" *not* a valid form of argument?

13. Most investigators try to get a conclusion that confirms what was predicted from their research hypothesis, even though the conclusion cannot be logically valid. How is this sort of information used?

14. Explain the frequently stated idea that hypotheses can never be proved right, they can only be disproved.

15. Explain why a collection of facts does not make a science.
    What is wrong with a scientist doing research by just studying the facts?

16. Where do ideas for good research come from?

17. Explain the point of view that science advances faster through good ideas than it does through the accumulation of facts.

18. Define a research hypothesis.
    How are hypotheses used in research?

19. What are some criteria for a good research hypothesis?

20. What are some ways for assessing the validity of hypotheses that cannot be evaluated by normal research techniques?

21. What does it mean to say that a research hypothesis should have "predictive power"?

22. What is the role of serendipity in scientific discovery?

23. If extensive research shows that a particular hypothesis is inadequate, why is the hypothesis not dropped from further consideration?
    Why are poor hypotheses retained even though they cannot adequately explain phenomena of interest?

24. What is the "law of parsimony" (Occam's razor)?

How is this idea of importance in research?

25.   Define and explain the differences among hypotheses, theories, facts, and laws. What determines whether a particular explanation is a hypothesis or a theory?

26.   Explain the idea that a scientific law is not a part of nature but is only science's way for understanding nature. Develop the idea that scientific laws are not discovered, they are made.

27.D What would a person have to do to prove that the Fagan theory of intelligence (mentioned above) is right?

28.D Why do some theories in psychology "take off" (become popular) and stimulate a great deal of research whereas others do not?

29.D It has been said that everyone has a "theory of personality." What is yours?

SMALL TALK

PART TWO

Measurement

Chapter
4

Special Topics in Measurement

Three procedures are common to all measurement:

1. identify and define the quality or attribute that is to be measured,
2. determine a set of operations by which the attribute many be made manifest and perceivable,
3. establish a set of procedures for translating observations into quantitative statements of degree or amount.

Thorndike & Hagen. (1969), p. 9.

CONCEPTS AND CONSTRUCTS

Peter and Jennifer planned to major in psychology when they went to college. To get a little preliminary experience they undertook a high school psychology project. They knew that an important task of psychology is to observe, describe, interpret, and ultimately to explain behavior. Peter had a new puppy, so he and Jennifer kept records of various things they were able to observe about him. They knew they might be ego involved while observing a pet they loved, but they promised themselves to be as objective as possible.

When first brought to the house the puppy was disoriented. After awhile he relaxed and began to wander around the room, examining things. The puppy seemed naturally curious, almost as if he had an instinct or a need to explore his environment.

Whenever Jennifer came to the house the puppy wagged its tail, which showed he was happy to see her.

To study his memory, they let the puppy watch while they hid bits of food. They held him for one minute, then watched to see if he went straight to the food when he was released. He nearly always did.

A psychologist friend was able to lend Peter and Jennifer a dog intelligence test,[1] which they enjoyed trying out. This experience led to several discussions about the nature of intelligence, and particularly, dog intelligence. The test did not show the puppy to be as bright as they thought he was. They concluded that the test probably was not valid. They tried to get some information on determining the reliability and validity of intelligence tests, but they had no knowledge of statistics so they did not get much out of the material.

The puppy quickly learned or was conditioned to come when they called him and held his leash. The leash seemed to signify he was going for a walk, and he enjoyed the walks very much.

The point of this little exposition is to show the large number of psychological terms we use in our daily discourse. A list of some of the ideas, although certainly not all of them, would include the following:

Disoriented	Relaxed	Curious	Instinct
Need	Happy	Learning	Memory
Intelligence	Eager	Validity	Reliability
Conditioning	Ego	Love	Bright

Terms of this sort are so well accepted, so much a part of the language of psychology, that we rarely question their meaning—except perhaps to wonder how learning could be speeded up or how memory could be improved to reduce the amount of forgetting. For most of us, words like "relaxed," "happy," "eager," "intelligence," and maybe even "ego," stand for something that has as genuine an existence as "gravity," "light," or "heat." We might not understand how memory works, but we know we have it. The familiar psychology words listed above have for us such a strong grounding in reality that it is difficult to accept that they, together with *all* psychological expressions, are "concepts" or "constructs." These are the names science gives to the terms it uses to summarize, identify, and sometimes even to explain its observations. Other terms that represent the same basic idea are "theoretical concept," and "hypothetical or theoretical construct."

In general, a concept or construct is something that a "scientist puts together from his own imagination, something that does not exist as an isolated, observable dimension of behavior." Nunnally (1970) continues:

---

[1]A "Dog Intelligence Test" developed by Kathy Coon was available in 1977 from: Dog, Inc., Box 14808, Baton Rouge, LA 70808. I do not know if it is still available. The test was thoughtfully designed and is more than a gimmick.

It is important to realize that all theories in science concern mainly statements about constructs rather than specific, observable variables.

> Scientists cannot do without constructs. Their theories are populated with them, and even in informal conversation scientists find it all but impossible to discuss their work without using words relating to constructs.
>
> (p. 139)

All attributes, terms, expressions, and names in psychology (or in any other science) are constructs. They are made-up names used to label or to help identify a set of behaviors. A short list of constructs that come immediately to mind could include the following.

Aggression	Hate	Love
Anxiety	Honesty	Lust
Bravery	Hostility	Pain
Depression	Humor	Patriotism
Ego	Id	Persistence
Fear	Insight	Personality
Feminine	Intelligence	Prejudice
Frustration	Learning	Reminiscence

It is an easy exercise to add many hundreds of others to the list.

Suppose I asked your opinion about someone. Is the person nice, friendly, well adjusted, of good character, artistic, possessing good taste, sanguine, phlegmatic, or resourceful? You could answer my questions only to the extent that you have had an opportunity to observe the person behaving in ways you can evaluate in terms of my constructs as you understand them. We can make a judgment about a person only by observing what that person does or, depending on the situation, does not do. Our own individual definition of a psychological construct determines how we evaluate the behavior we select for observation. We would have difficulty comparing our research findings on "persistence" if we discovered that you defined the construct using one kind of behavior and the situation I developed produced persistence in a markedly different way. Our disparate measurements might in fact be related, but we would not know that until we undertook a statistical comparison.

People often discuss intelligence without being clear whether the construct means the same thing to all of them. What does it mean for a person to say, "I have an IQ of 115"? Do all people with the same IQ behave in the same way? Are there different kinds of IQs? Do all IQ tests produce essentially the same score? Does IQ remain approximately the same throughout a person's life? How can we talk about—perhaps even try to compare—intelligence of different groups or different cultures? Intelligence is frequently characterized by an IQ, but could it be argued that "intelligence" and "IQ" are not the same? The point is, we cannot use psychological constructs for research, or even discuss them in a useful way, unless everyone involved knows what has been done to demonstrate the attribute in action.

"Intelligence" can be demonstrated by standard tests of many different kinds. Although results are likely to be related, there is no assurance that intelligence defined by one test will *necessarily* be the same as the one obtained from a different measuring instrument. Nor would performance on a test *necessarily* lead to an accurate prediction of behavior in a different situation—on a job or in school, for example.

OPERATIONAL DEFINITIONS OF CONSTRUCTS

Effective research requires investigators to define a construct by explaining what has been done to produce it. As we will see, the tasks of definition and measurement go together. The essence of measurement dictates that we show that some people have more of the construct and some have less.

> Identity, or sense of identity, is described as more than the sum of the childhood identifications. It is the accrued experience of the ego's ability to integrate all identification with the vicissitudes of the libido, with aptitudes developed out of endowment, and with opportunities offered in social roles.
>
> (Erickson, 1963, quoted in Cartwright, Jenkins, Chavez, & Peckar, 1983, p. 261)

If we wanted to evaluate this statement, we would be out of luck. Look at the words requiring definition: "identification," "accrued experience," "ego," "integration," "vicissitudes of the "libido," "libido," "aptitudes," "endowment," and "social roles." The only word here that could be employed in practical terms is "childhood"; unless all the other words and expressions can be adequately defined, it will be impossible to undertake any research on "identity." Or to recall Byrne's (1966, p. 26) succinct opinion, "Thus, if one cannot define a concept in terms of observables (hell for example), the concept is simply not open to scientific inquiry."

The problem of term definition is not one that is unique to psychology. If a physicist wanted to undertake research involving speed, how would she define it? How is mass defined, density, magnetism, gravity, light, time, or even electricity?

If I asked a reader this question, what answer would I expect? "Is there electricity available at your bedroom wall socket?" We can only learn if a household wall socket is "live" by plugging something into it. A lamp would do, a hair dryer, a radio, or a volt meter. Electricity becomes apparent only when it is called upon do something: light a light, heat a dryer, or play a radio. In this example we have demonstrated the presence of electricity by observing what it does.

Defining terms in physics is one of the problems Bridgman (1961) attempted to solve in his short but very influential book, first published in 1927, *The Logic of Modern Physics*. He illustrated his new way of thinking about concepts by defining "length." Before continuing, pause for a moment to consider what length is.

We could check what a couple of dictionaries have to say: "Extent in time, number, and quantity." "Measurement or extent from end to end." "The measure of how long a thing is." If a person undertakes an investigation that involves length, the construct must be clearly defined so that anyone who refers to the work will know precisely what the scientist means by "length." Bridgman solved the problem in this way:

> We may illustrate by considering the concept of length: what do we mean by the length of an object? We evidently know what we mean by length if we can tell what the length of any and every object is, and for the physicist nothing more is required. To find the length of an object, we have to perform certain physical operations. The concept of length is therefore fixed when the operations by which length is measured are fixed: that is, the concept of length involves as much as and nothing more than the set of operations by which length is determined. In general we mean by any concept nothing more than a set of operations; *the concept is synonymous with the corresponding set of operations.*
>
> (p. 5)

An appropriate operational definition of all constructs is a necessary precondition for successful research. Study the following statement until you fully understand its meaning.

To define a concept operationally, it is necessary to specify the measurable and observable acts that produce it.

To define the length of this page operationally, take an object—a pencil will do nicely—lay it down and count the number of lengths it takes to go from one edge to the other. When you show me the pencil and explain how it was used, I will have a complete understanding of what you mean by "length." Operational definitions provide an empirical way for identifying, defining, and explaining what a concept means to a particular investigator. I hope that we will now be able to make an easy transition from physical to psychological constructs. (Frankly speaking, I would rather measure the speed of light than "anger." The speed of light has already been measured—and I know the answer!)

Among many other things to be looked for in the evaluation of journal articles, one must identify the constructs that are being studied and note what procedures were used to define them operationally. Occasionally authors will name and operationally define their constructs. An article on "Explanatory Style as a Mechanism of Disappointing Athletic Performance," (Seligman, Nolen-Hoeksema, Thornton, & Thornton, 1990) lists two constructs: "explanatory style" and "disappointing athletic performance."

The abstract for their article gave their operational definitions. "Two university varsity swimming teams took the Attributional Style Questionnaire (ASQ) at the start of the season." Coaches used a 1- to 7-point rating scale of each swimmer's accomplishments on a competitive swim to determine an unsatisfactory performance. Those of us who are not swimming coaches would not know exactly what that means, but we could find out. With that information, and the ASQ questionnaire, we could replicate their study.

Another article in the same issue is less helpful. It simply states in its title that "Attractive Faces Are Only Average." A reader should immediately begin to wonder how attractiveness of faces was operationally defined. The authors state only that they had adults judge the physical attractiveness of faces by rating them. We do not know how or on what criteria. Following publication of this article, the authors published others that provided the operational definition we need (see the Endnotes).

An operational definition of a psychological construct requires an investigator to arrange standard conditions that produce an example—a sample—of the behavior to be measured. Measurement is very important to the scientific study of behavior; some psychologists might say that it is a central issue. Tests of various kinds—and psychology has produced a great many in a tremendous diversity—become operational definitions of psychological constructs.

PSYCHOLOGICAL TESTS AS OPERATIONAL DEFINITIONS

Throughout the following discussion, please understand that I use the word "test" in the broadest possible way. A test to me means a standard, structured situation that produces objective, measurable, samples of behavior, suitable for assessing individual differences. Naturally, an investigator tries to arrange a situation that will elicit the type of behavior he or she wants to use to define the construct operationally. If we want a test to define operationally, to measure, "sense of humor," we have a number of options.

We might use a group of 15 jokes that a test-development committee thinks are funny. Another group could collect 15 cartoons to make up their sense-of-humor test. A third group might draw cartoonlike pictures for which subjects would be asked to supply captions that would make the cartoons as funny as possible. We could collect a group of limericks, leave the last line off, and have the test takers provide new ones. These last two situations would probably measure a sort of humor-creativity construct. We might be interested in finding out if the personality attribute necessary for "creating" humor is the same as the one for appreciating it. How are these humor constructs related to "social" humor? Other psychologists interested in this area might examine humor by noting which people cause other people to laugh at parties. After we have defined and measured "sense of humor" we might want to compare those scores with measurements from other areas of personality.

If a test is to be of any use as an operational definition, it must produce scoreable differences in responses to it. This task is relatively easy if behavior can be scored as right or wrong. Scoring humor tests or other personality tests that do not have right or wrong answers presents a great deal of difficulty to the test developer. It is difficult indeed to show that designating 12 of the 15 cartoons from a particular group as funny is an operational definition of sense of humor that is meaningful in other ways that interest us.

Unless we were very careful in our selection, items on a sense-of-humor test might include subject-matter content that takers would respond to in ways completely unrelated to the sense-of-humor construct. Political items, those with a sexual content, items directed toward ethnic or other selected groups could all produce different results for that reason alone.

Even though jokes or cartoons are universally associated with humor, a *particular* set of jokes or other types of "funny" material might not produce an operational definition of the "sense-of-humor" construct. Responses to jokes or cartoons have been employed to assess aspects of personality other than humor. See the Cattell and Luborsky (1947) article on "Personality Factors in Response to Humor." Their work was later turned into the "IPAT Humor Test of Personality."[2] Yarnold and Berkley (1954) undertook an analysis of the test. Andrews (1943) also published relevant work, studying personality by analyzing responses to comic material. Eysenck (1943) published an experimental analysis of five "appreciation of humor" tests.

GENERAL TEST DEVELOPMENT

On any given day a psychology major might be involved with two different types of tests: typical classroom tests constitute one example, and there is another type we can broadly and loosely call "psychological" tests.

Tests of academic performance are "mastery" or "criterion referenced" tests, as is the one you take to get a driver's license. Items on these tests are scoreable as right or wrong (acceptable or not acceptable to the test developer.) There is no theoretical reason why everyone who takes a mastery test should not get every item right. Some psychology tests such as proficiency, achievement, or intelligence tests are made up of items scoreable as right or wrong, but meaning is given to each test's overall score in a different way, which produces operational definitions of different constructs.

The point of psychological testing is to identify subject differences. Items that everyone gets right (or wrong) are useless for discrimination among subjects. We want a psychological test, as opposed to a mastery test, to show that certain subjects have more or less of some attribute than others. The content of a test can be almost anything that can be made scoreable. A test can be a natural or contrived situation. The chief requirement is that it must be the same for everyone.

Before using a "test" a uniform testing procedure is established and scoring methods are developed. The test is given to as many people as possible in order to collect data to establish *norms*. This process is called "test standardization."

There are no predetermined standards for scoring "psychological tests," as we are defining them here; they are "norm referenced." This means that an individual's performance is given meaning by comparison with performance of the people in a standardization group. We must keep in mind the distinction between

---

[2]This test is available from the Institute for Personality and Ability Testing, 1602 Coronado Drive, Champaign, IL.

these tests and criterion referenced tests, which use investigator-established standards for interpretation.

Test Reliability

"*Test Reliability*," as the term is used in testing, means *consistency*. We usually talk about test reliability, but it is not the test that varies; it is the people who take the test. Test theory assumes that each person has a "true" score which the test attempts to estimate with an obtained score. A person's performance will vary from time to time as a result of almost anything that can affect people: test conditions, how we feel, how much we concentrate, mood, . . . whatever.

All measurement is subject to error—even measurements as simple as a carpenter's measurement of the length of a board. Variability of human judgment limits accuracy, so a carpenter's single measurement is only an estimate of a board's "true" length. Good carpenters understand human error in measurement, so careful ones always make several measurements before cutting. "Measure twice cut once" is the carpenter's saying. I'm afraid we are not nearly so careful in our psychological measurements.

Repeating a test in a brief period of time is a possible way of determining reliability. If people's scores on their second testing are about the same as on their first, the test is reliable. We would not, however, expect people to get exactly the same scores. If it is an ability test, takers would probably do better. They might remember questions, going over a problem the second time might make it easier, and experience might improve confidence.

Even reliable tests will appear to be inconsistent when the construct itself changes. Moods and emotions will vary from time to time; therefore, a test that accurately measures these constructs should reflect these changes just as a reliable thermometer shows variations of temperature.

The test-retest method is useful only for measuring characteristics that are not believed to change much over short periods of time, but time between the original testing and the retesting is always a relevant variable. If we repeat an intelligence test after a 2-week interval we would expect essentially, but not exactly, equivalent results. We would not expect a high correlation between two measurements separated by a 10-year gap.

We will again discuss statistical techniques for assessing reliability in Chapter 7, when we apply correlations to test analyses.

Test Validity

"The validity of a test concerns *what* a test measures and *how well* it does so" (Anastasi, 1988). The recurring question that psychologists must answer is easily stated, "How do we know that a test measures what we say it does?" If we state the question more scientifically we could ask, "How do I know this test provides a good operational definition of the construct I want to study?" The assessment of test validity is for me one of the most interesting areas in psychological measurement.

Although common sense suggests otherwise, experience forces us to acknowledge that just looking at the content of test items does not necessarily accurately reveal the construct that the items measure. Jokes or cartoons can be thought of as items for measuring sense of humor; but, as I discussed above, this reaction can be greatly influenced by the item content. It is the inescapable task of the test designer to demonstrate the nature of the dimension along which the scores are distributed.

A large portion of a course on psychological measurement studies the several different ways of determining test validity. We will see the topic again and study it in a different way in Chapter 7.

A simple way to "validate" a test is to correlate scores from a newly developed test with scores from another instrument that is already in use to measure a similar-appearing construct. The assumption is that if there is a large correlation between the two sets of scores, the tests are to some extent measuring the same construct. We might not know what the construct is, but whatever we decide to call it, both tests seem to be measuring it.

A second, different but highly correlated test would be useful if it were shorter, easier to give or score, or had some other advantage over the original.

"Content validity" is a type well known to every person who has ever been to school. A student has every right to expect that a given test will cover the announced course content. A test that asks questions from chapter 8, when only chapters 4 through 7 were assigned, would not demonstrate adequate content validity.

Personnel tests particularly are widely used to measure abilities or personality attributes that are presumed to be relevant for performance in certain situations. We give a test and then use its results to predict subsequent behavior, generally called a "criterion." This could be performance on a job, functioning in some special activity, or success in a training program. A valid test will permit at least moderately accurate predictions with errors that fall within reasonable, statistically defined limits. A test with perfect validity would be one that predicts criterion scores exactly, with no error at all. At the other extreme, accuracy of prediction from an invalid test will be so poor that we might as well make predictions by guessing.

"Concurrent validity" is a variation of predictive validity. Instead of making a prediction to some future time we twist the meaning slightly and "predict" some characteristic of "present"—i.e., concurrent—behavior. A test that has good concurrent validity can be used for diagnosis of mental states or physical conditions.

"Construct validity" is an estimate of the extent to which a test measures some hypothetical construct. This idea of validity is very relevant to the notion of operational definitions of constructs. A psychologist studying people with Machiavellian tendencies would have to demonstrate that the test of Machiavellian personality traits measured those and not other personality attributes, such as authoritarian characteristics.

Measurement by Human Judgment

Observers are often used as if they were measuring instruments. Examples of persons used in this way include judges of diving and gymnastics competitions, referees at sporting events, and members of committees that make hiring decisions.

Another example is a clinical psychologist making an evaluation of a person's mental state. Human judgment as a measurement involves the same questions of reliability and validity applicable to other measures.

Standardized Tests

Measurement problems can often be solved when an investigator has access to appropriate standardized tests. Professionally developed measurement instruments that follow the guidelines published in "Standards for Educational and Psychological Testing" (available from the American Psychological Association) will provide information on reliability and validity and other information on scoring and interpretation of test results. Test development is a major professional activity for psychologists. Tests are available to evaluate achievement and proficiency, abilities and interests, aptitudes, personality traits, and status of mental health—to list but a few of the more familiar types. Investigators should consult *The Mental Measurements Yearbook (MMY)*, which is available in most university libraries. These references will supply information about the representative tests that are available in any particular area. The *MMY* includes quite useful reviews of tests by people who have studied them. Their opinions will help a person to decide whether a test is suitable for an intended purpose.

Test materials that are published or distributed by the large publishing companies—The Psychological Corporation (Harcourt Brace Jovanovich) is an example—have a classification scheme that restricts the sale of certain materials to qualified people only. An untrained person cannot phone in an order for a "WAIS"[3] just because he or she thinks that it might be fun to have one. Tests that require special training and experience are restricted to purchase by only those people who can prove they are qualified. Information regarding registration to purchase restricted tests is given in each catalog.

Psychologists working in new areas often have to devise new tests that are primarily for research. Although they would not be suitable for general distribution, they might be just what is needed by someone else who is working in the same area. Sometimes these will be published in an article related to the original research, they might be available through a private firm, or one might be able to obtain information on the test by writing directly to the author. Usually we have no reason for going to the trouble to develop a new measuring instrument if something already available can be used.

Psychologists study a great many areas, including memory, perception, physiological psychology, and many others. All of them require apparatus for timing, presentation of materials, or for measuring physiological changes or reactions. Modern variations of the "Wheatstone Bridge"[4] can be used to identify

---

[3]Anyone who does not know that this is the acronym for "Wechsler Adult Intelligence Scale" is certainly not qualified to order one!

[4]This is a simple electric circuit that uses a meter to compare small currents through separate resistances. When resistance in one arm falls relative to the comparison voltage, as might happen to the skin resistance of a person who has become emotional, the meter will register an increase in current in one branch compared with the current in the other.

changes in skin resistance that are related to changes in emotion. A tachistoscope can show variations in visual response times. Photographs of the eyes can permit measurement of pupillary dilation, another physical response known to be related to emotion. Measurement of reaction time to variations of stimuli is now quite easy and accurate with microchip apparatus. "Hooking up" and programming equipment is, like modern automobiles, more complicated than ever. Skill and understanding are required to use current technology. Some physics departments offer courses on simple instrumentation for people who need to make use of apparatus, and a working knowledge of computers is now almost mandatory for psychology majors.

Medical Diagnoses as Operational Definitions

The American Psychiatric Association has published a definitive series of definitions of psychiatric disorders in books that people usually refer to as the "DSM—III" (or whatever the most recent edition is). The initials stand for *Diagnostic and Statistical Manual of Mental Disorders*. This publication has attempted to standardize diagnostic categories through carefully worked-out "diagnostic criteria." The illustration that follows does not refer to any particular illness. The manual nearly always lists several diagnostic criteria for the same illness. (Dementia, for example, has five—A through E—but most seem to be limited to two or three.)

DIAGNOSTIC CRITERIA

A. Frequent mood changes which can range from rage through intense depression. There is a loss of interest or pleasure in regular enterprises. Disturbances of mood are the most important feature. (List of diagnostic symptoms could be continued for a paragraph, or one or more pages.)

B. "At least four of the following symptoms have each been present nearly every day for a period of at least two weeks." In this area would be listed a series of specific behaviors which could be observed. These could include symptoms such as the following.

  (1) Loss of appetite and significant weight loss or increase of appetite with significant weight gain.

  (2) Change in sleep habits from sleeping too much to being unable to sleep at all during the night.

  (3) Loss of strength, lack of energy.

A great deal of individual judgment is involved in making these diagnoses, even though definitions have been carefully formulated to improve their reliability. The fact that the diagnostic categories are carefully explained does not make them operational definitions of sufficient precision to be used in research. When one reads that "Jughead Hurpur was diagnosed schizophrenic," we must recognize that this was a *judgment* not a *measurement*. Another equally well-qualified psychiatrist might not agree. Diagnostic categories are very important for some kinds of psychological research, but they are very difficult to use.

CRITERIA OF GOOD OPERATIONAL DEFINITIONS

With so many constructs that need definitions and so many definitions of what appear to be similar constructs, it is inevitable that some operational definitions will be better and some will be worse than others. The following guides will help select or create better operational definitions. As always with lists (or at least with my lists!) items tend to overlap. I have difficult finding a single item to illustrate a particular point. Real examples typically violate more than one of my rules.

1. They should not be trivial. To be of value, an operational definition should show a clear relationship to the behavior normally identified with the construct it was devised to define.
2. Operations that are intended to define the same construct should correlate with each other, but they should not correlate with measurements that are meant to define different constructs.
3. Operational definitions that do not correlate significantly with each other define different constructs and should be identified with different names.

We need look no further than a typical college classroom for examples of operational definitions applied to practical measurement. Instructors are regularly faced with the task of devising techniques that measure, and in that way define, student performance. Students' grades for a course are often based on various combinations of the following elements: examinations featuring short or long essay questions, multiple-choice and matching questions, and fill-in-the blanks questions; term papers or research projects; and classroom participation and attendance. Whatever techniques we instructors choose to evaluate student performance, we can be sure that not all students will approve of the selection.

I'm certain that I know more than your test showed.

I studied 5 hours for your test, and I still got a low grade.

I know all about the stuff in your course, but you just asked the wrong questions.

I haven't been doing very well in your course, so can I do some additional work to bring up my grade?

I prefer essay questions so that I can explain my answers.

I did well on all the tests, so that proves I know the material. But because I didn't do very well on the experiment the instructor lowered my grade.

What is the best way for an instructor to certify that a student has a full understanding of the course material? How should an instructor assess the differences that demonstrate "what a student really knows about the content of the course"? What is the best type of test or technique for measuring knowledge of course material? Take a minute to think through an answer before reading on.

These questions are deliberately misleading, and they cannot be answered—but thanks to all who tried! The deception was necessary to emphasize an important point. The questions ask about the relationship between test scores and a construct—i.e., knowledge of course material. A phrase such as, "what a student knows about the content of a course" is just another of psychology's many constructs. "It is meaningless to talk about the amount of correspondence between operational measures and the real variable, because there is no *real* variable" (Byrne, 1966, p. 26).

Each test or other type of measure *defines* course performance in different but generally highly correlated ways. Experience shows that students who do well on one type of test tend also to get high grades on other kinds. From this we can conclude that different tests are measuring—i.e., defining—the same construct.

Recall the earlier discussion on intelligence as defined by IQ tests. Intelligence is often used in our general conversations as if it were a single concept, even though we all know that there are different kinds of intelligent behavior. A statement of this sort, "In some ways he might be intelligent, he has a college degree for example, but he sure doesn't have any common sense," means that the speaker is defining intelligence in two ways: one is in terms of common sense and the other definition involves completing college. The person is presenting the opinion that these two operational definitions of intelligence do not correlate. Why should they? They are different constructs. Instead of applying the same "intelligence" term to such diverse behavior and then arguing about what it is, psychologists should agree on different names that recognize the distinctive qualities of each construct. We should, but we usually do not, give different names to constructs that are defined in dissimilar ways.

The second point means that three tests designed to measure anxiety should correlate significantly with each other. Three tests designed to measure depression should also correlate significantly among themselves. Tests of depression should not, however, correlate with anxiety tests—unless one is prepared to argue that depression and anxiety are related concepts.

Note how it was stated that it is the *tests* that do or do not correlate with each other. Popular usage often results in the following incorrect statement: "Anxiety tests should measure only anxiety, and depression tests should measure only depression." Statements of this sort suggest that we want to correlate scores on a test with the construct. As we have already seen, a construct is derived from observations of behavior.

ENDNOTES

What is Average and What is Not Average About Attractive Faces

Apparently a number of people raised questions about what it means to "average attractiveness of faces" so the authors wrote other articles to provide that information. They state that: "We demonstrated the effect of averaging faces on the perception of attractiveness by digitizing faces on a computer, mathematically averaging their matrices of image intensity values, and reproducing the facial images of the resulting averaged faces," (Langlois, J.H., Roggman, L.A., & Musselman, L. 1994).

They assigned a numerical value representing the extent of light to dark, the gray value, of each picture element (pixel). They averaged these values and had the computer create a new picture from them. The new averaged picture was generally seen as more attractive.

Langlois, J.H., Roggman, L.A., (1990). Attractive faces are only average. *Psychological Science, 1,* 115–121.
Langlois, J.H., Roggman, L.A., Musselman, L., & Acton, S. (1991). A picture is worth a thousand words: Reply to "On the difficulty of averaging faces." *Psychological Review.* 2, 354–357.
Lanlois, J.H., Roggman, L.A., and Musselman, L. (1994). What is average and what is not average about attractive faces? *Psychological Science, 5,* 214–220.

Identify the Operational Definitions of Constructs

The topic of constructs and operational definitions of them is, I think, a very important foundational element in the design of research techniques. A full understanding of these ideas seems almost to require a shift in thinking—and that takes a lot of work. I have noted frequently that many students are able to explain operational definitions but they cannot easily identify them in actual examples. Lack of practice seems to be their problem. The following exercise should help.

These examples are patterned after those we run across in the literature. They were not purposely designed to be difficult. For each of the following statements:

 a. Identify the construct and its operational definition, if there is one. If no operational definition is given, write "no op. def."
 b. Underline any *main* constructs.
 c. Put brackets [. . .] around any operational definitions.

Some examples might have constructs that are not operationally defined, and some operational definitions might not fit the listed constructs. I have worked the first five problems to illustrate what I have in mind. I should mention that my answers are not necessarily the *only* correct ones. Careful readers might well be able to develop a good idea I overlooked.

 1. The results from a study of the sociocultural factors in the development of <u>anorexia nervosa</u> showed that it and <u>excessive dieting</u> concerns were overrepresented in dance and modeling students.
     No op. def.
 2. The company's personnel office refused to consider my application because I hadn't finished college. They felt that [a college degree] was necessary to prove a person had the <u>ability to do the work</u>.
     The personnel office used "a college degree" as an operational definition of a person's "ability to do the work."
 3. We conceive of <u>stress</u> as a relationship between a system (either personal or social) and its environment such that <u>adaptive demands</u> placed on the system exceed its <u>normal homeostatic limits</u>.
     No op. def.

4. [A multidimensional measure] of <u>the fear of personal death</u> is related to the religious belief of <u>guilt attribution</u>.

   We do not know what this "multidimensional measure" is, but we could write to the author to find out. I presume it is an adequate measure of "the fear of personal death." "Guilt attribution" was not operationally defined.

5. The [Michil Adjective Rating Scale] was one of the measures administered to help Jones identify <u>the fractorily obese</u>.

6. Smith studied the effects of anxiety and defensiveness on children's ability to cope with stressful situations. A major objective of the study was to compare children's relative preference for toys that were either relevant or not relevant to the stressful surgery and hospitalization they had experienced.

7. The questionnaire given to identify people suffering from sleep paralysis contained questions like the following: "Have you ever experienced transient paralysis?"

8. Altruism is displayed by repeated acts of purposive behavior in which one animal helps another at some cost to himself (in material wealth such as food or in the expenditure of energy) when the behavior was not induced by reward or by the threat of punishment.

9. Sex-role typing is related to the acceptance of self, acceptance of others, and discriminatory attitudes toward women.

10. Alwitt found that individuals classified as androgynous on the Alwitt sex-role inventory are able to respond both instrumentally and expressively according to situational demands.

11. Social skill is the ability to generate effective interpersonal behavior.

12. Mayeux et al. described depressed Parkinson's disease patients, who had prominent complaints of sleep disturbance, fatigue, psychomotor retardation, difficulty concentrating, loss of self-esteem, and guilt.

13. Persistence has been defined as an objective feature of purposive behavior or as "the capacity for continued release of energy."

14. A scale to quantify hopelessness was administered to several diverse samples of patients to assess the test's psychometric properties.

15. Two types of pain were used in the experiment. The cold pain was produced by an apparatus similar to that used by Baber and Hahn.

16. The Bristol Social Adjustment Guide is a well-established instrument for detecting restless, outgoing, and anxious children. The data were factor-analyzed, and two stable factors emerged across both sex and social class.

17. Loneliness due to emotional isolation is characterized by the absence of a close emotional attachment, whereas loneliness due to social isolation appears in the absence of an engaging social network.

18. Empathy was studied by having subjects respond to each adjective on a continuum indicating how strongly they possessed the feeling described by the adjective.

Operational Definitions in Journal Articles: Library Assignment

This assignment will help you to solidify your understanding of operational definitions. It will also give you some experience in digging around in the professional literature.

The basic idea is to find constructs as they are used for research in psychology and then to look for their operational definitions. Pick a psychological construct that interests you and use it as a general heading to look up relevant articles in the *Psychological Abstracts*. Many constructs are listed in titles, and their operational definitions are sometimes given in the abstract. Select *two* articles that give good operational definitions of the psychological construct you have chosen.

Your instructor might want you to do something like the following to demonstrate that you know what you are talking about.

a. Make a photocopy of the page on which the operational definition is located. Identify the construct in some way (circle, highlight, or underline it) and label it "construct."

b. Next, identify the full operational definition *of that construct*. Circle, underline, or highlight it so it is clearly marked. Label it "operational definition." These must be precisely indicated so the instructor will be able to quickly evaluate the items you have identified. (Do not mark a whole paragraph in the hope that it might contain something the instructor wants!)

c. Write your name and/or other necessary identifying information at the top of the page.

d. On the blank side of the page copy the complete journal reference in accurate APA style. Use the bibliography at the end of the text for examples.

e. Repeat the process for the second article. Staple the pages together and hand them in at the beginning of the class period on the date the assignment is due.

STUDY QUESTIONS

1.   What are the three procedures common to all measurement?

2.D   What is the importance of concepts and constructs to the study of psychology?

3.D   What is wrong with dictionary definitions for research?

4.   What are operational definitions?
      How are they developed?
      What is their advantage over dictionary definitions for research?
      How are they used for research?

5.D   Explain the idea of a test as an operational definition of a construct. (Think of classroom tests.)

6.D   How do we know whether an operational definition of a construct is in fact an accurate definition of what the construct really is?

7.D   What does it mean if tests that presumably are defining the same construct do not correlate with each other?

How do we know which one is the "right" definition?

8.D   How can we determine which classroom test is best for measuring what a student really knows about the content of a course?

9.   What is the *DSM-III,* and how is it used? Discuss medical diagnoses as operational definitions of certain psychological constructs.

10.   What are some rules to be followed in developing good operational definitions of constructs?

11.   On tests in my class I have often asked students to write operational definitions of constructs like those listed below. Some can be answered easily, but others may cause trouble.

a. Hunger

b. Pain

c. Excessive TV watching

d. Fatigue

e. Lust

f. Math Anxiety

SMALL TALK

Chapter
5

Introduction to Measurement

. . . when you can measure what you are speaking about, and express it in numbers, you know something about it; but when you cannot measure it, when you cannot express it in numbers, your knowledge is of a meager and unsatisfactory kind.

William Thomson (Lord Kelvin)

IMPORTANCE OF MEASUREMENT SCALES

Teachers of experimental psychology are sometimes approached by students from other classes, "Pardon me, but I am doing a research project for Dr. ———. I've collected all of these data, and I don't know what to do with them. I wonder if you can help." In the best of all worlds, we would be able to design our research projects, step by step, right from the beginning. We would understand the type of information we would have available, what kinds of numbers we would get from it, and what statistic (or statistics) could be used that both satisfies the characteristics of the numbers *and* permits an evaluation of the research hypothesis posed at the beginning.

Research does not often happen in this way. Beginners are handicapped by a weak background, insufficient experience, and inadequate knowledge to do the job as well as they will be able to do it after they have had a few trials. That is the reason why many instructors require a research project in conjunction with a course like this one. But even people with a lot of experience can run into trouble when something unexpected happens (as it often does) that makes a readjustment necessary.

The guidance given by a good comprehension of measurement techniques helps to avoid the distress caused by the discovery that the data we laboriously collected cannot be evaluated by the statistic we had planned to use.

Even if we ignore the use of measurement for research, we should have an understanding of it because of the wide application of measurement concepts in all areas of the behavioral sciences. I have provided an endnote to illustrate the *practical* importance of measurement in the daily lives of a large part of our population.

People who do not have a satisfactory understanding of different measurement levels are prone to make interpretative errors. We might hear someone say something to the effect that a person's score on a neuroticism test improved 50% following therapy. Does this mean that the person is now half as neurotic as he or she was before? Is the person twice as close to being normal?

Suppose that a person had these percentiles on several different tests: 35, 15, 65, and 50. Would it be correct to average them in order to get a composite score? The answer to the percentile question is no; percentiles are "ordinal" measurement data, which is not suitable for evaluation by means.

If we have a psychological test made up of say, half a dozen subtests, would it be correct to average the number of correct responses on the subtests in order to get a combined score? One might conceive of a situation in which this would make sense, but generally the answer would be no. Teachers who determine a term grade by computing an average of the number of correct answers on each test make a similar mistake. Students who have had a first statistics course will here suddenly find useful some of the abstract material they learned. The correct technique converts the number of right answers on subtests to "z-scores," or some variations of them. A common way we have for summarizing responses in terms of "percentages" is a simple technique that is often misused (even if we assume that the person knows the difference between "percents" and "percentiles").

It has been my experience that a large number of the authors of the many measurement discussions I have read treat measurements as if the interpretation of them is fixed. I am prepared to argue that the numbers we obtain from the quantification of our data can have different meanings, and they can be interpreted in different ways. These different interpretations require an adjustment of the statistic we would use for data analysis. A number, say 9 for example, can mean one thing in one situation and something else when it is obtained from a another measurement technique. Or it can have different interpretations even when obtained from the same measurement. It is important for us to know these distinctions.

My emphasis on measurement in this text is partly explained by my consideration of its importance in scientific investigation. That explanation does not justify my fuller development of the simpler measurement types than is customary in a book of this kind. The reason for this is that I think beginners are better served if they understand the *foundations* of measurement by looking first at the simplest types. I also think—but I accept that the point can be argued—that a lot of behavioral science measurement is used at a higher level than it deserves to be. I would rather encourage a beginner to comprehend and correctly use one of the simpler measurement scales first. The kinds we need for advanced research are already covered thoroughly in many other places.

WHAT IS MEASUREMENT?

A reader would probably measure the heights of everyone in the experimental psychology class by attaching a tape measure to a wall in the room and having class members stand next to it. The values recorded would be only approximate of course, because measurement of height is not very accurate, and it varies from time to time. It is my understanding that we are taller in the morning than we are at bedtime. This operational definition of height would not be materially altered if measurements were in centimeters or any other arbitrary unit of length.

Now assume that instead of measuring the heights of the people in the experimental class in the normal way, we simply asked class members to organize themselves in a line according to decreasing height. The tallest person would come first, the next-tallest second, and so on, until the shortest person present found his or her place at the very end of the line. We would not know in measurement units how tall anyone was, but we could look over the group and see that some people were taller or shorter than others.

Does this procedure constitute a legitimate form of measurement? It does according to Underwood's (1966) definition of measurement, which we will use in this text. Instead of Underwood's term "scaling methods," it is close enough to think "measurement."

> When we refer to scaling methods we mean techniques for sorting stimuli according to the amount of some specified characteristic these stimuli are said to possess. If the sorting is reliable we say that the set of procedures leading to the scale constitutes the definition of a dimension. (p. 191)

Measurement in terms of units produces a generally more useful higher order of measurement, as we will see shortly; but ordered observations, such as ranks, are also important. The two ways of measuring height produced two kinds of measurement numbers. The higher order of measurement defined height by counting previously explained units (inches). Counting numbers, those that answer questions about *how many*, are called "cardinal" numbers. Ordered measurement by ranks produces "ordinal" numbers. Saying that something is 9 inches and that it is ninth in a sequence mean quite different things.

Each type of measurement discussed in the following paragraphs is analyzed with a statistic from either of two large classes: *parametric* or *nonparametric*. "Parameters," as the word is used in statistics, refers to the properties or characteristics of a population. The same properties of a sample are called "statistics." For our purpose parameters can be understood as means (averages) and standard deviations or variance. Statistics that can be used with data for which averages and standard deviations are meaningful are called "parametric statistics." If measurement produced other types of data we would choose a nonparametric statistic. Parametric statistics are the ones studied in most beginning statistics courses, although recent statistics texts now have a section on nonparametric statistics as well.

Judgment is involved in making a decision about the type of number scale that is obtained from research. The same numbers could mean one thing to one person and something different to someone else. Investigators are likely to want to interpret their data at as high a level as possible, but some of the time a higher level of usage will not be justified. We have to know the meaning of our data and the statistics that are appropriate for analyzing each type. Keep this idea in mind because it is fundamental to much of the discussion that follows: *It is always possible to move from a higher to a lower order of measurement if a more conservative evaluation seems appropriate.* Movement from a lower to a higher measurement scale is usually not recommended, even though statisticians have demonstrated a few instances in which it is possible.

The following discussion will approach measurement through a discussion of the simplest, the most primitive, form before we move to the most complex.

CATEGORY (NOMINAL) SCALES

General Characteristics

This scale involves *classification and assignment of observations into mutually exclusive groups*. We simply count how many examples from our original sample end up appropriately assigned to each category.

According to Underwood's definition this type of scale is not actually a measurement at all. The whole point of measurement is to *order* observations according to variations in amounts of some quality. Category scaling is not restricted to classification according to actual amounts of anything, although these can be used. They can also be formed by classification according to qualitative observations, for which variations in quantity are meaningless. Thinking of classification as premeasurement is appropriate because things cannot differ in amounts if they have not previously been shown to differ in kind.

This scale is widely known as the "nominal scale," which is the name Stevens (1951, p. 25) gave it when he organized measurement scales into the form generally used today. According to the original definition, this scale employed numbers only for identification. By this usage the number 9 would be just a label for one of the categories. This application seems to me to be a trivial use of numbers because categories can be identified with names, letters, or any other of symbol. In any case, cardinal numbers (counting numbers, numbers that tell how many) are the *values used for computation* on the so-called nominal scale. They tell us the frequency of observations that ended up being assigned in each category.

For reasons that are too involved and too rambling to go into here, I have decided to break with many years of tradition and call this type of measurement a "category scale." That name more accurately identifies the nature of the measurement principle involved.

All that category scaling requires is sorting—or classifying—observations into well-defined *mutually exclusive* groups. This means that classes must be so well identified that it will be impossible to classify an observation into more than one group. This scale requires, as do the others, that there be a common element running through all the classes. It must be reasonable to compare the items in one class with items in the others. Items can be sorted or classified and counted according to one attribute or another, but each change requires a new sorting.

The following sections will fully explain each of the several ways in which categories for research can be obtained or created.

Category Scales from Naturally Occurring Categories

Many ideas for research can take advantage of preexisting categories, but even though the nature of each class is immediately apparent, it is still necessary to define it precisely. There must be no ambiguity about where an observation is to be classified. The make of an auto is an example of an obvious, generally satisfactory, category. Country of birth, pregnant or not pregnant, college from which the first B.A. was earned are all categories that occur naturally as well-defined classes.

We must be careful to guard against classification schemes that seem workable until they are used with actual data. "Married" and "single" are legal terms that could be used if all we were interested in was whether each particular person was or was not legally married, but these categories probably could not be used for behavioral science research. Where would a person be assigned who is married but separated? How about couples of either sex who are not married but who live together as if they were? Is there a difference between being a divorced single or a widowed single? How about a single who has never been married? We can see that sorting according to marital status is likely to be more involved than it first appeared to be.

Developed Categories

When categories do not exist we might want to develop them, but we have to be sure the categories identify classes along a continuum. Psychological classifications of personality into types illustrate this usage: "There are three kinds of people. . . ." Sheldon's body types: endomorph, mesomorph, ectomorph constitute another example (Sheldon, Stevens, & Tucker, 1940). Classifying body types was a popular endeavor for awhile, used in trying to discover possible relationships between body build and personality.

Masculine, androgynous, or feminine personality traits might not be recognized at first as classification on a single scale. If we think of "gender orientation" along a dimension as the common element, the grouping process becomes obvious.

Logically Ordered Categories

Some classification schemes have an inherent logical order in the relationship of the classes to each other: instructor, assistant professor, associate professor, full professor. Second lieutenant, first lieutenant, captain is another naturally ordered sequence. These sequences show that classes coming earlier have less of some quality than those coming later, but these variations of amount are generally ignored in the statistical evaluation of category data. Even though student classes are ordered according to the number of courses that have been satisfactorily completed (freshman, sophomore, junior, senior), research questions typically used with these data look only at the number of students in each class, not at where it is ordered in a sequence.

Data from ordered categories are sometimes incorrectly treated as "ordinal" measurement, which is a higher level to be discussed later. When a logical order of classes already exists, it should be maintained, because it is helpful for interpretation of results. But a typical statistical analysis simply compares the numbers in each class with all the other classes. The order of the classes is generally irrelevant to statistical analysis, except for discussion.

Categories From Higher Orders of Measurement

Statistics texts identify certain kinds of data as "continuous"; the units of the scale progress evenly, or in small units, without breaks or gaps. This concept is applicable to *interval* data, which will be discussed later. These higher levels of measurement are very useful for many purposes, but situations exist in which it is better to drop from a higher to a lower order of measurement in order to simplify it for discussion.

Age provides a ready demonstration of the procedure for converting continuous data to categories. Days from birth are continuous data, an unbroken time sequence of evenly spaced intervals. The physiological and psychological changes that are concomitant with increasing age—the attributes that generally interest us for research—do not, however, form an even, linear progression. Psychologically speaking, an age change from 0 to 5 years does not have the same meaning as a change from 25 to 30 or from 75 to 80. Society has generally accepted the following age classifications as a better measurement scale: infants, toddlers, preschool, children, pre-teens, teens, adolescents, young adults, adults, middle-aged, and seniors. Boundaries of the classes would have to be precisely defined for actual use, but there seems to be a general understanding of age levels and the type of behavior to be expected within each group. Note that the original scale was "interval," which is the highest form of measurement, but for practical application we have dropped it to "category," the lowest form.

"Number right" from classroom tests is usually treated as continuous data. We could use the number of right answers on a test to indicate the level of performance, but we usually do not. The number right is more commonly formed into "letter grade" categories (A, B, C, D, F). Five levels of performance are generally adequate for indicating quality of academic performance.

IQ scores from intelligence tests are continuous data that are often used as interval data for statistical calculations. But when psychologists *describe* the levels of intelligence, they usually divide the IQ continuum into categories.

Classification of personality variables is a good way to deal with personality information because the scheme forces a recognition of the inherent unreliability of all tests. A single obtained score suggests a precision that is usually lacking in psychological or other social science measurement. Assignment to categories indicates lower levels of measurement accuracy, which in my opinion is closer to reality.

ORDINAL SCALES

This scale compares observations along a continuum, then orders them according to varying amounts of the underlying quality being measured. Often, but not always, ranks will be used. But when the quality of measurement units cannot be assured (i.e., the units are unlikely to be equally spaced), continuous data can be treated as *nonranked* ordinal data. This distinction will require extra study because I think it is important and it is rarely mentioned in measurement discussions. Ordinal scales constitute the lowest level of true measurement, according to Underwood's definition. An ordinal position indicates differences among items and also identifies the level of an item in terms of the amount of the underlying measurement continuum. The ordinal scale shows which item has more of some quality and which has less, compared to others in the group. Ordinal scales do not specify the *amount* of differences.

Ranks are one form of ordinal data. I always use a rank of "1" to represent the highest value in a rank sequence. The largest rank, which identifies the lowest or least satisfactory score as interpreted by the investigator, is set by the number of observations being compared. For 17 scores the last value would be 17. Note that on a rank scale we can always tell a high score by the small values: 1, 2, 3, . . . and it is assumed that every rank will be used only once. If a person got a rank of 19, we must know how many items were ranked in order to interpret that value. Having a rank of 19 out of 19 judgments means one thing, but a rank of 19 out of 225 has a different meaning. A rank of 1 always indicates the highest rank in the scale. I emphasize this point because I have often seen ranks in which the item of lowest value is given a rank of 1 and the item having the most is given the last rank according to the number of items being ranked. I think my arrangement makes more sense. Although ranks might seem to be too crude a measurement to be of value in research, be assured that they are not.

Ranks can be obtained directly by having a group of observations compared and ordered along a continuum, or they can be converted from a higher-level measurement. In one study cardinal numbers might show that Meg got 94 points right on a certain exam; Gladys got 96, Jim got 83 points right, Alice got 82 points, and Bernie got 89. Rank values, from low to high, can be assigned in place of the number right scores to get this result: Meg 2, Gladys 1, Jim 4, Alice 5, and Bernie 3. The number right is considered a fairly high order of measurement, so converting these numbers to ranks is an example of moving from a higher to a lower order of measurement.

Note that ordinal scale differences do not necessarily reflect actual score value differences. Gladys and Meg are 2 score points apart, Bernie and Jim are 6, Jim and Alice have a 1 point difference. In every instance the *rank difference* is 1, no matter what the score difference is. An equal rank difference does not necessarily indicate an equal score difference.

Ordinal and Ranked Data

Many statistics and experimental texts describe ranked data and ordinal data as if the terms were synonymous. There is an important difference. Although all ranked data are ordinal, *not all ordinal data are ranks*. Nonranked ordinal data can best be explained by what they are not. If a set of measurements is not category, which should be obvious immediately, and if it is not sufficiently precise to have equal intervals (to be more fully explained later), then a conservative interpretation will identify it as ordinal.

An instructor can measure a student's class attendance by the number of absences. At first this might appear to be a good measurement scale of a fairly high order; each absence is apparently worth the same amount as every other absence. I think these numbers should be treated as nonranked ordinal data. A deciding feature is, in my opinion, the point that short absences of 1, 2, or 3 days does not have the same meaning as absences that total 6, 12, or 18 days. I cannot assume that each day of absence has the same importance as their numbers increase. I could rank absences according to their number, but I would not have to. The values themselves, 2, 7, 8, 12, and 16 for example, produce an unranked ordinal scale. I would treat absences as ordinal but not ranked data.

Clothing sizes are an obvious example of ordinal data that are not ranks. A dress size of 16, within the same style and line, is larger than a dress of size 14, and both are larger than size 12. The amount of increase or decrease with each change of size is not equal, because sizes are determined by measurements of several different dimensions.

Statistics for Use With Ordinal Data

The following section is included for reference, for a person to come back to after developing a better background in statistics. I think it is important for readers to understand that certain statistics are used with certain types of numbers, even though one will not at this early stage achieve a full understanding of which statistic goes with which measurement. Statistics books usually do not explain the distinction between ranked and nonranked ordinal data carefully enough. One can easily make the mistake of assuming that any statistic suitable for ordinal data would work with ranks. Each statistic has to be studied very carefully to determine the nature of the original data for which it can be used. Some statistics require ranked data, and others cannot be used with ranked data. Following is a short list of a few better-known nonparametric statistics which require "ordinal" data but which cannot be computed with ranks.

Sign test

Median test

Mann-Whitney U

Kruskal-Wallis one-way anova

Kolmogorov-Smirnov two-sample

Wilcoxon matched-pairs signed-ranks

INTERVAL (EQUAL INTERVAL) SCALES

Unit differences along this scale are assumed to be equal. The change from 15 to 20 has the same meaning as a 5-unit increase or decrease anywhere else along the scale, say between 75 and 80.

This scale is the highest form of measurement we can normally expect from behavioral science research. It shows order, just as the ordinal scale does, but it has the additional desirable quality of having *equally spaced units*. For this reason, it is appropriate to call it an "equal interval" scale. That is a good term to remember, because it precisely identifies its fundamental characteristic. The same unit difference anywhere along the scale has the same meaning.

RATIO SCALES

A ratio scale is an equal interval scale that has the additional feature of an "absolute zero." The underlying quality of the scale is such that the attributes get smaller until they totally disappear. Having a zero on the scale is not enough; many scales have zero points on them. The important quality of a ratio scale is that the zero is "absolute," which means that no negative values are possible. This is the characteristic that permits the use of ratios. With a ratio scale we can say that a value of 84 is twice as much as one of 42. That is not possible with an equal interval scale. This distinction between the ratio and the interval scale is only of theoretical interest, because it does not in any way affect statistical computations.

Age, which was used previously to illustrate category scaling (the lowest measurement scale), can be used here to illustrate a ratio scale (the highest measurement level). The units of time are equal interval, and birth provides a zero starting point. Age ratios that are relevant to particular research can be meaningfully computed; a person who is 20 is twice as old as a person who is 10 and half as old as a person who is 40. I cannot think offhand of a situation in which incremental age progressions would be useful for research in the behavioral sciences.

Reaction time is an example that includes an element of ambiguity characteristic of measurement in the behavioral sciences. Reaction time is a measurement of how quickly an organism can react to a stimulus. Physics does not provide a zero reaction time; no reaction can take place infinitely quickly—if such a phrase makes sense. But it still seems reasonable to say that Person A can react twice as fast to a certain stimulus (0.3 seconds)—that is, A took half the time to react that Person B took (0.6 seconds). This is possible because the underlying quality, time, is ratio data.

The number of correct responses on a test will sometimes but not always give a ratio scale, as we will see in the following discussion.

WHAT IS THE LEVEL OF MEASUREMENT?

No distinction is necessary between interval and ratio data because the same statistics work with both. The only distinction is that we cannot discuss ratios with an interval scale.

Category data require nonparametric statistics. This scale can be readily identified, and it is not easily confused with other types of data. The primary distinction is usually between interval and ordinal but not ranked data.

People are often called upon to self-report certain information. "How old was your first-born son when he started talking?" "How much time does your child spend each week watching television?" Smokers might be asked, "How many cigarettes do you smoke a day?" "How many books did you read last year?" Responses to these questions will produce cardinal numbers that give the appearance of being equal interval. In every case we have counted something: years from birth, hours per week, cigarettes, and books.

For the cardinal numbers, such as "amount of television watched" and "books read" questions, there can be an absolute zero that could help form a ratio scale. We must, however, seriously question the basic accuracy of the figures. Some people responding to questions like these might want to hedge their answers a little to make them sound more socially acceptable, and there are other reasons why respondents might not be able to supply accurate figures. The inherent ambiguities of these types of data do not offer much confidence that the units of measurement are equal interval. In my opinion, they should be treated as nonranked ordinal measurement.

A scale formed by the age at which a child started talking is a little confusing. From one point of view there is no zero value on this scale, because no child can talk at zero years of age. One might, nevertheless, make a case for stating that a child who uttered his or her first words at 1 year took twice as long to do so as did one who spoke first at 6 months. This is possible because age, the underlying scale, is ratio data. We could get into an argument about whether the psychological units between 0 and 6 months have the same meaning as those between 6 months and 1 year. A conservative interpretation would call this ordinal data.

Suppose that a psychologist provides small pieces of candy to motivate children participating in her research project. Each additional piece was meant to provide an incremental increase in motivation, but does it? Although we can count the number of pieces of candy, we have no way to know if there is an equivalent increase in the underlying quality of their motivating value. Does a fourth piece after a third increase motivation by the same amount as a second piece did after the first? Is the motivational force from zero to one the same as one to two? I believe this scale should also be treated as ordinal.

Would counting the number right on a typical, 50-item, multiple-choice classroom test produce a ratio scale? Is it meaningful to say that Jones's 40 right is twice as many as Smith's 20? To say this requires an equal interval scale with an absolute zero. The fact that a person could get zero right on the test suggests an absolute zero, but an absolute zero on a test might mistakenly suggest that the person knew nothing whatever about the material being tested. We could not say that Jones *knows* twice as much as Smith, because the attribute being measured—knowledge of the course material—does not have an absolute zero. A person could miss every item on a 50-item test, but if the test had been longer he or she could have missed a larger number. The zero right is a function of that test, not the underlying measurement.

We can also reasonably question whether test items are in reality equal interval. Many instructors treat every multiple-choice question as worth the same amount, as I do—but only because it is convenient to do so. I am unable to make a case for saying that a question everyone got right should be worth the same amount in computing an overall grade as a more difficult question that only 10% of the test takers got right. These speculations suggest to me that typical classroom tests produce ordinal data, which I try to convert into sequential categories of A, B, C . . . , using some procedure that seems to make sense. In the end I can say only that a person who gets more questions right on my tests seems to know more about the material than does a person who got fewer questions right.

The same thinking can be applied to IQ scores. We would have difficulty defining an absolute zero point for intelligence scales, so stating that a person with an IQ score of 120 is twice as bright as a person with an IQ of 60 does not make sense. Dropping to the next level of measurement, we can ask if scores on intelligence tests are equal interval. I do not think they are. A 10-point change from 120 to 130 does not seem to have the same meaning as a change of 10 points from 90 to 100, and probably 10-point differences at other places along the scale are not all equal. A conservative investigator will treat IQ scores as ordinal data; but doing so would certainly place the person in a minority, because IQ scores are generally treated as interval data.

A measurement scale developed by Holmes and Rahe (1967) raised several interesting questions and stimulated a lot of research. They began the serious study of a topic that became so popular it continues to be discussed in magazines and newspapers as well as in the professional literature. They asked, "How do stressful situations affect our behavior?" One of their first tasks was to quantify stressful situations. To accomplish this, they developed a Social Readjustment Rating Scale to show the amount of stress various changes in our lives can cause. The original list contained 43 items. Death of a spouse is most serious, with an assigned value of 100. On the same scale a marital separation, worth 65 points, appears to be only a little worse than a jail term, worth 63 points—the same stress value as the death of a close family member. To analyze these data, it is necessary to determine the level of measurement. A scale of 0 to 100 suggests a ratio scale, but I would question the absolute zero. In my opinion, the decision seems to be between interval and ordinal.

Holmes and Rahe used the best techniques for developing the scale, even to the extent of "anchoring" the ratings. Their approach should produce an interval scale, and for many purposes it does work at that level. But other investigators might harbor a lingering doubt about the question of equal intervals. Does the 5-point difference between "a change in the number of family get-togethers" (15) to "a change of residence" (20) have an equivalent psychological value as the difference between "retirement" (45) and "getting married" (50), or "a vacation" (13) and "a change in social activities" (18)?

An investigator's assignment of a scale level is largely based on the assumptions made by the person using it. When we publish our work we should be prepared to defend our choices. In a later chapter we will look again at the options available to us as we try to match up a statistic with the other components of our particular research project. I will elaborate a little on the topic here, even though I realize that it will be necessary to refer to statistics many readers might not know about. It is the *basic idea* I want to develop; this is not intended to be a brief course in statistics. This preliminary discussion is to summarize our overview of measurement by calling attention to the special relevance of measurement scales and selection of statistics.

SELECTING A STATISTIC

Selecting a statistic is not easy because of the many characteristics of each research project we need to consider. The type of data is only one of them. Two markedly different approaches to research—correlational analyses and experimental designs—ask totally different questions that are answered in entirely different ways. Some investigators do not even consider correlations to be legitimate techniques for research, but I think they have important functions in the broad diversity of research questions we ask in the behavioral sciences.

After we have phrased our research hypothesis and selected the general class of statistic that would help us to make a decision about it, we still must assess the effects of several other relevant variables. The type of data is one that we will discuss in the next paragraph. We also consider the number of samples we will use, sample size, equivalence of variance among samples, and the shapes of their distributions.

Suppose we plan to do a simple experiment that involves two groups of participants. We want the relevant conditions for the groups to be as similar as possible so we can compare the actions of variable X, used for one group, with the action of variable Y, used for the other. If the measurement outcome produced interval data, we could compute the average score for each group. We might then select a "t-test" statistic to determine the significance of differences between the means. If we had a similar research design that produced *nonranked* ordinal data, we would probably select a statistic such as a Wilcoxon T[1] or a Mann-Whitney U. A similar research design that generated ranked data could use a Kruskal-Wallis One-way Analysis of Variance by Ranks, or a Friedman Two-Way Analysis of Variance by Ranks. Keep in mind that these are just old, well-known statistics. Keep alert for new ones that might come along.

When we learn how to use a statistic we also learn what types of data are appropriate to it and what restrictions apply to it. Statisticians are by no means unified on how important it is to be careful in deciding about the usable level of actual data. Investigators who are concerned that their measurements do not adequately meet requirements for a parametric statistic can always drop to a lower level and use a nonparametric statistic. Investigators try to get the most out of their measurements by using parametric statistics because these are more sensitive and make better use of the data. Statisticians point out that a great deal of work has shown parametric statistics to be quite "robust" (that is the word they use), so they work well enough even when the data do not entirely fulfil all the basic restrictions generally considered to be relevant to them.

What difference can it make to the science of psychology if a construct is analyzed as interval data when a more conservative evaluation says it should be treated as ordinal? Even experts disagree about the answer. Theoretical analyses and practical studies suggest that parametric statistics do their job satisfactorily even if the data being used are not quite right for them. It should not differ *markedly*, however, from the theoretical assumptions on which the statistic is based.

Nonparametric statistics are much easier to learn and usually quicker to use. They are more likely to conform to the level of measurements obtained from beginning research projects. "The non-parametric[2] techniques do serve a useful function under some circumstances, *viz.*, as 'screeners' to determine if the analysis should be considered complete or if further analysis by a suitable parametric test should be effected" (Gaito 1959).

Please permit a personal note about nonparametric statistics: I like them, and I think they are not used as often as they should be—particularly by beginners. One reason might be that instructors in the behavioral sciences do not normally study them because our educational time is limited, and the push is toward the more powerful and complex statistics. With computers we can easily and quickly analyze data that approximates the interval level. We do not need the extra step of ranking our observations or assigning them to categories.

This is true, of course, but my thought is that the further removed we are from our actual data, the less we seem to learn about them. Time spent physically working with and thinking about what we call "raw data" contributes a lot to helping us understand them. A beginner's mistakes are made more quickly, and

---

[1] The full title for this statistic sounds more confusing than it is: Wilcoxon matched-pairs signed-ranks test.

[2] There is some ambiguity about the spelling of this word. The more widely used spelling is without the hyphen, but in this quotation from Gaito a hyphen was used so I have kept it.

they are much easier to find in a simple undertaking. And we avoid the frustration that results when one invests a great deal of time in a project that does not work out. In this age of massive computer printouts, we often get more information than we have brains and time to interpret.

This should be all the justification necessary for learning a few applicable nonparametric statistics; they help us to keep in contact with our data. This is an opinion, of course, which can be justified only from my own experience and from discussions I have had with others who also believe that they have learned more from simple calculations they really understand than from complicated statistical analyses resulting from data they simply fed into a computer.

COMPARABLE WORTH: AN IMPORTANT PROBLEM IN MEASUREMENT

Working women must know that they and millions of others like them often are treated unfairly in the workplace. Let us put aside the problem of sexual harassment, important though it is, and limit this discussion to wages. It is well-documented that women as a group are paid less than men who do similar work or who have similar levels of training and responsibility. We can easily identify several reasons for this. The problem is partly one of tradition and custom. To some extent this situation represents beliefs about women in the workplace and perhaps even feelings about the status of women in our society. Women who need jobs work for less money, and they may not have strong unions to help them along. Improving wages for women also runs up against a major economic obstacle: An effective change would cost a great deal of money. The only portion of this large area of concern that is relevant to this chapter is the part that deals with *measurement* of comparable worth. We assume for this discussion that a person should be paid according to his or her value to an employer and that value should be related to the nature of the work and the amount of education and training required to do it. To make sense out of this requires a high level understanding of applied measurement—and a great deal of creativity.

The objective here is to introduce a measurement problem for discussion and consideration and to illustrate how complicated measurement becomes as we move from simple research projects to searching for solutions to practical problems that confront a large portion of the population. Despite the potentially huge number of people whose incomes might be altered by measurement decisions made in this area, the subject has not yet been widely studied by psychologists. However, judging from the literature, psychologists are actively involved in the work. I think that psychology, more than any other discipline, has the statistical foundation and expertise in measurement to do effective work in this area, but it is not easy.

I can think of no realistic way to assign an economic value to a person's work. An object or service is worth whatever someone is willing to pay for it. How much should an airline pilot be paid? How much is your physician worth? What would be a reasonable salary for a household manager? Why should chief executive officers of some corporations be paid ten or more times as much as the president of the United States? Why should Lee Iacocca, when he headed Chrysler Corporation, be paid $17.9 million in salary and stock options, bonuses, and other compensation (in 1988 dollars)? (This comes to over $143 per minute for an 8-hour day and a 5-day week.) Are all of your teachers worth the same salary? How could you determine scientifically how much each should be paid? How much is teaching worth compared to writing and research? Note what we are doing: We are thinking about ways to operationally define *worth* in *dollar* units.

Northeastern Illinois University is currently looking for a psychology teacher. The requirements include a Ph.D. degree in psychology, teaching experience (usually 5 years), and published research work. One may reasonably estimate that it would take 12 years of training and experience beyond high school to qualify for this position. The salary authorized by the state of Illinois is $25,000 for 10 months. Admittedly Illinois is among the lower-paying states for college faculty.

At the same time as an advertisement for the above position went out, Chicago beer-truck drivers were considering a strike to emphasize their contract demands. The average salary for beer-truck drivers is $30,000 to $35,000, with a small group earning as much as $80,000 to $90,000. A high school education should be adequate for doing this work. For anyone who might be thinking of going into college teaching in Illinois, the message should be obvious—at least if income is of any concern. I can imagine a very interesting discussion concerning which group is worth more to society: college teachers or beer-truck drivers!

The topic I want to emphasize here is not inherent worth but "comparable worth." The latter topic requires us to think about the distinction between ordinal (a comparative) level of pay and actual salary levels. Many "typically women's" jobs do not pay as much as jobs traditionally held by men, even though women's jobs might require as much or more training or education and have greater levels of responsibility. Comparable worth asks that people be paid by "ranking jobs on the basis of the skills and responsibility they require and their value to an employer." Apparently women have always had trouble getting comparable pay. The following paragraph is from a letter written in 1867 by the grandmother of Marilyn Gardner, who wrote an article on comparable worth for the Chicago Sun-Times (1985, January 17, p. 60).

> I am teaching here in town this winter. A Mr. Pope teaches the other school. I have 32 and he has 30 scholars. He gets $50 per month and I $25. They say he never taught before. . . .

"The Comparable Worth Controversy" by H. Remick (1981) is one of the earlier professional articles on this topic and is one of the best for explaining the problems and looking ahead to solutions. Remick gives evidence from study after study to show that male-dominated jobs pay more than those that primarily employ women. The "pink-collar ghetto" is what the employment area is called that limits women in their career choices and pays them less than their male counterparts. The facts of the case are not questioned.

The *APA Monitor* (1984, March) notes that the "Dispute Over Comparable Worth Places Burden on Evaluators." This discussion is an interesting one for pointing out the importance of having psychologists, particularly from the industrial/organizational area, involved in comparable worth disputes. They are more likely to be skilled in the type of measurement that is needed, and they are otherwise qualified for determining reliability and validity of the measurement instruments that are used.

The state of Washington was the leader in working out a solution to the comparable worth problem and succeeded, over several years, in narrowing the gap between the average salary for men and women, from 20 to 5 percent. "But as officials have found out, solving one problem can create others." Jobs that have by tradition been held by women are still held by women, and men still predominate in jobs that have traditionally gone to men. The practical problems have arisen partly because of the increased cost of paying a group of workers more than they had been getting before. And the higher-paid male workers lost salary advancements, which has caused them to leave state employment for higher-paying jobs in the private sector. There have also been difficulties in the assessment of job equivalence, which is the primary concern of my discussion.

J. Madigan's (1985) article helps us to appreciate something of the problem pointing out that ". . . the adequacy of job evaluation measures for determining the relative worth of jobs has not yet been established." He made the claim that validity coefficients as high as 0.95 (which are remarkably high for psychological measurements) "could still be inadequate for comparable worth job evaluation applications." There were several other shortcomings identified that caused measurements up to that time to be unsatisfactory. This article is an example of the types of work psychologists can do in this developing area.

Serious efforts in several areas have identified the difficulty psychologists have faced in their efforts to measure and compare employment skills as a step toward pay equivalence. And that has been the easy part!

In the summer of 1991 "after eight years of trying" and by a very narrow vote, the Illinois General Assembly passed a comparable worth bill to apply to state workers and to go into effect in the year 2000. The legislation would require the state to develop a system to ensure "equitable compensation" for jobs that are essentially equivalent, based on "composite skill, effort, responsibility, and working conditions." The cost of just determining salary equivalence is likely to be very large. Major business organizations in Illinois have argued that worker compensation should be determined by the law of supply and demand. The governor pointed out that the bill "would cost the state tens of millions of dollars during the next decade to adjust wages based on the comparable worth of shared skills among disparate jobs held by state and university workers."

The *American Journal of Nursing* (1991, July, pp. 70–71) briefly explained an instrument being used to analyze and ensure equivalence of Canadian nursing jobs. SKEW, the name of the document, considers ten factors: complexity/judgment, education, experience, initiative, result of errors, contacts, character of supervision, scope of supervision, physical/mental demands, and work conditions. Various point values are assigned to each factor, and points are totaled to achieve a score for comparison with other jobs. One of the problems with this system is that it does not adequately value the human caring factors in nursing and gives too much weight to management skills.

The bulk of articles on the comparable worth topic seem to have been published in *Public Personnel Management,* which is perhaps not widely read by psychologists. *Personnel Psychology* is the closest psychology equivalent, but it seems to have published fewer articles on the subject. The *Journal of Applied Social Psychology* has done a little better. When we consider that many topics in psychology attract hundreds of publications, it must be obvious that the interest of psychologists in the comparable worth issue is not very great.

In November 1993, 30 years had passed since the Equal Pay Act was signed, but the basic problem of getting equal pay for women had not been solved. Some salary improvements have been made in the area of starting salaries. No one is quite sure why the gap is narrowing. When the National Organization for Women made the pay differential a political issue in the mid-1970s, they argued that women earned 59 cents for each dollar earned by men. The revised figure for 1990 shows women earned 71 cents for each of the men's dollars. For young men and women who are entering the work force, the 22 cent difference in starting salaries that had been common just 10 years before had shrunk to only 10 cents. But to a woman who needs the money just as much as a man does, that is still a big difference.

Only after I researched the topic a little did I begin to understand. I should confess that I am old enough and I should have known better, but the problem is more complex than I had realized. The measurement difficulty is certainly there, but many other things—all of them psychological in nature—also deserve consideration.

If we look at a group of men and women who have the same levels of education and who start similar jobs at the same time at equal pay, we will find the equality does not continue. We will see that men tend to get promoted more quickly, their salaries increase faster, and the gap between men's and women's salaries tends to widen. Why is that? The obvious explanation is that women take time out to have children and raise families. After allowances have been made for those circumstances, the gap still exists. A further discussion of this point would take us away from this chapter's measurement orientation. I hope that interested readers will look further into the topic on their own.

Although readers might be surprised at finding this topic in a research textbook about a generally different subject, they should be assured that I had several reasons for including it. I thought it was time for us to get out of the classroom in order to broaden our understanding of measurement. I wanted to demonstrate a good—and I hope interesting—application of psychological measurement in an important area that affects a great many people. However, it is not one often discussed as a measurement problem in psychology. Our special interests tend to narrow our perceptions so much that we fail to appreciate the importance of psychological measurement in larger areas of human behavior.

Clarence M. Pendleton, Jr., who was at one time the chair of the U.S. Commission on Civil Rights, reserved for himself a place in history with the remark characterizing comparable worth as: "The looniest idea since Looney Tunes came on the screen." Time will show whether or not he is right.

ENDNOTES

So You Think You Know All About College Testing?

The following questions were written to encourage people to start thinking about measurement in a college environment. They involve subject matter that is familiar to every college student (tests, grades, and grading). Do not be surprised at how difficult it will be to explain your answers.

1. What does a grade on a test *really* mean?
2. What does a letter grade on a course tell about the person's knowledge of the course content?
3. If you learn that a person graduated from college, what does that tell you about the person?
4. An instructor could use a number of ways to determine a final grade when several tests have been given throughout a term. Assume that the instructor gave five tests, each worth a different number of points: 100, 35, 70, 140, 50. Which of the following techniques is best for computing a term grade?
   What is wrong with the others?
   a. Compute an overall average for the number right. Total the number right for all the tests and divide by their number (5 in this example). Compare this with the overall average for the class.
   b. Convert the number right on each test into percent right, then average the percentages.
   c. Convert number right into percentiles, then average the percentile ranks. (Note that percentiles and percentage right are not the same.)
   d. People who have had a course in statistics might want to review a little before helping their colleagues do this problem and the next. Convert the number right into "z-scores."
   e. Convert the number right on each test into stanines.
   f. Give each test a letter grade, convert the letters to numbers, average the numbers, then convert the numbers back to letters.
5. If a student got exactly 71 points out of 90 possible points on each of three different tests, would you say that he or she deserved the same letter grade on each of them?
   What would the grade be?
6. If every student in class missed the same question on a particular exam, should that question be thrown out?
   Should a question be dropped from a test if everyone gets it right?
7. Should difficult questions be worth more in computing a grade than easy questions?
   How can the difficulty level of a test question be determined?
8. How might an instructor determine whether a test is valid?
9. What exactly does it mean to "grade on the curve"?
   What is the logic of grading on a curve?

In what circumstances can the procedure be justified?

10. Assume that a student got 77 points right on a test with 90 possible points. What percent did he get *wrong?*
11. Justify the position that a student's term grade for a course should include information about attendance, class participation, extra work, class projects, opinions of other students, and scores on exams.
12. Should essay exams be graded for spelling, punctuation, sentence structure, and organization of ideas as well as for content?
13. If a person has not done well on exams, should he or she be allowed to do additional or outside work (such as writing a special report) to bring the grade up to a passing level?
14. If a cumulative final exam is given, how much more should it count in relation to the other tests (the same, 50% more, double, whatever)?
15. Justify the position that a grade on the final could be used to *raise* the term grade but not to *lower* it.
16. Justify the position that a student must pass the final exam to pass the course.
17. Justify the position that a student who is doing badly in a course should be given an incomplete so he or she can do work later to raise the grade. Should a student be permitted to repeat a test in order to raise the grade?
18. In computing a term grade from several test grades, should the lowest test grade be dropped? If so, how about also dropping the highest grade?
19. Should a term grade somehow include information about the fact that a student started badly but improved as the course progressed? Should special credit be allowed for students who were unable to reach satisfactory levels but who tried very hard?
20. Should students who are not adequately prepared for a course be judged by the same standards used for other students who have a better background?

Practice in Determining the Scale of Measurement

Indicate for each of the following the most appropriate level of measurement for its use in research: category, ordinal, interval, ratio. I have given my suggested answers after the list of factors. Several of the examples produce measurements that can be used in different ways, so there is plenty of opportunity for discussion. My objective here is to get readers to *think* about measurement, not to provide fixed answers.

1. Birth order.
2. Determine the relative merits of seven movies you have seen over the past year.
3. Age.

4. A naturalist counted the types of birds that came to a feeder during a 1-hour period.

5. Reaction time to a sudden loud whistle.

6. Clothing size.

7. Income in dollars.

8. Trials needed for a rat to learn a maze.

9. Passing a ten-item driving test.

10. IQ

11. Masculine/feminine personality characteristics.

12. Grade point average.

13. Color.

14. a. What measurement scale results from the number right on a 50-item multiple choice test?

b. What scale is the percentage right?

c. What scale is the letter grade?

d. What if the test were graded pass/fail?

STUDY QUESTIONS

1.D What is wrong with averaging percentiles?

2. Differentiate between parametric and nonparametric statistics.

3. Under what circumstances might it be appropriate to use nonparametric statistics?

4. What is Underwood's definition of measurement?

5. Differentiate between cardinal and ordinal numbers.

6. What is the basic idea of category scaling?

Explain why the category scale is not an example of true measurement according to the Underwood definition.

7. Explain three ways of developing categories.

Why is it important for categories to be formed along a single underlying quality or characteristic?

8. Why might we sometimes want to go from a higher to a lower level of measurement?

9. What are continuous data?

10. What are ordinal data?

11. Explain why all rank scales are ordinal, but not all ordinal scales are ranked data. Give an example of an ordinal scale that is not ranked.

12.D Understand the point that some statistics listed as suitable for ordinal data might not work for ranks.

13. What is an equal interval scale?

How does it differ from an ordinal scale?

14. How does a ratio scale differ from an interval scale?

15. What is the advantage of a scale that starts at an absolute zero?

16.D Explain why the number of correct responses on a test might not produce a ratio or even an interval scale.

17.D What are some of the things we would need to consider in deciding on a statistic for data analysis?

18.D What is your opinion of the comparable worth idea?

19.D Devise a scale to ensure that your teachers get paid according to "what they are worth."

What types of behavior would you consider and evaluate?
How would you evaluate a teacher you like, as compared to one you do not like but from whom you learned a lot of important material?

20.D Is the average salary of women teachers at your university about the same as the average salary of men?

Assuming there is a difference, how do you account for it?

21.D What is the relationship between salary and the academic rank of your teachers?

How much more are the full professors worth than the associate professors? How much differential should there be between the salary paid to a beginning teacher, and the salary for a person who has been teaching a long time? (Let us agree that length of teaching experience does not necessarily improve quality of instruction, however you want to define it.)

ANSWERS TO MEASUREMENT PROBLEMS

1. Although birth order might seem to be rank and therefore ordinal (first born, second born, etc.) I would treat it as category. For research, we are likely to compare order of birth in categories and count the *number* of first born, *number* of second born, etc. Several statistics are available to analyze both correlational and experimental studies that involve data like these.

2. This would be a rank and therefore ordinal scale.

3. Age could be treated as almost any scale, depending on how it is used. Probably for most research applications in the behavioral sciences I would use age as a category scale, but it would make sense to maintain the order of the categories.

4. Category.

5. Reaction time would be interval.

6. Ordinal.

7. I treat income as similar to age. It would appear superficially to be interval or perhaps ratio. For practical research, nonranked ordinal would make more sense. I

would have difficulty making the case that a $5,000 cut in salary has the same meaning for a person who earns $25,000 per year as it does for a person who earns $250,000. For a scale to be equal interval, the same units would have to have the same *meaning* at any place along the scale. I do not think income fits that definition.

8.   Interval, although there might be a reason for treating this as nonranked ordinal.

9.   Pass or fail is category.

10.   This probably should be treated as ordinal, but nearly everyone uses it as interval data.

11.   I think these characteristics are best expressed along a continuum. I do not see them as categories, so ordinal would apply.

12.   All registrars treat letter grades as interval data, otherwise they could not compute a grade point average. To do this legitimately we would need to be certain that the difference between an A and a B grade has the same *meaning* as the difference between a D and an F or between a C and a B. I am not sure the meaning is the same, so an ordinal use would seem to better fit the nature of the data—but don't tell the registrars!

13.   I have included this entity because it gets into the area of perception, which we have not mentioned yet. Color for many people would seem to be category: red, green, blue, for example. (These are the colors generated in the picture tube of a TV set to produce all the colors we see in our TV programs.) If we do research on color perception, we would most likely use colors in discreet units. The "Lúscher Color Test" is designed—so the cover says—to "reveal your personality through color." It uses little colored pieces of paper smaller than a playing card.

The physical characteristic of color is in fact continuous and ranges from the beginning visual experience of colored light at the infrared end of the spectrum to the ultraviolet end. The scale is formed and is measured by variations in wavelengths. These units are so small that scientists have substituted Ångstróm units for them. A much more convenient way of defining the continuous nature of color of light sources—which is a special concern in color photography—is in terms of "color temperature." This is the temperature of a heated black body that emits a color equivalent to the sample being studied. When a black piece of metal is heated it begins emitting color in the dull red range, through yellow orange, and finally to white hot. We often use the expression "red hot."

While we are thinking about vision, which is just one of our sensory modalities, how would you measure sound, smell, taste, and touch?

14.   a. I think nearly everyone treats this as interval, which makes sense only if we agree among ourselves that every questions is at exactly the same level of difficulty for every test taker. The nature of the data is clearly ordinal, but we get by well

enough treating it as interval. Some might argue for ratio on the grounds that a person could get zero right. Remember the discussion of this point in the chapter.

b. This is also ordinal, but we treat it as interval.

c. Depending on how we want to use them, letter grades could be interval, ordinal, or category (how many got A's, how many got B,'s etc.)

d. Category.

SMALL TALK

Nonexperimental Research Techniques

Chapter
6

Introduction to Research

Since the measuring device has been constructed by the observer . . . we have to remember that what we observe is not nature in itself but nature exposed to our method of questioning.

From Werner Karl Heisenberg. *Physics and Philosophy.* Quoted in a Little, Brown, and Co. advertisement for their text, *Assessing Individuals.*

Anyone who has ever been assigned a research project knows that getting started is the most difficult part. Selecting a reasonable topic for which there are enough literature references is just the beginning. Then we think about the design of the research project itself: What form will it take? What will I measure? how will I evaluate data? By comparison, practical difficulties seem almost easy. Availability of suitable subjects, a place in which to work with them, apparatus, equipment, tests or measurement scales—all require decisions. We try very hard to foresee and allow for difficulties that could cause the results of many hours of hard work to be ambiguous or inconclusive. As we know from *Murphy's Law,* "If anything can go wrong, it will."

The nature of the learning process requires the individual parts of the research strategy to be studied sequentially, but in application the various components of research designs are interrelated. Each decision we make in one area affects decisions made in others. Decisions are further complicated by the fact that research questions can often be evaluated in several ways. The direction of our research, as given in the phrasing of the research question, determines the general class of statistic that will be chosen. However, any particular statistic will work, for example, only with certain levels of measurement and with subjects who have been appropriately selected by number of samples and sample size. In order to select the statistic that works best for evaluating a particular research idea, one must have a good working knowledge of alternatives and the justifications for making each decision.

To simplify this integration, at least for students who have had a first course in statistics, I have organized the presentation of research techniques to follow the sequence used in many statistics texts. The order progresses from the relatively simple descriptive techniques to the sophisticated and complex experimental research designs.

INTEGRATION OF STATISTICAL CONCEPTS WITH RESEARCH METHODS

Statistics texts often divide their subject matter into three broad categories. Within each category there are several statistics to accommodate variations of designs, selection of subjects, types of data, and several other relevant conditions.

1. Descriptive statistics and naturalistic observation
   Graphing
   Measures of central tendency
   Measures of variability (dispersion)
2. Correlations (measures of relationship) and concomitant variation
   Includes regression and prediction.
   These can also be used as descriptive statistics for early stages of research.
3. Inferential statistics and experimental research designs
   Used to test for statistically significant differences between or among research groups.

The logical sequence in the ordering of the major research methods is rarely followed in research practice. The pattern suggests that tentative, not always very well-formed ideas are screened using simple descriptive statistics or possibly no statistical evaluation at all. The method might use observation in a natural environment, it might evaluate preexisting data obtained from records, or it might use any of many other variations, none of which permit control of the variables being studied.

If results from this approach are promising, a correlational analysis might be undertaken to test them further. When hypotheses have obtained enough supporting evidence at that level, experimental tests might be devised for a higher level of assessment.

Unfortunately, the complexity of the behavioral sciences does not make good research easy. We are often forced to use a simple research technique because the nature of our research questions do not permit an analysis in any other way. When we cannot manipulate our variables—which means to change them and try them out in different ways—we are forced to make the best use we can of what we have.

Cohen (1978) wanted to find out if "dark hair and light eyes" could be used as a "potential biologic marker for liability to psychopathology" for female college students. No one of the variables of interest to him (hair color, eye color, gender, handedness [left or right], and vulnerability for psychopathology) could be systematically manipulated in the way that would be necessary for an experimental design.

He got the idea for this research from "informal observation," and tied it in with other work on organicity which suggested left-handedness in females might indicate a predisposing factor for psychopathology. His brief, published report of this work presented results in simple tables that showed the percent of "target" students, those with dark hair and light eyes, who were either left or right handed. A chi-square statistical analysis demonstrated that the hypothesis could not be entirely rejected.

If we take an outlandish jump from the college classroom to evaluate hypotheses regarding how people react in a major crisis, a hurricane, tornado, earthquake, or large fire, the event itself will dictate what research options are available. We cannot devise cruel or inhuman situations for research. Naturalistic observation or a correlational analysis might offer the only options for research in situations that would be impossible to create. Even a study of less-dreadful events, failing a test perhaps, must use results obtained in the normal sequence of events. It would be highly unethical for an instructor to give unearned failing grades in order to study the resulting behavior.

Statisticians have developed a number of correlation statistics that can be used in special ways for research. Their general purpose is to statistically "describe" the extent of a relationship between or among sets of data. Descriptive applications of correlations are very important in the preliminary levels of research. Keep in mind also that correlations have an inferential function in the measurement areas of psychology. Some correlation statistics are flexible enough to be used in different forms both for describing characteristics of data and for making inductive inferences from it.

Both naturalistic observation and the correlation methods function in research primarily for screening hypotheses. They help investigators to pick out those hypotheses that seem to be worthy of further study. As knowledge of an area is accumulated, the next step is to develop research hypotheses and evaluate them using research techniques—if that is possible. When a researcher is clever enough to formulate a hypothesis suitable for direct experimental analysis, he or she would skip the preliminary screening techniques. A competent investigator would always go directly to experimental designs when that level of research is possible.

For this text, the inferential statistics applicable to "experimental" designs are the most important ones. I probably should point out that I apply a more narrow meaning to the word "experiment" than is common. I have limited the term to a specific type of research design. I reserve the word to identify a research technique having a specified structure. I do not call it "an experiment" when someone tries something out just to see what happens.

Inferential statistics get the most coverage in typical statistics texts. Recall from the logic chapter that an inference is drawing a conclusion from evidence. In research, we work with samples in order to make inferences—i.e., draw conclusions—about a larger group which the samples are presumed to represent. The logical process involved is "induction," so in research we are actually using these statistics for making "inductive" (as opposed to "deductive") inferences.

Only research methods that are roughly equivalent to the simplest techniques for statistical evaluation will be discussed in this chapter. In later chapters we will study correlational analyses and experimental techniques.

NATURALISTIC OBSERVATION AND DESCRIPTIVE STATISTICS

The method of naturalistic observation is descriptive in the way it functions. Because the technique is not precise in its determination of possible causes, it does not have much professional application in the behavioral sciences, but untrained people use it regularly. It is also valuable in special instances of medical diagnoses that involve a single cause for a specified set of symptoms.

The inherent character of naturalistic observation blends well enough with research questions that might not require a statistical analysis for evaluation. However, for most projects in the behavioral sciences, I think that we would at least use descriptive statistics to demonstrate the findings. This type of statistic is aptly named because it helps to describe, and in that way give meaning to, an unsorted collection of scores or measurements. Familiar statistics for distinguishing certain characteristics of data include, but are not limited to, measures of central tendency (means, medians, and modes) and measures of dispersion or variability (variance, range, interquartile or semi-interquartile range).

Descriptive statistics might not even be used if the data can be presented pictorially by drawing a graph or chart. Sometimes a lot can be learned by studying a graph, but if we want to work with our data rather than just looking at them, we will need a statistical presentation.

This section discusses the many ways we have of selecting, organizing, and to some extent interpreting observational data obtained from natural or natural-appearing situations. "Field research" is another name used for some aspects of this general method. In "natural" situations we usually do not have much control over the many extraneous conditions that could have affected our conclusions. This method requires a great deal of caution in the interpretation of our conclusions. As I mentioned earlier, the method is best used for preliminary study or for drawing only tentative conclusions.

Field Work With Animals

As a general rule, I hold that all research should be undertaken to evaluate hypotheses we have put forward for testing. In the earliest stages of research, when very little information is available about a topic, naturalistic observation might be our only choice. I am sure that anyone who looks carefully in the literature of science will find many examples of simple observation producing testable hypotheses. I know of a biology instructor who sent a group of students to a zoo with instructions to "just study the animals." The success rate for nondirected observational enterprises like that one is certain to be very low. I contend that if you do not know what you are looking for, you will not know when you have found it. If I do not have a background of information in an area, I will not have the information I need to make comparisons. How would I know that a particular observation is unexpected without having information available for making a comparison? Even in the preliminary stages of research I think progress is more likely if the work develops from a foundation of ideas obtained in other ways—a study of the literature perhaps.

If an investigator did not start animal observation with a question about whether or not animals use tools (it was popularly believed for a long time that they do not), instances of animals[1] using tools would be overlooked as unimportant or irrelevant. Once a research question directs attention to a particular idea, we are able to note evidence that contradicts it.

It turns out that there are many creatures that use tools. A finch on the Galapagos Islands puts a twig into a termite nest, then after a little, withdraws the twig and eats any termites clinging to it. The finch carefully selects a twig with a slight bow in it to better get around the bend at the entrance. Chimpanzees have been observed putting twigs into termite nests to collect termites for eating. Some of the apes go further. They actually create tools by stripping leaves off a twig they want to use, rather than just looking for a twig that is lying around. While thinking about primates, consider the bonobo species, which uses a "rock and a hard place" for cracking nuts.

Egyptian vultures come to mind as another example of tool-using creatures, but in a different context. Many times they have been observed using rocks to break the hard shells of ostrich eggs in order to eat the contents. They will hold the rocks in their beaks and hit the eggs, throw the rocks, or even fly over and dive-bomb them (Van Lawick-Goodall, 1968).

Note that in all these examples "just watching" is not enough. We have to observe creatively to integrate observations with other ideas we have about behavior—if observations are to be of value.

To illustrate how little progress we can make by using the method of undirected naturalistic observation, I present the following anecdotal examples. Note that my new and interesting observations might already be well known, but I would not know that without a background of information in the area.

I have from time to time watched birds at my wife's bird feeder and have noted the following: A male cardinal repeatedly selected a sunflower seed from the feeder, shelled it, carried the tidbit to a nearby branch, and fed it to a waiting female cardinal. In thinking back, I now realize that I noticed this behavior only in the spring. Could that be important?

Recently I have become aware of birds and squirrels feeding together, often eating just a few inches from each other.

---

[1] The word "animal" is used here to mean all living creatures except people.

One day a bird watcher called my attention to a bird going down a tree trunk head first, like a squirrel goes down. I had seen this many times, but I had paid no attention to it.

These three examples collectively illustrate several features of naturalistic observation. Regarding the male cardinal that kept shelling and feeding sunflower seeds to a nearby female that readily accepted them: Of course the behavior is cute, but we would know this *only in the context of what other birds do.* If all birds did this, we would think nothing of it. That is just the way birds are; that is what they do. An investigator must have a working knowledge of what is normal or typical in behavior in order to recognize what is unusual. Without further study we cannot say if this was just a peculiar pair of cardinals or if behavior of this sort is characteristic of their species—which I have heard it is.

Hundreds of times I must have observed squirrels and birds eating alongside each other, just as the reader probably has done. I have no idea what caused me one day to finally recognize this behavior as a research problem. How does a bird learn that squirrels will not harm birds? I can understand that over time one bird might, with repeated experience, learn this, but I cannot explain this observation with reference to whole groups of birds of different species. When our dog is in the yard birds will eat off the elevated feeders but not on the ground. When a cat is in the yard birds will not come into the yard at all. It takes only a minute or so after the cat has disappeared for the birds to come back and continue eating.

Since I hit on the idea of bird/mammal recognition I have found myself making many other observations. I have concluded that the birds living in my neighborhood are able to recognize and differentiate among the several types of mammals that live in or wander through our yard: squirrels, rabbits, woodchucks, cat, dog, raccoon, chipmunks. Although the woodchucks and cat are about the same size and color, the birds ignore the woodchucks. We can follow the cat's walk through the woods by the raucous calls of the blue jays. A bird that does not know the difference between a cat and other animals learns a lesson that cannot be passed directly to future generations.

As for the bird that goes down a tree trunk head first, it had never occurred to me that the behavior was unusual. Others had to point out that nuthatches are the *only* birds that do this.

It seems to me that some of the best animal research involving methods of naturalistic observation has been done with primates. This is understandable, partly because many primate species are endangered and need protection. But also, I think, we like to study primates because they are more like us. Three women have become particularly important in the area of primate study: Jane Goodall, Dian Fossey, and Biruté Galdikas. Their stories have been summarized in a very interesting book by Montgomery (1991), *Walking with the Great Apes.*

Of the three women involved in ape research, Fossey is the most notorious. Work of well over a decade produced a book (1983) and ultimately a well-received movie named "Gorillas in the Mist." Her war with poachers started, as many wars do, simply and with justification. Initially her objectives were to conserve and protect an endangered species. Poachers had long been a problem in the area, but with each new confrontation with them, the war became more personal and Fossey became increasingly belligerent. In the beginning she wanted only to prevent poaching activities by taking or destroying poachers' snares and spears. As more crimes were committed against her gorillas, her objectives changed from thwarting poachers to punishing them.

The many pictures in her book are sufficient for an outsider to appreciate the depths of her involvement in the protection of these intelligent and interesting creatures. One pair of pictures can summarize her intense frustration, which she admits turned to anger. The first picture is of "Digit," an important subject whose group she had been studying intensively. The photograph shows Digit, a handsome fellow on sentry duty a little distance from his group. The opposite photograph is of Digit's headless corpse. A note points out that he did not live to see his only sired infant. He had died "so that his family group could survive."

The very human side of the Fossey story can be read in *The Dark Romance of Dian Fossey* by H. T. P. Hayes (1990). This analysis helps to explain the personality of Fossey, the scientific investigator who became deeply involved in the politics of protecting the gorillas she had been studying. There were pressures from human population growth, but she did not back away from physical confrontations with poachers who cut off gorilla heads and hands for sale as trophies. She was outraged as members of her gorilla family—this is the way she thought of them—were slaughtered for the few dollars that their parts could bring. What had begun as a significant scientific study led to her vigorous defense of animal rights and ended when she was brutally murdered in her jungle home.

We can get a feeling of the naturalistic observation process by reviewing Fossey's initial day at work. "On my first full day in the field I had scarcely walked more than ten minutes away from camp before seeing a lone male gorilla sunbathing on a horizontal tree trunk that projected over a small lake nestled in a corner of Kabara meadow."

Before she could get her binoculars out, "the startled animal leapt from the tree and disappeared into the dense vegetation of the adjacent mountain slope." Fossey spent an entire day trying to catch up with the animal, but never did. She wrote, "Oddly enough that brief observation was the first and only one of its kind in which I encountered a gorilla resting in such an exposed area." Obviously, she did not know this when she made the observation, but she remembered it, and it served as a standard against which other observations would be compared. "How common is it for male gorillas to rest in exposed places?" became a research question for her.

I am fairly confident that Fossey did not begin her gorilla research with a checklist of items to be observed. First, she had to find the gorillas and allow them get acquainted with her so she could spend some time with them—and *they* determined what would be happening. Over many years of unstructured observation she developed a baseline of behavioral examples that would be the source of hypotheses more specific observations would help her to evaluate.

The following brief list of things Fossey studied suggests the complex nature of the behavior that she felt was important enough to comment on in her book: migration from one group to another, causes of death, breeding rights, injuries and recuperation, gentle fathering practices, group interaction, squabbles within groups, soil-eating binges, maternal behavior, play, disciplining infants, masturbation, vocalizations, and favorite foods.

If investigators have a great deal of time, an open-ended research protocol can produce many observations, but what observers look for is always determined by their objectives. Several independent investigators, studying the same group of animals, will likely evaluate different aspects of behavior. It is difficult to note behavior that answers questions we have not asked, but in the beginning, that might be the only approach we can use.

We must acknowledge, however, that research moves along faster if we narrow our perspective through the guidance and direction of testable ideas. For contrast with the work done by investigators in the wild, let us examine briefly a well-structured research project that looks basically at one psychological construct, *Peacemaking Among Primates* (de Waal, 1989).

Although the living environments of the various great-ape subjects were markedly different, all investigators used the method of naturalistic observation for the collection of data.

De Waal did the bulk of his work in several zoos and research centers. The use of captive animals who lived in a structured, institutional environment permitted better control of relevant variables, and this in turn allowed more definitive conclusions. Different zoos specialize in one or another of the different ape species, which allowed de Waal to easily contrast behavior in different ape groups and ultimately to compare his ape observations with human behavior. De Waal did compare his observations with those that had been made by observers of apes living in the wild when such comparisons were relevant.

The flavor of de Waal's observations on the ways animals keep the peace by making up can best be appreciated with an example. He explains that

> . . . it is not uncommon for a female chimpanzee to break the ice between adult males who, after a fight, stay close to each other but seem unable to reopen communication. Avoiding eye contact, the two males play the familiar game of glancing over when the other looks away. A female may approach one male, briefly groom or touch him, and walk over to the other with the first male following closely. This way he need not face his adversary. When the female sits down next to the second male, both groom her. Only a small shift is necessary for them to groom each other after the female has walked away. That the mediator knows what she is doing is clear from the way she looks over her shoulder and waits for a male who is reluctant to follow.

Captive Versus Field Studies

Although the reasonable use of captive animals made it feasible for de Waal to draw conclusions that would not have been possible from even a prolonged study of free-ranging animals, one must always raise a question about the relevance of captive animal behavior to similar animals living in the wild. At some point one must address the question, "Which type of animal do we want to find out about?" One might say that we are interested in explaining behavior as it occurs in the "real world," which would probably mean the animal's natural environment.

Someone else might present the point of view that behavior is behavior, so we could make a case for studying behavior in the simulated natural environment of a good zoo. What we must not do is to study zoo behavior, then use those conclusions to generalize to the animal's natural environment. Some topics such as inter-community relations cannot be studied in a zoo environment at all. The apes in Fossey's study lived in family groups that had their own identities, but she was able to study the migration of animals from one group to another.

Where we study behavior is to some extent a matter of convenience. Field research is time-consuming and requires a dedication that is often beyond the willingness of all but a very few people to undertake. Some behavior might not be much affected by captivity, and if frequent measurements or multiple daily observations are required, we must arrange to keep animals where we can watch them. The interesting work that has been done on teaching apes to communicate is a good example of this.

We should acknowledge from the beginning that we probably cannot be sure the behavior we see in captive animals is necessarily characteristic of the behavior in the wild. Bonobo apes often had been noted for being quite gentle in captivity. Field work discovered a large number of physical abnormalities among free-living bonobos. A long list of possible explanations for the deformities, particularly among adult males, was unable to rule out a link with aggression. De Waal noted that the same observation of gentleness had been made about gorillas and chimpanzees. The impression was dispelled when field studies disclosed otherwise.

Mook's (1983) article "In Defense of External Invalidity"[2] pointed out that good and important research can be accomplished in situations that are so artificial that results cannot, nor are intended to be, generalized to the real world: "Rather than making predictions about the real world from the laboratory, we may test predictions that specify what ought to happen in the lab." Some laboratory findings are interesting because they demonstrate behavior that can occur, even though we are never likely to observe it outside the laboratory setting. There has been so much emphasis on the necessity for arranging experiments that encourage and permit generalization of results to the general population of interest, that Mook felt it was necessary to call attention to a number of important experiments that produced results with no relevance to life outside the laboratory. Mook referred to the widely reported work by Harlow (1958, 1959, 1965, 1970) on mother love in rhesus monkeys. He questioned how research using mother figures made of wire mesh, rubber nipples, and terrycloth cylinders warmed with light bulbs could "possibly tell us about how monkeys with natural upbringing would behave in a natural setting." Mook's point is that we should use judgment regarding the meaning and interpretation of research findings.

Field Work With Humans

De Waal makes the case that many people mistakenly suggest that apes are just like children. Although there are many similarities, there are some remarkable

---

[2] This term will be explained later.

differences. "In summary, it is probably closer to the truth to say that humans look and act like ape children than apes look and act like human children." Let me use that observation to segue into a look at naturalistic observation applied to humans.

Peacemaking, the topic de Waal chose for study, gave him a lot of trouble because there is so little information on it. This complaint applied particularly to research in humans. He stated that except for a few reports on preschool children and "occasional anthropological accounts" he was unable to find information on reconciliation behavior in humans. He commented on the ". . . amazing lack of data on peacemaking in private human relationships." "I speak from years of frustration with the literature on human behavior. How do people actually behave?" He notes the tremendous amount of work that has been done on violence and aggression, but he could not find a single reference on peacemaking or forgiveness, except as the last word is used in clinical literature.

If we are to look briefly at peacemaking among humans we might begin with children, primarily because they are easier to study than mature adults. We learn from watching children that a number of forms of reconciliation can be identified. The list is in descending order of frequency (from de Waal, 1989).

> *Cooperative propositions*—statements of friendly intent and suggestions for collaboration, such as "I'll be your friend" or "You can help me build this house."
> *Object offering*—(discussed in the next paragraph.)
> *Grooming*—handholding, stroking, kissing, embracing, or other forms of touching.
> *Apology*—verbally expressed regret at the result of the fight.
> *Symbolic offer*—a promise, such as "I'm going to bring you my truck."

The list could in large part be duplicated by a list compiled from ape studies, but there is one pattern that apes do not use—gift giving. De Waal points out that "this peace gesture is unknown or very rare in other primates, yet common in our own species."

For a complete change of direction, let us study humor by unobtrusively making notes regarding the humor situations we all get involved in as we go about the business of living. In what circumstances do people laugh? What jokes do people tell each other? What humorous experiences do they relate? Are there differences among people in the extent to which they elicit laughter from others? We know that many people will laugh out loud when they see a funny episode at the movies. Do they laugh out loud if they see the film alone? (Is there a social facilitation of laughter?) Do people really laugh if someone slips on a banana peel and falls? (This is often mentioned, incorrectly I think, by humor theorists as a funny situation. When a person slips and falls, concern and an immediate offer of assistance would be the result—not laughter.) Is laughter used in social situations to soften the intensity of an unpleasant situation? Naturalistic observation would be the technique we would use to study the laughter behavior of humans as they react in a natural environment.

I consider smiling and laughter to be primarily a social phenomenon, that might or might not be related to an appreciation of a humorous event. I concluded that from observing people in natural situations. Many aspects of the humor construct are open to study, but it never would have occurred to me that additional work was necessary to verify that smiling means different things at different times. If that statement is changed to a question, Ekman and Davidson (1993) have given us an answer. They "used measures of regional brain electrical activity to show that not all smiles are the same. Only one form of smiling produced the physiological pattern associated with enjoyment." In addition they evaluated several ideas related to the interaction of facial expression and emotion, but these are irrelevant to this discussion.

Early work on sense of humor (actually humor appreciation) tried to equate laughter and enjoyment. In one study, researchers even went so far as to measure smiles in order to correlate these with whether or not certain jokes were said to be funny. Any thoughtful observer can, in a short time, draw what seem to me to be quite sensible conclusions about smiling, grinning, and laughter, as these occur in social situations. Watch a group of people at a party who have just been introduced. Their small talk will be punctuated with all the smiling and laughter required by the traditional expectations of a pleasant social situation. It can be observed quickly that the smiling has absolutely nothing to do with what is being discussed. Party talk is meant to be pleasant, and it involves lots of smiles, but is it humorous? Not usually. ("Well we have a beautiful night for the party, don't we? [grin, grin]" "Yes, it cleared off nicely. We can even see the moon. I wonder if the Wolfman is about! [ha, ha.]")

Important meetings that involve disparate, strongly held opinions that need to be resolved among participants, will often produce what the world calls "nervous laughter." That statement directs us to another topic that would take us too far afield if we were to pursue it. The idea is, "To what extent can humor (and laughter) be used to relieve feelings of frustration (anxiety, nervousness, whatever)?"

Observing adult behavior is much more difficult than observing children in a nursery or school situation, so investigators have compromised with reality. Instead of actually observing what people *do*, investigators often use a questionnaire to ask them what they *did*. Diaries, questionnaires, checklists are all ways to get the information we would like to get from naturalistic observation if it were possible to do so. Obviously, information collected this way is more convenient for the investigator, but the trade-off is that investigators are in large part dependent on respondents for data.

First we need to ensure, to the extent we can, that the forms returned are an accurate representation of the group we want to find out about. It is most unlikely that everyone will complete and return a questionnaire, so investigators will try to determine if there is a possibility of selective elimination. If we are studying eating habits, the very obese people might not want to respond. If particular groups are underrepresented in the final tabulation, the sample will not adequately represent the larger group we are studying.

Next, we should try to determine whether respondents are telling the truth. Many scales include some form of "lie" measurement to help identify a set of less-than-truthful responses.

Finally, we want to do what we can to get *accurate* information. This is different from just telling the truth, as it appears to the respondent. One might truly believe that a particular (false) response is true. When in doubt, people tend to put down what they think is the more socially acceptable response.

May, Hasher, and Stoltzfus (1993) used questionnaires to help them study "Optimal Time of Day and the Magnitude of Age Differences in Memory." They concluded that most younger adults were "evening or neutral types." The vast majority of "older adults were morning types." Marked performance differences between these age groups were noted when all participants were studied in the afternoon, a time when young people were at their peak. No age differences were found when both groups were studied in the morning, when older but not younger adults were producing their best performance.

While waiting to discuss a matter with the Dean of Students at my university, I picked up an old copy of a professional journal, *Journal of College Student Personnel.* Looking in other disciplines' journals is often a good way to broaden one's perspective, and that certainly was true in this case. I was immediately surprised at the large number of studies that derived their information from questionnaires or variations of them. Not that this is not a legitimate technique for research—it is; but I had just been looking in a recent issue of *Psychological Science* (a publication of the American Psychological Society) so the contrast was startling. To some extent, the subject matter was also different. In the personnel journal it seemed to be less theoretical and more appropriate to application by people who work in a specific situation (the office of student personnel). I have selected some of the titles that used variations of the method of naturalistic observation as a source of data.

"College Students' Attitudes Regarding Sexual Coercion and Aggression: Developing Educational and Preventive Strategies."

"College Students' Attitudes Towards Wellness."

"Time-Budgeting Practices of College Students: A Developmental Analysis of Activity Patterns."

"Activity Factors That Affect Transfer Student Persistence."

"Evaluation of a Program of Peer Helping for 1st-Year Students."

"Interpersonal Moderators of Depression Among College Students."

"Factors Affecting Alcohol Use by College Students."

At least one author of five of these seven articles indicated a psychology department affiliation at his or her university. These titles are all from volume 28, the 1987, July issue.

Naturalistic observation as a research tool comes up in several different ways in the text, as the conclusions are used to illustrate one point or another. Recall the Holmes and Rahe (1967) work on life crises discussed in the last chapter. All of their data came from reports that were related to actual life events. Near the end of this textbook, in an entirely different context, there will be a discussion of "The Tearoom Trade: Impersonal Sex in Public Places." The material for this study was obtained from direct observation of behavior in a men's washroom.

Technical Problems With Naturalistic Observation

Our opportunities for observing many aspects of human behavior are all around us, but unsystematic observation probably does not produce results we can rely on. Behavior varies a lot, as determined by where a person is, who she or he is with (if anyone), and what is being done.

If small groups of people are being studied, there are additional constraints on observation. Should the investigator be actively involved in the group? Do other participants know they are being studied, and how will this knowledge affect the group? These and many other procedural questions need answers before we can undertake research in certain areas of social psychology.

Volume 2 of *The Handbook of Social Psychology* (Lindzey & Aronson, 1968) is devoted to topics related to research methods for investigations in the social sciences. The chapter by Weick on "Systematic Observational Methods" in this volume is particularly relevant and should be consulted by anyone planning to work in this area. The content is dated, but the basic concepts are still sound.

Campbell and Stanley (1963) is another useful reference that discusses the collection of research data by observation. They emphasized the distinction between "experimental and quasi-experimental designs." The control an investigator has over extraneous variables and the ability to systematically manipulate the research variables are distinguishing features of the experimental method. Clever investigators have occasionally managed to contrive a social situation that closely approximates the controlled conditions of an experiment, but mostly the methods of naturalistic observation do not permit much in the way of controlled conditions. That accounts for the distinction between true experiments and quasi-experiments.

In situations in which an investigator cannot manipulate directly the research attributes to be studied, he or she can sometimes use preexisting variations. These could be something like the presence or absence of a particular life experience—finishing or not finishing high school, for example. With these data, personal "naturalistic observation" is not necessary because the information needed could be obtained from records and historical documents. Instead of watching subjects to see what they are doing now, we use records to see what they did in the past.

"The GRE Psychology Test as an Unobtrusive Measure of Motivation" (Ewen, 1969) is an example of a quasi-experiment. The basic hypothesis tested in this research was that motivation might affect success in graduate programs in psychology. Motivation was operationally defined by the score on the GRE-P test (the psychology part of the Graduate Record Exam). The thinking went like this: Highly motivated students are strongly interested in psychology, and they will develop a good background in the subject by taking and doing well in a number of psychology courses. This in turn will produce a good grade on the GRE-P. (The authors had a way of making an allowance for differences in ability.)

NATURALISTIC OBSERVATION OR LABORATORY: WHICH IS BETTER?

People taking their first physics class are regularly surprised at demonstrations that show familiar objects doing unexpected things. Everyday experience has long ago convinced us that a feather and a lead pellet do not fall at the same rate; the light feather floats down when dropped, but the lead pellet drops straight down. It almost seems as if gravity has a much stronger pull on the lead pellet than it does on the feather. The surprise comes when a feather and a lead pellet are put together in a long glass tube from which the air has been evacuated to form a vacuum. In that environment both the feather and the lead pellet fall at the same rate. This demonstration is unnatural in the sense that it is not typical of our everyday experience, but when we remove the influences of our natural environment (air in this example) we get a truer picture of how gravity operates. For physics, the terms "artificial" or "natural" have no meaning.

Life is not so simple for behavioral scientists. We can visualize the difference if we picture two rooms at opposite ends of a hall. One room is clearly labeled "Human Behavior Laboratory" and the other is the "Lounge." One end of the hall represents the "natural" world, with all of its numerous uncontrolled, varying, and interacting causal pressures. At the other end of the hall investigators try to eliminate extraneous variables in order to simplify the environment. Does what we learn at the "Laboratory" end of the hall help us to understand what goes on at the "Lounge" end? We would like to think that it does, but we cannot be sure.

Our environment and the causes of behavior are complex. When we simplify conditions to improve the quality of our research, we also tend to make the conclusions less relevant for explaining what real people do in real situations.

Clever investigators in the behavioral sciences will occasionally devise ways for doing their work in what we can think of in this analogy as a third room, perhaps halfway up the hall between the other two. This room offers meaningful controls that are necessary for quality research, but the conditions in it should not be so unnatural that they would restrict an experimenter's ability to generalize results to ordinary situations and everyday experience.

Cooper managed this with her experiments in "cognitive aspects of visual processing" (Kent 1990). Computers and particularly computer graphics have made it possible for her to achieve an experimental control in her work while economically simulating real-world events. She writes, "Lots of questions that people have wanted to ask for a long time are just now being investigated in a rich enough way to maintain the complexity of information in the world but in a controlled enough way to be scientifically acceptable."

"Experiments in group conflict," Sharif's work from many years ago (1956), gave psychology an example of good research that used a natural-appearing situation to simulate controlled conditions. A summer camp for boys provided the location and circumstances for the development of group conflicts that could be studied as various methods were tried to resolve them. Complex hypotheses were stated simply: ". . . when two groups have conflicting aims—i.e., when one can achieve its ends only at the expense of the other—their members will become hostile to each other."

Then, turning "to the other side of the problem," Sharif and his camp counselors asked the question: "How can two groups in conflict be brought into harmony?" He pointed out that bringing hostile groups together socially, to communicate "accurate and favorable information about one group to the other," does not always work very well: ". . . as everyone knows, such measures sometimes reduce intergroup tensions and sometimes do not." "What our limited experiments have shown is that the possibilities for achieving harmony are greatly enhanced when groups are brought together to work toward common ends." People the world over are still trying to implement that finding in the solution of their own group conflict problems.

Work with animals is much more easily carried out in a laboratory environment than with naturalistic observation. Homing in pigeons has frequently been noted, studied, and used in natural conditions; but only when pigeons were moved into a laboratory was there any progress toward an explanation (Keeton, 1974). Laboratory findings were able to upset previous explanations of the homing process. Other studies have since been carried out in natural conditions. One of them attached magnets to the pigeons to confuse possible sensory modalities for the earth's magnetism.

The better-controlled and managed conditions of a laboratory have encouraged (according to some psychologists) too much laboratory work to the exclusion of field research. Miller (1977) in effect issued a plea for psychologists to get out of the laboratory in order to study animals in their natural living conditions. He argued persuasively for an integration of the two types of research, but he also made the point that certain types of behavior—socialization of nonhuman primates is an example—can only or best be investigated in the natural environment.

Miller's recommendations were for the use of field conditions as a "natural laboratory." He did not find the casual study of nature for its own sake, of the "bird-watching" variety, to be of much value. But he went on to point out that, ". . . a trained and astute observer can begin to formulate questions that can be transformed into scientific problems," by watching animals "do what comes naturally" (Lehrman, 1971).

The Milgram (1974) study on obedience to authority is one that is still discussed because of the startling findings it produced—in a highly structured laboratory situation. Some psychologists have questioned whether the situation itself might not have partly produced the phenomenon it was designed to study.

"Eyewitness Testimony" (Buckhout, 1974) is just one example from among a great many that illustrate how behavior first observed naturally can be brought into a laboratory environment for more intensive study. Although eyewitness testimony is widely used, laboratory research shows it to be "remarkably subject to error."

The "prison" investigation by Haney, Banks, and Zimbardo (1973) had startling success in creating conditions for the study of complex psychological behavior. The environment they produced seemed to compress and speed up psychological reactions that would have taken a great deal longer to observe in an actual prison environment. Findings were so provocative that the experiment had to be ended before its scheduled completion time.

Naturalistic observation is difficult, time-consuming, and quite prone to observational errors, but it does reflect the world as we know and experience it. Laboratory experiments are much better for research, but the controls in the laboratory environment, together with other factors to be discussed later, tend to produce results that are difficult to generalize (assuming of course that understanding behavior in the everyday world is our objective). The dream of research psychologists is to create conditions that are normal and natural as far as the subject is concerned but which incorporate controls that are necessary for good research.

METHOD OF AGREEMENT AND NATURALISTIC OBSERVATION

This is one of the most widely used research techniques there is, but it is also one that is almost never discussed in the research texts. The reason is that it does not work well in *behavioral science* research. It does, however, have an important use in certain areas of medical research, as I will illustrate a little later. The fact that this research method provides at best only very weak validation for behavioral science hypotheses does not seem to restrict its use by nonscientific people for everyday applications. Several reasons might account for this. It is easy to use; intuitively it seems to make sense; and, a nice third point, it does not require statistical evaluation for drawing a conclusion.

The method of naturalistic observation is exactly the research design that suits the pseudo-science of "pop psychology." One can pull almost any book from the shelves in the psychology section of the nearest mall bookstore and find something like the following. (I have not quoted this excerpt exactly, but it is close.)

A chapter begins with the wandering thoughts of a woman who is suffering from the flu. She describes the room as feeling large and cold and unpleasant. As the hours pass she begins to remember herself as a little girl, "small, vulnerable, helpless." By the end of the day she feels "utterly miserable" in a way that is not so much a result of the flu, but of anxiety. She wonders what she is doing there, "so solitary, so unattached, so . . . floating." She feels cut off from family, from her busy and demanding life, she feels . . . "disconnected."

Then as a break occurs in her stream of thoughts, she comes to realize that she is always alone—a truth she has always tried to avoid. She does not like being alone but wants to be looked after, to feel safe, warm, and taken care of.

Since that day spent in bed I've learned that there are other women like me, thousands upon thousands of us who grew up in a certain way. . . . Everything about the way we were raised told us we would be a *part* of someone else—that we would be protected, supported, buoyed up by wedded happiness until the day we died.

As I diagram and develop this research pattern, the structure will seem obvious and familiar. We first identify a problem, a difficulty, a set of symptoms perhaps, as in this example. We then look around for examples of other people who demonstrate the symptoms we are studying, and we try to identify what characteristics they all have in common. We use these to explain the symptoms. As we know, nothing in the behavioral sciences works out exactly, so we lace our explanations with "generally, usually, often" or other similar terms to show that the observations seem to fit some but not all of the time.

The general forms of today's standard research procedures have had many hundreds of years of development. John Stuart Mill,[3] nearly 150 years ago published the *System of Logic,* in which he summarized and organized information on research methods as they were understood up to that time. Mill could not have foreseen the many techniques for statistical analysis that are now available, but several of his research methods follow the logical divisions of modern statistics texts surprisingly closely. That is why I am using three of his "methods of experimental enquiry" for the basic structure of this text.

Mill's "method of agreement" provides a useful structure for analyzing and deriving meaning from collected observations. The reason for the title will become clear as the technique is described.

Mill (see Nagel, 1950) recognized that we might sometime need to get data for our research from general observation, rather than from the careful manipulation in an experimental framework.

For the purposes of varying the circumstances, we may have recourse (according to a distinction commonly made) either to observation or to experiment; we may either *find* an instance in nature suited to our purposes or, by an artificial arrangement of circumstances, *make* one.

The method of agreement works in this way: An investigator has identified a condition that needs to be studied. Say that a number of people in a small town developed a stomach problem at the same time; this is the *effect*. The health authorities began a study to determine a *single* possible cause of all cases of the illness. People from different families were involved, but investigation disclosed that all of them had eaten food at a certain small restaurant.

The traditional use for this technique begins when there is a problem discovered, an effect, and we want to find the cause. The method is simplistic in operation and is applicable only when it can be presumed that there is a *single* cause/effect relationship. The method gets its name from the fact that *we look for the single causal entity on which all examples of the effect agree.*

The following contrived example demonstrates how the method might be used and what is wrong with it.

---

[3] The most readily available source of information today can be found in Nagel (1950).

A group of people attended a party at which something of value was stolen. Some but not all of the people in the original group attended another party, and something again was stolen. This was quite a partying crowd, so several more parties were held, each of which was attended by different groups of people. A theft occurred at each party. A careful study of the guest lists might disclose the thief. The procedure would be to look for the only person who had been present at every occurrence of a theft. Table 6.1 illustrates. Displaying data in this way makes it easy to select the relevant variable.

The initials represent a particular person's presence at that party. Person A attended every party except for the one on June 5. Person B missed May 23 and June 28. All the letters representing people are interpreted in the same way. Note that only one person, D, attended all the parties. D is the single entity on which all cases of thievery agreed. Person D is the presumed thief.

The logic of the method requires the investigator to select a number of examples having the same effect and then arrange *possible* causes to help identify the single characteristic all of them have in common. All other possible causes should differ from one instance of the effect to another. The method tries to eliminate possible causes by using the logic that *nothing can be the cause of an effect if the presumed cause is absent when a particular effect is present.* Mill expressed the idea in this way:

> If two or more instances of a phenomenon have only one circumstance in common, the circumstance on which alone all instances agree is the cause, or is related to the cause, of the phenomenon.

We can see from the example that the method does not work in cases of multiple causation. If there are two thieves the method would not be able to pick them out. Both A and B might have been the thieves, or E and F. If we can be sure that there is only one cause the method can *help* us to identify what it is. The method of agreement is an exploratory method for assisting an investigator to identify likely hypotheses that can be more carefully evaluated with other methods. This is the quality that makes it valuable for the analysis of data collected from naturalistic observation. For behavioral science research, it might be enough if we narrow tentative hypotheses to the two or three that seem most likely to be the correct ones.

Table 6.1

DIAGRAM OF MILL'S METHOD OF AGREEMENT					
Party Dates			People in Attendance		
May 3	A	B	C	D	E	F
May 23	A		C	D		F
June 5		B		D	E	F
June 28	A		C	D	E	
July 9	A	B		D		F

A brief news item in the *New Scientist* (1975, February 27, p. 493) called attention to Dr. T. J. Murray's early investigative work to identify the cause or causes of multiple sclerosis. This attempt to solve a medical problem nicely illustrates the method of agreement as it was applied in an actual situation. Dr. Murray studied all cases of multiple sclerosis that he could find in a small Nova Scotia community with a particularly high incidence of this disease. He looked at all the factors he thought might be possible causes, such as: water supply, personal contact, surgical operations including tonsillectomies, trace metals in the soil, vegetation, allergies, occupation, and childhood diseases, together with other conditions that were shared also by people who did not suffer from multiple sclerosis. "The only time in the past when all the patients lived in the vicinity at the same time was between 1961 and 1962. This coincides with a severe outbreak of polio in the area. . . . One other factor that the patients had in common was that they all had measles late in childhood, about the time of puberty." Note that observations of this sort are not proof, but they direct attention to worthwhile hypotheses that had not previously been considered.

The method of agreement works no better for illnesses that have multiple causes—high blood pressure for example—than it works in psychology for explaining aggression.

If space permitted, I would like to fully describe how well this method worked for medicine in discovering the causes of the "thalidomide syndrome." All I can do is to mention it in passing. After an unexpectedly large number of malformed babies were born during a brief period in Germany, physicians there gradually came to recognize a problem. Investigations were begun to evaluate a large number of possible causes. Various possibilities were rejected one by one because they could not have affected some of the women who gave birth to infants having the identified symptoms. In the end, they found one attribute alone was common to all instances of the phenomenon: All the women who had given birth to deformed babies had taken medication containing thalidomide during the early stages of their pregnancy. We in the United States were spared the tragedy of this near-epidemic because thalidomide had not been approved by the FDA and was not for sale in this country.

A great many of us are concerned about the possibility of heart attacks as we grow older. Many people exercise regularly (or at least know they ought to), take an aspirin every other day, or take vitamins; some of us take drugs for hypertension, and we all know that we should watch our diets. But there might be more that we should know. One way we might identify what is best is to study how people manage in other countries. Some investigators have selected France.

French people have a lower rate of heart attacks than do people in other industrialized countries. Why? One answer is that they drink more red wine. For one's health, a glass of red wine a day might not be too difficult for most people to manage—if they just think of it as medicine. Several years after red wine was selected as the likely cause of fewer heart attacks, other investigators concluded that it was not the red wine at all. In fact, it was because the French also eat more vegetables. This demonstrates how difficult it is to try to identify *the* cause, when any or all of several explanations might work.

ENDNOTE

Until I ran across the de Waal work on peacemaking, I had given only minimal thought to the processes of making up after a confrontation—and that perspective seems to be reflected in the behavior of a great many of my colleagues. De Waal makes repeated references to ". . . the amazing lack of data on peacemaking in private human relationships." If aggression is one of the major problems in society today, then peacemaking should be one of our major concerns.

Surely everyone is aware of the increasing extent to which seemingly trivial disputes lead to violent reactions. Such disputes are made markedly more dangerous by the ready availability of powerful firearms. The observation that people cannot always get along peaceably is certainly not a new one, but means of conflict resolution in earlier times were less aggressive and caused less harm both to the people involved and to bystanders. A great many people are killed each year because they happened to be in the area of conflicts in which they had no part. Nearly every day produces examples. Here are but a few:

> A careless or distracted driver made a quick turn in traffic to get into a parking lot. He cut off another driver and caused him to brake sharply. The offended driver came back to the parking lot to confront the driver who nearly caused an accident. The confrontation resulted in a shooting that missed the driver of the car but killed his little son.

> A teenaged girl, on a major Chicago intersection around noon on a busy Christmas-season shopping day, fired several shots from a pistol in a dispute with another group of young people. Amazingly, no one was hit.

> A young lady was trying to break up with her boyfriend. He critically wounded her, then killed himself.

> A father was killed when he tried to intercede in a quarrel between his daughter and her boyfriend.

Chicago school administrators recognize the seriousness of the inappropriate techniques people use for resolving differences. There is talk about offering special programs for teaching young people socially acceptable options for conflict resolution. This is a very good idea. One may wonder if it is not already too late.

STUDY QUESTIONS

1. Even after you have selected a research idea, why is it so difficult to get started on a research project?

2. Why is it important to plan a research project as a whole?

3. What are the three general areas of statistics and the three general types of research techniques that go with them?

4. Why is research in the behavioral sciences so difficult?

5. Describe the general idea of the method of naturalistic observation.

6. What are some advantages and disadvantages of the method?

7. Why is "bird watching" for its own sake not a method of science?

8.D What, if anything, is wrong with just observing nature?

9.D What is the importance in a couple of animals that were observed using tools?

10. Discuss and contrast animal research as carried out in a laboratory rather than in a field research environment.

11. What are some advantages and disadvantages of laboratory research compared to field research?

12.D To what extent can animal research be generalized to humans?

13. Identify some situations in which naturalistic observation might be the only method possible for research.

14. What are some advantages and disadvantages of field work with humans as a research technique?

15. Why are so many more research projects that involve naturalistic observation done with children than with adults?

16. What are some technical problems with naturalistic observation as it involves humans?

17.D What determines where and how one will do research?

18.D What is your opinion about which research technique is best—laboratory or field research?

19. What is the method of agreement?

    What is the logic on which it is based?

    What are some advantages and disadvantages of the method?

20. How is the method of agreement used with naturalistic observation?

21. Why is the method of agreement rarely used for research in psychology?

22. Why is the method of agreement so widely used, even though it does not work very well for behavioral science research?

SMALL TALK

Chapter

7

Correlational Analyses in Research

Intelligent use of the correlation coefficient is impossible without knowledge of its properties. It is not sufficient that we be able merely to recognize r *as a measure of relationship. It is a peculiar kind of measure which permits certain interpretations provided certain assumptions are tenable and provided we consider possible disturbing factors.*

McNemar (1969), p. 129.

A parent at a PTA meeting once commented on the deleterious affects of an "open campus." This was at a time when high schools were beginning to liberalize a little by letting students leave the school grounds when they did not have classes. The parent argued against continuation of the idea by pointing out that, "Last year, before we had this freedom for students to wander around, we had four national scholarship winners. Then you started the open campus, and this year we didn't have any!"

Nearly every daily newspaper carries examples of presumed cause-and-effect relationships inferred from associations. "Unhappily Married Men May Be More Prone to Disease, Study Suggests," is the headline on a clipping from a *Chicago Tribune* (1987, August 29) article. The inherent assumption in both of these examples is that when two sets of observations change concurrently, one of them is the cause of the other. In this chapter and in the one that follows we will see how to use correlations for research and how to compute and interpret them. We will also learn why relationships do not by themselves permit valid conclusions about causality.

GENERAL IDEAS OF CORRELATIONAL ANALYSES

This is the second of the three research techniques John Stuart Mill identified. Long before statistics for correlational analyses had been worked out, Mill understood the logical structure for using them. He called this way of doing research "the method of concomitant variation."

Correlations have always seemed to me to be both the simplest and the most complicated of the research statistics. They are simple in the sense that their statistical foundations are fairly straightforward and how they work can be easily understood. Fully understanding their different uses and *interpreting what they mean* makes for the complexity.

Most of the discussion in this chapter will be concerned with the employment and computation of the Pearson product-moment correlation, the one that regularly seems to find the most work. (See the Endnote for my guess about what the "product-moment" part of the name means.) The Spearman rank correlation will also be discussed briefly. It is computed with rank rather than with the interval data required for the Pearson correlation, but both are used and interpreted in similar ways.

In the general scheme of statistics, correlations are unique. Others can be classified reasonably as descriptive or inferential statistics, but a correlation can be used either way, as determined by the nature of the questions asked of it. The descriptive function, the way correlations most often are used in research, observes associations to help uncover or suggest *possible* cause-and-effect relationships.

The *inferential* application is important for the testing and measurement areas of psychology. In this application correlations might be asked to evaluate a test's "predictive validity," a form of inductive inference. Regression equations, derived from correlations, can utilize test scores for predicting behavior in some real-life situation. ACT scores are often used for predicting success in college. Assessment of test reliability and consistency is also an inferential process.

A correlation is always computed and interpreted in the same way, so whether we intend to use the results as an inferential or descriptive function is a logical decision we make. It is a little like using the same tool for many different jobs.

Several correlation techniques are available for use with any of the several types of data and for both simple and complex analyses. Some formulas can evaluate mixed measurements such as category and interval, and other techniques compute average intercorrelations among several groups. We will have enough to do if we master only the simplest applications, but other types will be mentioned later in the chapter.

An italic r with a subscript to identify the type of correlation seems to have become the standard symbol for correlations. The Pearson usually has the symbol r_P, and the Spearman symbol is r_S. Not every publication uses these symbols, but they are quite common. Authors should always identify the type of correlation used. If they do not, and in the absence of other information, we assume they have used the Pearson.

A Correlation Practice Problem

I have found that beginners seem to learn correlation analyses more quickly if they first understand how to compute them. Computation seems to emphasize the logic of what correlations do and how they work. Even though I said at the beginning of this discussion that the Pearson is the more important correlation and the one most widely used, I am forced to contradict myself immediately, as I use the Spearman rank correlation formula for the following illustration. It clearly and simply illustrates precisely how a correlation shows *extent* of relationship. Extent of relationship between or among sets of data is what we want to know, and that is the information correlations give us.

The Spearman formula requires two sets of *logically paired ranks.* Recall that ranks are ordinal measurements that can be obtained in several ways. If we start with interval data, which are often called "scores," we can get ranks from a downward conversion. It is always possible to go from higher to lower levels of measurement. We can also arrange the collection of data so ranks are obtained directly from observations. The following little exercise should help to review material illustrated in the measurement chapters.

Rank five of your friends in order according to your estimate of their intelligence, and then rank them in order according to your judgment of the size of their foreheads. Note that I need two judgments (i.e. measurements) for each of several people. By correlating these two sets of data we will get an idea about the extent of relationship between intelligence and forehead size. Many people believe that a high forehead indicates intelligence. Your data will tell us something about this idea.

Remember that conventions for ranking suggest that the largest observation has a rank of 1. The observation having the least amount of the entity being evaluated is given the rank equal to the total number of ranks being compared. In direct ranking we use each rank only once, so the ranks in this example would be 1 to 5 because we are ranking five people.

It is necessary for us to digress slightly in order to avoid a possible misunderstanding. I tend to think of both "ranks" and "number right" as scores. It is just as much a "score" for me to know that a person ranked 5 on a test that included 20 people, as it is to know the person got 57 out of 70 questions right. In fact, knowing that a person got the fifth-highest score out of 20 people tells me more about how the person did, relative to the other people who took the test, than the number right tells me. Without converting number right to some other value, I have no way of knowing whether 57 is a good score or not compared to how the others did.

I explain this point because there is a usage that separates "score" data, which are usually interval, from "rank" data, which we know are ordinal. Obviously, I need to know the kind of data I have in order to do the relevant calculations, but when I am just discussing performance, for me any level of measurement can be used as a score, even category. I know well enough what is meant if I am told that someone ranked seventh in the graduating class, and I also understand how delighted a person would be to be in the "top 5 percent," which is category scaling.

The example in Table 7.1 allows us to study the relationship between "motivation" and "academic performance." Let us agree that the X column will show the ranks of participants according to your estimate of their motivation. The Y column will show the ranks in terms of academic performance. X and Y are generic labels and are commonly used to identify separate columns of data.

Ranks show the ordered positions of judgments within their respective groups. The Spearman correlation notes the amount and direction of differences between paired ranks. In this example the pairs are formed by two sets of ranks for the same individuals. So long as the pairing "makes sense" (i.e., is not arbitrary or capricious), scores can be and often are paired in other ways as determined by the research question.

Both the Spearman and Pearson correlations compare the ordered position of a "score" (for a Pearson) or "rank" (for a Spearman) in one group with the paired measurement in the other group. Because the data are different—interval or ordinal—the computation formulas are quite different.

The Spearman (r_S) formula compares the rank position of a score in the X group with the rank position of the paired score in Y. The difference between these pairs of ranks is recorded in column D. Bill's X score was ranked 1, his Y score was ranked 2. Mary's rank was 1 on the Y scale but 2 on X. Bob's rank of 3 was the same in both groups.

Table 7.1

SPEARMAN *R* FOR RANKED DATA				
Subjects	Ranks		Rank Difference	Difference Squared
	X	Y	D	D^2
Bill	1	2	1	1
June	5	4	1	1
Mary	2	1	1	1
Joann	4	5	1	1
Bob	3	3	0	0
Sum of the squared differences				4 ΣD^2

$$r_S = 1 - \frac{6\,\Sigma D^2}{N\,(N^2 - 1)} = 1 - \frac{24}{5 \times 24} = .80$$

The D column shows the arithmetic differences between pairs of scores. We get the differences by subtracting either the X rank from Y *or* by subtracting the Y rank from X. The D value is squared for the D^2 column, so the sign of the difference disappears. You will usually have small groups when you use this formula, so just subtract the smaller from the larger number in each pair. N is the number of pairs of scores. The 6 in the formula is a constant.

The fairly large correlation computed from the above data suggests that in this sample motivation is highly correlated with academic success. The relationship is positive, which means that highly motivated people generally do better academically than people who are not highly motivated. Since a correlation is *nondirectional*, we cannot determine from information like this whether motivation is a cause of academic success or an effect of it. I might also argue, using the same data, that people who are already performing well academically are more highly motivated to do even better. Which is cause and which is effect is an ambiguity in correlation analysis we will leave for a later full discussion.

If in every pair of scores, the rank in the X group was identical to the rank in Y, the relationship would have been a perfect and positive +1.00. We could use the X rank to predict exactly and without error, the rank of the paired Y score.

If the value in one group of ranks was found to be exactly reversed so that the largest value in one group was paired with the smallest value in the other, and similar reversals were obtained throughout the list, the computed correlation would be –1.00.

Rank X	1	2	3	4	5
Rank Y	5	4	3	2	1

Note that even when ranks follow an expected pattern exactly (either the paired ranks are exactly the same, or they are exactly opposite), the positive or negative correlation they produce is *never* larger than ±1.00. This point is a very important one to remember.

A reader who has not yet done so might want to make up and work some practice problems. Compute a couple of correlations with numbers rearranged in random order to see what happens to *r*.

The Meaning of Paired Measurements

Correlations are typically applicable only to scores that are "logically" paired. The Spearman and Pearson correlations particularly answer questions about the extent of relationship between two sets of paired measurements. Pairing of scores must have a rational basis. Often we have two sets of scores for the same people: scores for people on Test X and scores for the same people on Test Y.

Although this arrangement is widely used, research is not restricted to paired scores for the same people. Correlation between measurements for different people can be used if they are paired according to some predetermined rule. We could correlate measurements for wives and their husbands to answer a question like this one: "Do women marry men who are of roughly the same level of intelligence as themselves?" Using measurements of other personality variables we could study the relationship for dating couples. Does athletic ability of sons correlate with the athletic ability of their fathers? In these examples, the measurement is the same in each pair, but the subjects are different. Note in my examples that I applied a consistent rule for the formation of each pair: husbands/wives, she/he dating couples, fathers/sons.

Pairing two sets of data in selected time intervals would work. That is the way we would study a possible relationship between availability of pornographic materials and the number of sex crimes during each of the last 30 years.

I have emphasized the importance of comparing logically related scores because experience has shown me this is an area students do not always understand or remember. I have seen students try to determine whether there is a relationship between unrelated pairs of scores, with each group of scores listed in sequential order. The person who arbitrarily lists data in this way is always delighted that the relationship is highly significant—as it would have to be between two sets of scores both listed in sequential size order. (See the Endnote for an additional comment on this point.)

Let us note the following to summarize major points made so far.

1. The Pearson or Spearman correlations require two sets of *logically paired scores*.
2. When both sets of data are ranks, the Spearman is the appropriate correlational statistic to use.
3. Both the Pearson and Spearman correlations answer questions about relationship. Computations show the *extent* (amount) of association between two sets of paired measurements.
4. The computed limits of r will never be larger than ±1.00.

USING A PEARSON CORRELATION FOR RESEARCH

Direct Manipulation of Variables

In the ideal case we would arrange a situation in which extraneous conditions are maintained equivalent between the two groups and all irrelevant potential causes are controlled. We would then systematically change one measured variable to assess concomitant changes in another.

Our inability to control extraneous variables in the behavioral sciences does not provide good illustrations of direct cause-and-effect relationships through investigator manipulation of one variable. Mood is a human condition that appears at first as if it might submit to systematic adjustment. We could formulate a reasonable expectation that when a person is in a good (happy) mood he or she would perform better on a given task than would be the case if the person were depressed. In order to control extraneous factors to some extent we would use one person for all the mood variations. All an investigator needs to do is to figure out a way for varying the mood condition, measure changes in some types of performance, and keep all other extraneous conditions equivalent from one day to the next. I am quite unable to think of a way for making a person 5 units happy on one day, 3 units happy on another day, 12 units depressed on a third, and 0 happy on a fourth! We could learn a lot from a study of this kind if anyone could figure out a way to do it.

One might argue that we could use naturally occurring mood swings, but in that situation we would be even less able to control extraneous influences that might interact with the attribute we want to study.

Anxiety, frustration, sexual arousal, and fear are some other variables that come to mind as possibilities for direct manipulation in order to study correlated changes in behavior, but measuring systematic variations of these variables is still a problem. In general, the kinds of psychological changes an investigator can cause with human subjects is limited.

We have a little more flexibility with the systematic manipulation of selected biological conditions that might be related to certain aspects of behavior. Muscle fatigue through measured amounts of exercise is one that comes to mind, and we could control the amount of sleep a person gets in order to study the effect of this on alertness for solving math problems. Learning could be studied at varied levels of noise or some other distraction. Variations in amount of ingested drugs can be added to the list of variables under investigator control.

Biology can provide a better example of the direct manipulation process and the control of extraneous variables. A laboratory technician could study the relationship between temperature and yeast growth in a brew mixture. A group of identical samples of brew mixture would be kept at different temperatures for a couple of days. Investigator-controlled variations of temperature would be the only difference among the samples. After a certain period of time, the technician would measure the number of yeast cells in each sample. We know from previous work that at very low temperatures there is very little yeast growth and too-high temperatures kill the yeast. Between these extremes we could study yeast growth in relation to changes in temperature.

Data From Observation: Pre-Existing Data

The things we study in the behavioral sciences are usually so complex that, in the early stages of research, we might not even know what observations might tend to go together. That is the time when a correlation can be useful. We organize our thinking, hypothesize a relationship, collect measurements, and then compute a correlation to test the hypothesis.

In the behavioral sciences, correlations are most often used for analyzing data from variations of naturalistic observation techniques. We often want to assess the extent of relationship between two sets of observations that are beyond our control to manipulate directly. We would have more confidence in our results if we could vary or manipulate whatever it is we are studying ourselves, but for the topics that interest behavioral scientists, that is not usually possible. Often data from naturally occurring observations will be all the information we have and all we can get. We collect instances showing variations of an entity and note variations on another measurement. In this way we try to evaluate relationships that would not otherwise be open to investigation. Effect of lead ingestion on mental development and intelligence would be an example.

A little thought will identify many areas of human behavior psychologists need to study, but for obvious reasons they cannot do so directly: long-term isolation, physical restraint, child abuse, death of a loved one, effects of rape or other physical assault, marriage to the wrong person, natural disasters, divorce, children raised with only one parent, effect of drugs on child development. This list identifies only a tiny number of many possible examples. (The Pearson correlation is not necessarily applicable to data obtained from all of these examples, but other correlational statistics are available to do the job.) For many research questions, historical records might be our only source of data.

Landy, Rosenberg, and Sutton-Smith (1969) studied the relationship between several aspects of having a father in the home (amount of time, time of day, and age at time of father's presence), and the later math proficiency of college-aged daughters. Evidence they collected seemed to suggest a positive relationship.

The relationship between the size of police force and crime (Press, 1978) is an entirely different type of question which can be answered by a correlational analysis of existing data. A person studying personality might ask a question about whether there is a connection between personality and birth order. Forer (1976) thinks there is a relationship.

We will study at length in the next chapter some major weaknesses of a correlation, but we should note one of them here. Whenever we try to establish a concomitant relationship of the sort illustrated above, we should recall the distinction between *functional* and *causal* relationships. Even when we discover that two sets of measurements tend to vary concurrently, we cannot conclude from that information alone that the observations are causally related.

Data From Measurements

A very large number of correlational analyses are based on *measured variations* of attributes or conditions. Possibly any personality variable will fall into this category. Suppose a psychologist wanted to study "depression." Since there are no suitable ways for varying "depression" in a laboratory situation, an investigator might try to get some idea of its effects by using an appropriate test to *measure* the amount of depression in 100 people. An alternate arrangement would measure variations in depression for the same person at different times. These scores could then be correlated with some other variable we think might be related to it. Studies of "seasonal affective disorders" fit this pattern. We study the relationship between mood and sunlight variations caused by seasonal changes. Unlike many other problems psychologists have to solve, we can address this one rather simply by providing large amounts of light to substitute for the sunlight that is missing.

Although we might not be able to manipulate levels of intelligence, we could collect suitable measurements of intelligence to study behavior thought to be correlated with it. Anderson and Rehm (1984) used correlational analyses for studying "The Relationship Between Strategies of Coping and Perception of Pain in Three Chronic Pain Groups."

Correlations can help to organize complex data and in that way assist in the discovery and identification of related (i.e., shared) elements.

Table of Intercorrelations

The computation formula for the Pearson correlation can be used only for studying relationships between two sets of data. The complexities of personality and behavior frequently lead to questions that involve comparisons among many sets of measurements. We cannot directly make multiple sample comparisons, but we have ways of getting around the restriction. One way of doing this begins with the computation of all possible *paired* relationships in the data we want to study. We then put them in a "table of intercorrelations." In that form we might use a complex statistical technique called "factor analysis" to help identify common elements among the correlations. Quite a lot of behavioral science research involves the analysis of batteries of test data, so we are likely to run across correlations presented in this form.

I should explain that "factorial design," a research technique we will study later in the text, and "factor analysis" are not the same.

In Table 7.2 I have developed some fictitious data to illustrate how investigators often organize correlations in the preliminary stages of their research. Various tests are identified by the letters: A, B, C, D, E, F. The numbers in the body of the table are correlations. I have followed the common practice of leaving out the decimal that is otherwise always included in the correlation figure. The value of the correlation between the A and B measurements is given at the intersection of the A row and the B column. The relationship between C an E is given at the intersection of the C row and the E column. That is the pattern followed throughout the table.

Measurements are arranged this way to help an investigator discover any common elements among them. We cannot tell by looking whether three measurements of insecurity are all measuring in varying ways the same underlying attribute, but intercorrelations might disclose whether they have something in common. Measurements that do not correlate are measuring (i.e., defining) different attributes.

Examination of the table discloses two "clusters" of measurements that correlate rather strongly with each other but not with the other measurements. A with B, A with C, and B with C are examples of this. A similar pattern is found

Table 7.2

A TABLE OF INTERCORRELATIONS					
Tests	B	C	D	E	F
A	42	53	–20	13	05
B		64	17	26	13
C			23	12	09
D				62	58
E					49

among D, E, and F. With real data we would not expect to find such obvious patterns. We would rely on factor analysis to disclose them to us. These data suggest that these tests have defined two quite different, unrelated, components of personality (if that is what we are studying).

In exploratory work, we use correlations to identify, organize, and give meaning to complex behavioral relationships. Hypotheses are screened to help identify those worth evaluation by other methods. Look at this example, an excerpt from the abstract of an important article in the area of personality research:

> Little is known about the genetic and environmental etiology of the association between specific cognitive abilities and scholastic achievement during the early school years. A multivariate genetic analysis of cognitive and achievement measures was conducted for 146 pairs of identical twins and 132 pairs of fraternal twins from 6 to 12 years of age.

Two tables of intercorrelations were developed by Thompson, Detterman, and Plomin (1991) to study "Associations between cognitive abilities and scholastic achievement: genetic overlap but environmental differences." Their work included seven measures of cognitive abilities and a measure of scholastic achievement. Because of the complex statistical evaluation involved in this work, it is difficult to simplify their findings. Let me just say that in part their work led to a conclusion that "there is a substantial overlap between genetic effects on scholastic achievement and specific cognitive abilities."

DATA REQUIREMENTS FOR A PEARSON CORRELATION

I think that one of the more interesting aspects of the kinds of data that can be used with a Pearson correlation is that the measurements can be in any units, so long as the data are interval and the general characteristics of the data meet the additional requirements to be discussed next. Many inexperienced investigators might have trouble answering these questions. Could I correlate high school teachers' salaries and quality of instruction? (I have heard it mentioned that teacher salaries have to be increased in order to attract and keep the best teachers.) How about correlating longevity and attitude toward life? (I think people with a good attitude tend to live longer.) How about exposure to humorous materials and speed of recovery from serious illnesses? (I have heard that humor is a great healer.)

Even though the measurements in every instance are quite different, the answer to all three questions is yes—providing . . . ! Teacher salaries in dollars can be correlated with quality of instruction, if we can agree on an operational definition of that construct that produces suitable interval data and if the salary spread is not too large. Longevity is adequate interval data as we are using it here, but we might have to work a bit to develop a good measure of attitude toward life. For the third question we would need to produce interval data that defines and shows variations in "exposure to humorous materials," and we need to search out some of the work that has been done to define and quantify seriousness of illnesses.

The reason all sorts of actual data can be used in a correlational analysis is statistically simple, but one probably should have had an introductory statistics course to understand the explanation. I think I can show something of the nature of what happens.

Assume we start with two quite different sets of data: a set of scores on the psychology component of the GRE and on-the-job ratings for the same people preparing to be clinical psychologists. This is an example of a way to evaluate a test's predictive validity.

In order to compute a correlation it is necessary for both measurements to be in the same units. One way to accomplish this with these data is to simplify it by converting *both* sets to ranks. The person getting the highest score on the GRE would be given the rank of 1, the next-highest score a rank of 2, and so on. We can do the same thing with the on-the-job ratings. Remember that it is always possible to change a higher order of measurement to a lower one, but this usually brings a loss in the quality of the original measurements. After the data transformation we would have two sets of ranks, which is what we need to compute a Spearman rank correlation. The result would be essentially the same as we would have had if we had computed the Pearson correlation directly.

We would not, however, normally go to the trouble of converting interval data to rank data just so we could use the Spearman formula. Even if we program our computers to make the changes for us, we still would be ill-advised to do it. Any simplification of this sort causes a loss of data accuracy. The Pearson formula is sensitive to and uses the additional information inherent in the original interval data.

The Pearson formula cannot directly use interval data that is in different measurement units. In order to compare measurements it is necessary for them to be in the same units. For Pearson calculations, both sets of measurements are changed to z-scores. A z-score gives the number of standard deviations a raw score is away from the mean of that distribution and, in that way, indicates the relative position of a raw score in the distribution. No matter what the original units of measurement were, z-scores always have the same parameters: the mean is 0 (zero) and the standard deviation is 1. I have expanded on this explanation in an Endnote.

It would be tedious to do it, but it is possible to go through the two distributions of measurements we want to correlate and change all of them to z-scores. Once scores are in that form we could easily compute the relationship using a very simple "definition formula" for the Pearson correlation. But, except to gain experience, we would never compute a Pearson correlation in this way. In normal usage, no matter what the original measurements units are, we simply use them in the "computation formula," and it automatically takes care of the conversion details for us.

Several other restrictions on the type of data appropriate for a Pearson calculation remain to be mentioned. Study these points carefully. They are important for obtaining meaningful results.

Both sets of data should be interval (or ratio).

Data should be symmetrically distributed. Skewed data should not be used. It is better for data to be normally distributed, but data that are evenly spread on both sides of the mean are satisfactory. A graph will show whether data meet these basic requirements.

When samples are randomly selected from a large population we should ensure that there has not been a "restriction of range" or a "truncated range." This subtle, easily overlooked complication can cause trouble when samples are *selected* from a special group. Assume that an original set of scores ranges from 10 to 100. The size of a correlation computed using only a part of the range, say the top scores from 80 to 100, is likely to be much smaller than if the whole range of scores had been used.

To see how the problem might arise, consider an official in the counseling department of a university with a highly selective student admissions policy. He or she wants to study the relationship between reading ability and academic performance. If the university official actually collected and correlated data from a student sample, it would be unlikely that the person would learn much of interest—except to give more thought to the nature of the data before computing a correlation. The range of reading ability for students at a university with restrictive admission requirements would be truncated. Anyone who was not a good reader would not have been admitted. At a university with a less-restrictive admissions policy, the spread of reading scores *might* be large enough for a meaningful relationship to be discovered, but even here results should be interpreted with caution. People admitted to any university probably read better than those people who have no interest in getting a university degree.

COMPUTATION OF A PEARSON CORRELATION USING THE RAW-SCORE FORMULA

We have already seen how a Spearman correlation works. It compares the relative position, the rank, of a score in the X group with the rank position of the paired score in Y.

The Pearson correlation works in somewhat the same way as the Spearman, except that it compares the z-score value in the X group with the paired z-score value for Y. As I mentioned earlier, the calculation, often called the "raw-score formula," does the conversion in the process of computation. Most people who use the Pearson formula do not even know what happened. I think the important idea to remember is that both the Spearman and Pearson correlations determine relationships in essentially the same way. They compare the relative position of a measurement in one sample with the relative position of a paired measurement in another sample. Ranks are used with the Spearman formula; z-scores are the common element for the Pearson formula.

A person who is looking for a computation formula for the Pearson correlation will find several from which to choose. They are algebraically equivalent, but they are not all equally easy to use. I have selected a formula that works well with the small calculators we are likely to use for practice calculations (see Table 7.3).

Table 7.3

RAW-SCORE FORMULA FOR A PEARSON CORRELATION

$$r_P = \frac{N \Sigma XY - (\Sigma X)(\Sigma Y)}{\sqrt{[N \Sigma X^2 - X)^2] [N \Sigma Y^2 - (\Sigma Y)^2]}}$$

Many beginners will think the correlation formula looks rather forbidding; take heart—it is not so bad as it appears. Once appropriate data are listed in logical pairs, computation becomes just another algebra problem.

The best way to speed the work along is to be systematic in your procedures. Keeping computations organized will help you to avoid mistakes, and it will be easier to find those that do occur. The use of a table like Table 7.4 is highly recommended. One needs only to fill in the required numbers and then substitute

Table 7.4

		r COMPUTATION		
X	Y	X^2	Y^2	XY
—	—	—	—	—
15	15	225	225	225
06	07	36	49	42
12	19	144	361	228
08	01	64	1	8
09	08	81	64	72
50	50	550	700	575

Summarizing Table for Computation

$\Sigma X\ 50\ \Sigma X^2\ 550$ $(\Sigma X)^2\ 2500$ $\Sigma XY\ 575$

$\Sigma Y\ 50\ \Sigma Y^2\ 700$ $(\Sigma Y)^2\ 2500$ $N\ 5$

$r = .75$

375

$2875 - 2500$

$$\frac{5\ (575) - (50)\ (50)}{\sqrt{[5\ (550) - 2500]\ [5\ (700) - 2500]}}$$

$\sqrt{(250)\ (1000)}$

$$r = \frac{375}{500} = .75$$

them in the formula for the final computations which can be easily done with even small calculators. Be clear on the difference between ΣX^2 and $(\Sigma X)^2$. Do not forget to take the square root of the denominator and remember to divide the numerator by the result. These are common mistakes, frequently made. N is the *number of pairs of scores*.

GRAPHING A RELATIONSHIP

Drawing a graph of correlational data, making a scatter diagram or "scattergram" as they are sometimes called, is a good way to illustrate a correlational relationship. Use the instructions and the data given in Table 7.5.

A sheet of quarter-inch-squares graph paper is good for drawing a scatter diagram. A preliminary look at the data on Table 7.5 shows that the X and Y scores are in different measurement units and they have a different range. Scores on the X axis range from 1 to 11. Scores on the Y axis range from 10 to 110. This large difference requires an adjustment to either one of the axes on the graph so the scores can be graphed in approximately the same distance. Interpretation of possible relationships would be difficult if one axis were drawn ten times longer than the other just because that was the way the scores came. Adjustments of axes to compensate for differently sized scores would not be necessary if z-scores were being graphed, because these are already in equivalent measurement units.

If the range of scores is not large, they should be spread out a little by leaving space between columns and rows of graphed scores. Label the X units along the horizontal axis and the Y units along the vertical axis. An assumed cause, if there is one, or an antecedent condition would be plotted on the abscissa (X axis), and a presumed effect would be plotted on the ordinate (Y axis). A graph of data to assess a test's criterion related validity would plot the predictor test scores on the abscissa and the criterion scores on the ordinate.

Table 7.5

			SOME DATA FOR MAKING A SCATTER DIAGRAM				
X	Y	X	Y	X	Y	X	Y
4	50	3	40	3	20	3	30
5	70	7	50	4	40	6	40
5	50	11	110	8	80	5	40
6	60	9	90	5	30	9	80
8	70	6	50	6	90	1	10
7	80	6	70	10	90	6	80
10	100	7	90	8	90	10	110
6	30	7	60	5	60	2	10
2	20	2	30	9	100	7	70
4	30	11	100	1	20	8	60

Making the decisions necessary for laying out a well-drawn scatter diagram is probably the hardest part; plotting the data is easy. The two scores in the first pair are 4 and 50. Go along the X axis to the column where the 4s are plotted, then go up the column, paralleling the Y axis, to the row for the 50s. At the box formed by the intersection of column 4 and row 50, put a dot or a small x. Repeat the process with every pair of scores until all have been plotted. Compare your work with my interpretation given in Figure 7.1. They should look similar overall, but if you made different decisions from mine they will not be exactly alike.

One reason for making a scatter diagram is to give a researcher a chance to look at the general configuration of the spread of scores. A large positive relationship is shown by an elongated bunch of scores spread from the lower left to the upper right corner of the graph, if scores have been laid out in the usual way. Scores for a large negative relationship would be distributed from the lower right to the upper left corner of the graph.

Another reason for looking at graphed data is to make sure the relationship is "linear." A Pearson correlation is appropriate only for determining a linear—straight line—relationship. We can see the scores appear to form a fairly even elongated bunch. If a graph of scores shows them to take some other form—that is, U-shaped perhaps or possibly J-shaped—a Pearson correlation would not adequately describe the extent of the relationship. The size of the correlation would be underestimated.

The way in which scores are bunched gives an idea about the extent of the correlation. The narrower the spread of scores, the larger the correlation. Figure 7.1 shows what a large $r = .89$ correlation looks like.

Figure 7.2 illustrates a number of different patterns of scores for practice in interpretation. In diagram A all of the scores fall exactly on a theoretical straight line. This is how a perfect correlation between two sets of data would look. Note that there is no score variability at all around the central line. The

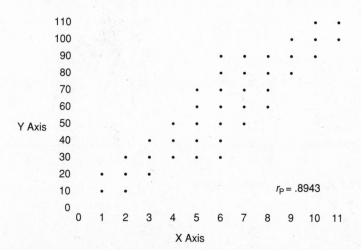

FIGURE 7.1 Correlation Scatter Diagram

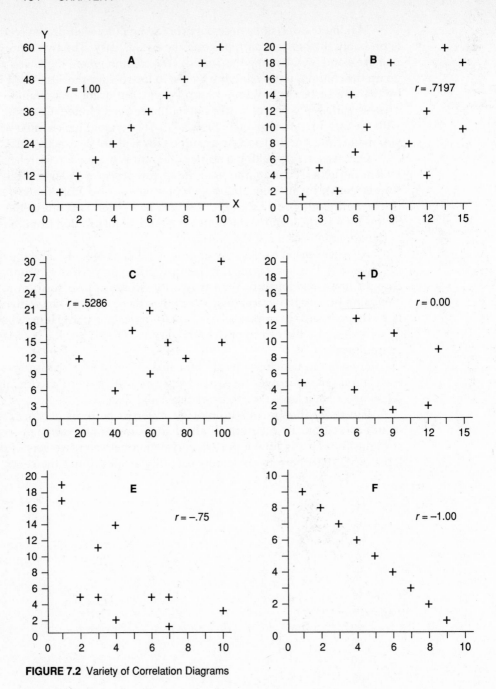

FIGURE 7.2 Variety of Correlation Diagrams

consistent increase in value of each Y score with an increase in the value of the paired X score indicates a positive relationship.

Pattern B shows a large but not perfect positive relationship.

Diagrams A through D together show how different amounts of scatter produce varying levels of correlational relationships. Approximate correlational values are shown on each graph. Note how the extent of the relationship is reduced when there is a large spread of scores. In graph D the $r = 0.00$ correlation shows that there is no relationship at all. The scatter of scores forms a crude circle rather than being spread in a linear fashion. A person who has studied scatter diagrams for awhile can get a good idea of the size of a relationship by looking at a scatter diagram.

Recall from the discussion earlier in the chapter: No Pearson or Spearman correlation ever produces a value larger than ±1.00.

MEANING OF NEGATIVE RELATIONSHIPS

A positive relationship is one in which changes in one variable have parallel equivalent changes in the other. A large X value would generally be found with a large Y; a smaller X would typically go with a smaller Y. Whether a value is "large" or "small" would be defined by the investigator with regard to the meaning of the data.

The standard way for graphing scores is to start with low values for both sets of measurements at the lower left corner. Measurements are normally shown as increasing in value as they go toward the right for X and up for Y. A scattergram of a positive relationship shows an elongated cluster of scores extending from the general area of the lower left to the upper right corners.

People are so accustomed to this arrangement that any spread of scores that goes from the lower right to the upper left, such as diagrams E and F on Figure 7.1 is immediately identified as a "negative correlation." In standard usage, a negative correlation has a different meaning from a positive one, but to draw that conclusion an investigator must be sure the scores are logically equivalent and that they have been listed in a comparable way.

Generally speaking, scores on my classroom exams are positively and significantly correlated. The proportion of questions a student answers correctly on one exam will be representative of the person's score on others. If I graphed the number right for a group of students on two exams I would get a typical lower-left/upper-right distribution of scores. I would get an identical distribution of scores if I graphed the number wrong for both tests. People who got more wrong on one test would likely get more wrong on another.

If I graphed the number wrong for one test and the number right for the other, the relationship would be *negative*. This makes sense, of course, because a person who gets a lot of questions right on one test will probably get few questions wrong on the other.

A correlation's *statistical significance* is determined by its size (and the number of pairs of scores). Whether a correlation is positive or negative is important only for helping us to understand what the relationship means.

The large and interesting area of personality measurement offers many examples of correlational analyses. First, let us agree that personality traits can vary independently of each other. Although a great many of them are known to correlate positively among themselves—a high measurement on one tends to be found with a high measurement on another—we might be able to identify a few negative relationships. Recall that whether a relationship is positive or negative is determined by which characteristic on a measurement scale the author selects for the high end. If we search a bit we could probably locate a scale to place individuals along a dominance/submission dimension. If we also measure concern for others among the same individuals in our sample, we might discover a negative relationship between the two personality scales. High-dominant people may also be the ones who tend to have relatively low levels of concern for others. The reverse is true for people who measure lower on a dominance scale.

Some psychologists have suggested that when we are faced with frustrating situations there are three very general ways in which we can react: We can blame others for the predicament, we can look for solutions without blaming anyone, or we can blame ourselves. We might hypothesize that reactions to frustration would correlate negatively with measures of inner strength or feelings of self-worth. People who are secure within themselves have the resilience to accept responsibility for their own actions.

Tolerance for pain and level of mental health might produce a negative relationship, but that would depend on the direction of scoring either of the two variables. We quite likely would find an inverse relationship between the number of hours of TV a child watches per week and the grades he or she gets at school. The more hours of television viewed, the lower the child's grades.

The scatter diagrams in Figure 7.2 are so oversimplified that they do not adequately demonstrate a correlation diagram of real data. Plotting data that have no duplicate values encourages the perception that graphed scores are thinly spread over a two-dimensional surface. Large samples will have a number of instances of identical scores. A true representation of this information would require a three-dimensional space, because multiple scores would be piled up on each other to form a density of similar scores.

A three-dimensional graph of all the Y scores for a particular column X, in an ideal case, would form a little normal curve. A three-dimensional display of a large number of positively correlated scores would probably look something like a mountain range. The mountain peaks are produced at the points of greatest score frequency (density). I seem to have a better understanding of correlational data if I think of it in three dimensions rather than just as a scatter of dots on a sheet of paper.

THE PEARSON CORRELATION IN TESTS AND MEASUREMENTS

The correlation statistic is of inestimable value in psychological measurement. It can be used in so many ways that I believe the field of psychological testing as we know it today would not exist if correlations had not been invented. This discussion will expand a little on material already mentioned in Chapters 4 and 5.

Reliability

We generally think of reliability as consistency. If we gave the same test over again at a later time we would have "test-retest" reliability. A group of people who get certain scores on a reliable test today should get similar, although not necessarily identical, scores on a retest given soon after. Instead of giving the same test over again we could give another test as similar to the first one as we can make it. The use of an equivalent test is named "alternate-forms" reliability.

The most common estimate of reliability given for published tests is a third type, named the "split-half" method. Since we usually do not have alternate forms of the same test, test makers get similar information by splitting one test in half. This gives two logically equivalent shorter tests. Each half of the test is scored separately for each person, and the two sets of scores are correlated. The correlation shows the extent of relationship between scores on the two halves of the same test.

Shorter tests tend to be less reliable than longer ones. The smaller correlation is corrected—made larger—by using a simple statistical modification that gives an estimate of the reliability we would expect if each half of the test were twice as long as it actually is.

If you think about the information provided by the so-called split-half reliability computation, you will note that correlating two halves of the same test does not tell us anything about reliability, as we normally think of the term. Reliability usually suggests similarity over time. Correlating two halves of the same test does not allow this temporal distinction. What we get is a measure of item homogeneity—the extent to which the items on the two halves measure the same entity, whatever it might be.

If we determined test reliability using the test-retest method we probably would find the average of scores for the second test was higher than the average the first time the test was taken. It seems to make sense that if we take the same test over again, we would be likely to do better on it. The difference between scores can mislead people into believing that when the averages are quite different between two sets of measurements, they will not be significantly correlated. The example given earlier in this chapter demonstrates that two sets of scores can be highly correlated even when the data are markedly different. Score differences, if they are consistent, do not affect the interpretation of reliability because neither the Pearson or Spearman correlation is sensitive to actual score values. If people did *uniformly* better on the second testing, the scores could be higher but the relative order would not have changed.

Validity

Correlations are the foundation statistic in the several different ways we have for defining test validity.

Psychologists commonly evaluate "predictive" or "criterion" validity by giving a test, and after an appropriate period of time, they correlate the test scores with a measurement called a "criterion." This is often performance in a training program or success on a job. This technique will be discussed in the following chapter in connection with the use of errors in prediction as a way of understanding the meaning of relationships.

Recall that test validity is generally understood to be a measure of the extent to which a test measures what it is supposed to measure (or what the test developer says it measures). "What is the extent of the relationship between a test and a construct?" When a test is used as an operational definition of a construct, the question cannot be answered. To do so would be like using a word to define itself.

Construct-related validity is the most difficult to determine and the most difficult to explain. I will be able only to suggest the nature of the problem here. We can get a rough idea of a test's construct validity by showing that tests that we presume to measure the same construct correlate with each other. Scores from a joke test and a cartoon test, for example, should correlate significantly if they do in fact measure the same sense-of-humor construct.

Suppose the relationship is not statistically significant. This would tell us that whatever the tests are measuring—and we can only speculate about what that is—we know they are not measuring the same thing. We have no easy way to know which of them—or perhaps whether either one—is measuring sense of humor as we otherwise understand and use the construct.

SEVERAL TYPES OF CORRELATIONS

Although we have so far limited our discussions of correlations to the Pearson and Spearman, we should also be aware that other correlational statistics are available. These differ in the type of data they use and the number of samples that are correlated.

Point-biserial and biserial correlations, r_{pbis} and r_{bis}, are particularly interesting because they evaluate the validity of individual test questions. (The Pearson correlation determines one or another kind of validity for the test as whole.) Question validity evaluates the relationship between a right or wrong answer on a particular question and performance on the test as a whole. A good question is one that people earning grades of A and B on the test are more likely to get right and people earning a D or E, as determined by the test as a whole, are more likely to get wrong. C-level people would go about half and half either way.

There is a statistical distinction between a biserial and a point-biserial correlation which is of no importance for this discussion. The logic for their use is essentially the same. How they work can be guessed at by their names. Two different types of data are involved; the "bi" tells us that there are two groups of category data, which in this example means getting a question right or getting it wrong. The "serial" number is a person's score on the test as a whole. Computations have to be done for each question, of course.

I should also mention two other statistics that are frequently mentioned in the literature. Both multiple correlations ($R_{1.32}$) and partial correlations ($r_{12.3}$) are more relevant to psychological testing, but they could have a tangential place in research.

A multiple correlation, sometimes called a multiple regression equation, is applicable in situations in which there are several measurements that will be used for making a prediction to a "criterion" (the same idea we have already studied, but this time we will use several measurements for making the prediction). The subscript 1 in the symbol indicates a criterion we are predicting to. Let's take "success as an athlete" for this example. The subscript numbers 2 and 3 represent several predictor variables. A coach might use measurements of motivation, general athletic ability, physical strength, and speed, or whatever is relevant for the sport.

A multiple correlation would help the coaching staff to determine how much to "weight" the various predictor variables to get the best prediction. The predicted success of an athlete could be estimated by statistically combining his or her weighted scores on the predictor variable measurements. Coaches might find that motivation is worth more in predicting success than ability, and both should be given more consideration than physical strength.

Coaches, clinical psychologists and other professionals, as well as people on the street often make decisions that require us to combine different sorts of information. We might need to balance a job interview against letters of recommendation and job history. Colleges and universities commonly use multiple correlations with high school grades and ACT scores for predicting academic success. In some instances this information will determine which people are admitted.

A partial correlation, the second one we will look at, estimates the extent of relationship between two variables with the effect of a third variable "partialed" out. Suppose that many observations have shown a decline of certain intellectual abilities with age. Older people just do not perform as well on intelligence tests as younger people do. We might be tempted to conclude that the difference in mental ability is the result of increasing age, but doing so would ignore the fact that a significant relationship between two variables does not necessarily mean that they are themselves *causally* related. An alternative explanation would suggest that poor health, which often comes with advancing years, could account for the lower performance on the intelligence tests. We might want to make allowance for differences in educational opportunities; many in the older generation did not finish high school. Slower physical speed of reaction is a third variable to be taken into account. A partial correlation statistically could balance out the potential influence of poor health, level of education, or other variables in order to study the relationship between age and IQ more directly. A partial correlation deletes the influence of third variables in order to better study the relationship between two others.

If we plan to use only category data, we have several variations of relationship statistics that are based on the "chi-square." A tetrachoric correlation requires two independent categorical variables, at two levels. These form a "two-by-two" table. More categories, say three-by-three (3×3), would be analyzed from a table that looks like one used in playing tick-tack-toe (naughts and crosses). Larger tables also can be analyzed for relationships using the same formula.

ENDNOTES

Using the z-Score Formula for Calculation of a Pearson Correlation

Following is a review section primarily for students who have had a statistics course and need only to brush up on basic ideas that they might have forgotten. Other students probably will need to work very hard to make sense of this abbreviated presentation, but I would urge all readers to try. Statistical concepts are nearly always more difficult to learn than they are to use, but learning about the Pearson correlation will greatly improve one's understanding and appreciation of how it works. A Pearson correlation is rarely computed using the z-score formula I will discuss next, but I think readers who know something about statistics will find that it is worthwhile to follow along with the work.

No matter what the original units of measurement were, they will be comparable when they have been changed to z-scores, because z-scores always have the same parameters. Anyone who does this work will find the most troublesome aspect of using the z-score formula for computing a Pearson correlation is the tedious work required to make the conversion of raw scores to z-scores, but the translation is an integral part of how the formula works.

The mean of a set of z-scores is always zero. A positive z-score shows a raw score was larger than the mean, and a negative z-score indicates the original raw score was smaller than the mean. A z-score uses the standard deviation of a distribution of scores to show the position of each raw score relative to the mean of the same distribution. The numerical variation of z-score values is very narrow; in a normally distributed group of scores the largest z-score would rarely exceed ±2.5, which tells us that scores are rarely larger or smaller than 2.5 standard deviations from the mean. Most scores would be less than ±2.0.

We begin the computation of z-scores by first computing "deviation scores" for each set of data. These scores give the position of each raw score relative to the mean of the distribution, in the units of the original measurements. To determine how far a score is from the mean we simply subtract the mean from the score. Deviation scores are converted to z-scores by dividing the deviation score by the standard deviation.

Accuracy[1] of z-score computations can be checked by taking their sum; it should always be zero. This makes sense because they are computed around the mean, which is, by definition, the point of balance in a distribution. The sum of the positive deviations must equal the sum of the negative deviations.

$$z_x = \frac{X \text{ (raw score in Group X)} - M \text{ (mean of Sample X)}}{SD_x \text{ (standard deviation of the X distribution)}}$$

The same formula would be used for the computing z-scores for the Y distribution. Just substitute the Y values.

After you have converted data to z-scores, you can compute a correlation directly. A Pearson product-moment correlation is defined as *the mean of the*

---

[1]This method does not produce proof of accuracy, because there is always the possibility that offsetting errors will balance each other.

cross-products of the paired z-scores. Multiply the z-score in the X column by the paired z-score in the Y column; add these products, then divide by the number of pairs of scores (N).

$$r_P = \frac{\Sigma \text{ (the sum of) } [z_X][z_Y]}{N \text{ (number of pairs of scores)}}$$

Computing at least one problem this way helps to improve your understanding of what a Pearson correlation does and how it works. Table 7.6 demonstrates a worked problem for study.

These data were ranked to give the rank values used for demonstrating the Spearman correlation in Table 7.1. Interval data are a higher form of measurement than ranks, so correlations computed with interval data should more accurately represent the extent of relationship. The two correlation computations will not usually be exactly the same, but they should be close.

Note that the Y values in Table 7.6 are much larger than the X values. This demonstrates the point made previously, that score values can be quite different in a correlational analysis, providing they meet other data requirements.

The "Product-Moment" in a Pearson Correlation

The "product" part of the title is clear enough. That is the result of multiplying numbers together. When a multiplier is multiplied by a multiplicand, a product results.

Table 7.6

PEARSON CORRELATION COMPUTED USING z-SCORES				
	Raw Scores		*z-Scores*		*Cross-Products*
	X	Y	X	Y	$z_X z_Y$
Bill	15	90	1.58	0.79	1.25
June	06	42	−1.27	−0.47	0.60
Mary	12	114	0.63	1.42	0.89
Joan	08	06	−0.63	−1.42	0.89
Bob	09	48	−0.32	−0.32	0.10

Sum $z_X z_Y$ = $\overline{3.73}$

Summarizing data for computation of means, standard deviations, and z-scores[2] used to compute r with a z-score formula

$\Sigma X = 50$ $\Sigma X^2 = 550$ $(\Sigma X)^2 = 2500$ $M_X = 10$ $SD_X = 3.16$

$\Sigma Y = 300$ $\Sigma Y^2 = 25{,}200$ $(\Sigma Y)^2 = 90{,}000$ $M_Y = 60$ $SD_Y = 37.95$

$z_X z_Y = 3.73$ $N = 5$ $r_P = .746$

[2]Refer to any standard statistics text for information on how to compute these descriptive statistics.

A person who questions such things might wonder what "moments" are, for Pearson to be able to take the product of them. One guess about the origin of the term holds that it is derived from physics, which used the word "moment" in an expression dating back to the early 1800s. "Moment of inertia" deals with the force or torque applied on a lever perpendicular to the axis of a rotating body. The amount of twisting is proportional to the applied force and the square of the distance. We have less trouble tightening a nut with a long-handled wrench than with a short one. If we double the length of the handle, the same amount of applied force will quadruple the amount of torque.

In statistics, the word is applied to the moments of deviation scores around the mean. A deviation score, sometimes symbolized by a small italic x, is the difference between the mean of a sample and any score, X.

$$x = X - M$$

The first moment is the mean of the deviation scores; this is the sum of the deviation scores in a sample, divided by their number, N. Other moments are similar, but the deviation score is raised to different powers.

1. First moment:

a. $\dfrac{\Sigma x}{N}$

2. Second moment:

b. $\dfrac{\Sigma x^2}{N}$

3. Third moment:

c. $\dfrac{\Sigma x^3}{N}$

Formula b might be recognized as the formula for the variance, which is the square of the standard deviation; or actually with this formula the variance is computed first, so the standard deviation is the square root of the variance. It is the second moment that is relevant to a correlation.

A slight variation of the z-score definition formula is given below, and the one we used is given next for comparison.

$$r = \frac{\Sigma xy}{N\sigma_x\sigma_y}$$

Since $x \div \sigma_x$ is a z-score, the formula becomes:

$$r = \frac{\Sigma z_x \Sigma z_y}{N}$$

The Importance of Pairing Scores for Correlational Analysis

As I stated in the discussion in the body of the chapter, I know from work with many students that inexperienced people often do not fully grasp the idea of paired scores. I am unwilling to accept that it is only my students who have this problem, but as far as I can recall, Senter (1969, p. 416) is the only other person who has mentioned it.

Senter emphasized that the Pearson (and Spearman) correlations must "*always* be calculated from matched pair data. Scores *must* be arranged in pairs according to some *a priori* rule." Then, in a footnote, Senter expanded on the point.

> This fact might seem self-evident from previous discussion, but after seeing one graduate student try to correlate *totally independent* groups of scores by pairing them in the order they happened to appear on the page and seeing another student rearrange his scores and form pairs in order of magnitude (highest X with highest Y, and so on), the writer deems it appropriate to emphasize the fact that *matched pairs* are necessary.

Are These Data Suitable for a Pearson Correlation?

The following proposals for correlational analyses were submitted by students for class projects. Assume that constructs could be measured. Identify which examples would provide data appropriate for analysis with a Pearson correlation. Answers follow the study questions.

1. Is there a relationship between the age of car salespeople and their sales volume?
2. There is likely to be a significant relationship between the signs of the zodiac and certain personality attributes.
3. I would like to study the relationship between men's and women's intuition.
4. There should be a reduction in deaths as a result of cyclists wearing helmets.
5. Grades on the final exam for the experimental class should correlate with the grades for the statistics class.
6. It is not true that "opposites attract." People who get along best generally have similar personality characteristics.
7. I am sure that the breakdown of family life is the cause of many of the problems in the world today.
8. I believe there is a relationship between love of nature and the way people treat children.
9. There is very likely to be a relationship between the community in which a family lives and income.
10. The more time a person spends studying, the fewer dates he or she will have.

STUDY QUESTIONS

1. What is the general idea of how correlations are used in research?
   What types of research question can a Pearson correlation be used to answer?

2. Differentiate between "descriptive" and "inferential" applications of a correlational analysis.

3. Explain the computation of a Spearman correlation.
    What type of data is used?
    How is it organized?

4. Explain the idea that interpretations of correlation results are "nondirectional."

5. What is the importance of pairing scores in a correlational analysis?

6. Explain the process of correlational research in which one variable is manipulated directly to determine its effect on another.

7. How are correlational relationships discovered through the analysis of observations and measurements?
    What are some advantages and disadvantages of this approach?

8. Differentiate between "functional" and "causal" relationships.

9. What is a table of intercorrelations?
    In what circumstances would you use one?

10. What are some restrictions for the data to be used with a Pearson correlation?

11. How is it possible to determine the extent of relationship between two entirely different types of data?

12. Why is it not necessary for scores used in a correlational analysis to be in the same units?

13. What is a "restricted" or "truncated" range? How might the size of a correlation be affected by data from this source?

14. How might a truncated range of scores affect the size of the resulting correlation?

15. How is a correlation used in determining reliability?

16. Know how to graph a correlational relationship and how to interpret the graph.

17. What are some reasons for graphing data?

18. Explain a negative relationship.
    Which correlation is larger: –.47 or .39?

19. Explain how correlations can be used to demonstrate a test's reliability.

20. What is the general idea of test validity?
    What are some ways correlations can be used for expressing it?

21. Explain the idea of "predictive validity."

22. Name and briefly explain some correlations, other than the Pearson and Spearman, that you might run across in the literature.

23. Assume that you have been given two sets of paired scores. Know how to lay out a scatter diagram, identify and label all the parts, and know how to plot the measurements.

24. What is a negative—an inverse—relationship, and how would one be illustrated? Give an example of one from your own experience.

25. How do ranks make it possible to correlate data in quite different units of measurement? Illustrate using the ranked quality of teachers (based on student evaluations) and the number of articles published during the preceding 5 years.

26. With raw data provided by your instructor, compute a Pearson r using the raw-score formula.

27. Would a set of appropriately paired negative scores produce a negative correlation?

ANSWERS TO THE CORRELATION EXERCISE

1. Both age and sales volume are interval data, so the arrangement might be all right, except that age might be truncated. Because of restrictive hiring practices, most of the sales people might be around the same age.

2. Not possible. Signs of the zodiac are categories.

3. Not possible. Groups of men and groups of women are not paired scores.

4. No. Wearing or not wearing helmets is category measurement.

5. This would satisfy the statistical requirements. Doing this would provide a kind of validity for instructors' grading practices.

6. If we could quantify "personality characteristics" this would work. We would need to develop measurements that show individuals having equal intervals of some personality attribute, and then we could correlate husbands' and wives' scores.

7. I do not have a good idea how we might quantify "breakdown of family life" or "problems in the world today." If either of the two measurements cannot be adequately quantified, the Pearson cannot be used.

8. This would work if both these features of personality could be adequately measured.

9. Not workable. Communities are category data.

10. This would probably work, assuming both measurements are interval data. The quesion here is, which is cause and which is effect?

SMALL TALK

Chapter
8

Interpreting Correlations

Correlation is a necessary *but not a* sufficient *condition to establish a causal relationship between two variables.*

Runyon & Haber (1988), p. 213.

I attempted in the last chapter to introduce some of the behavioral science applications of correlations. They are widely used in testing, and they have an important function in the early stages of research.

In this chapter we will study what an investigator does after the data have been collected. Now is the time to figure out what the data mean so that we can draw some conclusions from them. The flexibility of correlational analyses, which is so useful in certain contexts, contributes to the complexity of interpretation. The method used for analyzing a correlation in one situation will not necessarily be applicable in another.

The procedures for data interpretation are nearly always discussed with reference to statistics used for analysis of data from experiments. My different approach attempts to integrate statistical considerations with the research methods with which they are used. We are studying correlations, so this is the first opportunity we will have for the discussion of "statistical significance." When we study the "*t*-test" later, we will find there is carryover from this preliminary introduction. That is all to the good.

The sentence quoted below, from the Thompson et al. (1991) article mentioned in a different context in the last chapter, is typical of the sort we would find in any publication which had used a correlation for data analysis.

Genetic correlations among the cognitive and achievement tests ranged from .57 to .85, shared environmental correlations were essentially zero, and specific environmental correlations were low (.00 to .19).

Our job in this chapter is to learn how to give meaning to numbers like that. "Statistically significant" is a phrase we see repeatedly in the literature—and even in the daily newspaper with reference to statistical evaluations. Significance does not mean that the results are important, or even meaningful or worthwhile, as a person who has not studied statistics might think. When there are different ways to interpret a statistic, as there are with a correlation, we might find the same statistical results can be and indeed will be interpreted in different ways.

Before we get involved with the complexities of significance interpretation, I need to clarify two areas that sometimes cause confusion. First, in the behavioral sciences, correlations are not interpreted as "percents." We should not say that an r of .37 shows there is a 37 percent (37%) relationship between the two sets of data. When correlations are used in a special way for test interpretation or when an investigator makes assumptions that are generally not relevant to the behavioral sciences, as can be done in certain biological analyses, correlations can legitimately be interpreted as percents.

Second, correlational values are not equal interval. A difference of .10 points between two numbers at the high end of the possible range—take $r = .70$ and $r = .80$ for example—is much more important than an equal .10 point change between $r = .20$ and $r = .30$. Equal changes at higher levels produce greater increases in statistical significance. That explains why correlations cannot be averaged.

We might be tempted to collect correlational values from several different sources and average them to get a typical value, but doing this directly would be incorrect. To combine several correlations to get an average we would first convert them into z-scores. We would get these values from tables included in many statistics texts. The z-scores are averaged in the normal way. The z-score table would again be consulted to convert the mean z-score back into a correlation.

REJECTION OF NULL HYPOTHESES

We will begin with an interpretation of correlations that determines "statistical significance through rejection of a null hypothesis," because that is the one most widely used. Recall the logic section in which I explained that the only logically correct way to evaluate hypotheses is to reject them.

Research hypotheses (symbol H_a) are often called "alternate hypotheses." Even though testing research hypotheses is the primary reason for doing the research, they are not tested directly by statistical evaluations. Another hypothesis, obtained entirely from statistical reasoning, is the one directly tested by a statistical analysis. For every statistic a "null hypothesis" (symbol H_o) is set up for the sole purpose of rejecting it, if that is possible. The statistical decision is made about the null hypothesis, and what we conclude about the research hypothesis follows from that decision. Research guidelines allow only two decisions about hypotheses: Either we can reject them or we can fail to reject them. One thing we can never do is to "prove them right."

Null hypotheses and research hypotheses are nearly always stated as opposing each other.[1] They both cannot be right. When we are unable to reject a null hypothesis, we routinely reject the research hypothesis.

USING A PROBABILITY TABLE

The statistical determination of whether a null hypothesis should be rejected is undertaken in a roundabout way. Statisticians first ask a question about whether the results are likely to have resulted from random variation. Statistical analyses do not provide clear-cut yes/no or right/wrong answers. Probability values form a continuous scale with no definite logical decision points. (Think of how you would make a decision about how fast is fast, if it were your job to set speed limits along the highway.) We are forced to make a decision about whether we will or will not reject the statistical null hypothesis we are testing. Statisticians and research investigators have agreed on certain probability values they will use, and these will be explained later. At best these decision points only recommend that rejecting a null hypothesis with these data is a better course of action than not rejecting it—but the conclusion is always made with the understanding that some of the time it will be wrong.

The concepts of probability are so important for understanding the processes of statistical evaluations that I will take a little time and space to illustrate the basic ideas.

Suppose that a person threw seven coins on a table and four of them turned up heads and three tails. This would not be unexpected, it seems reasonable, and it is likely to happen fairly often. If another person threw seven coins and all seven turned up heads, the question would be, did the second person cheat in some way? To evaluate whether cheating was likely (we never know for sure unless we catch the person deliberately doing something irregular) we would need to know the probability that seven coins would all turn up heads (or tails) on one toss. If the probability of seven coins coming up heads at the same time is low, we might want to use that as evidence that the person cheated. If seven heads on one toss were found to be a common occurrence, we would just call it luck and conclude that chance does things like that sometimes.

If it is "reasonable" to explain an event (such as this one) as a chance happening, we say that we have failed to reject chance as an explanation. Null hypotheses are explanations in terms of what is likely to occur by chance, so our failure to reject chance as the explanation is the same as failing to reject the null hypothesis. The alternate hypothesis states that the person cheated. The null hypothesis states that we can explain the result as something that can happen fairly commonly by chance. When we are unable to reject chance as a reasonable

---

[1] It is possible to make a case when this is not true, but examples of both the research and null hypothesis being in the same direction are very rare.

explanation, the research hypothesis we are studying is automatically rejected. In this example, we are testing the research hypothesis that questions whether it is likely the person cheated. Rejecting the research hypothesis expresses our conclusion that the person did not cheat.

We cannot predict exactly what will come up on any particular coin toss, but the algebra of probability can tell us what combinations are more likely. There are 128 different possible heads/tails combinations that describe how 7 coins can fall. The approximate probability for each combination is given in Table 8.1. There is only a .008 probability of expecting 7 coins to all come up heads and the same probability for them all to come up tails. There is an approximate .54 (54%) chance that they will come up with either 4 heads and 3 tails *or* 3 heads and 4 tails (27% + 27% = 54%). Numbers in the second row show the probability of any particular event occurring.

Numbers in the second row of Table 8.1 are the frequency of occurrence out of 128 possibilities for any particular event. With 7 coins we can see that there are 35 ways for them to fall with 4 heads and 3 tails, and there are also 35 ways for them to fall with 3 heads and 4 tails. This is a total of 70 possible ways for either event to occur. Percent probability is computed by: 70 ÷ 128 = .5469 (ignore rounding error).

Table 8.1 shows that some random events are more likely to occur than others. The same concept is applicable to research. Most statistical probabilities are not determined from this table, but the logic of interpretation is no different. With a probability of less than 1 in 100 that seven heads will be thrown at one time, we would, according to the tradition of research, reject the null hypothesis and look further at the possibility that the person might have cheated. Seven heads will come up with an average frequency of about 4 times in 500 trials. Throwing seven heads at one time will happen, according to probability theory, but not very often.

The algebra of probability gives only a general *theoretical* idea based solely on mathematical calculations. It is not of any help at all in predicting what will happen on a particular toss when we actually toss seven coins. We do not know whether one of the four predicted seven-heads occurrences will come up on the first trial, the last trial, or perhaps never in 500 trials. Suppose we tossed seven tails on the 149th trial. What would be our expectation that we would get seven heads again on the 150th toss? The laws of probability say the odds for this would be just the same. To believe otherwise is committing the "gambler's fallacy." I will not further slow the flow of this discussion to note the difference between the theory of probability and what actual data seem to produce, but see the endnote for some thoughts on the topic.

Table 8.1

PROBABILITIES FOR A SEVEN-COIN TOSS									
Types of Possibilities									
	7H 0T	6H 1T	5H 2T	4H 3T	3H 4T	2H 5T	1H 6T	0H 7T	Total
Percentage	.8	6	16	27	27	16	6	.8	100
Frequency of Occurrence	1	7	21	35	35	21	7	1	128

The following little exercise will demonstrate the process for interpreting a correlation in terms of probability. Write the numbers from 1 to 20 on two different sets of slips of paper and put all the numbers for each set into separate containers. With a hand in each container, simultaneously draw out numbers to form a pair. Record the selected numbers, put the slips back, mix them up, and draw another random pair. Continue drawing and recording numbers until you have chosen 20 pairs.

We have no reason to assume there would be a "significant" relationship between these randomly and independently selected pairs of numbers. Repeating the exercise hundreds of times and computing a correlation after you have selected each set of 20 scores would produce a large number of near-zero correlations. Some of the r's would be slightly larger, but according to the *theory* of probability a correlation as large as ±.45 for 20 pairs of scores would be very rare indeed.

I should mention that although we will often see references in statistical discussions to "the" null hypothesis, the expression does not mean what it says. Each statistic has its own way for stating the null hypothesis that is applicable to it. Since there are many statistics, there are many ways for stating the applicable H_o. Part of what we do when we study a statistic is learn how to state the null hypothesis suitable to it.

The null hypothesis for a correlation states that the obtained value should be zero $(r = 0.00)$.[2] Randomly selected samples from a hypothetical population would not normally produce a correlation of precisely zero, but to satisfy the null hypothesis the obtained values should not be far off. An appropriate table of p (probability) values, found in many standard statistics texts, provides values that help to decide whether a null hypothesis should be rejected. If the table gives a high probability that a particular result would occur fairly frequently by random variation, we do not reject the null hypothesis. The value of the obtained correlation is small enough (is close enough to zero) for us to conclude that it is most likely a chance occurrence. There does not appear to be a *statistically significant* relationship between the measurements.

The probability level statisticians have selected as the cut-off value for *rejecting a null hypothesis* is .05 or smaller (e.g., .04, .02, .01). When we reject a null hypothesis, we fail to reject the research hypothesis we are testing. For a correlation we would conclude there appears to be a statistically significant correlational relationship between the two sets of measurements. Later in this chapter I will discuss the point that even when a relationship has been found to be statistically significant, it might be of only limited value in practical applications.

A tabled value of .06 or larger, (e.g., .07, .10, .25, .40.) leads to the conclusion that we fail to reject the correlation null hypothesis, so we directly reject the research hypothesis.

We *never know for sure* whether a research hypothesis is true. We might conclude that it is probably true or that it has a high probability of being true, but we never know for certain. There is always a chance that the experimenter's decision

---

[2] This is a simplified idea that is good enough for practical applications. The usual assumption tested is that the *population* correlation is zero.

is wrong, and some of the time it will be. When it is reported in the literature that a correlation is statistically significant, the statement means only that the correlation is so large, for the sample size, that it does not seem very probable it could have occurred by chance. *Statistical interpretations are only guesses with certain levels of probability of being right; they are not facts.*

A table of "critical values," as they are called in statistics texts, is entered with two numbers: the size of the computed correlation and a value related to the number of pairs of scores. Some tables can be entered with the sample size (N) directly.[3] Tables that use "degrees of freedom (df)" get that value by subtracting 1 or 2, depending on the table, from the number of pairs of scores (N).

Probability tables for correlations should also be checked to note whether values listed are for a "one-" or a "two-tailed test." The logic here seems to be that if a hypothesis permits a prediction, prior to the collection of the data, of our getting *either* a positive *or* a negative relationship, we would use a one-tailed interpretation. In instances in which we make no prediction we would use a two-tailed interpretation.

Statistics texts are often not very good at helping us to understand how to use their tables. Some probability tables for correlations are given with values for both one- and two-tailed alternatives. When only one set of values is given, it is often for a two-tailed analysis. I have seen tables that do not state whether probability values are for a one- or two-tailed interpretation. We can easily compute one- or two-tailed probabilities from whichever value is given—if the given value is identified.

Probability values listed for a one-tailed test are half the two-tailed values. For a two-tailed probability, multiply the listed one-tailed value by 2. Conversely, if a two-tailed value is listed it can be divided by 2 to get the one-tailed value. The write-up of results should always state whether the reported probability values are for a one- or two-tailed interpretation.

The ethics of research suggest that investigators make a decision about whether to use a one- or two-tailed interpretation *before* the data are analyzed. A one-tailed interpretation produces a higher level of statistical significance, which we usually want in research. But we should not wait until our data have been analyzed and then make a statistical decision according to whatever best supports the hypotheses we are studying.

Investigators doing research that involves only a small number of variables would probably know enough about their measurements to predict whether a relationship will be positive or negative. In that situation a one-tailed interpretation would be appropriate. If a large number of correlations are computed among a great many measurements an investigator will probably not be able to make a reasonable prediction in advance regarding the direction of the expected relationship between every two sets of measurements. In that situation, two-tailed interpretations would be in order.

Table 8.2 illustrates an abbreviated probability table that is like the complete tables found in statistics texts. The two probability levels of principle interest for

---

[3]Makers of probability tables could subtract the constant for us and arrange the table so it can be entered directly with N, the number of pairs of scores. A few tables are given this way; it is difficult to think of a good reason why this has not been done for all of them.

Table 8.2

SOME CRITICAL VALUES FOR A PEARSON CORRELATION (ONE-TAILED TEST)		
N	.05	.01
05	.805	.934
10	.549	.716
20	.378	.516
42	.257	.358
82	.183	.256
102	.164	.230

the determination of statistical significance are the .05 level (pronounced "point oh five"), and .01 ("point oh one"). For this table, "N" is the number of pairs of measurements. If the N of your sample does not appear on the table, use the next lower value. If the table you are using requires degrees of freedom, follow the instructions for that table.

When there is a small number of pairs of scores r has to be larger for the same level of significance. A small correlation of .164 is all that is needed for significance at the .05 level when N = 102, but an r = .805 is required when N = 5. The effect of sample size on significance can be seen by running one's eye down the columns and noting that as sample size (N) increases, the size of the correlation necessary for the same level of significance is reduced.

Note also how the size of a correlation necessary for significance at the .01 level is larger than a correlation necessary for significance at the .05 level. Smaller correlations will be produced by random variation five times more frequently than larger correlations necessary for significance at the .01 level.

When a correlation exceeds the size necessary for rejection of the null hypothesis at a minimum .05 level, it is said to be "statistically significant." A correlation must be *equal to or larger than* the tabled value to reject the null hypothesis at the selected level. When N = 20 an r of .378 is statistically significant at the .05 level; an r of .354 would not be significant. Any value between .378 and .500, when N = 20, would be significant at the .05 level but not at .01. Study the table until it is clear that every correlation significant at the .01 level is also significant at the .05 level for the same sample size but that the reverse is not necessarily true. When N = 10 a correlation of .715 and .549 are both significant at the .05 level, but only the larger r value is also significant at .01.

Investigators often report their results by listing correlations in a table of intercorrelations, and they identify statistically significant relationships with symbols. Typically, a single asterisk (*) means the correlation is significant at the .05 level, ** means .01, and *** identifies a correlation that is very significant at the .001 level of probability. Correlations not specifically identified as being statistically significant are understood to have a probability larger than .05.

The very words "statistically significant" have an authoritative sound to them that can easily mislead a person who has not studied statistics. The determination of statistical significance does not guarantee that a true relationship exists between the two measurements, nor does the finding affirm that the relationship is large enough to be useful for any practical purpose. If this confuses untrained people, consider the following dispute involving professionals.

The Environmental Protection Agency expects that perhaps 4,000 nonsmoking people die annually from lung cancer caused by secondhand cigarette smoke. Tobacco companies have called attention to a thesis written by a doctoral candidate. That work supposedly showed, according to the article I read, "... that nonsmokers do not face a statistically significant increase in lung cancer risk from exposure to other people's cigarette smoke." A cigarette company's "review of the scientific literature says only 5 of 23 studies since 1981 show a statistically significant link between secondhand smoke and lung cancer." This is from an article in a large daily newspaper, so we can be reasonably sure that most of the people who read the article did not understand what it means for a correlational relationship to be statistically significant.

On June 22, 1993, a combination of tobacco firms filed a suit in a federal court challenging the EPA report on the harmful effects of secondhand smoke. The tobacco industry believed the EPA report to contain serious statistical and procedural flaws and asked the court to have the report withdrawn. A tobacco firm stated, "When the EPA could not otherwise reach its predetermined conclusions using generally accepted scientific and statistical practices, the EPA simply changed the rules." An EPA representative stated that the report "has gone through extensive review by scientists inside and outside the EPA."

THE USE OF r^2 FOR CORRELATION INTERPRETATION

Prediction of behavior is a very important part of a psychologist's work. In the first part of the following introduction I will highlight ideas of prediction with relevance to psychological tests, but that is not our major concern in this discussion. Ideas related to accuracy of prediction are directly involved with ideas of statistical interpretation of correlations. These are a little easier to understand after first looking at them as they apply to the field of psychological testing.

A high school student takes an SAT test. A university will use this measurement, in conjunction with other information (a written application, interview data, high school grades, and letters of recommendation), to help predict the applicant's chances of successfully completing that university's educational program. The predicted chances of success will help determine whether or not the applicant is admitted.

Most people would probably accept that it makes sense to assume the larger the relationship between two sets of data, the more accurately we can predict a score on one measurement (usually Y) from a given score on the predictor (X) variable. The truth of this idea can be illustrated easily when both sets of data have been converted to z-scores. All a person needs to know about z-scores at this point is that they can be compared directly because they are in the same units. z-scores are obtained from suitable interval measurements, and they are statistically changed to a scale that is independent of the original measurement units.

z_Y (predicted score) $= rz_x$ (predictor score)

The predicted z_Y is determined by (is a function of) the size of the predictor z_X score and by the size of the correlation between the two measurements. For this discussion, we are primarily interested in the influence of correlations of different sizes.

Let us pick several correlation values to study what happens to the predicted Y score for a given X. When the correlation is $r = 1.00$ and $z_X = 1.5$, z_Y will also be 1.5. This simply confirms what we already know: When the relationship between two sets of data is perfect (and they are in the same units), we can predict Y scores exactly. When the correlation is .75, a z of 1.5 will predict a score of 1.25. For $r = .50$ the predicted score will be .75, and when $r = .25$ the predicted score becomes .375. When $r = 0.00$, the predicted Y score is 0.00, which is, of course, the mean of z scores.

This demonstration makes it easy to see the "regression"[3] of predicted scores to the mean as the magnitude of the relationship decreases. When there is a very small relationship between two sets of scores, the best prediction we can make is the mean of the group to which we are predicting. Whenever we know nothing whatever about a set of data, the mean gives us our best guess for a predicted score.

Accuracy of predictions from one set of measurements to another set is determined by the extent of the relationship between them. A large correlation tells us they have a lot of "variation" in common, so predictions from X to Y will be fairly accurate. We can say that a lot of the variability of the Y scores is "explained" by variability of X. One way to think about the meaning of a correlation is in terms of explained and unexplained variance, as given by the following formula:

explained variation/total variation $= r^2$

The r^2 value expresses the amount of variance in one measurement that can be accounted for, explained, by the other. The amount of variance the measures have in common, as given by r^2, decreases as r decreases from 100% when $r = \pm 1.00$ to 0% when $r = 0.00$. When $r^2 = 0.00$ none of the variation in Y can be explained by variations in X. Obviously, we cannot make accurate predictions from one measurement to another when they have very little variance in common. The statement of percent when we are using r^2 is correct, but recall we cannot interpret r in terms of percent.

Assume that a psychologist wanted to assess the relationship between leadership ability and success as a politician. To do this, 739 politicians were measured for both leadership ability and for their success as politicians. Accept that the correlation between these measured attributes was .30. A correlation of this size does not show a high level of statistical relationship, but with such a large sample it is highly significant, as statistically defined using probability tables as previously discussed.

---

[3]Regression is the source of the "r" symbol for correlations.

Think of the many variables that go together to produce the leadership construct; some of them are: intelligence, having a good way with people, listening and incorporating disparate ideas in group plans, physical height,[4] a good appearance, well-thought-out group goals and objectives, being a good judge of people, and an ascendant personality.

A similar look at the characteristics of a successful politician might include: being a good judge of people, having a good way with people, an ability to attract followers who will work on one's behalf, an ascendant personality, understanding what people want to hear and offering it to them, being physically strong to withstand the rigors of campaigning, being able to attract people with money to fund the campaign, and a good appearance.

Note that a politician needs some of the characteristics of leadership, but there are matters of concern to politicians—raising money for example—which are not necessary in the leadership definition. And we might also note that people who have good leadership traits have some, but not all, of the qualities that could help them to become politicians.

The square of the correlation, .09 in this example, gives the proportion of the qualities necessary for being a good politician that were predicted from the leadership measurement. The square of the correlation measures the proportion of the Y variance which can be attributed to variation in X. In this example, r^2 shows the proportion of variance the measures of leadership have in common with being a successful politician.

Klein's (1987) work is typical of correlational studies in the area of personality. She evaluated the relationships between scores on temperament tests and the ways in which young adults adapt to change. The temperament tests were the predictor variables, and the criteria consisted of three measures of adjustment with the general titles of loneliness, involvement, and affectivity. Each of these had three subcategories of adaptation measures. All together the work produced 63 correlations.

Klein's sample of 167 participants was large enough for relatively small correlations to be statistically significant according to the generally accepted principles for rejection of the null hypothesis. I do not have a table that gives the probabilities for 167 subjects, but N = 152 (two-tailed test) is adequate. For this sample size, $r = .159$ is large enough for statistical significance at the .05 level, and $r = .208$ is all that is required at the .01 level. Her sample was larger than 152, so r's required for significance would be smaller than those I have given. A total of 36 correlations out of 63 (about 57%) were statistically significant at either the .05 or the .01 level. This information was sufficient for Klein to report that, "Overall, the results demonstrate the relationship between temperament characteristics and adaptation outcomes."

Klein did not note that 43% of the correlations were not significant, and concluding a relationship with those correlations that were significant does not acknowledge the fact that many of them were quite small. Only 5 were .40 or larger, and 12 were .19 or less. Although Klein's interest in this research primarily involved the descriptive application of correlations, the idea of prediction was also

---

[4]There is some evidence to suggest that leaders tend to be slightly taller than average.

clearly relevant as indicated by this observation. "Mood was the best predictor for all three affective areas."

Correlations as low as .30 are common in psychological research. A sample size of a modest 45 pairs of scores is enough for a correlation of .30 to be significant at the .05 level. But a correlation of $r = .30$ has only 9% of the variance in Y that is associated with or "can be explained by" variance in X. A large 91% of the variance *has not* been explained by the relationship. *"This brings about a major point in the interpretation of r: A correlation coefficient* may be *significantly* (and *highly*) *different from zero* and still be *worthless* as a predictive index," (Senter, 1969, p. 431, italics by Senter). Squaring a correlation is a simple, practical way to demonstrate that large samples might produce statistical significant correlations that are nevertheless so small that they should be interpreted with caution.

By squaring the correlations given in the Klein research we get a different understanding of the findings and conclusions. The *largest* correlation listed was –.54. The normal interpretation of r^2 tells us that whatever it is that the "mood" test measures, it accounts for only .29 (29%) of the variance of the "depression" part of the affective scale. Let us reason that all of the factors that cause depression total 100%. The mood scale measurements account for only 29% of the total, which leaves 71% of the variance that was accounted for by other factors not identified by this study.

One-third (12) of the correlations that were statistically significant were equal to or smaller than $r = .20$. When we square .20 the variance accounted for is only .04 (4%), which leaves 96% of the variance unexplained. Two statistically significant correlations were as small, $r = .15$, $r^2 = .023$ (2.3%); and the smallest statistically significant correlation was only $r = .13$, $r^2 = .017$ (1.7%).

The point of this discussion is to urge research people to look more carefully at what constitutes reasonable conclusions from data analyses. The standard way of interpreting correlational relationships, in terms of probability, fails to take account of all the data have to tell us.

ACCURACY OF PREDICTION

Another way of thinking about the meaning of a correlation is to consider errors in prediction, a topic closely related to the r^2 interpretation. When we compute the relationship between a set of X observations, possibly a test, and some other behavior Y, we are in effect determining "predictive validity" of the X measurement.

Statisticians could use these preliminary data to establish a "regression line." This is most easily visualized with reference to a scatter diagram and a single straight line that goes through the overall cluster of scores so the two halves balance. The regression line is a computed straight line that takes account of all the X values[5] in a distribution and gives the best possible fit among the means of

---

[5]A similar line can be computed for Y values, but prediction has generally been standardized to predict Y from X.

the vertical columns of data. For a typical scatter plot of reasonably correlated data, the means of the low X values will be near the lower left-hand corner. The means of the larger X scores will be near the upper right. A straight regression line will not go through the mean of every column of X values, but taking the data overall, it will be computed to come as close as possible. It is the best way we have of summarizing correlational data. If a correlation is not perfect, measurements will scatter around the regression line. The smaller the computed relationship, the larger the amount of variation.

After we have obtained representative data from preliminary research, we can use an appropriate statistical formula to predict Y scores from X values. The "standard error of the estimate (SE_{est})," is a measure of variability that gives an idea of the amount of scatter of "predicted" scores (i.e., errors in prediction) around the regression line.

The algebra for determining the standard error is quite simple. We will define errors in prediction as unexplained variance and compute it by subtracting the r^2 value from 1 to get an estimate of variance *not* accounted for by the relationship.

$$\frac{\text{unexplained variation}}{\text{explained variation}} = 1 - r^2$$

Let SE_{est} stand for the standard error of Y as estimated from X. S_Y is the standard deviation of the distribution of Y scores, and r is the validity coefficient, obtained from an earlier study.

$$SE_{est} = S_Y \sqrt{1 - r^2}$$

We can better understand what the SE_{est} is telling us about data if we work several problems using our own substitutions.

Suppose a psychologist has developed a new type of test which she would like to use for predicting success in an ambassador-training program sponsored by the State Department. Assume the standard deviation of the behavior measurements in the training program is 16. Use the standard error of the estimate formula and compute the standard error resulting from each of the following correlations: $r = 1.00, .75, .50, .25,$ and 0.00. The standard errors in the same order would be: $0.00, 10.58, 13.86, 15.49,$ and 16.00. These data show what we have already come to expect: The smaller the correlation, the larger the error in prediction. When the relationship is perfect, we would make no errors in prediction. When the relationship is zero, the best we could do would be to guess that every score was equal to the mean of the Y measurements.

McNemar (1969, p. 141) notes that ". . . compared to a correlation of zero, an r of .60 reduces the error of estimate by 20 percent." A correlation must be as large as .866 before there is a 50 percent reduction in the error of estimate.

> . . . the difference in reduction between an r of .70 and an r of .90 is approximately the same as that between .20 and .70. This interpretation of r is most useful and at the same time most disturbing, since errors of estimate for r's in the vicinity of .40 to .70,

values usually found and utilized in predicting success from test results, are discouraging large.

Study Table 8.3 to see how this works. The difference in error reduction between *r*'s of .70 and .90 is .278, which is approximately the same as the difference of .266 between *r*'s of .20 and .70.

Table 8.3

	EFFECT OF A CORRELATION SIZE ON ERROR REDUCTION		
r	$\sqrt{1-r^2}$	*r*	$\sqrt{1-r^2}$
.00	1.000	.70	.714
.20	.980	.866	.500
.60	.800	.90	.436

SAMPLE SIZE AND A CORRELATION'S USEFULNESS FOR RESEARCH

Even though a correlation derived from a large sample might be statistically significant according to the manner of interpretation described earlier in this chapter, interpretation with the standard error of the estimate can show that it has little value when we try to put it to practical use in a research situation. Significance, as the term was used in the earlier discussion, was based on both the sample size and the size of the correlation. Large correlations obtained from small samples and small correlations obtained from large samples both could be statistically significant at the same level. Recall the discussion regarding Table 8.2. A little thought at this point will disclose a contradiction. A small correlation from a large sample might be statistically significant and still be so small that it is of little value for making accurate predictions.

The summary in Table 8.4 will recall the previous discussion. A standard deviation of 16 is assumed for the Y variable, the one we are predicting to. All the correlations given in the table are significant at the .01 level using a two-tailed interpretation.

Table 8.4

	SAMPLE SIZE AND SIZE OF STANDARD ERROR OF THE ESTIMATE	
N	*r*	Standard Error of the Estimate
05	.959	4.534
12	.708	11.299
42	.393	14.713
102	.254	15.475
402	.128	15.868

We know that it is the *size* of the correlation that reduces the errors in prediction. Therefore, as the table shows, a large correlation derived from a small sample will be of more practical use for prediction. Table 8.4 shows that small correlations derived from large samples will reduce errors in prediction by only a very small amount.

CAUSE AND EFFECT AND THE POST HOC FALLACY

Find Adultery Causes 46% of Marriage Counsel Cases

Storrs, Conn.—Adultery is the cause of nearly half the problems marriage counselors deal with, according to research by the president of the American Assn. of Marriage and Family Counselors.

(Chicago *Sun-Times*, 1977, April 11)

Education Good for Health: Study

Chapel Hill, N.C.—A national study of lifestyle and heart disease indicates that higher education may be good for your health, researchers say.

(Chicago *Sun-Times*, 1982, January 4)

Come Out Smoking:

Teen-aged girls who smoke are more likely to engage in sex at an early age than their nonsmoking counterparts. So finds a study published in the *American Journal of Public Health*.

(*Moneysworth*, 1984, Autumn)

Links Degree, Pay to Stable Match

Washington—Married persons with college degrees and family incomes of at least $20,000 a year are more likely to have stable marriages than couples with less education and money, a Census Bureau report showed Friday.

(Chicago *Sun-Times*, 1977, September 10) [Note: 1977 salaries would have to be adjusted to today's standards; $50,000 perhaps?]

These are all examples of how correlations are used in our daily lives. Sometimes they might only describe a relationship without any suggestion of a causal connection; but in other instances a cause and effect relationship is clearly implied, even if it is not directly stated. The use of correlations to suggest, indeed encourage, the notion that observations are causally related is perhaps the most common form of argument in the popular forms of communication. Correlations provide valuable assistance in identifying and isolating hypotheses that might be worthy of study in other ways, but they are of little *direct* value in research. The reason is, a presumed cause might be just a *sufficient* rather than a *necessary* condition. It might be just *a* cause rather than *the* cause, or *they might not be directly related at all.*

Several difficulties with the correlational reasoning make it impossible to verify cause and effect conclusions. Attempting to do so is such a common logical mistake that it has been given its own name, the *post hoc fallacy.* Some readers will recognize this as an abbreviation of the complete phrase *"post hoc ergo propter hoc"* (after this, therefore because of this). It is a mistake in reasoning caused by the assumption that just because two things go together, one of them is *the* cause of the other.

Sometimes mistakes in reasoning from a presumed cause to a presumed effect will be obvious, as in the examples given at the beginning of this discussion. But for many other presumed relationships the connection is more subtle. There seems to be evidence that men who commit sex crimes have an interest in pornographic materials. That observation ignores the point that there are many men, and women, who enjoy the same materials but who do not commit sex crimes. Writers have made a case for calling sex crimes crimes of violence. It has been very difficult to demonstrate that the availability of pornographic materials (if these can be defined) is *the,* or even *a,* major cause of sex-related crimes. Government commissions, certain religious groups, and many individuals have worked very hard to establish this connection.

Whenever it is necessary to make sense from complex relationships, an investigator must find ways for answering both of the questions discussed below. A failure to provide answers to either of them makes it very difficult to establish a causal relationship between the two variables.

Which Is Cause and Which Is Effect?

In the behavioral sciences it is very difficult—usually impossible—to control all relevant variables that are involved in any set of presumed relationships. Even when we can establish that two sets of observations consistently go together, it is not always possible to know which is cause and which is effect. Is infidelity a major cause of unhappy marriages, or do unhappy marriages cause infidelity? Does watching pornographic movies or buying raunchy literature cause men to become sexually aggressive, or is it just that people who already have established inclinations select reading materials and watch the sorts of films that fit their interests? It is unlikely that people who are not interested in religion, or golf, or philosophy, or experimental psychology will buy and study materials in any of those areas.

Correlations are entirely nondirectional. It is just as reasonable, *from the statistical point of view,* to argue that X is the cause of Y as it is to say that Y is the cause of X. When there is a clearly established sequence of an event coming at one time and a second event coming later, the second event could not have been the cause of the first. This is the technique used in the Eron, Huesman, Lefkowitz, and Walder (1972) article on viewing television violence (see the endnote). Boys who watched a lot of violence on television when they were in the 3rd grade tended to show more aggressive behavior when they were in the 13th grade.

Just because we know the order of correlated observations does not guarantee they have a causal connection. Obviously, we cannot argue that aggressive behavior observed in the 13th grade caused boys to watch violent television programs 10 years before. But we might argue that *both* aggressive behavior in the 13th grade *and* interest in watching violence-oriented television programs shared a common element. In this example, a personality trait that involved an interest in violence might explain both aggressive behavior in the 13th grade and interest in watching violence-oriented TV programs when the observer was a third-grader. The Eron research was designed to rule out this possibility, but it could not do so completely.

Is It Certain That ALL Other Potential Causes of the Same Effect Have Been Eliminated?

A person who does not consider alternative explanations might make this mistake. Both of the related X and Y variables could be the result of an unknown third variable. Figure 8.1 illustrates that situation.

Having a good education and a good income might not be *the* cause of a successful marriage. Personality factors that made it possible for a person to finish college and then get and hold a good job might also be advantageous in the development of a good marital adjustment. Or it might be argued that the only contribution a good education makes is to improve a person's chances for earning a good income, and a shortage of money is a major cause of quarrels in marriage.

The same cultural factors and changes in our society as a whole that stimulated growth of "the women's movement" might also contribute to an increase in divorce and a general breakup of family life.

Based on the following observations it is tempting to argue that nudism should be encouraged. The Maryland chapter of the American Heart Association found that "nudists had fewer cases of high blood pressure than the national average" (Chicago *Sun-Times*, 1977, September 9). The presumption is that nudism is the cause of lowered blood pressure. Anyone can identify a number of conditions that could account for both an interest in nudism and a generally lower blood pressure. More frequent periods of relaxation at a resort, a greater general interest in health and exercise, and enjoying the company of other people with similar interests are obvious candidates.

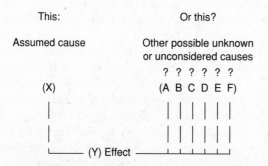

FIGURE 8.1
A Third Variable as a Possible Cause

Even if a particular investigator is unable to identify a third condition that could explain a relationship, it cannot be argued that there is none. In attempting to make the point that we have exhausted all possible explanations, we call up the specter of another logical fallacy, *argumentum ad ignoratiam*. The name means that ignorance of the facts is not a good foundation for supporting a particular point of view. The argument can take this form in discussion: "If you can't think of a better idea, my proposal must be right." "Evidence we do not have can hardly be considered a relevant argument" (Little et al., 1955, p. 20).

SOME POINTS TO KNOW AND REMEMBER ABOUT CORRELATIONS

1. What sorts of research questions are correlations used to answer?
2. How are correlations used in research?
3. How are correlations used in tests and measurements?
4. Computation and presentation of results:
   a. Understand how to draw and interpret a scatter-plot.
   b. Understand the principle of r in terms of ranks.
   c. What types of data are required for the computation of a Pearson correlation?
   d. How are correlations computed?
5. Interpretation:
   a. Reject null hypothesis when probability is .05 or less.
   b. Extent of common variance is given by r^2.
   c. Standard error of the estimate evaluates extent of expected errors in prediction

$$(SE_{est} = SD_Y \sqrt{1 - r^2})$$

   d. Correlations are not "percent."
6. Correlation and causation (post hoc fallacy):
   a. A correlation is statistically nondirectional.
   b. In many observed relationships it difficult to determine which is cause and which is effect.
   c. Explain how two sets of data could be correlated because both are correlated with a third factor (that might not even be known.)

ENDNOTES

I will close this discussion with a short critique of a major article about an important topic. I will use it to illustrate in a practical way that research is an ongoing process. Different investigators can legitimately interpret data in different ways that lead to different conclusions. Behavioral science research is not yet sufficiently mature so that everyone who studies the journal articles will necessarily agree on what the conclusions are or what they mean.

Many people have been and are quite concerned about how viewing violent television programs might affect the behavior of children who watch them. An article by Eron et al. (1972) is an example of work on this topic. Their study was complex and extensive, both in what they attempted and in what they accomplished. Their objective was to determine whether there is a significant relationship between the preference for watching violent television programs and aggressive behavior. Data were collected at the start of the study and 10 years later. They found, among a great many other observations, that ". . . there exists a highly significant relationship between a preference for violent television in the third grade and aggressive habits in the thirteenth grade." The correlation is .31.

The age difference is important because it removes one of the difficulties in the determination of causal relationships. A later event cannot be the cause of something that happened earlier. The delay also made it possible to check the idea that observing TV violence will not necessarily affect present behavior, but it might have a delayed effect that will show up later.

Regarding the low .31 relationship, the authors called attention to it in this way:

> While the correlation between third-grade preferences and thirteenth-grade peer-rated aggression explains only 10% of the variance[6] in aggression, 10% is impressive when one considers the probable limitations on the size of the correlation imposed by the skewed distributions of the variable, the large number of variables affecting aggression, the comparatively small explanatory power of these other variables . . . , and the ten-year lag between measurement times.

Note that only 10% of the predicted aggressive behavior variance was explained by the correlation; 90% remains to be explained in all the ways other than viewing violence-oriented television programs.

There is another point I believe to be important. I do not think it is appropriate to argue—as was done in the preceding quotation—that although a correlation was not very good, this can be at least partly explained by inadequacies of the data. By implication, if the data were better, the correlation would be larger. We have to work with and draw conclusions from the data our research produced. We should not speculate about possible results we might have obtained if the data had been better suited to a correlational analysis.

Several of the correlations given in the study *did not* support the hypothesis of a causal connection between viewing TV violence and aggressive behavior, but these were mostly ignored. A good scientific study should give equal weight to evidence that fails to support the research hypothesis.

This article has been widely discussed and frequently quoted as evidence that viewing violence-oriented programs on television is a cause of subsequent aggression, but other published research both supports and contradicts the evidence of this one.

Turner, Hesse, and Peterson-Lewis (1986) have summarized a number of "quasi-experimental" studies on the effects of naturally occurring media violence. They concluded that "the balance of the findings is consistent with the hypothesis that TV produces a long-term increase in the aggressive behavior of boys but not of girls."

---

[6]The 10 percent is an approximate value obtained by squaring the .31 correlation; $.31^2 = .0961$.

Freedman (1984) has published a contrary opinion. He reviewed a large number of articles on the possible relationship between exposure to TV violence and later aggressive behavior and concluded that the field studies produced only mixed results. He found little evidence to support the idea of a causal relationship between the two.

Friedrich-Cofer and Huston (1986), in an article entitled "Television Violence and Aggression: The Debate Continues," raised objections to Freedman's conclusions and defended what they considered to be majority consensus opinion "that there is a causal relation between viewing TV violence and aggression."

Freedman (1986) responded by emphasizing his original conclusion and arguing that "there are sound reasons for exercising caution in generalizing from laboratory results and that research outside the laboratory provides only weak and inconsistent support for the causal hypothesis."

In 1993, the federal government became concerned about violence in computer games and considered ways for keeping the more egregious examples away from children.

In December 1993, the *Chicago Tribune* carried a series of articles that included a discussion on "How the Brain's Chemistry Unleashes Violence." (The series was titled "Unlocking the Mind.") The general presentation supported the idea that much aggression seems to have a physiological component which is amenable to manipulation by drugs.

This discussion illustrates the complexities of psychological research when it is applied to the "real-world" experience. We can see that there is considerable disagreement about statistical interpretations, general explanations, findings, and conclusions. I also wanted to illustrate the self-correcting procedures of the scientific process. Its procedures are self-correcting so that in time we should be able to work out all the difficulties and the truth will be affirmed.

Long before the attorney general issued a formal opinion about the effect of smoking on health, I knew a wise biology teacher who had this opinion about smoking, "I do not know exactly what the long-term effects of smoking are, but whatever they are, they are not good." With a slight transposition, that statement summarizes my opinion about the apparent glorification of violence that seems to be so prevalent in our society today.

Exercise In Correlational Analysis

This exercise will demonstrate that you understand how correlations are used in psychological research.

1. Make up and state a research hypothesis that can be tested with a correlational analysis using a Pearson correlation.
2. The following is a fairly simple exercise, so two weeks would be more than enough time for its completion.
   a. Make up and list two columns of appropriate data. Ten sets of logically paired measurements should be enough. Identify the nature of

the measurements for each variable. Make sure they meet the requirements for a correlational analysis. Keep the numbers small to reduce errors in computation.

b. Compute the Pearson correlation. Show all work. Use an appropriate table to determine statistical significance.

c. Since data will be available, compute and interpret the standard error of the estimate.

THE USE OF CORRELATIONS IN JOURNAL ARTICLES

Your task in this assignment is to locate journal articles that show examples of correlations being used in research articles.

1. Check your library for the psychology journals it has available. Thumb through several different ones to find those that tend to publish articles involving correlational analyses. Titles of articles will sometimes suggest the study of relationships. Look only for the Pearson correlation: r not R. Articles that study personality will often include a "table of intercorrelations."

2. Two articles are required to fulfill this assignment. Research involving a study of relationships usually involves the computation of several. Select only one from each article. Copy a page from each that shows the correlation. State in your own words what the correlation was found to mean according to the way it was used in that article. Was it significant? What level?

STUDY QUESTIONS

1. Explain the idea that a large correlation is a necessary but not a sufficient condition for the determination of causality.

2. Explain the distinction between a correlation used as a descriptive statistic and one used for making an inductive inference.

3. What is the interpretation of a −1.33 correlation?

4. What is the difference in meaning between a positive and negative correlation of the same size?
   Which is more important?

5. What would you say to a person who stated that there was a 57 percent relationship between lifetime income and the number of years of education satisfactorily completed?

6. Explain the idea that values of correlations are not equal interval.

7. Would it be all right to combine several correlations in order to compute the average? Explain.
   What other way is available for computing an average of several correlations?

8.   What is a "null hypothesis"? How is the null hypothesis for a correlation stated?

9.   What does it mean to reject a null hypothesis?

10. How are decisions regarding a research hypothesis affected by decisions made about the null hypothesis?

11. Know how to use a probability table to determine statistical significance.
     How is the p value affected by the sample size? by the size of the correlation?

12. Explain this statement: An observed relationship for a sample of a certain size was found to be "statistically significant at the .025 level."

13. If a correlation is found to be significant at the .05 level, is it also significant at the .01 level?
     If it is known to be significant at the .01 level, is it also significant at the .05 level?

14. Explain the relationships among sample size, size of the correlation, and statistical significance.

15. What is the standard error of the estimate? How is it computed?
     What does it tell us about the significance of a relationship?

16. How is the standard error of the estimate affected by the size of the correlation?
     How are errors in prediction affected as the size of a relationship increases?

17. In what circumstances might a highly significant correlation be relatively useless for practical applications?

18. How is r^2 used to interpret a correlation?

19. In terms of the relationship between two variables such as a Graduate Record Exam and subsequent performance in a psychology graduate program, what is "error variance"? Give some examples.

20. Even when two variables are highly correlated, why is it difficult to demonstrate a cause-effect relationship between them?

21. What is the "post hoc fallacy"?

22. Explain the idea of *argumentum ad ignoratiam*.

SMALL TALK

I've computed a correlation of -1.47 between the use of sarcastic statements in conversation and scores on a self-esteem test. People who had the lowest measured levels of self-esteem were also the people who most often used sarcasm in trying to be funny. That proves that low self-esteem is the cause of sarcastic behavior.

It only proves that you made a mistake in computation. The negative relationship might be O.K., but a correlation can never be larger than ± 1.00.

It was just a minor slip. I have redone and checked the calculation and find the relationship is higher than I thought. It is now -.74, which for my sample size is statistically significant at the .01 level. My concluding statement hasn't changed. Low levels of self-esteem unquestionably cause a person to be sarcastic. This is probably a compensation mechanism. People who have good self-esteem do not have to be sarcastic.

Post hoc ergo propter hoc.

Are you trying to be sarcastic?

PART FOUR

Experiments in Psychology

Chapter
9

Logic of Experimental Designs

An experiment is a research procedure that requires the controlled manipulation of at least two possible causes, or one possible cause manipulated in at least two ways or amounts. During all the trials for all groups, extraneous potential causes are maintained as equivalent as possible. The effects are evaluated using the same measuring procedures for all the conditions. Statistical significance of differences are determined using standard formulas that are appropriate for the data, number, and selection of samples.

An experiment designed and carried out by Louis Pasteur well over a hundred years ago, is an often cited prototype for good experiments. It is an important one in the history of medical science, but no ethical researcher would do an experiment like this today. I have been unable to find another example that illustrates so well and so simply the points we will be discussing in this chapter. The structure of the experiment is correct, good control of extraneous conditions was possible, and the results were unambiguous.

In the experiment twenty-four sheep, one goat, and six cows were inoculated on May 5 with five drops of living attenuated culture of anthrax bacillus. On May 17 all these animals had been revaccinated with a second dose of a less-attenuated culture. On May 31 all the immunized animals were infected with a highly virulent anthrax culture, and the same culture was injected as well into twenty-nine normal animals: twenty-four sheep, one goat, and four cows. When Pasteur arrived on the field on the second day of June with his assistants Chamberland, Roux, and Thuillier, he was greeted with loud acclamations. All the vaccinated sheep were well. Twenty-one of the control sheep and the single goat were dead of anthrax, two other control sheep died in front of the spectators, and the last unprotected sheep died at the end of the day. The six vaccinated cows were well and showed no symptoms, whereas the four control cows had extensive swellings at the site of inoculation and febrile reactions. The triumph was complete (Dubos, 1960, p. 118).[1]

While studying chicken cholera, Pasteur made a major biological discovery. He found that when chickens were injected with an anthrax serum that had deteriorated from age they became ill but they did not die, and they subsequently developed an immunity to the virulent form of the disease itself. When his work with anthrax had advanced sufficiently, he made a public announcement of his findings and was met with considerable criticism. He readily accepted a challenge to prove his theories in a public demonstration set for May 2, 1881 at Pouilly-le-Fort. The quotation gives the results of that demonstration. Pasteur's still-limited knowledge of immunology, and a lot of beginners' luck, were enough to carry the day. Nothing occured to ruin his demonstration.

1. Note first—and this is an important point—that experiments require comparisons between at least two conditions. We evaluate the effect of one variable by comparing it with another. Vaccination with a weakened vaccine was compared with a no-treatment condition in this example. All extraneous conditions that might affect one group differently from the other were maintained equivalent. Had Pasteur run trials using only the vaccinated group, people could argue the animals would have lived anyhow. With an experimental design we do not have to speculate about what might have happened in the alternate condition. This design shows us what would happen.

2. The use of *groups* of animals was important. There is so much variation of all sorts in living organisms that we can never be sure that a few examples are necessarily representative of the larger group we want information about.

   Although so-called lower animals are not identical to each other, it is accepted as safe to say that one sheep of a certain breed is very much like another of the same breed. We assume that all the animals were healthy and similar in other ways at the beginning of the experiment. Just to be sure that extraneous variations would even out, animals were randomly assigned to one or the other research conditions.

3. To rule out possible effects of treatment such as diet, living conditions, handling, diseased drinking water (whatever), all the animals were kept in the same field, had the same care, ate the same food, drank the same water, and shared the same environmental conditions. And we should also make note that the farmers looking after them did not know which animals had been inoculated.

---

[1] This event is an unusually dramatic experimental presentation, so it has been described in many different places. I have seen another version in Haggard (1946) and a third in de Kruif (1953). Variations of it are probably given in every history of medicine, biology, or science.

People who have had some training with experiments might notice that Pasteur made no statistical analysis of his data, and no one seems to have questioned his conclusions! Pasteur could not have evaluated his 1881 experimental results statistically even if he had wanted to; a suitable statistic had not been developed yet. The results of the anthrax experiment produced category data—either the animals lived or died. He probably would have used a chi-square or some other nonparametric statistic if there had been one. The inventor of chi-square, Karl Pearson (the same one who did our correlation), had been born 24 years before, but the bulk of his work in statistics was not published until after 1890.

The deadly nature of anthrax permitted no ambiguity about the outcome. Work in behavioral sciences rarely (perhaps never) produces such a sharp distinction between the effects of the experimental variables. In our work statistics are always necessary. Suppose that a few of the nonvaccinated animals had not died, perhaps because they had somehow previously developed an immunity by having come in contact with a weakened strain of anthrax. Pasteur was just learning how to develop the vaccine, and he did not fully understand the process. He might have produced a batch of vaccine that was not sufficiently potent for all the vaccinated animals to develop immunity. As a result, some of them might have died. If some animals had died in both groups, Pasteur would have needed a statistic for data analysis—just as we do in behavioral science research.

An "experiment," as the word is used in this text, has a much more restricted meaning than seems to be common. People think they are doing experiments when they do something one way and then change to a different way or even when they do something once to see what will happen. A great deal more is involved in an experiment than planting beans in a garden one year and peas the next, to determine which does better. That is research, but it does not fulfill the requirements of experimental design. Much of the material to follow in this chapter will help to define what experiments are and how to do them.

THE DIFFICULTY WITH "ONE-CONDITION" RESEARCH

When we collect data from a single group of subjects and use that as evidence, we do not have an experiment. A psychologist would not adequately demonstrate the effectiveness of his new therapy by using it on 17 of his patients and then pointing out that 14 of them improved.

Suppose I have an idea that a hot breakfast is important for the intellectual development of growing children. I could try to demonstrate the validity of my hypothesis by showing that children generally do well academically when they come from families in which some adult in the family gets up early each cold winter morning and fixes a hot breakfast before sending them off to school. This would not be an experiment because I would have failed to take account of and to allow for other factors that might be relevant.

In addition to the hot breakfast, it is likely these families differed from cold-breakfast or no-breakfast families in many ways—all of which could have an effect on the children's school experience. Parents who are concerned about their children's health and general welfare try to arrange their schedules so they can do what they think is best for the children. More is involved than just fixing a hot breakfast. Parents might use a moment to discuss the coming day's activities; offer support or encouragement for success in some coming event; and check that assignments, belongings, and supplies are collected and ready to go. The "hot breakfast" might not be the important point. The hot breakfast might be only a characteristic of a family that works together. To test a hypothesis that it is just the hot breakfasts that contribute to good academic performance, we probably could arrange to have hot breakfasts served from a vending machine!

One-condition research designs do not function as experiments and provide very little useful information, because effects of other "sufficient" conditions do not get canceled out. Recall that sufficient conditions are alternate causes, any one of which can by itself produce an effect. Experiments are designed to balance out, and in that way cancel effects of other possible causes, so the effects of *the* cause we want to study can be emphasized.

STRUCTURE OF A SIMPLE EXPERIMENT

The structure of a simple experiment is opposite to the *method of agreement*. That design, which is applicable to naturalistic observation, examines a number of instances in which an effect occurs and looks for the *single* entity on which all instances *agree*. There must be nothing else that is found to be common in all examples of the effect.

J. S. Mill's *method of difference* works in a way that is directly opposite to the method of agreement. An investigator manipulates, varies, or changes an "independent variable" to determine its effect on a "dependent variable." All other extraneous conditions in the two (or more) groups are kept as equivalent as possible. In an ideal experiment the *only* entity on which the conditions *differ* is the independent variable, the construct the investigator is studying.

There are three parts to a simple experiment. The two or more forms of independent variable are what we study to compare their effects. The dependent variable is the measurement of the experiment's outcome; this measurement is the same for all forms of the independent variable. Controlled conditions, potential confounding variables, are maintained as equivalent as possible in order to partial out any extraneous influence they might have on the dependent variable.

Table 9.1

STRUCTURE OF A SIMPLE EXPERIMENT			
Research Groups	Independent Variable	Controlled Conditions	Dependent Variable
First conditions	30 units	A B C D E	Test score
Second condition	75 units	A B C D E	Test score

The foundation in logic for controlling extraneous potential causes by maintaining them equivalent in all the conditions of the experiment can be briefly stated: *Nothing can be the cause of an effect if it is present both when an effect occurs and when it does not.* A young pianist carried a rabbit's foot and won a piano competition. A second pianist also carried a rabbit's foot, but he lost the competition. If a rabbit's foot was carried by both a winner and a loser (a given effect occurs in one case and does not in another), obviously the rabbit's foot is not a consistent cause of winning.

INDEPENDENT VARIABLES: SELECTION AND MANIPULATION

The independent variable is the one being studied. The word "variable" is an all-purpose term to mean anything that changes or that can be manipulated, modified, altered, or eliminated. These include attitudes, personality states, an emotion, or an experience. We could study objects of different colors, shapes or sizes, words with different meanings, or different amounts of money; different drugs would work, or different states of mind. Altered educational methods, different childhood experiences—or hundreds of thousands of other measures or observations would work.

Experiments that produce the most dependable results are those in which the variations of the independent variable are entirely under the control of the investigator while maintaining equivalence among all groups in everything else. In the previous example, I facetiously suggested a possible way of serving hot breakfasts to some students. That would not produce a good experiment, because I would be unable to control the complex family variable I think is important. As a last resort, we could select and compare families by *measuring* family differences we think are meaningful. The complex nature of behavioral science research often makes it difficult, even impossible, for investigators to systematically regulate the research variables being studied. As we will see, the alternate ways we have of getting around this frequent difficulty do not produce very good experiments.

I am often confused by an inconsistent way different writers have of describing the *independent variable* in the structure of experiments. A simple experiment has two conditions, but do we think of these as two independent variables, or two forms of one independent variable? I suggest that we standardize on the latter usage.

A psychologist could design a simple experiment in which he or she compared two varieties of fonts (printing types), Roman or Gothic, to determine which one was easier to read. The psychologist would need to operationally define ease of reading to include elements of both speed and accuracy. The fonts should be the same size, density, and, except for style, equivalent in other ways.

I do not recommend the labelling used by some investigators who would say that we are dealing with *two* independent variables—Roman and Gothic fonts. I prefer a more general expression which will work with simple experiments and be equally applicable as experimental designs become more complex. I recommend that simple experiments should be said to have" "*one independent variable with two or more 'levels.'"* I prefer to say that "variations of fonts" identifies the independent variable in the above experiment, and the levels are Roman or Gothic.

Suppose our object of study is learning during sleep by having tape-recorded material played back softly. Half our participants would listen to taped material they wanted to learn as they slept, and the other half would not listen to anything. I propose a term such as "material played during sleep" to generally identify the independent variable, and "present" or "absent" would be the levels.

Later we will look at complex experiments that involve two or more independent variables, each of which is present at different levels. A "2 × 2 (two by two) factorial design" would be an example of a complex experiment that has *two independent variables, each of which has two levels of manipulation.*

TYPES OF INDEPENDENT VARIABLES

A useful expansion and clarification of independent variables identifies three distinct types.

Variable Present or Absent

The simplest arrangement consists of having one variable present and another absent. This is the arrangement that is often taught as the only experimental design. A person either does or does not participate in a particular type of therapeutic program. We could study the personality correlates of people who do or do not seek psychotherapy or counseling. Students do or do not regularly use study questions in preparing for their tests. Drug experiments can supply easy examples of an independent variable as present (a drug was used) or absent (a drug was not used).

In most experiments it is not sufficient to do nothing as an alternate level of an independent variable. In drug research, for example, the group that is not involved in the active treatment should be administered a "placebo," a similar-appearing but otherwise innocuous substance or treatment. If a group of patients improves after taking a drug, it might be because of the drug's beneficial effect or it might be because of the suggestion resulting from the administration of something patients *thought* would help them. It could be the expectation of treatment rather than the treatment itself that produces the improvement. This reaction has been observed so often that it has been named the "placebo effect." This is an important extraneous condition in experimental design which must be controlled if valid conclusions are to be achieved. See the Endnote for an expanded illustration on the importance of placebos for drug research.

Finding a meaningful equivalent for the active variables in psychological experiments is much more difficult than it is for drug studies. Psychologists studying how viewing sexually explicit films influences subsequent behavior would need to do a great deal of thinking before selecting a second film. For the alternate level of the independent variable a film is needed that will be just as emotionally stimulating to the viewers as the X-rated films, but without the sexual orientation. It would not be satisfactory to use a film for one sample, provide nothing for the other group, and just say it is the control. Experiments that are of most interest to psychologists are generally also among the most complex. One recurring problem is to assess the effectiveness of psychotherapy. What is an appropriate control condition for the "nontherapy" group? It would be wrong to say that one group received psychotherapy and the other did not, because psychotherapy can take many forms: Talking to a neighbor, a minister, a teacher, or a friend might be of therapeutic value, as might taking a course in psychology or reading a book on the subject. The passage of time itself seems to have a curative effect on some people. We could be sure the second group did not receive a *particular* psychotherapy, but the alternative to one type of psychotherapy is not "no psychotherapy."

Variable Present in Different Amounts

Independent variables that can be *measured* permit allocation in varying amounts. Examples include improvement of mental health after varying periods of psychotherapy and academic performance as a function of number of homework assignments completed.

Time, weight, and length illustrate continuous variables, those that have no gaps. These can be contrasted with discrete variables that occur naturally in fixed units, such as the number of cars in the parking lot. The process of measurement forces continuous data into discrete units. Although length is a continuous type of variable, measurement of the length of an object produces a figure that is discrete.

When a variable such as time is to be used as an independent variable in an experiment, it is necessary for the investigator to divide it into discrete units in a meaningful way. Previous experience with the variable should suggest values that meet the practical consideration of not requiring too many research groups.

A study of the effect of sleep loss on performance might assign participants to groups having increasing 1-hour increments of sleep deficit. Such an experiment would be possible, but too many people would be needed for so many levels of the independent variable. "Amount of sleep" is the general independent variable which can be measured. Even though the measurement base is continuous, three levels of the independent variable can be developed easily: normal number of hours of sleep, 3 or 6 hours less sleep than the person normally requires.

Variable in Different Forms

Independent variables that come in different "forms" permit a third way of varying levels. This is a change of "kind" rather than a variation of amount or presence/absence. Suitable category differences might occur naturally, or they might be created by the investigator. The selection of fonts in the experiment mentioned earlier is an example of this arrangement.

Suppose we wanted to do research on the interesting topic of how group leadership affects the behavior of the group participants. We could do worse than to follow the design worked out a long time ago by Lippitt and White (in Barker et al., 1943). They studied the "'Social Climate' of Children's Groups" by randomly assigning children to groups having three different types of leadership: authoritarian, democratic, or laissez-faire. Groups met for the same lengths of time, and they worked on the same types of projects, but the style of leadership was varied.

Test designers have long assumed that easy items should be presented first on a test and more difficult, complex, items should be brought in later. A person who is frustrated early by difficult items might waste too much time working on them, or otherwise react differently to the later, easy items. This would, it is supposed, result in a lower score.

We could test the hypothesis by designing two tests. The items on them would be identical, but the order of items, according our estimate of difficulty (difficult to easy or easy to difficult), would be different. As always, subjects would be randomly assigned to one or the other group.

CONTROL CONDITIONS IN EXPERIMENTAL DESIGN

Basic Idea of Control

The following discussion will expand on the "Controlled Conditions" category illustrated in Table 9.1. Controlling extraneous variables is possibly the most difficult task facing an investigator who is designing an experiment. The job is to ensure equivalence of *all* variables that might affect one group in a way that is different from the other groups. We try to arrange the research design to do this, even when we do not even know what the possible relevant extraneous variables are.

The basic idea in experiments is that we try to design them to allow only the levels of the independent variable to change. If something else were to change concurrently, we would have trouble knowing whether we caused an observed difference in final results or whether "something else" did it. These "intervening variables"—confounding or secondary variables, or "confounds" as some people call them—are the troublemakers in research. When Underwood (1966, p. 32) introduced the term "confounding variables" in his text he explained:

> While "confounded" is a technical term as used here, its literary affective tone is perfectly appropriate for the situation. Thus, a confounding means that two or more stimulus variables have changed concurrently so that the results cannot be said to be attributable to a single stimulus variable. A confounded experiment is one in which the rule of allowing one and only one variable to change is broken.

Confounding variables act as alternate independent variables which experimenters would like to eliminate entirely from experiments if they could. An experiment becomes confounded if the experimenter fails to ensure equivalence of extraneous conditions among all research groups. In a confounded experiment there is no way to know which of several possible causes was *the* cause of an effect. Understand that investigators might not even be aware of some conditions that should be controlled. Table 9.2 illustrates that when extraneous variables have not been appropriately equated between the research groups, we cannot be sure what caused an obtained difference.

If the investigator in the fonts experiment mentioned earlier were not very competent, something like the following could happen: The professor used the students in the morning General Psychology class (the one required of all psychology majors) to do the reading exercise using Gothic fonts and the afternoon class (for nonmajors) to read the material in Roman type. Based on the reading measurement scores given in the "Dependent Variable" column, the professor concluded that the Gothic fonts were much better.

That conclusion failed to take into account possible confounding differences between the two groups of people who took part in the experiment. I think I could argue that psychology majors were, on the average, much better readers than an unselected group of freshmen taking the beginning course. This difference in basic reading skills could be enough to account for the observed difference in reading performance—it might not have been the font difference at all. Lack of control in subject selection produced a confounded experiment. The experiment might have worked had the investigator randomly assigned students from the same class to one or the other of the fonts.

The letters B, C, and D suggest that other extraneous control conditions were correctly maintained equivalent between the groups.

Some experiments—those in perception for example—might be arranged to use the same participants, who will respond to each of the independent variable manipulations. Advantages and disadvantages of this arrangement will be studied in a separate chapter. Many experiments are designed to use different subjects in the separate research conditions. If one group's participants are collectively different from people in other groups, the dissimilarity could become a confounding variable. That is the error I wanted to illustrate in the font experiment. Experimenters work very hard to select and assign subjects in an appropriate way to ensure group equivalence on what we call "subject variables." More on this point later.

Holding Experimental Conditions Constant

Anyone who has had even a very superficial introduction to experimental designs probably learned that an experiment "consists of an experimental group and a control group, an independent variable, a dependent variable, and all other conditions that are held constant."

Table 9.2

EFFECTS OF CONFOUNDING VARIABLES

Independent Variable	Control Conditions	Dependent Variable
IVX (Roman) P.M.	Poor readers B C D	35
IVY (Gothic) A.M.	Good readers B C D	45

This expression is so widely used it deserves a separate discussion.

> An essential part of an experiment that enables inferences to be made about causation is *experimental control.* One wants to isolate just the variable under investigation while holding all other variables constant."
>
> (Rubenstein, 1975, p. 21)

Although that reference happens to be from a general psychology text, similar statements can be found in experimental texts, as well as in texts for other disciplines that discuss experimental methods.

The fact is, there is very little in behavioral science experiments that can be "held constant." Certainly the state of the participants changes markedly from one time to another as the experiment progresses. Conditions in the physical environment come close to being held constant, but within a small range even light and temperature are always varying. The maintenance of "constant" conditions is neither possible nor necessary.

Underwood and Shaughnessy (1975, p. 16) provide a better way of understanding the idea of experimental control.

> When we say that we hold all variables constant except one, we must understand that literally we do not hold all variables constant.
>
> Rather, we devise our procedures in such a way that any effects of these uncontrolled variables will influence the behavior equally under the different levels of the independent variable. . . . we do not allow these potential independent variables to act differentially on our conditions of interest.

Investigators rightly devote a great deal of attention to maintaining research conditions and other relevant variables as equivalent as possible among the various levels of the independent variable. They know this is important, even though they also recognize that they will never achieve exact equivalence. A well-designed and appropriately executed experiment will help to reduce "error variance," but it cannot be entirely eliminated.

Control Groups in Research

Typical definitions of experiments often imply that the independent variable is limited to two conditions. The condition in which the variable is present establishes the "experimental group." A condition in which the variable is absent defines the "control group."

Some experiments *do not* require "control groups," *as the term is generally used.* The discussion on the various ways for manipulating independent variables noted the presence or absence of the independent variable as only one of the three alternatives. In psychological studies it is relatively uncommon for one of the groups to receive no treatment at all. The meaning of "control group" should be broadened to include concepts of what is ordinary, standard, or typical. When we do something to one group and leave the other group to do whatever is normal for it, the second group is the control.

I prefer not to use the term "control group" at all, because the term can be misleading and it suggests to inexperienced investigators that all experiments must have a control group. By definition, experiments have at least two groups. Identifying one of them as the control will sometimes make sense—drug studies are an obvious example—but the label adds nothing to our understanding of the experiment, and it is not necessary. Levels of the independent variable often take the form of different amounts or different kinds, none of which necessarily represent an everyday, nontreatment condition. Even the simple font experiment did not have what I would call a "control group."

The Dependent Variable

The dependent variable is a measurement used to assess the outcome of an experiment. Recall from the study of the hypothetical syllogism that the consequent—the dependent variable—is the result that was predicted by the antecedent/hypothesis. The dependent variable is a measurement of some operationally defined construct that identifies whatever it was the experimenter expected to change. This measurement is called the "dependent variable" because its value is presumed to *depend on* the action of the independent variable.

The dependent variable is the same for all participants in an experiment, no matter how many independent variables or how many levels of them have been manipulated. This statement partly defines "an" experiment in the sense that if several research studies had different dependent variables, they were in fact different experiments.

Much as investigators would like to personally arrange the variations of the independent variable for each experiment, that is not possible in many areas of behavioral science research. Quite often topics of interest can be studied only with data obtained from happenstance and accidents of nature or through *selection* by measurements or classification. The form of ex post facto research, to be discussed next, resembles experimental designs, but the technique is used in situations that do not permit independent-variable manipulation. Investigators are limited in the extent to which they can control extraneous variables, so results from this type of research are more ambiguous than they would be in a well-designed experiment that was under the control of the experimenter.

EX POST FACTO EXPERIMENTAL DESIGNS[2]

"Ex post facto designs" are a kind of experiment because they are based on an experiment's logical foundation as described in this chapter, but they lack the controls that are the bones and muscle and strength of true experiments. Some authors call this a "quasi-experimental design" because it has only some of the characteristics of experiments. Ex post facto (after the fact) designs are widely used in the behavioral sciences, because we frequently have no other way of

---

[2] Kerlinger (1973 and more recent editions) and Dunham (1988) both provide a more detailed exposition of this topic than coverage here will permit.

studying many of the topics that interest us. When a preexisting condition deter-mines whether a participant is *selected* for membership in one or another research group rather than being randomly assigned, we have an ex post facto research design.

Psychology often wants to study how behavior has been affected by a situa-tion that cannot be recreated. Many factors, including moral and ethical consider-ations, make it impossible for the investigator to alter levels of certain indepen-dent variables for study. Examples would include early experience, traumatic events, living in special situations, isolation, and deprivation, to mention a few. Ex post facto research designs are the only way we have of studying how present behavior has been affected by variables the investigator cannot experimentally manipulate.

The experimental method often uses random distribution for placing partic-ipants in research groups. Random assignment is a good way of balancing—and in that way canceling—the influence of extraneous, possibly confounding, vari-ables. In this way we will try to make the groups equivalent.

Subjects placed in groups because they already have the different levels of the independent variable the investigator wants to study might also differ in other ways that can affect the outcome. The situation is similar to correlational studies in the sense that extraneous variables are not controlled. This inherent difficulty should cause us to be very careful in our interpretation of ex post facto studies.

In a general way there are three forms of ex post facto research. The first method studies a "historical antecedent" to compare present behavior with possi-ble causes that came earlier. This technique is used in either of two ways. We could select participants in terms of defined or measured differences in present behavior and then examine records to identify conditions that might have caused them. Or we might reverse the order, according to our interest, and select subjects with reference to early conditions they were subjected to, then try to determine how these differences affect present behavior.

Goldman (1948) and Goldman-Eisler (1951) studied the "oral character" in personality and sought to identify its cause in the quality of breast feeding and the age of weaning. The 1948 article on "Breastfeeding and Character-Formation" pointed out that, "The description of adult character in terms of childhood experi-ence is one of the basic principles of psychoanalytic characterology, and indeed the (childhood experience) approach to human personality is the essence of the theory and method of psychoanalysis." Ex post facto analyses are widely used for studying the impact early experiences might have had on characteristics of per-sonality or behavior that came later.

If we wanted to study how long people lived "in the old days" compared to how long they live now, we could go to government offices and look at old records. But it might be easier, and likely more interesting, to just visit some old cemeteries. The birth and death dates on the tombstones would give us the infor-mation we need, but thoughtful observers have noted that cemeteries can provide even more information about the lives of people who lived in earlier times.

Many of the tombstones in Glasgow graveyards are obelisks. These come in a range of heights from about 6 feet to more than 30 feet. If one makes the appropriate assumption that rich people were buried under the taller obelisks, which were known to cost more, it would be possible to compare the life span of poor people and rich people at a time that predates modern medicine. When researchers did this, they found that on average the rich people did live longer. It might be interesting to speculate why this was so.

The second usage for the ex post facto method involves *measurement* of attributes in a way that allows for subject classification. Jenkins, Rosenman, and Friedman (1967) studied the "Type A" personality classification in connection with an increased tendency to have heart attacks. They developed an activity scale to classify people according to "Type A" or "Type B" personality profiles. Type A people seemed to be more prone to heart attacks. These are people who, when under pressure, will react with impatience, unnecessary hostility, and competitive reactions.

The concept of coronary-prone behavior was very appealing and produced a great deal of research. Rosenman (1978) provided an interesting "History and Definition of the Type A Coronary-Prone Behavior Pattern." Work by Ortega and Pipal (1984) should be consulted for more recent information.

The third general way of using ex post facto designs classifies subjects according to broader, rather than personal, characteristics: political affiliation, position within a company, attitude toward abortion—all suggest the idea.

Today there are many situations in which no adult is at home when the children return from school. Some of the time this happens because both parents are working, or the one parent in a single-parent home is working. How are children affected by this experience? An ex post facto analysis might provide an answer. Obviously there is no way that a laboratory situation could be created to duplicate the actual conditions of a child coming home to an empty house, day after day. To understand what the effects are, it is necessary to collect information from real cases, just as was done in the following studies. Here are two headlines to suggest answers.

LATCHKEY CHILDREN BIGGEST CLASSROOM PROBLEM, TEACHERS SAY

Most public school teachers in a national survey rated the widespread practice of leaving children on their own after school as the biggest cause of youngsters' difficulties in the classroom.

(*Chicago Tribune*, 1987, September 3)

CHILD GAINS IF MOM WORKS, STUDY FINDS

Children of working mothers tend to do better in school, are absent for fewer days, and have better communications skills, according to nationwide study by four Ohio researchers.

(*Chicago Tribune*, 1986, August 26)

Still another clipping provides a different point of view:

Cornell University researchers found that a mother's working has a salutary effect on girls but a negative effect on boys.

A little thought will uncover many ways in which families of latchkey children will differ from the family situation in which an adult caregiver is usually at home when the children return from school. These differences identify, indeed highlight, the weakness of ex post facto studies. When we *assign* subjects to research groups according to preexisting conditions, we cannot be sure that they are equivalent on extraneous variables that might also affect the dependent variable.

The complexity of "real-life" research, the inability of investigators to control extraneous variables, and the variety of entities measured could all account for the inconclusive findings of research in this area. Note the contradictions suggested in the above headlines. Rodman, Pratto, and Nelson (1985) summarized their work by noting that there was no significant difference between matched samples on personality variables they measured. "Results suggest that the growing public and professional concern about the negative effects of self-care arrangements may not be warranted." Messer, Wuensch, and Diamond (1989) also found no significant differences on personality and academic achievement measures. Padilla and Landreth (1989) have reviewed and summarized the literature on this topic.

To further illustrate the process of ex post facto research we could study a condition that is particularly relevant for college students. When do you study? Educators have often said that the best time to study course material is as soon as possible after the class has met. We would be faced immediately with an unsolvable problem if we wanted to do an "experiment" to determine whether this idea is true. We would start with a sizable group of college students, to be randomly assigned to several research groups. People in one group would be *required* to study immediately after class. People in a second group would be *required* to study only on weekends. A third group would be *required* to study only on the night before the major exams. People in each group would be permitted to study only at the assigned time, but everyone would study for the same number of hours. The dependent variable could be the grade earned on the exam.

I cannot think of any way at all to enforce these study arrangements on any randomly selected group of college students I have ever known. We might, however, learn something useful from an ex post facto research study. We could pay students in a large class to keep a diary or to complete a checklist of their study habits, and then we would group them according to their responses.

Basically we want to find out, "When do you usually study for major tests in this class?" The hypothesis is that grades will be better for people who study as soon as possible after class meetings. I do not know how we could check to be sure that what students report is in fact what they do. (Note that this is an example of a situation in which there is no "control group.") When data have been tabulated a table like Table 9.3 might result.

We can see that there are test performance differences among the groups, but we would be wrong to conclude that they were caused by differences in study arrangements. There might be advantages to studying immediately after class while the information is still fresh, but we can also speculate that people who do this are those who are interested, highly motivated, and whose schedules permit them to put their academic work first before everything else.

Table 9.3

EXAMPLE OF AN EX POST FACTO DESIGN EXPERIMENT

Experimental Groups	Independent Variable	Controlled Conditions	Dependent Variable*
Group Tom	After class	? ? ? ? ?	47
Group Dick	Weekend	? ? ? ? ?	44
Group Harry	Night before exam	? ? ? ? ?	38

*Average of the scores on a major comprehensive examination.

The question marks under "Controlled Conditions" are to emphasize that we do not know what relevant extraneous conditions have in fact been controlled, if any. Subjects have been selected for inclusion in one or another of the groups because of their reported study habits—a "pre-existing" condition. We have no assurance that groups are otherwise equivalent.

Students in Group Harry, those students who said they did their studying the night before the exam, on average got the lowest grades. We do not know if studying only before an exam is the worst way to study for a college exam. Students in this group might have been so busy with work, sports, or other commitments that they had no other time. These people might have been too tired to use the study opportunities effectively. The lower performance might also be accounted for by personality factors or levels of interest that caused them to postpone studying until the very last minute, when they could no longer avoid it. (People have been known to deal with their income taxes in this way.) It is not unknown for students to put off working on material for a class they do not like.

In some situations it is possible for an investigator to improve the quality of ex post facto research by pairing or matching subjects on qualities that he or she thinks could affect the results. Articles sometimes state that subjects were matched according to items such as the following: gender, year in school, socioeconomic level, and general ability. This might help a little to improve equivalence of the research groups, but we can never be sure that items selected for matching are the only important ones. Extraneous variables can be controlled only if we know what they are and only if we have a way to maintain them equivalent among all the groups.

Ex post facto studies cannot provide definitive answers to many questions that interest investigators in the behavioral sciences, but they are often the only technique that can be used. Despite the limitations, ex post facto research can be useful for the identification of functional rather than causal relationships. The method's primarily descriptive role places limitations on interpretation, but as long as we understand these restrictions we can take advantage of the research possibilities the method opens up for us. See the Endnotes for an example from medicine of an ex post facto experimental design.

LONGITUTINAL AND CROSS SECTIONAL RESEARCH METHODS

These two methods seem to me to be an extention or variation of the method of naturalistic observation because the independent variables to be studied are not under the control of the investigators. A common objective of both methods is to study changes that occur over long periods of time.

For the production of useful data the longitudinal method is possibly the better of the two. To use it we would select a large beginning sample and evaluate what happens to the subjects over the duration of the study. This is an excellent way to study what actually happens to people as they grow older, but the method has some serious defects.

I almost hesitate to point out a major defect in the longitudinal research method because it is so obvious—it takes a long time! If we need information today, we should have started working on it 40 years ago. But at that time we might not have known what to do. Anyone who has ever been involved in developing even a simple questionnaire for a survey (or who has ever completed one) knows how difficult it is to think of important, uncomplicated questions.

The longitudinal method works only if investigators ask the right questions and take the right measurements at the beginning of data collection. This establishes the baseline against which later measurements are compared to identify changes produced by the passage of time. Science is not much advanced by an investigator suddenly having an idea that should have been considered half a century earlier.

The "Framingham Heart Study," which was begun in 1948, continues to provide medical science with a great deal of useful information about what happens as people age. Over 5,200 men and women between the ages of 28 and 62 were enrolled in the study when it began. A number of physiological measurements related to cardiovascular conditions were taken at the beginning, and participants have been reexamined every 2 years since the study began (Dawber, Kannel, & Lyell, 1963).

One finding that might be important for older readers (Sagie, Martin, Larson, & Levy) was published in the New England Journal of Medicine in 1993. It helped to give guidance to physicians who needed information on when to begin treatment for hypertension (high blood pressure). Medicine has established "normal limits," but there is a lingering concern about whether to treat or not to treat people who are on the borderline. The investigators found that, ". . . after 20 years of follow-up, 80 percent of those with borderline isolated systolic hypertension had progression to definite hypertension." This increased the risk of cardiovascular disease sufficiently to warrant the recommendation to begin treatment sooner than had previously been the practice.

Conclusions of this sort, and a great many others that have come out of the Framingham study, could not have been made except through a longitudinal evaluation. Although long-term studies like this one are very expensive, the results they produce can be of consideral importance to a great many people. If psychology, with the backing of the government, undertakes to implement American Psychological Society recommendations for "psychological research for productive aging," the longitudinal method will become very important. See "The Graying of America: An Aging Revolution in Need of a National Research Agenda" (Cavanaugh & Park, 1993). The special issue in which this discussion appears features four priorities or directions for studying older people and the many characteristics of the aging process.

A graduate student who wants to study memory changes as people age should have started a long time ago if he or she wants to use a longitudinal evaluation. Since that is not possible, the *cross-sectional* method would be the next-best choice. Instead of studying people at regular intervals as they age, say every 5 years from 20 to 80 years of age, the investigator might just measure, compare, and evaluate differences among people of designated ages.

The difference between the cross sectional and longitudinal methods, in terms of the data each produces, becomes clear if we look at possible changes in intelligence that presumably result from increasing age. It would be easy enough to give intelligence tests to people of different ages to identify a possible divergence. We would not, however, have the very important initial base line to guarantee the subjects were at equivalent levels of intelligence when they were all at the same age. If older people seem to be less intelligent, it might be because of a mental deterioration, or it might be because of poor health, motor deficiencies, or an inadequate educational background, any of which could affect test results. Older people who differ from younger people in intelligence are often different in other ways as well as age.

HOW TO IDENTIFY INDEPENDENT AND DEPENDENT VARIABLES

Readers who want to make sense out of journal articles must learn to differentiate between independent and dependent variables. It is easy to explain the difference between these two elemental parts of an experiment, but the task of identifying them can be quite confusing when a reader is faced with actual examples from the scientific literature. Research is sometimes complicated, the space available for description and discussion is always limited, and the writing in journal articles is not always so clear as it might be. We would more easily understand a piece of research if authors would identify the major parts for us, but they rarely do.

The task of identifying variables can be even more difficult in the occasional experiment in which the variables have a different function at different places in the research. A dependent variable for one part could later become an independent variable. This sort of twist keeps readers alert.

Perhaps I could suggest some hints to help identify independent and dependent variables. The "IV" is the entity the researchers are studying. The levels of the independent variable may be "manipulated" or selected to be different. The independent variable is the entity the researcher wants to find out about by determining how its different levels affect something else.

The dependent variable is normally a measurement or observation that attempts to determine what changes or differences were likely to have resulted from differing levels of an independent variable. No matter how many levels of a *single* independent variable were manipulated in any one experiment, the outcome would be measured by a single dependent variable. I find it is easier to use the number of dependent variables rather than the number (*not levels*) of independent variables in a study to identify the number of separate experiments.

PRACTICE IN INDEPENDENT- AND DEPENDENT-VARIABLE IDENTIFICATION

Following are some paragraphs of the sort we would find in the *Psychological Abstracts*. Some of these are derived from actual examples. The task here is to identify the independent and dependent variables for each experiment. In the process, one is likely to discover that memorizing definitions and knowing how to use them are not the same thing. There is no substitute for practice.

Instructions

In the following paragraphs identify and copy the *independent variable and its several levels* and the *dependent variable* for each experiment. Some examples might include several different independent (IV) and/or dependent (DV) variables. Only one dependent variable is used in each separately defined experiment. Variables might sometimes have to be inferred when they are not named directly. Material that was learned earlier about constructs and their appropriate operational definitions now becomes important. If a measurement of some sort is mentioned, it is useful to be aware of the construct it defines. A Binet test, for example, is an operational definition of intelligence or "IQ" as it is referred to colloquially.

Example

1. This experiment compared how studying with the radio on or with it off affected a person's grade in the experimental psychology class.

Answer

IV	Levels	DV
Study conditions	Radio on	Experimental psychology grade
	Radio off	" " "

2. Some students with high IQs are successful academically, while other equally intelligent students are not. This observation suggests that academic performance involves more than intellectual ability. Science

achievement, for example, has been shown to be different for people who have good or poor levels of abstract thinking, flexibility of approach, and creativity. These findings can be interpreted as demonstrating the importance of "intellectual style" in science achievement. Important gender differences were also observed.

IV	Levels	DV
Abstract thinking achievement scores	Good	Science course grade
	Poor	" " "
Flexibility of approach achievement scores	Good	Science course grade
	Poor	" " "
Creativity achievement scores	Good	Science course grade
	Poor	" " "
Gender	Male	Science course grade
	Female	" " "

Examples for Practice

1. Reading achievement of pupils who had received computer-assisted instruction in reading was compared with pupils who did not. Twenty-two pairs of first-grade boys and girls were matched on Generic Reading Readiness scores. Separation of girl and boy matched pairs was maintained to allow cross-sex comparisons.

2. Students in a beginning statistics class were classified into two groups according to the way they studied: a logical group and a mnemonic group. Students in the logical group received significantly higher grades on several different academic criteria, which included: course grade, examination grades, class participation, and individual reports. The two groups were statistically equivalent on six measures of ability. Removal of these measures from consideration did not reduce performance differences between the groups. Differences in learning strategy indicate differences in learning processes. These results suggested that it may be possible to develop learning techniques to improve learning on specified tasks.

3. Both attitudes and behavior of members of a commune and members of a fraternity and a sorority were compared on appropriate measurement checklists. Commune members, as predicted, showed considerably more favorable attitudes toward nontraditional values, whereas their fraternity/sorority counterparts viewed traditional concepts more favorably. More commune members chose cooperation rather than competition on a strategy game test.

4. Systematic desensitization was compared with training in efficient study methods for reducing test anxiety among subjects selected on the basis of two types of self-reported anxiety. Subjects reporting high levels of emotion prior to or during examinations were expected to benefit more from treatment by desensitization. Subjects reporting high levels of worry but not emotion were expected to profit more from training.

This hypothesis was not supported. Desensitized subjects reported significantly less anxiety during a final examination than did no-contact control subjects. Control subjects received higher examination scores than did study-skills subjects. Desensitization offered more promise as a treatment method for test anxiety than did training in study skills.

5. All members of 11 experimental families and 9 lecture-control families were evaluated before and after seven weekly counseling sessions and again at a 6- to 8-month follow-up. Parents in both groups showed a significant increase in perceived marital adjustment at posttesting and at the follow-up. The finding suggests that for educated, middle-income families, the critical components in parent counseling may be the mere presentation of information and didactic instruction.

6. Situational factors that might influence the manifestation of dominance (DO) were investigated by pairing subjects according to high or low scores on a CP dominance scale. Pairs of subjects interacted on tasks in which one had to lead and the other had to follow. In experiments using a "masculine" industrial task and a sexually neutral clerical task the following subject pairs were studied:

Group 1: High and Low DO men

Group 2: High DO men and Low DO women

Group 3: Low DO men and High DO women

Group 4: High and Low DO women

Assumption of leadership by the High DO women in Group 3 was significantly lower in both studies. This was attributed to sex-role conflict inhibiting the manifestation of DO.

ENDNOTES

Importance of Placebos in Research: Aspartame

When aspartame, distributed under the trade name NutraSweet, became widely used in foods there were at least 3,500 complaints to the FDA commissioner that the product caused headaches and sometimes mild dizziness. To study this condition, NutraSweet was tested on a group of 40 people who had complained to the manufacturer about their reactions to the sweetener.

> Researchers gave the subjects capsules containing NutraSweet or identical-looking capsules containing cellulose. No one knew until the study was over which capsules contained NutraSweet.... Eight people complained of headaches after ingesting NutraSweet, while 12 suffered them after taking the neutral capsules. Six got them after both kinds of capsules.
>
> (Chicago *Tribune*, 1987, November 5, p. 18)

It was concluded that it was not possible to attribute headaches to the consumption of NutraSweet.

Attention should be called to an important and easily overlooked phrase in this account: "No one knew until the end which capsules contained NutraSweet."

It is obvious that the subjects themselves should not know whether they are taking NutraSweet or the placebo, the control substance. They should be "blind" to which level of the independent variable has been given to them. Research experience has shown that experimenters who know which subjects are receiving which treatment can also affect an experiment's outcome. Investigators who are actually running experiments should be protected from letting their expectations bias experimental results by withholding details of the treatment conditions from them. The "double blind" term sometimes seen in reference to experiments means that both the subjects and the experimenters who actually carry out the experiment should be "blind" regarding which subjects had which treatment. The participant in the drug study must not know whether he or she is getting the drug or the placebo, but neither must the clinical investigator.

Because medication can be administered in many different ways—by tablet, capsule, syrup, ointment, or injection—placebos must also be created to take the same form. If a product has a distinctive odor, color, taste, or texture this makes it more difficult to create a placebo for it. Of course, if a drug can be put into a capsule there is no problem. A particularly bad-tasting syrup would be difficult to duplicate with a placebo. Drug companies pay a great deal of attention to the development of fakes that seem real. The requirement that the placebo seem real is applicable to everyone who comes into contact with the product, and it extends even to the type of packaging.

A psychologist who does research with humans must have their approval for participation. As part of this approval process, participants should be told as much as possible about the experiment—and that is sometimes the difficulty. Much of the research of interest to psychologists requires that some relevant information should be withheld from them. We want to be ethical, but the reality of our work does not always give us the option of a full explanation before the experiment.

Suppose you were hired by a drug company to study the side effects of a new medication. A person would not have to be a psychologist to predict what the results would be if subjects were given these instructions: "I want to give you two different kinds of pills on alternate days in order to study their side effects. The red pills are more effective as a treatment, but we need to establish whether they do—as we suspect—cause more headaches than the white ones."

Accepting what psychology already knows about the "placebo effect" it follows that a full disclosure of possible side effects in drug experiments might actually produce the effects the experiment was being conducted to find out about. The ethics of psychological research require us to inform prospective participants what to expect in an experiment. Some subjects who have been told to be on the lookout for headaches, stomach upset, lethargy, or muscle cramps are more likely to experience these symptoms, even with a placebo, than would have been the case had they not been mentioned. Loftus and Fries (1979) have written an editorial for *Science* to point out that "Informed Consent May Be Hazardous to Your Health." Fully explaining what harmful effects a participant might expect in an experiment might become an independent variable that would actually produce the results the subject was being warned to be on the lookout for.

Ex Post Facto Research in Medicine:
Puerperal Fever

Medical research tends to be more involved with naturalistic observation (and Mill's method of agreement) than with the experimental method. When a disease has a single cause, simple techniques of discovery are often sufficient for practical identification. Naturalistic observation offers useful but not entirely convincing evidence for causal relationships. Well-controlled ex post facto experiments are relatively rare, but an example of an important one follows.

This illustration is from a chapter in H. W. Haggard's book, *Devils, Drugs, and Doctors,* (1946 and earlier editions). "Gentleman With Clean Hands May Carry the Disease" is the chapter to read (although I cannot see how a person would limit his or her reading to only one chapter of this very interesting volume). I have now read this chapter many times, always with fascination and surprise that people could not have seen what now appears to be obvious. A bright high school student who has had a course in biology could probably put the facts together that were known to the people in the 1700s and suggest a cause. Many hundreds of women needlessly died during childbirth because no one integrated the facts that were available to them. New information was not necessary; they only needed good ideas.

The disease known as childbed or puerperal fever had been known from ancient times, but only as an occasional occurrence. The outbreaks of the disease greatly increased as medical practitioners working in lying-in hospitals became more common. During a 200-year period following 1652, the number of epidemic outbreaks averaged one a year. It was thought to be caused by the weather.

A scientist of about the time of our Declaration of Independence had a number of clues with which to work. A doctor could have concluded that there was something about lying-in hospitals that was the cause. Note that evaluation of the following information would follow the method of agreement.

1. The increase of the disease roughly paralleled an increase in the lying-in hospitals of Europe.
2. Childbirth itself was not the cause, because expectant mothers who did not use the lying-in hospitals were not nearly so often affected.

Oliver Wendell Holmes probably should be credited with being the first to have a fundamental understanding of the nature of child-bed fever. He is perhaps best know as a writer, but he was also a physician and a professor of anatomy at Harvard Medical School. His paper on "The Contagiousness of Puerperal Fever" (1843) was not well known in Europe where the disease was more serious. Holmes argued that the disease was caused by physicians with dirty hands who carried it from one patient to another. His disclosures were not well received in the medical community even in the United States.

He reported an instance in which a doctor attended a dissection of a patient who died of puerperal fever, and in the process he examined and handled some of the diseased tissue. The doctor's next four patients were affected with puerperal fever, and the doctor had not previously seen the disease in his practice. Other people had also observed that incidence of the disease tended to run in cycles of a few successive cases for a doctor and then it would not occur for a period of time.

Semmelweis is normally given credit for identifying the nature of child-bed fever. He both made his discovery and tested it using an ex post facto experimental design. The assignment of Semmelweis to a maternity hospital in Vienna gave an opportunity for the experiment. The hospital was divided into two divisions. Medical students were trained and instructed in one division, and women who were studying to be midwives were trained in the other. In the division where the medical students were trained there were between 68 and 158 deaths from puerperal fever for each 1,000 births, which averaged about 99 over a 6-year period. In the division for the training of midwives the average was 33.

The accepted idea that the weather was somehow the cause of the disease can be rejected because the weather was the same in both divisions. Crowding of patients could not be the cause, because patients were equally crowded in both divisions. Religious observances were altered, so a possible differential influence they might have had could be eliminated. Many other possible causes, such as dirty laundry, ventilation, diet, and characteristics of the patients were eliminated from further consideration by noting that they were equivalent in both divisions. Even the assignment of patients to one division or the other was random. The only difference was that medical students as part of their training were sometimes required to work on the bodies of women who had died of the puerperal fever. They also made internal examinations of women. The unwashed hands of the doctor as he went from one patient to another could be the mode of disease transmission. Even when hands were normally washed with soap and water as was the practice, the odor remaining on them was evidence that they were not really clean.

With these observations in mind, Semmelweis required the medical students under his care to wash their hands in a solution of "chloride of lime" before making medical examinations. The death rate from puerperal fever was 120 per 1000 patients in the medical training division at that time. After careful hand-washing procedures were instituted, the death rate dropped during the following 7 months to 12 per 1,000. "In that year there were 2 months in which not one single death occurred" among the patients in that division. For the first time in the history of the hospital, the death rate for patients in the physician-training unit were below the rate in the division for the training of midwives.

Semmelweis was the first to recognize that puerperal fever is the same disease we now call "blood poisoning," and he died of it from a puncture wound to his finger during an operation. His death occurred on August 13, 1865, not quite 6 months after the conclusion of our Civil War.

STUDY QUESTIONS

1. What is an experiment?

2. What are some of the characteristics that identify a good experiment?

3. Explain some differences between the Pasteur anthrax experiment and typical experiments in psychology.

4. Why are statistics so important for research in psychology? Why were the results of Pasteur's experiment not questioned, even though he did not use statistics?

5. Explain the difference between an "experiment" as the word is used in this text and the way it is more commonly used.

6. What are some difficulties with one-condition research designs, and why are they not suitable for behavioral science research?

7. Why are experiments usually carried out with groups of subjects?

8. Why do experiments always require at least two types of research conditions?

9. What is the basic structure of a simple experiment?

10. What is the "logic" of a simple experimental design?

11.D Explain the "method of difference" and contrast it with the "method of agreement."

12. What does it mean to "nullify the differential effects of extraneous variables"?

13. What are three different ways for introducing variations of an independent variable?

14.D What determines how many levels of an independent variable an investigator will use?

15. What is the basic idea of experimental control?

16. What is "confounding" in an experiment? What are some techniques we use in trying to avoid it?

17. What does the following phrase mean in reference to confounding? ". . . its literary affective tone is perfectly appropriate for this situation."

18. What is the problem when two or more stimulus variables change concurrently?

19. Except for the independent variable, why is it important to maintain experimental conditions equivalent among all research groups?

20. Explain why it is not necessary to hold conditions in an experiment "constant," as long as they do not differentially affect one or another of the groups.

21. What type of independent variable is necessary in order to call one of the experimental groups the "control group"?

22. What are two correct uses of the "control group" identifying label?

23. What is a "dependent variable," and what is its function in experimental designs?

24. How many different dependent variables could be used in a single experiment?

25. What is an ex post facto research design?
What are some advantages and disadvantages of this method?
What is a common defect of all of them?

26. Explain subject selection by measurement in ex post facto design.

27. What are some other ways for selecting subjects for an ex post facto research design?

28. How might one explain the several different conclusions from studies of latchkey children?

29. What are some rules you can give for the identification and differentiation between independent and dependent variables?

30. What is the "placebo effect," and how is it important in psychological research?

31. What is a "double blind" research design, and what is its importance for research?

SMALL TALK

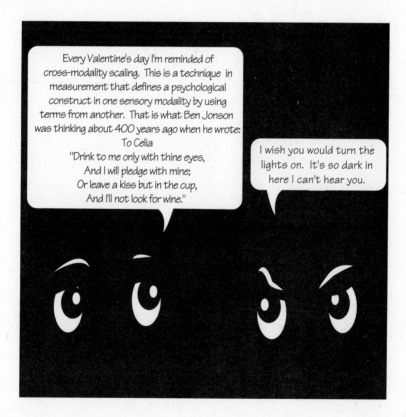

Chapter
10

Random Assignment for Control of Subject Variables

The only way to have real success in science, the field I'm familiar with, is to describe the evidence very carefully without regard to the way you feel it should be. If you have a theory, you must try to explain what's good and what's bad about it equally. In science, you learn a kind of standard integrity and honesty.

Feynman & Leighton (1988), pp. 217–18.

VALIDITY IN EXPERIMENTAL DESIGNS

"Validity" is a very important word for the behavioral sciences. It must be—we use it in so many different ways. Early in this text we discussed the validity of syllogisms. I felt it was important to show that logical arguments might be "true" but if there was an error in the structure of the argument we could not depend on the conclusion always being true.

Although psychological testing is not the focus of this text, it has been necessary to mention test validity. In a general way, test validity identifies the extent to which we can rely on the test to do the job of measuring what it claims to measure. The idea of test validity is simple enough, but its demonstration and application with real tests can get quite involved.

We need to pause here briefly to introduce a third type of validity into our vocabulary. The discussion of experimental designs becomes more meaningful when we include some concepts of validity that are applicable to experiments. The structure of an experiment, like the structure of a syllogism, must be set up correctly so we can depend on the results. Readers of this text will already know the general characteristics of a good experimental design. The difficulties that face investigators are practical ones. We might know what a good experiment looks like, but putting one together provides a never-ending challenge for those who undertake research in the behavioral sciences.

Internal Validity

"Internal" and "external validity" are two terms that are likely to be seen often as we read the literature of psychology. Campbell (1957), and Campbell and Stanley (1963) divided research validity into two logically different but interrelated forms: internal and external. "Validity" here means the extent to which we can rely on the results of our research to be accurate and true.

When miscellaneous extraneous conditions have been well handled so their influence is essentially alike for all levels of the independent variable, we would say the experiment has good *"internal validity* . . . the basic minimum without which any experiment is uninterpretable" (Campbell & Stanley, 1963, p. 5). Experiments must have a high level of internal validity if they are to be of any value. Internal validity of an experiment is a necessary but not a sufficient condition for good research. We must have internal validity, but that is not all we need for practical research.

External Validity

Normally (although not necessarily always) we want to generalize results of experimental findings to a similar group in "the real world." The extent to which this can be accomplished depends in part on the content of what was measured— i.e., the dependent variable and what we expect to do with the results. Experiments in perception, which are designed to study similarities, would be handled in a different way from those that study small-group processes, for example. The customary objective is to select subjects so they adequately represent a larger group to which we want to generalize the findings. Experiments that permit this are said to have "external validity." We will come to appreciate the importance of using a good random sample of subjects from a defined population. Good work in this area will permit results from an experiment, which was based on samples, to be generalized back to the population.

EQUATING SUBJECT VARIABLES

The preceding chapter established the structural foundations for experiments. It explained the reasons why experiments need at least two research conditions, and it emphasized the importance of keeping extraneous conditions equivalent among all levels of the independent variable.

The careful control of research conditions will be largely useless if subjects in one research group differ markedly from subjects in the other one. Differences among participants are uncontrolled variables. Inadequately selected or improperly assigned subjects reduce the internal validity of experiments and make it difficult to be sure that observed differences in the dependent variable were caused by the controlled variation of the independent variable. The font experiment was an example of this error.

I can further illustrate this point with an example that is ridiculous in the extreme. Suppose a not very good investigator, wanting to study the effects on behavior that result from viewing pornographic films, compares these with the effects of emotional films that are not pornographic. The researcher puts all women subjects to observing one type of film and all men subjects observing the other. Readers can decide which gender saw which type of film! This "experiment" would not permit a decision about the effects of viewing pornographic/emotional films because two research variables were allowed to change concurrently: the type of film and the gender of the viewer. A better approach requires that we maintain equivalence of subjects for all levels of the independent variable. Each type of film would be viewed by subjects of each gender.

Gender is only one of a great many "subject variables," as they are traditionally called, that could have an effect on the outcome of an experiment. The term, "subject variables," includes any and all of the myriad of ways subjects can differ. There are, of course, far too many characteristics to think of listing them, but even if we were to list a few we would have to think of each person's chemistry, biology, physical structure, personality, cognitive ability, background, training, experience, age, culture—and the list goes on. Some of these will be important for certain experiments, but others will be irrelevant and can be ignored. Subjects' academic background might be an attribute to evaluate for a learning experiment, but height is not likely to be of any consequence to the outcome. In other experiments height might become an important extraneous variable that must be taken into account.

Subject variables cannot be eliminated from experiments, but their influence can be moderated by keeping them at equivalent levels for all groups. "Nothing can be the cause of an effect if it is present both when the effect occurs and when it does not." Experiments that permit two or more sets of characteristics to change concurrently violate the most basic rule for good experimental design.

The last chapter explained that one of the difficulties of ex post facto research designs involves this very point. Subjects who are *selected* because of preexisting differences we want to study might also be dissimilar in other ways that could affect the outcome.

This chapter will look at ways for *assigning subjects* to form experimental groups that are as similar as possible on subject variables. *Random methods* will be studied first, then techniques for *matching subjects* will be studied in another chapter. The best techniques that can be devised cannot guarantee subject equivalence among samples. Only when we use twins who have been carefully studied to be certain they are identical can we have solid confidence regarding equivalence of our groups on subject variables. In all other cases the investigator is responsible for assigning subjects appropriately to ensure that research groups are comparable on subject variables.

COMBINED RANDOM SELECTION AND ASSIGNMENT PROCEDURES

The selection and assignment of participants to research groups can be understood as a two stage process. First, an investigator identifies a group of possible participants for an experiment. In the second stage they are assigned to research groups. Work by May and Hunter (1988) has demonstrated that many people, both students and faculty, confuse the roles of random sampling and random assignment. Most participants in their study correctly associated random sampling with external validity, the accuracy with which research results can be generalized. The greatest number of errors of interpretation occurred when people reported that random assignment of subjects to research groups was done to improve generalization of results. This chapter will attempt to make it clear that random assignment of participants to research groups is done in order to balance out subject variations and in that way help to remove that source of error to internal validity.

One of the oldest names for subject assignment is "random-groups design," but the newer "randomized groups" title seems to be replacing it. "Random assignment," "unbiased samples," or "unrelated samples" are other titles that are sometimes seen. Statistics texts often use entirely different terms to describe the same method: "independent groups," "uncorrelated samples," or "unpaired designs."

When an investigator can select the people to participate in an experiment, strategies for subject assignment can be incorporated in the procedures. Sampling techniques satisfactory for internal validity should distribute subject variables evenly among samples according to their proportion in the population. External validity requires that samples as a group should represent the characteristics of the population, so generalization of research findings will be appropriate.

Picture a "population" as an unbounded irregular group of many possible participants. My mental image is something like the one illustrated in Table 10.1. Let each letter represent a person who has certain characteristics. We use a suitable method for pulling individuals (letters) out of the population so subject characteristics will occur an equal number of times in the samples.

Pretend that we wrote each letter on a slip of paper and put all of them in a box. We pulled out three groups of 15 slips each to form three samples. We counted the number of letters (people) of each type in each group. The values in the f(requency) column show the number of times that particular letter was randomly selected for inclusion in that group. The sum of the f's equals 15 (N=15), the sample size.

At the same time that subjects were randomly selected, they were also being randomly assigned. One person was selected and assigned to the X group. Another person was randomly selected and assigned to the Y group, and a third person went to Z. The important letters selected for illustration here are distributed

Table 10.1

A HYPOTHETICAL RANDOM SELECTION AND ASSIGNMENT DIAGRAM

VAAH
EEIWADESTAVEN
EIGHAJAKLSAUCACVABEEN
AZECIVABEONSAELIKJAHEGIFADAOSADZAA
EMANEEBAVVAOICAXZESLAJUAKEOFIEDWAQAWRATEQ
AAWEERTAYEEDVABUANAMMOEANEEBAVCXE
EFAGEHAGIFEADGIHAAWIEQAAQFAQIWARS
ZAIXASTEVAUBIMAOZXWAAAEERAWRISADIFGAH
VAACIAXESAAAVOSADEGAGOHAWRWAIIAZXAAEDAEIGA
AQWEAORTAYIPAASAEDAUSAAEDFAGFIZXCAVBO

Sample 1		Sample 2		Sample 3	
X		Y		Z	
f Item		f Item		f Item	
8	A	9	A	4	A
4	E	3	E	5	E
2	I	1	I	3	I
1	O	2	O	3	O

approximately as follows in the population: 80 A, 40 E, 20 I, and 10 O, (150 total), together with a miscellaneous assortment of uncounted other letters that are not assumed to affect the experiment.

Sample 1 illustrates a theoretically ideal random selection and assignment of 15 subjects. The proportion of subjects in the sample was identical to the proportion of possible subjects of the same type in the population. Not every sample will turn out so well, but they should be close. Most of the time they will be. Samples 2 and 3 are more nearly typical of the way in which samples vary. Even though they are not all identical, they are probably close enough for useful work.

The assumption necessary for statistical evaluation holds that at the beginning of an experiment sample means (based on relevant measurements) will be approximately equal to each other and close in value to the mean of the population. The *possibility* of biased, nonequivalent samples keeps good experimenters constantly on guard against an enthusiastic interpretation of research findings.

Recall from statistics that randomly selected subjects do not need to be in groups of exactly the same size, but we should try to get them as close as possible.

RANDOM ASSIGNMENT TECHNIQUES

Lottery and Counting Methods

Investigators in the behavioral sciences do not often have the opportunity to select participants randomly from a large group of potential subjects. More commonly, we make use of all the people we can get. In that situation the investigator's task becomes one of assigning participants to research conditions in a way that is appropriate to equalizing subject variables.

The reason why random assignment techniques are often the preferred method might not be obvious. Justification for the method rests on the widely accepted idea that laws of chance will, over many trials, balance out differences and irregularities. Even the best techniques of random selection and assignment will not always produce equivalent samples, but they will do so most of the time, *if samples are large enough*. We must keep in mind that even a procedure that will be right most of the time must also be wrong occasionally. This should not happen often, but it will happen.

One of the easiest ways to randomly assign subjects to research groups, when one has a list of potential participants, is to select every fifth or every tenth person—or whatever proportion is necessary to produce samples of appropriate size. This method would be satisfactory when it is safe to assume that relevant subject characteristics are evenly spread throughout the list.

Sequential Random Assignment Using Random Number Tables

This is a reasonable place to introduce random number tables and explain how they are used. The basic idea of these tables is simple; they list a large number of digits in a random sequence. A person would find it very nearly impossible to make up a random number series because favorite or preferred numbers would keep getting listed in the same order more frequently than they should. The best way to avoid this is to use one of the published random number tables.[1] Complete tables are given in many experimental or statistics texts. They differ somewhat from each other, but their basic method of use is similar. Table 10.2 shows a sample of a *continuous random sequence* of digits 1 through 9. The space was left after each five numbers to help keep track of locations. The idea of a continuous sequence has been emphasized to differentiate this method of presentation from a method of *block randomization* to be discussed later.

Assume that an experimenter has the following group of 12 people to be randomly assigned to three groups, labeled 1, 2, or 3.

Karen	Bill	Rachel	Henry	Mark	Doris
Carol	Bonnie	Duke	Ana	Ralph	Allen

Because only three experimental groups are required, numbers 1, 2, and 3 will be the only numbers used. All other numbers will be skipped and ignored. The idea in the selection procedure is to put a finger on a name and ask the random number table where that person is to be assigned. Start anyplace at all on the table and go in any direction, but be consistent. It would be appropriate to begin each row at the left side and read across to the right or start on the right and go across to the left. We can start each row at the same end, or we can zigzag. It makes no difference. To make this example easier to follow we will start in the upper left corner.

---

[1] Computer programs are available, and even some calculators can produce a random number sequence.

Table 10.2

TABLE OF RANDOM NUMBERS—CONTINUOUS SEQUENCE									
73489	19778	49916	64853	27619	34291	97784	42161	16972	75334
87751	45356	94948	25551	98453	83591	81489	83316	88941	35836
22632	45394	97694	75577	48516	27817	37235	84255	29728	88562
35402	58466	62773	57367	37522	13267	97215	86371	49877	46324

With a finger on Karen we run our eyes along the random number sequence and find that 3 is the first number that appears from the 1 or 2 or 3 digits we are using. Karen's name would be written in the 3 column of Table 10.2. Bill will be assigned to Group 1 because 1 appears next. Continuing, Rachel goes to Group 1, Henry to 3. Next Mark is assigned to 2, Doris to 1, and Carol to 3.

Although nearly all investigators recommend random assignment as the best way of achieving equality of subjects in research groups, actual experience with random number tables clearly shows a defect in the method. Numbers in a short sequence of random digits nearly always form "runs," in which the same numbers appear more often than chance says they should.

Table 10.3 illustrates what usually happens when assignments are made from a short continuous sequence of random numbers. I have done this exercise many times using many different random number tables, and I have *never* found an instance in which the three groups end up with equal numbers of people in them. After reading *Innumeracy* (Paulos, 1988), which will be discussed briefly in Chapter 11, I have become aware that a continuous random sequence of digits works only over a very long list of thousands of numbers. Although the idea is to end up with equal numbers in each group, that rarely happens when assigning a small group of subjects. If the same numbers sometimes follow each other in rather close order, that is just the way random numbers are in short runs. All numbers should turn up equally often in a very long sequence, but not in a short list. A quick look along the first row shows there are only two 5's listed, compared to eight 9's. In the second row there are nine 5's, including one group of three together, but only six 9's. Because a random number table does not work well for a small group of assignments, the technique of *block randomization* was developed to deal with small groups.

Table 10.3

ASSIGNMENT USING A CONTINUOUS RANDOM NUMBER SEQUENCE		
1	2	3
Bill	Mark	Karen
Rachel	Bonnie	Henry
Doris	Ana	Carol
Duke		
Ralph		
Allen		

Block Randomization

The same table can be used, but this time people are selected in "blocks." For convenience in studying the example, the names are reproduced below together with the first row of numbers from Table 10.3. Again use only digits 1, 2, and 3.

73489   19778   49916   64853   27619   34291   97784   42161   16972   75334

Karen	Bill	Rachel	Henry	Mark	Doris
Carol	Bonnie	Duke	Ana	Ralph	Allen

Begin block assignment in the same way that was used for random assignment. Put the first person on the list in a group according to the first number (1, 2, or 3) that appears in the random sequence. The next *different* number will be used to identify where the next person will be listed. The third person in the block will be put in whatever group has not yet received a person. Stop after the first two assignments have been made and assign the third person in the block to the remaining group. Karen would be assigned to Group 3 and Bill would go to Group 1, just as they did before. Groups 1 and 3 have had assignments, so Rachel automatically goes to Group 2 because she is the third person in the block and that group has not yet received a subject.

After the three people in the block have been assigned, we start over using whichever number (1, 2, 3) comes next after the first two numbers used for assigning the first three people. Henry would go to Group 1, Mark to 3, and Doris to Group 2 because that is the Group left for an assignment in this block. It just happened in this series that 2 would have been the next number anyhow. Starting over again, Carol goes to 2, Bonnie to 1 and Duke to 3. In the last series Ana goes to 3,—which was not used for Duke even though it was the next number—Ralph goes to 2, and Allen goes to 1. This procedure for assigning subjects in blocks produces a better assignment schedule, as Table 10.4 shows.

Table 10.4

ASSIGNMENT BY BLOCK RANDOMIZATION		
1	2	3
Bill	Rachel	Karen
Henry	Doris	Mark
Bonnie	Carol	Duke
Allen	Ralph	Ana

A table that presents a random sequence of digits within blocks is easier to use. Table 10.5 gives an example showing every digit used once in each block. Numbers that are not used are ignored. After one subject has been assigned to each research group (three in this example), move to the next block and assign three more subjects. In this table, spaces are used to separate blocks.

Table 10.6 shows how subjects would be assigned according to the random block sequence given on Table 10.5.

Table 10.5

					RANDOM NUMBER TABLE FOR BLOCK ASSIGNMENT						
A	B	C	D	E	F	G	H	I	J	K	L
7	4	9	4	5	7	2	9	4	3	4	8
6	5	8	2	1	1	3	7	9	5	2	7
4	3	4	3	2	8	3	6	5	4	3	5
8	6	5	6	7	2	4	4	1	8	5	1
9	9	3	7	9	6	5	5	6	9	6	4
1	8	1	8	6	9	9	8	8	1	9	3
5	2	2	9	8	5	7	1	2	7	1	6
3	1	7	1	4	3	1	3	7	2	7	2
2	7	6	5	3	4	8	2	3	6	9	9

Table 10.6

1	2	3
ASSIGNMENT USING RANDOM NUMBERS IN BLOCKS		
Karen	Rachel	Bill
Doris	Mark	Henry
Bonnie	Duke	Carol
Allen	Ana	Ralph

Stratified Samples

This is a variation of random sampling techniques, but it employs a more formal structure that makes a deliberate attempt to create a sample which is as representative of the parent population as we can make it. Stratified sampling can be used only with a population made up of clearly identified important and relevant subgroups or classes; think of these as layers or "strata," as the term is used in geology. A well-developed stratified sample offers a better opportunity to generalize results back to the parent population than would be possible with other methods. Subjects for various groups are randomly assigned from the equivalent category in the population. Table 10.7 illustrates a stratified sample based on a college population.

Table 10.7 is easier to use after the frequencies have been converted to proportions, as shown in Table 10.8. It shows that a little over half the students (.542) are men, and .458 are women. (The total equals 1.00.) Only about 1 in 20 men (.054) are seniors, which is almost identical to the proportion of women seniors. Approximately a third of the students at this university are freshmen and sophomores (.327 and .327).

Table 10.7

NUMBER OF COLLEGE STUDENTS BY CLASS AND GENDER

	Freshman	Sophomore	Junior	Senior	Total
Men	260	195	130	065	650
Women	132	198	154	066	550
Total	392	393	284	131	1200

Table 10.8

PROPORTIONAL CLASSIFICATION OF COLLEGE STUDENTS BY CLASS AND GENDER

	Freshman	Sophomore	Junior	Senior	Total
Men	.217	.163	.108	.054	.542
Women	.110	.165	.128	.055	.458
Total	.327	.327	.236	.109	1.000

Students would be randomly assigned to groups until the proportion was approximately equal to the proportion in the population. We can appreciate the process if we think of a layer cake that has several layers of different flavors with different types of frosting between them. Each slice of the cake should be an accurate representation of the cake's structure.

Assume that a sample of 60 students needs to be divided into three experimental groups of equal size. Approximately 33 should be male and 27 female. Classes represented in the 33 males should be approximately as follows: 13 freshmen, 10 sophomores, 7 juniors, and 3 seniors. The 27 women would be divided into the following groups: 6 freshmen, 10 sophomores, 8 juniors, and 3 seniors. After random assignment to three experimental groups something like the arrangement shown in Table 10.9 should result.

Stratified assignment procedures are designed to reflect more accurately the characteristics of the population than is likely with random assignment techniques. We have to accept that more work is involved and that the method requires knowledge of relevant population characteristics. When the population does not have stratified characteristics that might affect the results of an experiment, the method is not applicable.

If the method is used in an appropriate situation, it can yield better results than would have been possible with a random selection method. A group of people working in The Infant Health and Development Program studied ways to enhance the development and reduce the health problems of underweight premature infants. Their findings were published in the *Journal of the American Medical Association* (1990, pp. 3035–3042).

Previous research had shown that low birth-weight babies were more prone to many difficulties than were their normal weight counterparts: Their development was delayed, they had more medical difficulties in infancy, they tended to have lower scores on tests of cognitive functioning, they had more difficulties with behavioral adjustment, and they had problems in learning and poorer academic achievement.

A comprehensive early intervention program was introduced to identify ways to alleviate the extensive difficulties of these children. The program in-

Table 10.9

	Group 1		Group 2		Group 3	
	M	F	M	F	M	F
Freshman	4	2	5	2	4	2
Sophomore	4	4	3	3	3	3
Junior	2	2	2	3	3	3
Senior	1	1	1	1	1	1

STRATIFIED ASSIGNMENT OF STUDENTS TO EXPERIMENTAL GROUPS

cluded an educational curriculum focused on child development together with family support and pediatric follow-up. Studies done earlier had shown that programs of this sort could be helpful, but these studies had been done only at single sites, with fewer subjects, and they looked only for short-term benefits. Approximately one-third of the children eligible for inclusion in this program were to be treated, and two-thirds were to be kept as a comparison group.

This research design "included stratification by eight sites and two birth-weight groups." The sites were located in a number of different places around the country; stratification by site seemed necessary because of large site differences. The investigators also attempted to maintain a balance between the groups for birth weight, gender, maternal education (less than high school graduate, high school graduate, some college, or more), maternal race (black, hispanic, white/other), and primary language in the home. The study showed that the early intervention program was able to produce significant improvements.

INAPPROPRIATE ASSIGNMENT TECHNIQUES

The logic of the method of difference requires that research groups should differ only on the various levels of the independent variable. Research groups that are not equivalent are called "biased samples." Like other sins, these are easy to commit unless one is vigilant and special precautions are taken to avoid them. When something in the assignment process tends to include selectively or eliminate certain types of candidates, biased samples will result. Good techniques will reduce—but cannot entirely prevent—occasional errors.

Readers are asked to make a not uncommon assumption that a particular graduate student is in need of subjects for a research project. The instructor of a large, 100-student, experimental psychology class felt the project was worth using class time for, and *all* students in the class agreed to participate. This is a simple situation which only requires the investigator to divide students into research groups. All candidates for inclusion are known, and they are all available. Assume that 75 people are to be divided equally into three groups labeled S, T, and U. The following discussion is to identify some ways that should *not* be used for subject assignment because they could produce biased groups.

1. When an alphabetical class list is available subjects could be assigned by taking the names of the first 25 people and putting them into the S group, the next 25 into T, and the third 25 into U.

   Comment: Alphabetical lists do not rule out the possibility that ethnic difference might be related to names. People with those names, and with whatever other characteristics might be relevant, would be grouped together. (Note however that random assignment from the list would work fine.)

2. Students could be assigned to research groups in the order of their appearance on the day of the experiment. The first 25 could be assigned to group S and the second 25 to group T. The first 25 of those who came late would be assigned to group U, which was being kept as a comparison group. Everyone else would be left out.

   Comment: The people in both the two early groups probably differed in several ways from people who came late or who did not come at all.

3. Participants could be assigned according to where they sit in the classroom. The S group would be made up of students who sit near the front of the room; the people sitting midway would go to the T level. The U group would be formed from students sitting near the back of the room.

   Comment: A quick analysis of grades and seating arrangement, for situations in which students choose their own seats, is likely to show that the average grades of students sitting near the front will be higher than the average grades of students sitting near the rear of the room. Students in the middle will fall between. [2]

ADVANTAGES AND DISADVANTAGES OF RANDOMLY SELECTED SAMPLES

Advantages

Experiments developed around randomly selected subjects are frequently used in research—primarily because the method is simple, easy to put into effect, and it generally works. When samples are large enough and if subjects have been appropriately assigned to research groups, one can be reasonably confident that the groups will not differ very much.

External validity should also be good when large samples have been selected using a suitable random method.

Random selection does not require any prior data about participants. People can be selected without the experimenter knowing anything at all about them.

---

[2] Assuming this logic is true, and it seems to be, it presents an interesting problem of cause and effect. Do students who get the higher grades get them because they sit near the front of the room, nearer the instructor—the source of truth and light and wisdom? Could it be that students who have the interest and ability for getting higher grades choose to sit near the front in order to be more involved in the class? Students wanting to avoid eye contact with the teacher and the possibility of being asked to answer questions for which they do not have answers might choose to sit inconspicuously toward the rear.

Methods that involve matching, which we will study next, require data on which to match or pair participants.

Disadvantages

Although the probability for a faulty selection of samples is small, it is nonetheless real. The method does not always work correctly, and there is no way to know which experimental findings are erroneous. If samples are not similar prior to the application of the experimental treatments, the experiment will lack internal validity.

Randomly selected samples must be fairly large.

The next point probably requires a knowledge of statistics for full comprehension. Variability among randomly selected samples tends to be large, which produces a large standard error of the mean. When the standard error is large the difference between sample means must be large to produce a statistically significant difference.

STATISTICS FOR ANALYSIS OF SIMPLE EXPERIMENTS

Three Types of *t*-Tests

Statistics texts are not always so helpful as they might be in organizing, comparing, and describing statistics that are similar in some ways but different in others. The *t*-test is an example of this. Readers who have already had a course in statistics will find the following discussion easier to understand, but others should still be able to work their way through it well enough to distinguish among the three *t*-test applications.

The evaluation of a statistic involves making a decision about its null hypothesis. The process is very similar to the one already studied with correlations. Following the calculation of a *t*-test we look up the result on the applicable table to determine whether or not the null hypothesis will be rejected. We use .05 and .01 probability levels, just as we did with correlations. Interpretation according to a one- or two-tailed test is much more relevant for *t*-test than it was for a correlation.

All *t*-test applications determine statistical significance by computing the ratio between the obtained mean difference and the standard error of the difference between the means. The standard error in this formula is an estimate of the population standard error obtained by taking the square root of the combined sample variances. (Do not be concerned if this is not crystal clear!) The standard error, the number that goes in the denominator, estimates a range of normal, likely, variations of mean differences. If an obtained mean difference is greater than the estimate, we conclude that the difference is statistically significant.

Statistical conclusions try to make inferences about the nature of the populations the samples represent. The *t* leads to a determination of the probability that the obtained means from two samples were randomly selected from the same population. If the difference between the means is so large, relative to the standard error, we assume it is unlikely that they are random samples from the same population. Whether or not a computed *t* meets the rules for statistical significance is determined by the sample sizes, in terms of the degrees of freedom and the size of the computed *t*.

Two *experimental* applications of the *t* statistic are possible. Both evaluate the difference between sample means of two groups of subjects who have been treated in different ways. The alternate forms depend on how subjects were selected. The most common *t* procedure in the behavioral sciences involves two independent and unrelated samples of randomly assigned subjects. These are the kinds of subjects we have been discussing in this chapter. When someone talks about an "experiment," this is probably the form the speaker has in mind.

The second *t*-test application, which will be discussed in the following chapter, is also an experimental design, but subjects are selected in a different way. In that arrangement participants are paired on relevant subject variables. The intent is to duplicate, as precisely as possible, pertinent characteristics of one group with those in the other. Participants in the samples are arranged in logically equivalent matched pairs. The arrangement is similar to, but not exactly the same as, the one required for computing a correlation. The advantage of this method is that it is more sensitive. A smaller *t* is more likely to be significant when samples are highly correlated.

To review briefly, both *t*'s just discussed compare the means of two *samples* of subjects who have been treated in unlike ways. The methods separate according to the way in which subjects have been assigned to their respective groups. The most common way is to assign subjects randomly. The other method assigns subjects in selected pairs. Both these methods try to form a conclusion about the probability that they are random samples from the same population.

A third application of the *t*-test is not widely used in behavioral science research because we do not often ask the form of research question it is designed to answer. This method is applicable when we want to compare a sample mean with a population mean. Instead of using an actual population mean, which might not be available, we would use an estimate of one, derived in part from some hypothesis we want to test. A comparison is made between a sample mean and a population mean. This arrangement tries to determine the probability that a particular sample, having a certain obtained mean, was drawn randomly from a population having specified parameters. These are often labeled μ (mu) and σ (small sigma). Note that only one sample is used, hence its name, "one-sample case" or "single-sample mean." Instead of comparing the means of two samples, we compare the mean of a sample with a specified mean of a population.

In the course of one's studies of statistics we will discover that the term "standard error" is used in three different ways. The standard error used in *t*-test computation has already been mentioned, even if its meaning is not yet clear. This standard error is not the same as the other two standard errors that are seen more often in tests and measurements applications. We studied the *standard error of the estimate* earlier as a way of evaluating the significance of a correlation. This standard error is important for determination of test validity as it is defined by making predictions.

The *standard error of the measurement* is studied in connection with test reliability and shows the expected variation of test scores around the presumed "true" score for an individual. If a test had perfect reliability, obtained scores from repeated testing would have no variation and would equal the true score. All measurements are unreliable to some extent, so obtained scores are only estimates of the true score. Tests with good reliability have a relatively small standard error.

The *t*-Test Formula (t-Ratio)

The size of a computed t is determined by the amount of difference between means and by the size of the standard error in the denominator. Decreasing the standard error makes an experiment more sensitive because the same amount of difference between obtained means will produce a larger t. As with any ratio, if the denominator increases, the quotient, which is t in this case, will decrease. The following examples show that a smaller denominator (i.e., standard error) produces a larger t. This helps to emphasize the importance of good experimental design, which reduces variance in the denominator and makes the standard error smaller.

$$t = \frac{12}{3} = 4 \quad t = \frac{12}{6} = 2 \quad t = \frac{12}{12} = 1$$

The t-test formula and details for t computation for uncorrelated (randomly assigned samples) are given at the end of this chapter.

Interpretation of Results

Our research work is not over after the statistical computations have been completed. We have the results, but now we need to interpret them and decide what they mean. The procedures for doing this are complex and require a chapter of their own. Readers who need to know right away how to interpret t-tests should move ahead to read Chapter 12.

Nonparametric Difference Statistics

In the following paragraphs I have listed the names and brief descriptions of nonparametric statistics that are easy to use and quick to compute. They are designed for data that are not interval. The statement of the null hypothesis will, of course, differ from one statistic to another, but research hypotheses can be evaluated in the normal way, using the table that applies to that statistic. I mention these statistics only to give names to them so readers who do not have suitable interval data, which a t-test requires, will know what other statistics to consider as they consult a statistics text for additional information. Older statistics have been emphasized because they are the ones for which information will be more readily available.

These statistics are applicable to uncorrelated samples. All of them assume a lower order of measurement than interval. They cannot compare differences between means, because the mean is not an appropriate statistic for their data.

The *Mann-Whitney U* statistic is the one closest to the t-test. It also evaluates whether two randomly selected groups are likely to have come from the same population. It is applicable when the data are at least ordinal but not ranked. If one has data that are not normally distributed and the units are not quite equal interval, this would be the statistic to use.

The *Median test* compares the scores above or below the median for two randomly selected groups. Nonranked ordinal data are required.

The following statistics are applicable to related, correlated, or paired samples, which will be studied in the next chapter.

The *Sign test* requires ordinal but not ranked data. Each pair of observations is examined to determine if the first score is larger. If it is, record a +. If the first score is smaller than the second, record a –. The statistics analyzes the column of + or – values. The test looks only at the direction of the differences, not the amount.

The *Wilcoxon matched-pairs signed ranks test* is an old standby. The data required are ordinal but not ranked. It compares the values in each pair of scores and takes account of the amount of difference between them. This is a more powerful test than the sign test, because it incorporates more of the information from the data.

HOW TO COMPUTE A *t* FOR RANDOMLY SELECTED SAMPLES

If the Y sample mean is larger than the mean for the X sample, the negative difference in the numerator will produce a negative *t*. The sign should be ignored; the meaning of the *t* is not affected. Some authors recommend subtracting the smaller mean from the larger so the value in the numerator will always be positive..

The *t*-test, like all statistics, has several restrictions for its use. Data must be at least interval, preferably normally distributed. Sample variance for each group should be approximately equal. Samples should be of approximately the same size.

Make calculations for each of the following symbols or formulas that appear in Table 10.10. Organizing work ahead of time in this way improves accuracy. Computations are also much easier to check for errors. In addition to the general plan of computation, I have provided a worked problem. Substitute figures in the formula and compute the *t*. Interpret the results.

ENDNOTES

When Random Selection Isn't

Students doing research projects as a course assignment will sometimes include a statement like the following in their report, "Subjects were randomly selected from the student population; 27 men and 27 women were used." That statement shows that these beginning researchers did not understand the basic idea of random selection. The point is, it would be exceedingly unlikely that a college population of students exists that is precisely 50/50 for males and females, and it is even more unlikely that a random sample would produce precisely the same ratio. At my university the female/male ratio is perhaps in excess of 2/1, so a randomly selected sample of this student population would produce something closer to 36 females and 18 males. If there happened to be a special reason for having equal numbers of each gender, a statement on "subject selection" should have indicated that groups of 27 women and 27 men were each randomly selected from the student population.

Table 10.10

t COMPUTATION: RANDOMLY SELECTED SAMPLES			
X	Y	X^2	Y^2
19	9	361	81
5	8	25	64
12	6	144	36
13	5	169	25
17	7	289	49
9	3	81	9
11	—	121	—
86	38	1190	264

N_X _____ $\quad \Sigma X$ _____ $\quad N_Y$ _____ $\quad \Sigma Y$ _____

M_X _____ $\quad M_Y$ _____ $\quad M_X - M_Y =$ _____

$df = N_X + N_Y - 2$ _____

ΣX^2 _____ $\quad (\Sigma X)^2$ _____ $\quad \Sigma Y^2$ _____ $\quad (\Sigma Y)^2$ _____

$\Sigma(X)^2 \div N_X$ _____ $\qquad\qquad (\Sigma Y)^2 \div N_Y$ _____

$\Sigma X^2 - \dfrac{(\Sigma X)^2}{N_X}$ _____ $\qquad \Sigma Y^2 - \dfrac{(\Sigma Y)^2}{N_Y}$ _____

$$\frac{M_X - M_Y}{\sqrt{\left[\dfrac{\left(\Sigma X^2 - \dfrac{(\Sigma X)^2}{N_X}\right) + \left(\Sigma Y^2 - \dfrac{(\Sigma Y)^2}{N_Y}\right)}{N_X + N_Y - 2}\right]\left[\dfrac{N_X + N_Y}{N_X N_Y}\right]}}$$

N_X 7 $\quad \Sigma X$ 86 $\quad N_Y$ 6 $\quad \Sigma Y$ 38

M_X 12.28 $\quad M_Y$ 6.33 $\quad M_X - M_Y$ 5.95

$df = N_X + N_Y - 2 = 11$

ΣX^2 1190 $\quad (\Sigma X)^2$ 7396 $\quad \Sigma Y^2$ 264 $\quad (\Sigma Y)^2$ 1444

$(\Sigma X)^2 \div N_X$ 1057 $\quad (\Sigma Y)^2 \div N_Y$ 241

$$(\Sigma X)^2 - \frac{(\Sigma X)^2}{N_X} = 1190 - \frac{7396}{7} = 133.43$$

$$(\Sigma Y)^2 - \frac{(\Sigma Y)^2}{N_Y} = 264 - \frac{1444}{6} = 23.33$$

$$\frac{5.95}{\sqrt{\dfrac{(133.43) + (23.33)}{11}}\,[.31]} \qquad \boxed{t = 2.843}$$

Design a Simple Experiment That Uses Randomly Selected Subjects

At this point in the course readers should be able to design a simple experiment to demonstrate their mastery of the material studied so far. There is probably not enough time left to undertake a genuine research project that involves actually doing an experiment and collecting data from real subjects. I have found that a simple derivation of the real thing works quite well for its intended purpose.

In lieu of specific instructions from the teacher, the following instructor should be followed. Do the exercise neatly and carefully to hand in at the beginning of the class period on the due date. If the material is well thought out and properly organized, a brief two-page report should be enough. It must be neatly typed (double spaced of course) with wide margins. The satisfactory completion of this exercise will demonstrate that you understand how to design a simple experiment and how to analyze the results.

It is not necessary to collect any actual data. All the numbers you need should be made up to produce a "statistically significant difference between sample means." Small numbers will help to reduce errors in computation, and they will work just as well to demonstrate to your teacher that you know what you are doing.

Carefully label and complete each of the following sections. At the top of the paper write your name, section number, and any other identifying information required at your university.

Label the sheet: "Experiment Demonstration—Random Assignment." The following example identifies most areas that teachers like to include. A much more comprehensive report would be required from students who are doing research projects for course credit.

1. *Title:* Give the title of your experiment.
2. *Reference:* Make up a complete reference to your article in correct "APA" style. (Use yourself as the author.) See the references at the end of this text for examples.
3. *Abstract:* Write an "abstract" of your article in the style of the "Psychological Abstracts."
4. *Research hypothesis:* Select an independent variable that can be manipulated in two levels. Ex post facto designs can be used, but they are not recommended. Do not use drugs, chemicals, or physiological variables. Emphasize psychological attributes. In a sentence or two explain what you are going to study.
5. *Construct and dependent variable:* Identify the major construct you will be studying, and give its operational definition.
6. *Selection of subjects:* Briefly state how your subjects were randomly selected to ensure their equivalence. Assume that *six subjects will be used for one group and seven for the other.* (The use of small samples will make it easier for someone to check your work.) Call attention to any special and relevant problems of control you might need to solve.
7. *Data:* On a separate sheet show your "made up" data for the 13 pretend subjects (6 and 7) in the experiment. Show all scores.

8. *t-test computation:* Compute a *t*-test, using the appropriate *t* formula; show all work.

9. *Interpretation of results:* Use a two-tailed test and an appropriate table to determine statistical significance. State whether *t* is statistically significant and explain findings in terms of the original hypothesis.

STUDY QUESTIONS

1.D Explain the idea that a researcher who studies white rats is not usually interested in *those particular* white rats but wants information on white rats in general.

2. Explain and understand the distinction between random selection and random assignment.

3. What is the "logic" of random selection procedures?

   How can properly selected random samples balance out subject variables?

4. What are biased samples?

   How might they be obtained, and what difficulties might they cause when interpreting experimental results?

5. What are subject variables, and how do they affect experiments?

6. Identify some correct and incorrect procedures for random selection of subjects.

   Give some examples of selection techniques that are likely to produce biased samples.

7. Explain some random selection techniques that do not use tables of random numbers.

8. Explain how a table of random numbers is used for subject assignment.

9. What is a major disadvantage of a continuous random number sequence for selection of small groups of subjects?

10. How are subjects assigned according to "block" randomization?

    What is the advantage of this method?

11. What is a stratified sample?

    When would it be appropriate to use one?

    What is its advantage over other random selection techniques?

12. What are some advantages and disadvantages of randomly selected samples?

13.D What, if anything, is wrong with randomly selecting 50 men and 50 women as a random sample to represent a university's student population?

14. How is the standard error for *t*-test computation affected by the use of randomly selected subjects?

15. Explain three different uses for a *t*-test.

16. How does the size of the "standard error" affect the size of *t*?

17.   What factors determine whether or not a particular *t* is statistically significant?

18.   What kinds of data are necessary for a *t* computation?

SMALL TALK

Chapter
11

Matching to Control Subject Variables (Matched Subjects Design)

One pair of identical twins is worth 20 subjects who have been randomly selected.

As we continue the study of research topics, the convoluted nature of the discipline begins to intrude. I have been unable to identify a logical linear order for the presentation of everything it seems to me is important. Subjects coming later in the text are not more or less essential than those studied earlier. Much of what was studied earlier becomes clearer after the later chapters have been mastered. Inevitably, when there is so much material to be mentioned, we are left to find a place for discussion of a number of small topics that are important but not complex enough to have a chapter of their own. This chapter will be used to bring together several miscellaneous topics that cannot easily be placed elsewhere.

In addition to explaining "matched subjects design," I will include in this chapter an assortment of other topics—pretest/posttest design, for example—that did not find a place in other chapters. The general nature of the topics makes them applicable in several areas, so they could have been included earlier or later in the presentation. They are discussed in this chapter after we have first examined a second technique for controlling subject variables.

The last chapter proposed random selection and assignment as one way of controlling subject variables in order to help ensure group equivalence. Normal irregular variations among subjects are used to balance out possible group differences. This chapter looks at a different technique which requires the investigator to match and pair participants on relevant variables. Spreading matched participants among all levels of an experiment helps to balance their individual characteristics so equivalence among groups is improved.

Authors of experimental texts sometimes call this a "matched groups" design. I believe that name is misleading because it suggests it is groups that are matched, rather than pairs of participants. "Matched subjects" or "matched pairs" comes closer to identifying what is happening. Statisticians tend to emphasize that samples are "correlated" or "dependent." These are relevant concepts for statisticians because they emphasize a fundamental difference between statistics used for correlated and uncorrelated samples.

Procedures for matching subjects can be time-consuming, and the difficulties are increased considerably if an experimenter tries to match on more than one subject variable. These considerations urge the restriction of this design to two groups. There are three different ways of selecting pairs of subjects for a two-group experiment.

The best method, which involves identical twins, is least often used because of difficulties and expense of obtaining adequate numbers of identical twin subjects. The advantage of twin studies rests on the assumption that the biochemistry and other genetic, physiological, and psychological characteristics of identical twins will be more similar than they will be among unrelated people. Anyone planning to do research with identical twins should be careful to follow the rules for twin studies in order to be sure that every set has enough characteristics in common to verify equivalence. Although twins would be quite an advantage in routine psychological research, they are a luxury that most researchers cannot afford.

I should note first that one of the most widely publicized research programs involving twins does not use the experimental method. The objectives of that research are different. Television programs, newspaper, and magazine articles give popular exposure to the serious scientific work being done by scientists who use identical twins to study inherited characteristics. Professor Thomas Bouchard, director of the Minnesota Center for Twins and Adoption Research (at the University of Minnesota) is a leader in this work. See also any of the recent articles by David Lykken. Twin studies done to note how alike twins are, even when they have been reared apart, follow the general form of Mill's method of agreement. This research application tries to identify common characteristics that can be attributed to heredity, in situations in which as many other variables as possible were different.

When twins are not available for experimental designs, subjects can be paired using score data for some relevant variable. One form would be similar to a correlational analysis that measures the same people twice, as in a before/after design. Subjects are first tested, subjected to an independent variable, and then retested. Subjects' performance before the independent variable is compared with performance following it. Subject variables are equivalent because the same persons are used for both the before and after measurements.

Another way for pairing subjects requires direct matching of people to form pairs that are equivalent on measured subject variable(s) the experimenter thinks are important. Only people who can be paired on appropriate measurements are used in the experiment. A person in the subject pool who cannot be matched with another person would not be used.

LOGIC OF MATCHED SUBJECTS DESIGNS

The following little exercise should illustrate the advantages of pairing. The task here is to find the misspelled words. One word in each pair in the "Paired Words" columns is misspelled. Finding the one with the incorrect spelling is easy—assuming the correct spelling can be recognized. Words in the "Randomly Mixed" columns are meant to represent a situation involving randomly selected subjects. The misspelled words are all mixed in with different words. One has to work harder to get the same result with this arrangement. The analogy is not perfect—they rarely are—but the difference between the two methods should be clear.

TECHNIQUES FOR MATCHING

Selecting all participants for both groups on a common characteristic such as gender, age, year in school, or some other attribute that seems to the experimenter to be relevant is a worthwhile way for controlling certain variables that are easily observed and have a restricted range. Some authorities call this procedure "holding conditions constant," because they can be the same for both groups. The selection of groups having a common characteristics on one variable is not, however, what is meant by pairing or matching subjects.

Paired Words		*Randomly Mixed*	
knighthood	nitehood	assimulate	astrology
omnivorous	ommivorous	assidous	assertion
parenthesus	parenthesis	hororscope	hospital
hospitabil	hospitable	complacence	combustibile
complacence	complasence	parenthesis	parturation
assimilate	assimulate	omnivorous	knitehood
assiderous	assidous	protaganist	prognosticate

Testing subjects on a relevant variable is a common way of getting data for subject matching. Scores obtained from a pretest that provides data known from other work to be relevant can also be used.

Because measurement involves extra work and expense, it is important to match subjects only on variables that are known to affect the outcome. Some researchers will state quite arbitrarily that, ". . . subjects were matched on the basis of . . . [several variables the investigator identified]" without presenting any information to justify the matching. If matching was irrelevant to the independent variable, the relationship between the groups will be low and the computed t will be close to what it would have been if the subjects had not been matched. If matching is not definitely known to have a potential value in a particular experiment, the random method should be selected.

Table 11.1 illustrates the principle of matching by presenting fictional score data collected from a dozen people. The task is to assign these people randomly to three experimental groups. Normally we would not use the paired subjects technique with three groups, but this is the best way I can think of to demonstrate the principles involved. The data have been simplified to sharpen the illustration. Note the scores have been listed in sequential order. Names show that each number is a score for an identified person.

A simple and obvious, but incorrect, way of sorting subjects is to go down the list and assign people sequentially. Table 11.2 shows how this approach produces inadequate results.

The reason for matching is to increase the likelihood that means for the three groups will be statistically equivalent before subjects are exposed to the action of the independent variable. This example shows that sequential assignment, when scores are ranked according to size, does not accomplish the desired result.

A second wrong way to match subjects involves a variation of the first method, but instead of assigning them sequentially by order of subject scores (1-2-3, 4-5-6, 7-8-9), a systematic reversal is introduced to give: 1-2-3, 6-5-4. This procedure and its results are demonstrated in Table 11.3.

Table 11.1

TEST SCORES FOR SUBJECTS TO BE MATCHED	
1. Jan	10
2. Robert	20
3. Aldus	30
4. Ben	40
5. Dylan	50
6. Cathy	60
7. Ruth	70
8. Mary	80
9. Allen	90
10. Karen	100
11. Rose	110
12. June	120

Table 11.2

	PAIRING BY SEQUENTIAL ASSIGNMENT		
	Group A	Group B	Group C
	10	20	30
	40	50	60
	70	80	90
	100	110	120
Sum	220	260	300
	55 <--Means-->	65 <--Means-->	75

Table 11.3

	PAIRING BY ALTERNATE REVERSAL		
	A	B	C
	10	20	30
	60	50	40
	70	80	90
	120	110	100
Sum	260	260	260

This time the sums are all equal at 260, and therefore the means are 65 for each group. Although the data look good enough to fool the not-so-watchful eye, they hide another error.

The range is a simple statistic that shows the "spread" or variability of a set of numbers. Assuming the range is the difference between the largest and smallest score, the scores in Column A range from 10–20 = 110; for B the range is 20–110 = 90; and for C the values are 30–100 = 70. In comparing ranges, 110 with 90 and 70, it is obvious that scores in the various columns are not equally variable.

The standard deviation is a descriptive statistic that shows variability or dispersion more accurately than does the range. The standard deviations for these data are: A = 45, B = 38.7, and C = 35.1. The t-test requires samples that have at least roughly equivalent variances (standard deviations squared). You can see that this method of sorting subjects to form equivalent groups is not a satisfactory one.

A standard matching process requires that measurements be listed initially in sequential order. A quick look down the list will show whether there are any aberrant scores that cannot reasonably be matched. These scores should be dropped before you begin assignment.

When you are assigning subjects to only two groups, simply tossing a coin *might* produce satisfactory results; heads go to one group and tails go to another. As I pointed out before, you cannot rely entirely on chance to produce an even random distribution. After the assignment of the first person in each pair, assign the second person to the other group. This implements a simple form of block randomization, which keeps the groups equal in size.

If you are using a table of random numbers for assigning subjects, designate groups as 1 or 2. Assign subjects to Group 1 when an odd number comes up on the table and to Group 2 when an even number comes next on the list. Run a finger down the list of measurement values, stopping on each one, then check the random number table to determine if the next assignment should be for the odd or even group. Remember that random number sequences often contain runs of digits that will produce errors in assignment of small samples.

ADVANTAGES AND DISADVANTAGES OF MATCHING SUBJECTS

The statistical advantage of pairing subjects has already been explained. When subject pairing is done in a meaningful way, so that paired scores are highly correlated, the standard error of the difference will be reduced, the t will be larger, and it is more likely to be significant.

The advantage of matching is blunted somewhat by differences in interpretation caused by looking up significance using the smaller degrees of freedom (df) applicable for correlated samples. The df for a t-test on a randomly assigned subjects experiment is two less than the total number of subjects (combined for both groups). When subjects are matched the df is one less than the *number of pairs of scores*. For this reason the df for matched subjects experiments will always be smaller than for the same number of people who have been randomly assigned.

Statistical significance is determined by both the computed size of t and the degrees of freedom. A computed t is more likely to be statistically significant for a larger df than for a smaller one. Or expressing the idea in a different way: When the degrees of freedom value is smaller, t must be larger for the same level of significance. As the samples are increased in size, say to 30 or more people in each sample, the effect becomes less important.

Subjects can only be paired on some sort of measurement or observation which is known to be relevant for the experiment, and the information must be available in advance of the pairing. Recall that no special information is required for random groups. The pairing procedure is itself an added step in the research sequence, so if investigators have a choice about which method to use, they will have to decide whether the expenditure of time and other resources is justified by the gain in sensitivity the method is capable of producing.

Possible loss of external validity is another disadvantage of the paired subjects method. The process of matching eliminates those subjects for whom pairs cannot be found. Assume that you have available a group of 70 volunteers. After you have eliminated 30 people because they cannot be paired, you must question whether the remaining 20 pairs of subjects (a total of 40 people) adequately represent the characteristics of the original group. It is harder to match subjects in the "tails" of a distribution where there are fewer people, so the spread of scores in paired groups is likely to be restricted to the middle of the range.

Both sample size and external validity are reduced if more than a few subjects leave the experiment. The *t*-test for this method analyzes *pairs* of subjects, so if one person in a pair leaves, the person with whom he or she was paired must also be dropped, further reducing the sample size.

There have been discussions in the literature about whether or not matching or pairing subjects is ever a legitimate research design. Campbell and Stanley (1963) state that, ". . . while simple or stratified randomization assures unbiased assignment of experimental subjects to groups, it is a less than perfect way of assuring the initial equivalence of such groups. It is nevertheless the only way of doing so, and the essential way." This negative point of view seems to rest in part on the observation that the matching technique is usually very badly implemented. Campbell and Stanley explain that random selection methods do everything the paired subjects design can do, and better. Their dogmatism is softened as they go on to state:

> This is not to rule out matching as an adjunct to randomization, as when one gains statistical precision by assigning students to matched pairs, and then randomly assigning one member of each pair to the experimental group, the other to the control group. . . . But matching as a substitute for randomization is taboo. . . .

I suggest that no method should be rejected without a full consideration of its merits for each application. If knowledge of behavior can be advanced by a paired subjects experiment, that should be the one chosen.

COMPARISON OF RESULTS FROM CORRELATED AND UNCORRELATED SAMPLES

The amount of improvement in statistical significance that results from pairing scores is determined by the relevance of the pairing measurements to the experiment and by the extent of the relationship between the groups. The use of the correlated samples formula, when there is not a large relationship between the samples, can produce a lower *probability value* than would be obtained if the uncorrelated samples formula were used. As I pointed out a few paragraphs back, the smaller df we get for matched subjects, the larger the *t* must be for the same level of significance. Note that if subjects are well matched on a relevant variable to produce a significant correlation, the size of the computed *t* will be larger than it would have been if the unselected-subjects formula had been used.

I believe we can understand that point more easily by studying what happens when we use alternate formulas to evaluate the same data. Table 11.4 demonstrates how the extent of relationship produces different-sized *t* values for data that are otherwise identical. Note that the means and standard deviations are the same for all four examples, but the *t* computed by the correlated samples formula increases considerably as the correlation between the samples increases.

A careful study of the table is important for understanding the following points.

Table 11.4

DIFFERING RESULTS FROM CORRELATED AND UNCORRELATED SAMPLES

$M_x = 15$ $s_x = 7.74$ $\Sigma X^2 = 1080$ $SS_x = 180$ $(\Sigma X)^2 = 600$ $\Sigma X = 60$
$M_y = 6$ $s_y = 5.16$ $\Sigma Y^2 = 224$ $SS_y = 80$ $(\Sigma Y)^2 = 576$ $\Sigma Y = 24$

df = 6 for all random samples computations.
df = 3 for all correlated samples computations.

	X	Y	
Example A	26	12	$r = .938$
	8	0	t (random) = 1.934
	14	8	t (correlated) = 5.196
	12	4	
Example B	26	12	$r = .667$
	14	0	t (random) = 1.934
	12	8	t (correlated) = 3.11
	8	4	
Example C	8	12	$r = 0.00$
	12	0	t (random) = 1.934
	26	8	t (correlated) = 1.934
	14	4	
Example D	14	12	$r = -.667$
	26	0	t (random) = 1.934
	8	8	t (correlated) = 1.521
	12	4	

The t computed with the "random" formula (for unselected, unmatched, un-correlated samples) is the same in every instance. The formula for randomly selected subjects does not include the r factor, so it produces the same t regardless of the extent of relationship between samples.

A second major point demonstrates the underlying reason for this chapter. Subjects are matched to better control extraneous variables, and in that way the technique increases the sensitivity of the t test. The examples show that if samples are highly correlated, the matched subjects formula will produce a larger t, which is more likely to be significant *even when the actual difference between means is the same.* When the relationship between the scores is not high, such as in example C, the value of the computed t drops to the same value obtained from the uncorrelated samples formula. But the probability value we will obtain from the t table will be lower when the samples are small because of the smaller df used with the paired samples formula.

Example B shows the effect when the correlation between the samples is large but not statistically significant. The computed t of 3.11, using the correlated formula, is large enough to be on the borderline of significance, whereas t of 1.934, computed using the "random" formula, is a long way from significance.

Example D demonstrates an anomaly in which the correlation is negative and the *t* computed with the correlated formula is smaller than it would have been using the formula for uncorrelated samples. I cannot imagine a situation in which an investigator would be so incompetent that the deliberate pairing of scores to make them as equivalent as possible would result in a negative relationship.

In conclusion, let us note that if our samples are well paired, the action of independent variable manipulations will be in the direction of producing a larger *t*. Pairing should not be undertaken casually, however, because it requires extra work. If samples are small, or if pairs are not properly matched on an applicable variable, the extra work will not produce an improvement over the random assignment formula.

HOW TO COMPUTE A *t* FOR PAIRED SAMPLES

Table 11.5 illustrates the computation of a *t* for paired samples. Keep in mind the following important points:

Samples must be logically paired on some attribute of importance to the experiment.

Table 11.5

t COMPUTATION: PAIRED SAMPLES

X	Y	D	D²
19	11	8	64
5	8	−3	−9
12	7	5	25
13	6	7	49
18	8	10	100
9	10	−1	1
11	5	6	36
87	55	32	284

Number of pairs of scores: N = 7

ΣX 87	ΣY 55	M_X 12.43	M_Y 7.86	$M_X - M_Y$ 4.57
ΣD 32	ΣD^2 284	$(\Sigma D)^2$ 1024	$(\Sigma D)^2/N$ 146.286	

$\Sigma D^2 - \dfrac{(\Sigma D)^2}{N}$ 137.71

N (N − 1) 42

df 6

Formula	Computation
$$\dfrac{M_X - M_Y}{\sqrt{\dfrac{\Sigma D^2 - \dfrac{(\Sigma D)^2}{N}}{N(N-1)}}}$$	$$\dfrac{12.43 - 7.86}{\sqrt{\dfrac{284 - \dfrac{1024}{7}}{7(7-1)}}}$$

$t = 2.52$

The greater the correlation between the samples on the matching variable, the more sensitive the test becomes for discovering a significant *t*.

The *t* test requires interval data, normally distributed.

Be sure to take the algebraic sum of the paired score differences for computation of (ΣD).

"N" is the number of pairs of scores.

PRETEST/POSTTEST DESIGN

At this point a shift of reading gears is required, as I introduce a new topic. The different research design to be examined next has no logical connection with the matched subjects design just completed.

A pretest/posttest design is a variation of a standard experiment with the advantage of providing data that help the investigator to assess group equivalence before an experiment is begun. In a regular experiment we can only assume that random assignment has worked its magic to form equivalent groups. When pretest scores can be obtained without a great deal of difficulty, they can help make a tighter experiment. The pretest could be either the same type of test as that used later to measure experimental effect (the dependent variable), or it could be a measurement that is known from previous work to be highly correlated with it.

The research design to be discussed in this section is not what I earlier identified as a *one-group pretest/posttest* design. In that arrangement a single group of people would be tested, subjected to an independent variable, and then retested. That procedure does not constitute a true experiment, because extraneous variables have not been controlled. Many conditions in addition to the independent variable could explain changes between the pre- and the posttreatment measurements.

Table 11.6 illustrates a suitable arrangement for recording data in a pretest/posttest design. Note that scores were available prior to the experiment for both samples. Groups were subjected to two levels of an independent vari-

Table 11.6

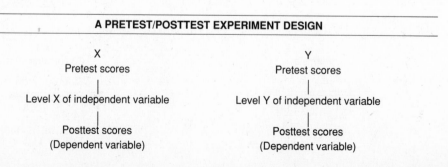

A PRETEST/POSTTEST EXPERIMENT DESIGN

X	Y
Pretest scores	Pretest scores
|	|
Level X of independent variable	Level Y of independent variable
|	|
Posttest scores	Posttest scores
(Dependent variable)	(Dependent variable)

able, then results were determined by a dependent variable. This arrangement differs from a simple experiment only by having pretest data available.

Figuring out how to analyze data for this design is probably its most difficult characteristic. As Table 11.6 shows, there are four sets of scores available. Three evaluation procedures are possible. The first two seem reasonable, but neither is the best method to use. The third method—the best choice—is more subtle.

One method would determine whether there is a significant difference between pretest and posttest scores using two *t*-tests, one for each group. The correlated scores *t* formula (the one just discussed) would be the formula to use, because we are comparing scores for the same people. An investigator might reasonably expect a strong treatment effect would produce a large, statistically significant difference between the pretest and posttest scores for the "experimental" group but not for the "control."

A second way to analyze the data also requires the computation of two *t*-ratios. The *t* here is computed with the formula for randomly selected, uncorrelated samples, because those in the X group are compared with those in the Y. The first *t* would verify that there is no significant difference between the pretest means. (If the samples were significantly different before we even began the experiment, we would be in trouble!) The second *t* would assess the effect of the independent variable by determining whether there is a statistically significant difference between the posttest means.

Neither of these two ways of evaluating pretest/posttest data are recommended, because they do not use all the available information provided by this arrangement. Neither method makes a complete assessment of *differences* or changes between the pre- and posttest scores. They do not pick up differences when both groups changed significantly but one group changed more than the other. There would be the same effect if neither group changed significantly but the change for one group was larger than for the other. What we want is an answer to the following question. Was the *change* between the pre- and posttest scores for the X group significantly different from the *change* between the pre- and posttest scores for the Y group? We would conclude that there was no treatment effect if both groups changed by the same amount. A significant *t* would result if the treatments caused one sample to change a lot and the other sample changed very little. This is what we would expect to happen if there were a treatment effect.

To get this information, we begin by computing "change scores," the difference between the pretest and the posttest scores for each person. Although the mean of the change scores is the same as the difference between the pre- and posttest means, the actual score differences between each pair of scores has to be listed because these are required for computation of *t*.

Next we *compute a t-test to determine the significance of the difference between the change scores*. The correct statistic is the *t*-test formula for *random groups data*. Do not use the formula for correlated samples unless subjects had been matched. The procedure is easier to understand when actual numbers are used (refer to Table 11.7).

The numbers we need for *t* computation are those values listed in the middle column for both groups; the one marked "Change." We are interested only in

Table 11.7

"t-TEST" COMPUTATION FOR A PRETEST/POSTTEST DESIGN							
X Scores				Y Scores			
Pretest	Change	Posttest		Pretest	Change	Posttest	
1	2	3		1	2	3	
2	3	5		2	–1	1	
3	1	4		3	1	4	
4	2	6		4	–1	3	
5	2	7		5	0	5	
Pretest	M_X	3.0		Pretest	M_Y	3.0	
Posttest	M_{X1}	5.0		Posttest	M_{Y1}	3.2	
Change				Change			
score	M_C	2.0		score	M_C	0.2	

the change or difference between the scores, so it does not matter whether the pretest scores are subtracted from the posttest scores, or vice versa. Whichever method is selected should be followed for both samples; it is important to be consistent. Negative values must be retained because the algebraic sum is necessary for determining the means.

The average change score for the X group in Table 11.7 is 2, and the average change score for the Y group is .2. The t is 2.71. When df equals 8, as it does in this example, a t of 2.306 is necessary for significance at the .05 level (for a two-tailed test). An experimenter would therefore conclude that there is a significant difference in the amount of change for the X group compared to Group Y.

SPECIAL TOPICS RELATED TO EXPERIMENTAL DESIGNS

Experimenter Effects

The logic of an experiment's design is easy to learn and to understand. By this point in the text readers should know that if several conditions vary concurrently—levels of an independent variable and uncontrolled extraneous variables—it is not possible to interpret the outcome correctly. The control of extraneous variables is a practical task all investigators have to deal with—made particularly troublesome because the investigators might not even recognize some of the difficulties. The experimenter is an extraneous element that can, in any of several ways, affect the outcome of an experiment or the interpretation of the results. The various ways in which experimenters can influence experiments are called "experimenter effects."

If experiments are carried out with one person handling a group subjected to one level of an independent variable and a different person handling the other group, we clearly have the possibility for confounding and a violation of internal validity. In a task as simple as collecting information, it can be easily shown that different investigators will get different responses. Rosenthal (1976) found that male investigators more frequently smiled than did female investigators, but the smiling was done more often in the presence of female rather than male respondents. The interaction of the gender of an investigator and the gender of a subject was only one area in which the effects of experimenter differences could be identified. Personality differences might, depending on the nature and purpose of the activity being studied, have a marked effect. Any of the following could also influence results: race, age, physical build and appearance, and an investigator's amount of experience.

Rosenthal and Fode (1963) were early investigators of what has come to be called "expectancy effect." They have shown that experimenters can sometimes produce the results they expect to get. Two groups of six experimenters were given randomly assigned rats to run on a simple "T" maze. The group that was told their rats were "maze-bright" got significantly better maze performance from their rats than did the other group of people who had been told their rats were "maze-dull." The rats were of course essentially the same. Differences in performance might have resulted from experimenter expectations being transmitted through their care, handling, and patience in animal treatment, and possibly also from their readings and interpretations of performance.

Kintz, Delprato, Mettee, Persons, and Schappe (1965) summarized many of the ways in which experimenters have demonstrated a far-from-passive role in carrying out research. They believe that whenever there is a subject-experimenter relationship there is a possibility for the experimenter to confound his or her data through many different ways. "By relating some of the findings of clinical and social psychologists . . . it is hoped that experimental psychologists will no longer accept on faith that the experimenter is necessary but harmless."

Although the situation is not quite the same, the effect of gender differences in a psychotherapy has been receiving more attention in recent years. An article by Fisher (1989) is an example: "Gender Bias in Therapy? An Analysis of Patient and Therapist Causal Explanations."

The Effect of Volunteers on Validity

A large amount of research in psychology is obtained from volunteer subjects. Suppose that nearly 1,000 people were available for a particular research project, but only 100 of them volunteered to participate. Do these volunteers accurately represent the larger group? There is no way to know for sure. If we went ahead and used these people for the experiment, at one time it might make no difference at all but at another time volunteers could cause misleading results. Depending on how they are used, volunteers can affect both the internal and external validity of experiments.

Internal validity can be challenged if volunteers participate for some levels of an independent variable and nonvolunteer subjects are used for others. We should not, for example, compare the academic performance of volunteers who participated in a learning experiment with a "control group" made up of people who did not volunteer. The rule is, never mix volunteers and nonvolunteers in the same experiment.

Possible threats against internal validity can be avoided by careful design, but whether volunteers accurately represent of the parent population is a more difficult question to answer. There has been a lot of work done on this topic, and the evidence generally shows that in several ways the personalities of people who volunteer are not typical of other people in their respective populations. They tend to be brighter, less conventional, and more sociable. Rosenthal's chapter in *Research Problems in Psychology* (Badia, Haber, & Runyon, 1970) provides an excellent summary of this topic, but there are many other references available.

In addition to personality differences, we can identify several reasons why people do or do not volunteer for participation in experiments. Basically, of course, a potential volunteer wants to know:

What will I get out of it? What's in it for me?

How long will it take? Do I have the time to spend in that way?

What do they want me to do? Does it sound interesting?

Can I do it well? (People tend not to volunteer for projects in which they might not perform at their best.)

The amount and kind of reward offered, if any, could also introduce a selective factor. Some students might volunteer for an experiment just to find out what experiments in psychology are like so that they will be better prepared when they have to undertake an experiment of their own. That information would be reward enough. Experiments that will take quite a lot of time will likely require a tangible reward of some sort. Class or course credit is one option, but for other types of research a monetary payment might be necessary in order to get "volunteers." These projects would attract people who have the time and want the money, so in effect they are being hired. Can we consider these people volunteers?

Past experience with volunteering is also a relevant variable. People who have volunteered and felt they got something worthwhile out of the activity are more likely to volunteer again than will people who had an unpleasant experience.

How the request for volunteers is issued can affect both the number and the types of people who volunteer. We are more likely to volunteer when the request comes from a person we know and like— particularly if we feel we can help him or her. People volunteer more readily in social situations in which others are volunteering and particularly if group pressure is brought to bear on holdouts. It has been noted that different recruiters visiting different sections of the same course can attract quite different numbers of people to participate in research projects.

College Students as Participants

Many people have sought answers to one of psychology's most perplexing questions: How do we get people other than college students to participate in research projects?

The existing science of human behavior is largely the science of the behavior of sophomores.

(McNemar, 1946, p. 333)

Often ours seems to be a science of just those sophomores who volunteer to participate in our research and who also keep their appointment with the investigator.

(Rosenthal & Rosnow, 1969, p. 110)

After quoting these two statements Oakes (1972) continued with a discussion of his work regarding "External Validity and the Use of Real People as Subjects." The first time Oakes mentioned students as contrasted with "real people," the term was in quotation marks, but not later: "The difference in the results of research when psychology students, as contrasted with real people, are used as subjects again makes one question the external validity of research using psychology students."

It seems safe to accept that college students are not typical of "people in general." They are more highly motivated, they are brighter, better educated, probably in better health, and have access to more money than the average person.

One may question whether students at a particular college or university who take courses in psychology, other than an introductory general course, are a reasonable representation of all students at that institution.

Students from one college are not necessarily equivalent to students from other colleges and universities. Admission requirements, fee structure, and specialty areas tend to differentially select certain types of people for admission. A sample from a particular university could be so highly selected that findings should not be generalized even to students at other universities or perhaps not to students at the same university but in a different subject major.

The advantages of college students as participants in experiments can tempt experimenters to take shortcuts that could be detrimental to scientific investigations. The seriousness of the effect is a topic of considerable discussion. The use of college students in many projects might not make much difference, but in other projects it could cause a serious distortion in our understanding of behavior. It is a task for the scientific community to evaluate the nature of participants used for research projects with the same critical appraisal that would be used for judging other features of the research.

The Problem of Subject Loss

Not everyone who begins an experiment will finish it, but having said that, it is difficult to provide guidance for understanding what the statement means. If people begin an experiment and then drop out midway, it might or might not make a difference.

Assume that an experiment is being conducted with two groups. If the subject loss is not large, and if the loss is evenly distributed over both groups, it probably would not make much difference in the conclusions. It would be helpful to have a simple rule for identifying how large a difference would be permitted before we start worrying, but I do not have one to offer. Investigators have to make their decisions in terms of their own work.

If the loss of participants is markedly larger in one of the groups than in the other, the observation strongly suggests that a complication has developed that might warrant the cancellation of the experiment. The difficulty, strangely enough, is not so much with the people who departed but with those who stayed.

> The problem posed by a loss of Ss [subjects] after they were assigned originally in an unbiased manner, is whether or not the remaining Ss are representative of the original groups. Is the number of Ss lost in the various conditions systematically related to the effects of the independent variable?
>
> (Underwood, 1966, p. 119)

Table 11.8 illustrates two groups that are well matched on subject variables at the beginning of the experiment. Each letter represents a person having an unusual amount of a certain characteristic. Group X had three people with a strong component of a B factor, but B is not a confounding variable, because these subjects were balanced by three B people in Group Y. The same would be true of people with characteristics identified by other letters. People with the same characteristics have been grouped together to illustrate sample equivalence on subject variables.

Suppose that three people with characteristics B, C, and E dropped out of Group X and an A and E person dropped out of Y. The proportion of dropouts from such a small group is fairly large, but the subjects were well spread out, so they probably would not affect the overall interpretation of the experiment. If a number of people left the same group, say C, C, C, and C left Group Y and no one dropped out of Group X, there is a difficulty. What causes concern is the *differential* elimination of a whole class of subjects from the Y group; with all the Cs gone, the groups are no longer equivalent, so any observed differences could have been caused by that fact rather than by the action of the independent variable.

Nonequivalent groups could develop through the action of the independent variable itself. Assume that a psychotherapist has a new active aggression therapy that he feels is very promising. He devised it after observing that some patients need to develop self-assurance and confidence in dealing with today's increasingly hostile urban environment. In therapy sessions the therapist was argumentative, quarrelsome, and belligerent until patients learned to deal with that type of behavior more calmly and more rationally—in the process, improving their mental health. During the progress of the experiment several people dropped out of the new treatment group. No one left the group that was being

Table 11.8

WELL-SELECTED SAMPLES AT THE BEGINNING OF AN EXPERIMENT						
Group X	AAAAA	BBB	CCCC	DD	EEEEEEE	FFFFFFF
Group Y	AAAAA	BBB	CCCC	DD	EEEEEEE	FFFFFFF

treated with the therapist's normal nonthreatening treatment method. By the end of the treatment period the therapist had invested so much time in the experiment that he went ahead and analyzed his data despite the loss of participants from the aggression therapy group. He was especially pleased that results were favorable and strongly supported his ideas about the new therapy—but did they?

People who were most in need of therapy might also have been those who were most intimidated by the treatment. The nature of their illness prevented them from coping with the aggression the psychologist had designed to help them, so they gave up the therapy. They were in effect forced out by the treatment. The weakest people withdrew to find another therapist, leaving the strongest people to complete the experiment. It is not surprising that the results turned out to appear so favorable. Any time a difference develops that could alter the initial equivalence of the research groups, the experimenter must be particularly cautious in interpreting results.

Demand Characteristics

Many years ago Pierce (1908) noted the active involvement of research subjects in doing what they could to help experiments turn out right. The act of agreeing to participate in a psychology experiment carried with it an understanding that the subject would fully cooperate and help the experimenter in every way possible. Subjects would try to do whatever they thought was necessary to fulfill the experimenter's expectations. Orne (1959, 1962) expanded on these ideas and investigated them scientifically. Orne has shown that participation in psychology experiments is not something people undertake lightly and without thought. College students in particular hope their contribution to an experiment will help in the advancement of science. Students expect that their participation will be important and that they should therefore do their best to cooperate fully with the investigator.

The mystique of participating in research under the supervision of a reputable scientist carries with it an implicit agreement that the subject will undertake to do whatever is requested without questioning the purpose or objective. Orne explains this willing compliance by the subject's "identification with the goals of science in general and the success of the experiment in particular." Participants want to be good subjects. Whatever hypothesis the investigator is testing, college students as subjects want to contribute to its verification.

This active subject involvement encourages participants to try to guess the true purpose of the experiment in order to make a more worthwhile contribution to its success. Subjects' guesses about the hypothesis "become significant determinants of subjects' behavior." Discovering the hypothesis requires the participant to take full advantage of suggestions, hints, and clues that are let slip by the investigator or anyone else who has come into contact with the research, as well as careful observation of what is being done in the experiment itself. "We have labeled the sum total of such cues as the *demand characteristics of the experimental situation*" (Orne, 1959).

The commitment subjects make when they agree to invest their time in a research project is enough to encourage them to look for objectives, implications, and meaning in what they will be asked to do. Orne is very strong in emphasizing that it is "inconceivable for [subjects] not to form some hypothesis about the purpose, based on some cues, no matter how meager; these will then determine the demand characteristics which will be perceived by and operate for a particular subject."

"It is futile to imagine an experiment that could be created without demand characteristics. . . . Rather than eliminating this variable then, it becomes necessary to take demand characteristics into account, study their effect, and manipulate them if necessary" (Badia et al., 1970, p. 9).

Demand characteristics operate in a special way to affect experimental results. Internal validity would be prejudiced if demand characteristics differed from one group to the other. It would be simply a case of not appropriately controlling relevant extraneous variables. The difficulty could be alleviated by a better management of experimental conditions.

Demand characteristics cannot be eliminated from experiments, but their influence can in part be dealt with by estimating their impact. Orne (1969) recommends the generally worthwhile practice of interviewing subjects after an experiment has been completed. Participants would be questioned on what they thought the experiment was about and why it was done. If deception had been employed, this would be the time to explain the deception and try to assess the extent to which participants were actually deceived. If postexperimental interviews are well managed, and preferably carried out by a different person, investigators can develop a better understanding of the extent to which their results have been affected by demand characteristics.

Relationship or Difference: *r* or *t*?

We have now completed our study of the two major research methods: correlations and experimental techniques. Students might find that a review is helpful at this point, to integrate the material and to identify areas of confusion. Inexperienced investigators sometimes have difficulty deciding when an experiment with a *t*-test analysis should be the method of choice and when a Pearson correlation is the technique to use. We should know early in the design of our research projects whether our research question requires a difference or relationship evaluation.

A Pearson correlation—with appropriate data, of course—answers questions about the *extent of relationship* between two sets of logically paired scores. "Relationship" is derived from the idea of covariance, the amount of agreement between a score's relative position in one sample compared to the relative position of the paired score in the other. A correlation is very useful in the early stages of hypothesis evaluation or when the research questions cannot be studied with experimental techniques. All correlational findings must be interpreted with caution. The tendency to infer cause and effect from a significant relationship is very great.

A *t*-test is the statistic used to determine the significance of the difference between sample means in an experimental design. It helps to assess the presumed effects of various levels of an independent variable.

A correlation is not used to assess differences between means.

A *t* cannot be used for determining relationships.

The Pearson correlation ignores numerical differences between paired scores, which—as I have noted several times—might in fact be in different measurements. Data for analysis with the *t* statistic must be in the same measurement units. This makes sense if we recall that experiments are designed to evaluate the effect of the different levels of an independent variable on a dependent variable—which is the same for all the samples.

I try very hard to keep separated the concepts of *relationship* and *difference*. I believe this distinction contributes to a better understanding of the procedures and statistic to be used for data analysis. My good intentions are often thwarted, however, by the flexibility of the English language, which permits investigators to infer relationships from the identification of differences.

The admissions committee at a particular university designed an orientation program to help improve the retention rate for new students. After several years the committee concluded that the program worked because 72.4% of the orientation program participants were still enrolled one year after admission, compared to 36.5% of an equivalent group of students who had not participated in the program. A *t*-test would evaluate this simple experimental design for significance of the difference. I do not like the usage, but members of the admissions committee would probably say, "There is a significant relationship between orientation program participation and remaining in college." I believe clarity is emphasized when "relationships" are strictly limited to correlational analyses. Calling the observed difference "a relationship" contributes nothing to our understanding of what happened.

People often mistakenly assume that when data are highly correlated, the values in each pair will be very similar. This conclusion confuses difference and relationship. One must work a little to understand that large correlations can result from data that a *t*-test shows are significantly different.

The test/retest method of determining test reliability illustrates this. We give and score a test for 100 people. The average score is 78. After two weeks we give the test over again. This time the average score is 96. Everyone had improved by approximately 18 points. The second set of scores were significantly higher than the first set, but since everyone's score changed by approximately the same amount, the measurements were highly correlated. We would say the test is quite reliable, even though no one got the same score the second time. Table 11.9 illustrates how data can be different but highly correlated, and uncorrelated but not different.

The *t* of the second group, using a correlated sample formula, is 2.81, which is significant at the .05 level for a two-tailed interpretation. An examination of the data will show why the significant difference is no surprise.

Table 11.10 includes examples of several alternatives of relationships and differences. Study the data carefully until you clearly understand the concepts of relationship and difference.

Table 11.9

CORRELATIONS COMPARED TO SIGNIFICANCE OF DIFFERENCES						
Difference Is Not Significant				Difference Is Significant		
Subjects	Scores			Subjects	Scores	
	X	Y			X	Y
Bill	15	15		Bill	15	90
June	06	07		June	06	42
Mary	12	19		Mary	12	114
Joann	08	01		Joann	08	06
Bob	<u>09</u>	<u>08</u>		Bob	<u>09</u>	<u>48</u>
Means	10	10			10	60

Correlations: $r = .75$ $\qquad\qquad\qquad\qquad$ $r = .75$

ENDNOTE

A Note on Statistical Reasoning

A short book by Paulos (1988) on *Innumeracy* has created a lot of interest. In it, he presents many examples and arguments to justify his conclusion that we Americans are not very numerically literate.

Of the many topics he discussed, one was particularly relevant for this text. I have been aware for a long time that a short list of random numbers does not produce a good random sequence. Numbers tend to be bunched up so that 6 might be found three times in 7 numbers and some numbers appear hardly at all in the first 25. Numbers will sometimes come up much more frequently than they should—I thought, by random selection alone.

It had always seemed reasonable to me to expect that even in a short sequence of heads or tails, perhaps 100 tosses, the number of heads should be close to the number of tails, although one would not expect them to be exactly equal. Paulos does not agree. He thinks that if we keep track of a long random sequence the proportions of heads/tails will rarely be close to 50 percent. That surprised me.

Assume that a fair coin is tossed 1,000 times. If heads had come up 519 times and tails 481 in 1000 trials, heads can be considered the leader. He makes the point that once a leader (winner) situation has been established "... it can take a long, long time for the lead to switch, longer often than the average life."

> Perhaps the reason this result is so counterintuitive is that most people tend to think of deviations from the mean as being somehow bound by a rubber band: the greater the deviation, the greater the restoring force toward the mean. The so-called gambler's fallacy is the mistaken belief that because a coin has come up heads several times in a row, it's more likely to come up tails on its next flip.

Paulos gave a computer-generated random sequence of 262 Xs and Os. The number of Xs was 177, compared to 85 Os. I counted the frequency of odd num-

Table 11.10

VARIATIONS OF RELATIONSHIP AND DIFFERENCE	
X	Y

A

X	Y
2	10
4	8
6	6
8	4
10	2

Negatively correlated scores; no significant difference

$r = -0.999$

$M_X = 6; M_Y = 6$

B

X	Y
2	22
4	42
6	62
8	82
10	102

Correlated but significantly different

$r = 0.999$

$t = 4.399$

$M_X = 6; M_Y = 62$

C

X	Y
2	8
4	2
6	10
8	6
10	4

Not correlated; not significantly different

$r = -0.199$

$M_X = 6; M_Y = 6$

D

X	Y
2	80
4	20
6	100
8	60
10	40

Not correlated; difference is significant

$r = -0.199$

$t = 3.726$

$M_X = 6; M_Y = 60$

bers compared to even numbers on a table of random numbers. Of the 220 numbers I examined, the frequency of odd numbers was 117 and even numbers, 103.

Paulos explained that what is found to result from many hundreds of trials is not clearly discernible from a short sequence. This seems to me to argue for an attitude of healthy skepticism about the infallibility of random number sequences.

STUDY QUESTIONS

1. Why are experiments that use identical twins more efficient than similar experiments that use randomly selected subjects?

2.D Why are twins not used more often in behavioral science research when it is well known that work with them can produce better results?

3. In addition to using identical twins, what are some other ways of getting paired subject data?

4. What is the logic of matched subjects designs? How does matching help to control a relevant subject variable?

5. What is the statistical advantage of matching subjects?

6. How does matching reduce the standard error of the difference between the sample means?

7. How is t affected by the size of the standard error?

8. What is wrong with matching by sequential assignment (1,2,3/4,5,6)?

9. How are assignments altered by reversing direction every other sequence (1,2,3/6,5,4)?

10. How are subjects assigned to experimental groups using a random number table?

11. What are some advantages and disadvantages in matching subjects for an experiment?

12. How might an experiment's internal and external validity be affected by pairing subjects?

13. How does the extent of relationship between two sets of data affect the size of the t for paired samples?

14. Know how to compute a t-test for paired samples.
    Contrast the two kinds of t-tests that have been discussed.
    When should each type of t-test formula be used? How is the correct one selected for each particular situation?

15. Explain the difference between a before/after single-group design and the pretest/posttest experimental design.

16. Diagram the basic structure of a pretest/posttest experimental design.

17. Why is the third method for a pretest/posttest data analysis the preferred one? What is wrong with each of the other two?

18. What are experimenter effects?
    How might they affect experiments?

19. How might the use of volunteer subjects affect both the external and internal validity of an experiment?
    How might our knowledge of psychology be affected by the large number of psychology students who are used as subjects in psychology experiments?

20. How might the loss of subjects by dropping out affect the conclusions of an experiment?

21. How are experimental results affected by subject loss when subjects have been matched?

22. What are demand characteristics, and how might an experiment be affected by them?

23. Understand how two sets of data can be highly correlated even when the X and Y means are significantly different.

SMALL TALK

Chapter
12

Interpreting Data

[Some psychologists] consciously reject scientific methodology in favor of subjectivity, intuition, and unconscious "understanding." There can be no argument here; those who look for religion, faith, beauty, or other non-scientific values need fear no scientific criticism. Neither, on the other hand, should they make any claims to having established scientific truths; they cannot reject the methods of science and claim its results.

Eysenck (1960), p. 226

The first part of this chapter provides an opportunity to summarize and review general features of the *experimental* method before we study the logic for data interpretation. If some of the material in the following discussion sounds familiar, it should. We have already studied statistical significance with reference to correlations, and some of the concepts learned at that time will be relevant here. There are, however, several important differences which require a separate evaluation of procedures for interpreting data from experimental designs.

According to the logic of research, investigators identify a problem, develop a possible solution for it, then test the solution to see if it works. All experiments begin with the statement of a testable research hypothesis that states the assumptions to be tested and predicts the outcome to be expected from an experiment. The proposed hypothetical solution (or explanation) becomes the antecedent for a hypothetical syllogism. A consequent, a prediction, is developed from the hypothetical assumptions. Research evaluates the prediction to determine the likelihood that the hypothesis is wrong.

If experimental results affirm the predictions (the consequent in the original hypothetical syllogism), an investigator might be tempted to use this as proof that the hypothesis is true. Recall that affirming the consequent does not guarantee the truth of the antecedent. Research never permits accurate determinations of proof. The best we can get are varying levels of probability that the hypothesis is right.

Early in a statistics class students often make an observation that surprises them. Statistical conclusions are not very accurate; a person cannot always depend on them to be right. Before one discovers that truth about statistics, a sure way to win any argument is to say, "Statistics prove that. . . ." and then carry on to make whatever observation one wants to convey. As politicians and others in the selling business know, very few people understand enough about statistics to challenge statements that are said to be based on statistical conclusions. By the time errors are discovered and publicized, it is much too late to change opinions.

Readers of this text who are not already sufficiently knowledgeable about statistics to exploit, abuse, and misapply statistical conclusions for their own advantage might want to consult Kimble's (1978) *How to Use [and Misuse] Statistics*, or Huff's (1954) *How to Lie With Statistics*. These are just two of several books that have been written on this general subject. They teach a lot about applied statistics by showing how they are misused. Learning what statistics can and cannot do is the best way we have of defending against statistical abuses.

Assume for the following discussion that the work involved in carrying out a research project has been completed. It involved a simple experiment that used two groups of subjects. The research hypothesis predicted that the mean of the X group subjects should be larger than the mean of the Y group—but how much larger? How large a difference must be obtained before it will be possible to reject a statistical "null hypothesis of no difference"?

The limitations behavioral scientists face in controlling extraneous conditions and the complexity of the behavior they want to study make it necessary to use statistics for data analysis. We might want a better technique, but statistics are all we have, so statistics are what we use. The brief exercise that follows illustrates why a statistical analysis of experimental data is necessary.

Assume that we have the results of a simple experiment involving two groups of randomly assigned subjects. One group included 18 participants, and the other group had 15. Let us also assume the experiment was well-designed and properly carried out, so subject variables and all extraneous conditions were essentially equivalent between the two groups. Interval measurements permitted the computation of means. We want to know if the action of the X level of the independent variable produced a mean that was both larger and "significantly different" from the mean of the Y group.

If the mean of X was 147 and the mean of Y was 147, a statistic is not needed to verify that the mean of the X scores was not larger than the mean of Y (as predicted by the research hypothesis) and the difference was not significant. These data would force the conclusion that the research hypothesis was wrong.

To illustrate the extreme reverse alternative, assume the mean of X was 147 and the mean of Y was 0. With these data we would probably conclude that something produced a difference so large that we would have trouble explaining it except in terms of the independent variable differences. We would be happy to use these data to "prove" that our hypothesis is true, but "proofs" given in this way are not dependable. The data fail to reject the research hypothesis—or we might say they tend to support it—but they did not prove that it is right.

Interpretation of less extreme differences of the sort obtained from real data are a great deal more troublesome. To see the difficulty, study the following numbers to select the smallest difference that you would say is "statistically significant": (a) 147 for X and 140 for Y; (b) 147 and 135; (c) 147 and 120; (d) 147 and 100; (e) 147 and 75. The truth is, we cannot make a decision about significance by "looking" at data. This chapter studies how to determine statistical significance and develops the logic that helps us to understand what it means.

The *t*-test, or *t* ratio, is one of the most widely used statistics for evaluating data from simple experiments, so it will be the focus of this discussion. The basic principles for all statistical interpretations are similar, so concepts learned in the study of the *t*-test can be expanded and applied to other, more advanced, research designs.

NULL AND RESEARCH HYPOTHESES

Research (Alternate) Hypotheses

These are the guides we use for research. They ask the questions and offer tentative answers. Statisticians refer to research hypotheses as "alternate hypotheses," even though they are the reason for conducting the research in the first place. Common symbols for research (alternate) hypotheses are: H_a or H_1.

Research hypotheses are not dealt with directly. What we do with them depends on the statistical decision about rejecting the null hypotheses (H_0). A null hypothesis is a statistical hypothesis designed for the sole purpose of rejecting it, if possible, following an evaluation of the data.

In a great many places a null hypothesis, without reference to any particular statistic, is loosely and incorrectly referred to as "the" null hypothesis, as if there is only one. There are as many statements of null hypotheses as there are inferential statistics. When one learns a statistic and how to compute it, one also learns how to state its null hypothesis.

Null Hypotheses

The null hypothesis for a *t*-test asserts that the mean of the dependent variable measurements for the population from which the X sample was selected is the same as the mean of the population from which the Y sample was selected. Another way of expressing the same idea is, the difference between the dependent variable mean for Population X and the population mean of Y is zero. The formulas would be: $\mu_X = \mu_Y$ or $\mu_{X-Y} = 0$. The symbol for a population mean is μ.

Note that we are comparing the population means, not sample means. This distinction is important. We cannot study population means directly, so we use samples to draw inductive inferences about them.

To understand the logic of null hypothesis interpretation we might do well to follow the thinking of statisticians. They start by assuming that subjects used in an experiment are *random samples from the same population*. Statisticians have worked out what to expect if an infinite (or at least very large) number of samples, all of the same size, were randomly selected from a given population. A frequency distribution for all these sample means would form a normal curve called a "sampling distribution of means." The mean of the sample means will equal the mean for the population. The variability among the sampling means is the "standard error of the mean." This provides the information we need for estimating the amount of variability we can expect from random variation. The standard error of the mean is the value that goes in the denominator of the t ratio.

Most sample means will cluster around the mean of the population, so the means of any two typical random samples will not normally be very far apart. Very rarely will a sample be randomly selected that has a small mean, and the mean of the other sample will be large. Statisticians have calculated the probability of this happening and have given us the figures in a table. We can ask the table, "What is the probability of randomly selecting two samples that have this large a difference between their means?" In effect, we want to know the probability of drawing random samples with various differences. Specifically we ask how large the difference must be in order for us to conclude that the probability of it being a chance occurrence is only about 1/20 (.05), or perhaps 1/100 (.01).

When a difference between sample means exceeds the limits statisticians have set for defining random variation, we conclude that the probability of it being a chance occurrence is small. It seems more likely the samples are *not random samples from the same population*. Some condition other than chance variation is a better explanation of the difference.

REJECTING A NULL HYPOTHESES

Statistics offers only two ways of dealing with null hypotheses: either they can be rejected or they can *fail* to be rejected. The correct logical analysis wants us to reject a null hypothesis if we can, but failing to reject a null hypothesis is not the same as "accepting" it.

These ideas, like many others in statistics and experimental design, sound more confusing when they are described than they need to be in practice. Consider this explanation from an excellent text on nonparametric statistics by Siegel and Castellan (1988).

> The *null hypothesis* is an hypothesis of "no effect" and is usually formulated for the express purpose of being rejected; that is, it is the negation of the point one is trying to make. If it is rejected, the alternative hypothesis (H_1) is supported. The *alternative hypothesis* is the operational statement of the experimenter's research hypothesis.

A research hypothesis and a null hypothesis are, in all but the rarest instances, stated in opposite ways, so both of them cannot be rejected at the same time. The decision we make about a null hypothesis determines the decision we make about the research hypothesis. Null hypotheses are given the right of first rejection in data analysis. For a *t*-test, *a null hypothesis tries to identify the probability of occurrence of observed differences between means, assuming that the null hypothesis is true.*

Probability values for null hypothesis rejection have been set arbitrarily because the continuous nature of underlying sampling distributions does not identify a cutoff value for significance. Later we will see that a specific difference might, or might not, be "statistically significant." The conclusion would depend on the level we chose for rejecting the null hypothesis, and on other decisions we make about the nature of the research hypothesis.

EVALUATION OF NULL HYPOTHESES

Assume that a *t* has been computed and needs to be evaluated for statistical significance. As I stated earlier, the statement of a null hypothesis will vary according to the statistic, but the general pattern of interpretation discussed for the *t* will apply to other statistics as well.

The size of the probability value given in a *t* table (usually titled something like "Critical Values for *t* Distributions") will be partly determined by the sample size. We cannot use the table directly by entering it with sample size, however. First one must determine "degrees of freedom," which are related to, but are not the same as, sample size. The normal curve table is applicable with "population" data, or very large samples. The *t*-test is generally used with small samples.

Degrees of freedom for a random group's *t*-test is the number of scores in the X group, plus the number of scores in the Y group minus two $(N_X + N_Y - 2)$. (This is sometimes stated as $[N_X - 1] + [N_Y - 1]$).

Degrees of freedom for a matched subjects *t*-test is the number of *pairs* of scores minus 1. Matched, related, or correlated designs require pairs of subjects who are matched in some way.

If the degrees of freedom for a particular experiment is not listed on the table, use the next smaller value that is listed.

For the present, ignore the concept of a "one or two-tailed test" and assume the use of a two-tailed interpretation. You will need to consult Table 12.1 during the following discussion.

The figures in the body of the table are values of *t*. The figures across the top give the decimal probability that an obtained *t* for a specified degrees of freedom could have resulted from chance.

Table 12.1

		PROBABILITY VALUES FOR *t* (TWO-TAILED TEST)				
df	*.50*	*.20*	*.10*	*.05*	*.02*	*.01*
5	0.727	1.476	2.015	2.571	3.363	4.032
15	0.691	1.341	1.753	2.132	2.602	2.947
25	0.684	1.316	1.708	2.060	2.485	2.787

Degrees of freedom are given in the df column at the left. Looking at the row for df = 15, we see t values that range in size from 0.691 to 2.947. These numbers and those in between relate to the probability values given across the top and are read like this: When df is 15, a t of 2.132 is necessary for significance at the .05 level. This means that a t of that size for df = 15 will on the average, in a large number of trials, occur about once in 20 times even if there is no effect from the experimental conditions being studied.

A statistic must be equal to or larger than the value in the body of the table to achieve significance at the value given at the top of the table. A t of 2.602 or larger is significant at the .02 level, when df = 15. What is the level of significance for a t of 2.678 when df = 25? The answer is .02. The obtained t is not large enough for significance at the .01 level.

Two points should be noted about the relationships among t, df, and probability. When the sample sizes remain the same, a larger t produces a smaller probability value. For a given t value, larger samples will, up to a point, produce smaller probability values. A t does not have to be large to be significant if the df is large. A larger t is necessary for significance when the df is small.

This idea can be emphasized with a little practice. Note how the value of t necessary for significance at a specified level, say .02, gets smaller as the df is increased. Go to the .02 column and see that a t of 3.363 is required when df = 5; 2.602 is necessary when df = 15; but a t of 2.48 will be large enough when df = 25.

This relationships between the size of t and df is not linear; the effect is much greater when df is small. After df = 40 the t value necessary for the same level of significance changes very little as the sample size increases. For df = 40 a $t = 2.423$ is required for statistical significance at the .02 level. If the sample size is increased to infinity, a slightly smaller t of 2.326 is statistically significant at the same level. Increasing sample sizes beyond 40 produces only a slight improvement in statistical significance for t values of the same size. (These figures are from a larger table than the one given above.)

Reading the table is the easiest part; interpreting what the figures mean is more complicated. A probability value of .05 or smaller indicates statistical significance sufficient to justify *rejection* of the null hypothesis and *failure to reject* the research hypothesis (H_a). Failing to reject the research hypothesis supports the idea that the hypothesis could be right. Probability values of .06 or larger tell us that we do not reject the null hypothesis. Values such as .08, .15, and .53 indicate an increasingly large probability that results are attributable to chance variation.

Published statistical conclusions usually state a finding was "not significant," or a specific probability value of .05 or smaller is indicated. A fairly standard code for identifying the level of statistical significance is sometimes seen in the literature: one asterisk * means .05 level, ** means .01, and *** means .001.

When a null hypothesis is rejected it is tempting but not entirely correct to assume that the findings confirm the research hypothesis; Bartz (1988, p. 254) explains:

> The statistical procedure allows us only to reject the null hypothesis, since such a decision is based on the probability of a difference occurring by sampling error. The

researcher cannot go any farther than that and use this approach to prove why a difference exists.

ONE- OR TWO-TAILED TEST

The idea of "directional hypotheses" and alternate ways for interpreting them are applicable to simple experiments that have two levels of an independent variable. The wording of the research hypothesis for simple experiments allows three ways of interpreting results. The mean of Group X is predicted to be significantly larger than the mean of Group Y. The mean of Group Y is predicted to be significantly larger than the mean of Group X. The third alternative is "nondirectional." The hypothesis expects a difference between the two means, but the direction of the difference was not predicted by the experimenter.

The "one- or two-tailed test" expression refers to the tails of a probability distribution. The area in one tail will be used to obtain probability values for a one-tailed test. A *t* probability distribution is symmetrical, so the areas in the tails are identical and can be combined for a two-tailed analysis. Tables publish probability values for one-tail, two-tails, or both. Tables should indicate whether the given probability values are for one or two tails, but not all of them do.

The selection of a one- or two-tailed test is a matter of considerable controversy, because the decision about which interpretation will be used can alter conclusions. The computations are not changed by the decision; a computed *t* is the same value no matter how the research hypothesis is stated. There will, however, be an effect on the determination of statistical significance.

One may safely take for granted that an investigator undertakes an experiment to test a hypothesis that he or she expects to turn out in a certain way. If the resulting difference between means is found to be statistically significant at the .04 level, the investigator will be pleased because the experiment tended to support the hypothesis. A probability level of .08 puts the hypothesis outside the normally accepted .05 or smaller level for statistical significance. But whether the probability value is .04 or .08 is a matter of interpretation that depends wholly on whether a one- or two-tailed interpretation has been used.

When you have a probability value for a one-tailed test and need a probability value for a two-tailed interpretation, multiply the one-tailed value by 2. If the table only provides probability values for a two-tailed interpretation, you can obtain the one-tailed value by dividing the two-tailed value by 2. The procedure is obvious, but confusing. A two-tailed interpretation needs the combined area in both tails. A one-tailed interpretation uses the area in only one tail—which is, of course, half the area in two tails.

After a little study these ideas should be clear enough, at least until you have to answer this type of question: "A student applied a one-tailed interpretation to some data and found the results to be significant at the .04 level. The instructor decided that the hypothesis required a two-tailed interpretation. Is the new value .02 or .08?" (Two tails incorporates the area in both tails, so it is twice as large as the .04 value given in the one-tailed interpretation. The correct answer is .08)

Assume here that a researcher completed an experiment that resulted in a .10 tabled probability value for a two-tailed test; not nearly enough for significance at the standard .05 level. After reviewing the data, he decided that he could make a case for a one-tailed interpretation. Without altering a single item of data and solely through interpretation, the same results suddenly became significant at the .05 level. Is this a legitimate procedure?

The point is an important one, and it has aroused a lot of discussion. How is it possible for exactly the same data to be statistically significant, and also not? The original data and all related calculations have not changed. No wonder people who have not studied statistics can get confused.

An investigator generally wants to obtain a significant difference between means in order to demonstrate the differential action of the two levels of an independent variable. This is more easily done with a one-tailed test, because the probability in one tail is half as large as a two-tailed interpretation.

Clearly there is an advantage in using a one-tailed interpretation. The decision about whether a one- or a two-tailed interpretation is the correct one should be determined from the research hypothesis. Research integrity requires that justification for a one-tailed interpretation should be established before the experiment is begun. Ethical investigators would not study the data and revise their thinking just to take advantage of a one-tailed interpretation. Perhaps this is a good place to insert a reminder: Even though it is the research hypothesis that identifies the direction of the interpretation, it is the null hypothesis that is actually being interpreted through the statistical analysis.

Statisticians have strong feelings about directional interpretations, apparently more so than experimental psychologists. Senter (1969), a respected writer of an excellent statistics text, makes the following statement rather forcefully:

> This writer feels that one-tailed interpretations of the t ratio should generally be avoided unless the circumstances under which the data are collected *firmly* and *undeniably* indicate their use. Such "firm and undeniable" circumstances rarely occur, especially in the behavioral sciences.

Scientific journals seem to encourage nondirectional analyses because the more conservative interpretation reduces the probability of rejecting null hypotheses that should not be rejected. One would also use a two-tailed analysis in situations in which the investigator has either no control or only a limited control over extraneous influences. When the experimental variables and assignment of subjects has not been managed by the investigator, as is the case with "ex post facto research designs," he or she might not have sufficient information for a directional statement about the outcome.

Two-tailed interpretations are often used in exploratory work, when a test or a test battery produces so many subtest scores that the investigator cannot have an opinion about all of them. When many measurements are available, investigators typically do not make predictions about the outcome of each test. A common practice is to report results by noting and discussing only the tests that showed significant differences.

Whenever it is possible to make a number of evaluations at the same time, it is probable, by their numbers alone, that some of them will reach statistical significance. The foundation of statistically significant differences is probability, and the probability of something happening is increased by expanding the number of trials.

A one-tailed prediction might sometime, though rarely, produce an interpretive anomaly. Suppose an investigator made a one-tailed prediction from the research hypothesis that the mean of the X group would be significantly larger than the mean of Group Y. Suppose there was a significant difference between the means of the two groups, but it was in a direction *opposite* to the one predicted: $M_X = 63.2$ and $M_Y = 84.2$. How should the investigator interpret these results?

When a research hypothesis clearly states the direction of a predicted difference, and when results are in the opposite direction, the *research* hypothesis should be rejected even if the difference is statistically significant. An investigator in this situation would want to reexamine the original hypothesis and the nature of the experiment to determine how a result could have been obtained that was opposite to the one predicted.

WHAT DOES A SIGNIFICANT DIFFERENCE REALLY MEAN?

Table 12.2 presents scores as they might have been obtained from a simple experiment. The data were contrived to illustrate some major points. Score values have been arranged in the form of crude curves that make it easier to note differences between the groups.

A *t*-table shows that this *t* is significant at the .05 level (two-tailed test). The probability of getting a 13-point difference between averages by chance selection of subjects is in the neighborhood of 1 in 20.

Table 12.2 shows in a rough but generally useful way the large overlap that can exist between two groups of scores, even though their *averages* are "significantly" different. Only one person in Group X got a score lower than anyone in

Table 12.2

MEASUREMENTS FROM A SIMPLE EXPERIMENT								
				50				
Y			40	50	60			
		30	40	50	60	70		
	20	30	40	50	60	70	80	
			40					
X		30	40	50				
	20	30	40	50	60			
10	20	30	40	50	60	70		

N = 16 for both groups

ΣX	640		ΣY	848
ΣX^2	29,600		ΣY^2	49,184
SD	16.32		SD	16.81
Mean X = 40			Mean Y = 53	

$t = 2.21$

Group Y, and only one person got a score in Y that was higher than anyone in Group X. Except for one person, everyone in Group X got a score identical to at least one person in Group Y. The observation that many scores in the X group—the group with the lower average scores—were higher than many scores in the Y group is an important point in statistical interpretation of significant differences that is frequently overlooked.

Suppose the psychologist who collected these data published an article in which it was stated that, "Group X in my experiment got significantly lower scores than did the people in Group Y on the UVW Test of Emotional Adjustment." Many people seem to mistakenly think of a "significant difference" as if it represented two separate and distinct groups, often with no overlap at all. A person who has had no training in statistics has difficulty understanding that even when there is a very large difference between the average scores of two groups, this does not necessarily mean that everyone in one group did better than everyone in the other.

Behavioral scientists who do the research, evaluate the data, and write the journal articles are trained to understand statistical interpretations. When the work is discussed in other articles and particularly when the work is reviewed by people who do not understand statistics, the observed difference can easily become a headline: "Scientist Finds Lower Scores on Emotional Adjustment Scale for Latchkey Children. Mental Health Seriously Harmed by Parental Absence." Newspaper bits of this sort distort the original findings. When a research result is labeled by an author as "significant," there is a strong temptation to conclude that a new law of nature has been identified. Anyone who has read this far in the text knows that science is not so simple.

The word "significant" is one of the causes of interpretive confusion, because the word can be used in two ways. Statistical significance has a clearly defined, rather narrow meaning that only a person who has studied statistics would understand. General readers tend to translate "significant" into "worthwhile" or "meaningful," or even "important," terms that do not represent the statistical meaning. Bakan (1967) has filed a strong objection to rejecting a null hypothesis and then concluding that the result is significant. He believes that

> . . . one of the most injurious things that has happened in the history of psychological research is indicated by that term. The word significance carries a surplus meaning of somehow being important. In point of fact, when we get a significant difference it only means that the difference in the population is not zero, which may hardly be significant at all.
>
> The fact remains that a difference between means, including the difference between means in the population, which is all that we are ever testing, is simply a difference between means, no more and no less, and as such it says very little.

Bakan is only one of many writers who have challenged conventional techniques for interpretation of research data. Rozeboom (1960) has called particular attention to psychology's normal way for evaluating hypotheses. (See "The Fallacy of the Null-Hypothesis Significance Tests"). One of his points notes that probability values are obtained along a continuum, so there is no inherently logical point for making such a sharp distinction between significant or not significant. The cut value at the .05 level is entirely arbitrary. He has argued for degrees of judgment, or as he states his view, "Decisions vs. Degrees of Belief."

> . . . the primary aim of scientific experiment is not to precipitate decisions, but to make an appropriate adjustment to the degree to which one accepts, or believes, the hypothesis or hypotheses being tested.

TYPE I AND TYPE II ERRORS IN INTERPRETATION

The .05 level (the alpha level) for rejecting a null hypothesis is a convention that accepts that investigators occasionally will incorrectly reject a null hypothesis.

An investigator could reduce the probability of making this error by choosing a smaller level than the usual .05 alpha level—say .02 or .01; or perhaps he or she would go even further to the .001 level. There is still a possibility for error, but at this value it is quite small. The chances of being wrong are reduced, but this also reduces the investigator's chances of identifying a true difference, or relationship when correlations are used. The behavioral sciences nearly always produce data with a lot of overlap, so real average differences might not be easy to identify if too narrow an interpretation is used.

An adjustment in the conservative direction might, if it goes too far, fail to identify a "true" difference. We will make a mistake if we are too liberal and assume a significant difference when in fact none exists, and we will make a mistake if we do not recognize a significant difference. These alternatives have been summarized in Table 12.3.

A correct decision results when an actually false null hypothesis is rejected. This is the case when an independent variable, not some uncontrolled condition, did in fact produce an observed difference. False null hypotheses should be rejected.

Correct decisions also result when true null hypotheses are not rejected. A null hypothesis asserts that chance is the best explanation. If chance factors were in fact the cause of observed differences, and we recognize the null as being true, then we have made a correct decision. Errors occur when we fail to reject a false null hypothesis or reject a true one.

Table 12.3

TYPE I AND TYPE II ERRORS			
		The Experimenter's Decision About the Null Hypothesis	
		Reject H_0	Do not reject H_0
Factual state of null hypothesis (truth of nature)	True	Type I error	Correct decision
	False	Correct decision	Type II error

Leary and Altmaier (1980) called attention to another area in which Type I errors appear to be excessive. The .05 level as used for interpretation of experimental findings means that on the average we will expect to be wrong in about 1 out of 20 experiments *when only one statistical test* is used for the same set of data. The computation of more than one statistical analysis—*t*-tests, for example—will increase the probability of making a Type I error to beyond the .05 level.

> In the case of perfectly uncorrelated tests, the actual probability of Type I error is equal to 1-(1 – alpha)^c, where $"c"$ is the number of comparisons performed (Kirk, 1968). Thus, if 10 independent *t*-tests are performed on a group of data, each at alpha = .05, the probability of making at least one Type I error is not .05 but 1-(1 – .05)^{10} = .40.

The increase in the number of unexpected Type I errors can occur when an investigator analyzes data from research that included more than one dependent variable. Leary and Altmaier (1980) analyzed all the full-length articles that appeared in the *Journal of Counseling Psychology* in 1978 and 1979. They found that "approximately 60% have inflated rates of Type I error due to less than ideal statistical analyses." Their solution is to urge broader use of multivariate statistics. Instead of analyzing each of several dependent variables with a *t*-test, analysis of variance or multiple analysis of variance (manova) should be the statistic used. These statistics analyze the group of data as a whole.

I consider a Type I error to be more serious than Type II. I believe the history of science shows that a great deal more effort is expended overthrowing incorrect hypotheses than is needed for testing new ones. If I had a choice, I would rather have no explanation of a phenomenon than an incorrect one.

All sciences have difficulty with hypotheses that seem to fit observations some but not all of the time. They are not very good, but neither are they totally inadequate. Evidence for these hypotheses in psychology can be seen by the "often"s and "usually"s or similar modifiers that are included with very nearly every explanation of behavior.

Behavioral science is a young area, so no one should be surprised by its many mistakes and false hopes. We need not be concerned that the science of psychology still has some growing up to do. Time and hard work will take care of that. I am concerned that we sometimes act as if we know a great deal more than we do. If psychology must make a mistake in its headlong rush to maturity, the error should lean toward the side of extra caution—at least in my opinion.

Kahneman, Fredrickson, Schreiber, and Redelmeier (1993) published research that involved a simple experimental design. Their report carried a somewhat enigmatic title: "When More Pain is Preferred to Less." Pain, or discomfort, was measured in response to the feelings of keeping one's hand in a tub of water maintained at a temperature of 14°C. They compared this response with a response that started at the same temperature but went longer, with the water consequently getting slightly warmer. The second trial finished with a less painful response, but the pain went on over a longer period of time. Quite a few subjects seemed to prefer that. "An on-line measure of discomfort was obtained using a "discomfort meter," which consisted of a potentiometer and a linear array of 15 light-emitting diodes (LEDs)." The level of discomfort was indicated by altering the number of lights turned on by the potentiometer.[1]

The mean response for one condition was much lower than for another: $t = 6.80, p < .01$.

> The comparative ratings that subjects provided after stating their choice were usually consistent with decisions, but not always with facts. Thus, most subjects indicated that the long trial had caused less overall discomfort ($t = 2.12, p = <.05$), was less cold at its most extreme moment ($t = 1.90$), and was less tough to cope with ($t = 2.90, p < .01$).

There! That should demonstrate the importance of understanding statistical evaluation if one is to make sense out of journal articles.

PRACTICE PROBLEMS

(Answers are given at the end of the chapter.)

1. Assume that a certain research hypothesis required for its acceptance a significant difference between the means of two samples. Do we interpret the t using a one- or two-tailed test?
2. For the same t and sample sizes, which produces a higher level of significance, a one- or a two-tailed test?
3. If a p value of .03 was obtained for a one-tailed test, what would the p value be if the same data were interpreted as a two-tailed test?
4. A research hypothesis stated that the M_X should be less than the M_Y. The X group mean was 37 and the Y group mean was 48, and $p = .07$ (two-tailed table). What decision do we make about the research hypothesis?
5. Suppose that in Problem 4 the results were 114 as the mean of X and 103 as the mean of Y, $p = .04$ for a one-tailed test. What decision do we make about the research hypothesis?
6. A student looked up a p value for a certain t with a specific df and found the p value to be .06 for a one-tailed interpretation. The instructor in charge of the project decided that the data should be interpreted using a two-tailed test. What is the final conclusion the student would make about the project's statistical significance?
7. a. If a t value is known to be significant at the .05 level, is it also significant at the .01 level?
   b. Is a t that is significant at the .01 level also definitely significant at the .05 level?

For each of the following explain whether it should be interpreted using a one- or two-tailed test.

---

[1] A great deal more was involved than I have hinted at. My purpose in selecting this article was to show how data of the sort we have been studying are reported in journal articles.

8. There is no difference of lifetime incomes between college and noncollege graduates.
9. Women have a higher level of intuition than do men.
10. The effect of motivation is to increase the speed of response.
11. There might or might not be a difference between extroverts and introverts on the XYQ test.
12. The obtained difference in scores on a sense-of-humor test between people classified as having high or low levels of insight is about 32 points.

ENDNOTE

Misunderstanding Statistics

A statistic is nothing more than a number computed in a certain way. The number itself is neither good nor bad, honest nor misleading. How the number is interpreted, understood, or given meaning determines its value in understanding the features of the world we are studying. Often, as in the following example, we have to know some fundamental information about the characteristic of the original data. If we do not, we might use the statistic to make an interpretation that is not reasonable. This example is like one in Paulos's book *Innumeracy: Mathematical Illiteracy and Its Consequences* (1990).

We can easily conclude from the following (fictitious) data that a particular graduate college accepts a greater *percentage* of its male than of its female applicants. Although the same number of students was accepted, the number of women who applied was much larger so the proportion accepted was smaller. This could be a cause for concern about the college admission policies.

	Males	Females
Total number of students who applied for admission	300	500
Total number accepted	170	170
Percent accepted	57%	34%

The addition of the following information markedly alters the meaning of these data. We should understand that graduate students specialize in certain areas or departments, and it is into these areas that they are admitted. Now study the following data.

	Males	Females
Engineering or Math		
Number applied for admission	200	30
Number accepted in the program	140	21
Percent accepted	70%	70%
Psychology, English, or Social Studies		
Number applied for admission	100	470
Number accepted in the program	30	149
Percent accepted	30%	32%

The overall picture of admissions shows that relatively few women applied for training in the engineering and math areas, but of those who did, the proportion of men and women admitted was the same.

Most of the women (470 out of 500) applied for admission to programs in the psychology, English, and social studies areas. A slightly larger percentage of women compared to men who applied for admission to this program were admitted. A person wanting to distort the meaning of the data might point out that five times as many women as men were admitted into the psychology, English, and social studies areas (149/30). This is true, of course, but five times as many women applied. If these statistics were real they ought to be used to encourage women to shift their areas of interest from psychology, English, and Social Studies to engineering and math, where there is much less competition for admission—and the salaries for final employment are likely to be higher.

STUDY QUESTIONS

1.D What is wrong with using "gut reactions," personal feelings, and opinions as evidence in support of scientific theories?

2. What is a null hypothesis?
    Where do null hypotheses come from?
    How are they used?

3. How is the null hypothesis for the *t*-test stated?

4. Differentiate between a null and a research hypothesis.

5. Explain the procedure for determining the validity of a research hypothesis by rejecting a null hypothesis.

6.D What does it mean to reject a null hypothesis?

7. How do we look up the probability value for determining statistical significance of a *t*-test?

    What information is required?

8. What does it mean to say that the difference between two averages is "statistically significant"?

9. How does the size of the samples affect the decision of statistical significance?

10.D Which is better, a large *t* and a small sample or a small *t* and a large sample—or might they produce essentially the same results? Explain.

11. Which shows a higher level of statistical significance, a large or a small *p* value?

12. Explain the difference between a one- and a two-tailed interpretation of a null hypothesis.
    How does a person determine which to use?
    How does the decision affect the determination of significance?

13.D When a battery of tests is used as dependent variables, what is wrong with just going down the list and discussing significant differences?
Why should we bother with differences that are not significant?

14.D How would you explain to someone who does not understand statistics what a significant difference between two averages really means?

15. Explain the distinction between "statistical significance" and the idea of being important or meaningful.

16. Explain and differentiate between a Type I and a Type II error.

17. How can analysis of several experiments with a *t*-test increase the probability of Type I errors?
What statistical analysis is recommended to avoid this?

18. According to the author, which is the more serious type of error, I or II? Why?

19. What is wrong with hypotheses that are only partly right?

ANSWERS TO PRACTICE PROBLEMS

1. Two-tail. The direction of the difference was not specified.

2. One-tail. The probability for one-tail is half the value for two-tails, therefore it will be half as large. The smaller the p value, the greater the level of statistical significance.

3. .06.

4. Reject the null at .035. This is a directional hypothesis, so use half the table value for a two-tailed test.

5. Do not interpret the null hypothesis. The research hypothesis clearly stated a specific direction for an outcome. The results are the *opposite* of what they should have been. Reject the research hypothesis.

6. Do not reject the null hypothesis.

7. a. A *t* that is significant at the .05 level might or might not be large enough for significance at the .01 level.

    b. The .01 level is more significant than .05. These questions are a little like saying, "I have at least a quarter in my pocket; do I have a dollar? The answer is we do not know. (If I tell you that I have a dollar, you can be certain that I have at least a quarter.)

8. Two-tail. Direction of expected difference is not specified.

9. One-tail. Direction is specified.

10. One-tail.

11. Two-tail.

12. Probably two-tail. Direction of difference is not specified, but the investigator might have expected that high-insight people would have a better sense of humor than low-insight people.

SMALL TALK

Chapter
13

Factorial Design

*It is the faith of all science that an unlimited num-
ber of phenomena can be comprehended in terms of
a limited number of concepts or ideal constructs.
Without this faith no science could ever have any
motivation. To deny this faith is to affirm the primary chaos of nature and the consequent futility of
scientific effort. The constructs in terms of which
natural phenomena are comprehended are man-
made inventions. To discover a scientific law is
merely to discover that a man-made scheme serves
to unify, and thereby to simplify, comprehension of
a certain class of natural phenomena.*

Thurstone, 1935.

"Younger Wives, Longer Lives . . . " was the title of a discussion in "The Sexes"
section of *Psychology Today* magazine (1984, September p. 12). "Those men
married to younger women generally lived longer than expected." Later in the
discussion the direction changed to consider another situation in which
". . . Older wives, better lives. Older men may live longer if they have younger
wives, but there are reasons to suggest that the quality of life may be better in
marriages between older women and younger men."

"Dynamic interaction" is a summarizing phrase that expresses the true
nature of influences acting on behavior: complex, subtle, and tangled. The interrelationships among psychological forces operating in real people have driven

psychologists to move beyond simple experiments to more elaborate designs. Experiments discussed so far have had only one independent variable with two levels. The study of experiments having at least two independent variables, each with two or more levels, moves experiments into the area of "factorial design."

This beginning discussion will permit only a limited and superficial introduction to a complex topic. Enough information will be included so that anyone reading a journal article that includes comparisons of several independent variables will be able to understand the nature of the research well enough to evaluate the conclusions.

Statistical techniques for data interpretation from factorial designs will not be included. *Analysis of variance* (anova) identifies a category of statistics for use with factorial experiments, but these are well beyond the prescribed limitations of this beginning text.

Factorial design, which is studied in this chapter, is not the same as "factor analysis." The terms can be easily confused. Factor analysis is a statistical technique for analyzing a table of correlations to discover and identify interrelationships and common elements among the measurements.

An older naming practice used the name "factors" for what this text has been calling "levels" of an independent variable. The name "factorial designs" identifies a complex experiment in which there are at least two independent variables, each of which has at least two levels, or four factors all together.

Two independent variables with two levels each, form a simple "two by two" design—which is as complex as this chapter will get. Four factors is the minimum number of groups in a simple factorial experiment, but experiments can be designed to include three or even more independent variables, and three or more levels for each of them. I have selected diagram techniques for interpretation of factorial experiments, but complex experiments are impossible to diagram in a useful way.

A FACTORIAL DESIGN EXPERIMENT

A study to determine which combinations of old men/young women or old women/young men make for the best marriages might be interesting, but the resulting ex post facto design project would quickly develop into a much too complicated example for a simple introduction.

For this demonstration assume that a psychologist wants to learn more about boys' and girls' personality differences. Her preliminary observations suggested that boys and girls did not react in the same way to computers. Boys seemed to approach them with a more relaxed manner; when playing computer games they were almost aggressive in the way in which they used the computers to win. The psychologist thought that girls were generally not so interested in computers as the boys were. When girls played arcade computer games they did not seem nearly as forceful as the boys did. She concluded that girls typically react more strongly to people when they play games, whereas boys react more strongly to inanimate competition as characterized by computers.

The experiment she outlined had two "independent variables" with two levels of each: gender of the participants (boy or girl), and the type of opponent (a person or a machine in the form of a computer). We must exercise a little caution in thinking of gender as an independent variable with male and female forming the two levels. Gender is an ex post facto variable, because it is not under the control of the investigator. Gender differences were earlier called "subject variables," which in many experiments we would like to control. Although it is an arguable point, I have no trouble in thinking of male and female differences as levels of an independent variable that differ according to type. When we select subjects according to a pre-existing condition we should keep in mind that differences we observe might not have been caused by the condition itself but by attributes related to it.

Subjects for a simple factorial experiment are randomly assigned to each of the four levels if all of the levels can be varied by the investigator. When one (or both) of the independent variables is a pre-existing condition, subjects cannot be randomly assigned. That is the case with gender in this example. Participants within each boy or girl group would, however, be randomly assigned to the levels of the independent variable that are directly manipulated by the experimenter (i.e., whether a subject thought that he or she was playing against another person or against a computer program as the opponent).

The psychologist developed a computer game for this experiment, in which performance was more strongly affected by concentration and desire to win than by practice, learning, or inherent skill of the players.

One level of the "type of opponent" independent variable was arranged so half of both the male and female participants thought they were playing the computer game against a human opponent who was at the controls of another linked computer in the same room at the same time. This was a misdirection because the computer program was, in fact, always in control for all trials with all subjects. This arrangement was necessary to standardize conditions and to remove the element of variability caused by a human opponent. Supposed human opponents were always of the same gender as the participant in order to avoid an additional complexity of opposite gender competition.

The second half of the participants played against the computer, with the understanding that no human participant was involved. During these trials no human opponent was in the room.

Assume for the remainder of this discussion that all normal research conditions have been met in terms of selection and assignment of participants, standardization of conditions. All other factors that could affect the outcome were also appropriately controlled.

This example is greatly simplified, but even with two independent variables and only two levels of each it will seem to be sufficiently complex for an initial introduction. The two levels of each of the two independent variables are given with their symbols in Table 13.1. The same dependent variable that operationally defines the outcome is used for each of the four groups.

Table 13.1

INDEPENDENT VARIABLES IN A FACTORIAL DESIGN EXPERIMENT			
Independent Variables		Levels	
A	Gender of participant	A 1	Girl
		A 2	Boy
B	Apparent form of opponent	B 1	Person
		B 2	Computer

The following alternatives identify the four different groups of subjects, as they appear from the subject's point of view:

A1 B1	Girls playing against a girl opponent
A1 B2	Girls playing against a computer
A2 B1	Boys playing against a boy opponent
A2 B2	Boys playing against a computer

FACTORIAL DESIGN ANALYSIS

A typical factorial design experiment (in which both independent variables were under the control of the experimenter) would probably have 15 or more randomly assigned subjects in each of the experimental conditions. Groups would not be required to be of exactly the same size, but they should be close. For the following discussion, assume that all four groups are of equal size, 15. Analysis is a little easier to understand if the N's are the same for all groups.

Each of the 60 participants involved played the game five times; the total of five game scores was each subject's final score. The average of these scores for each group was the dependent variable measurement. The group averages are given in the "Scores" column of Table 13.2. An analysis of variance could be computed to determine whether there are statistically significant differences among the means, but quite a lot can be learned by studying the graphed data.

Each block, or cell (to use an alternate name), at the intersection of a row and a column consists of a sample involved with the attributes of that row and that column. A2B2, for example, identifies the group of boys who played the game against the computer as the opponent. A1B1 identifies the group of girls who played the game against what they presumed to be a person as the opponent.

The hypothesis for this experiment expects that girls will reveal themselves to be more people-oriented than boys. It is likely that observed differences are the result of learning from the innumerable lessons and examples society provides to show boys and girls how to behave—as boys and girls. The hypothesis does not require, nor does it encourage, a biologically founded explanation. We might be able to show in this experiment that girls react differently from boys, but the experiment will not be able to explain why. I have no

Table 13.2

TABLE FOR FACTORIAL DESIGN ANALYSIS				
		Scores		Scores
B2 Computer	A1 B2 Girls/computer	122	A2 B2 Boys/computer	172
B = Type of Opponent				
B1 Person	A1 B1 Girls/person *A1* *Girls*	164	A2 B1 Boys/person *A2* *Boys*	107

A = Gender of Participants

expectation that biological science will one day discover a gene that controls gender differences for how boys and girls play computer games!

GRAPHIC REPRESENTATION OF FACTORIAL PROBLEMS

A plot of all the data from Table 13.2 would be too confusing a display to face directly, so we will study a simpler graph first. Figure 13.1 graphs the scores for girls and boys when the *type of opponent is ignored*. We have in effect dropped one of the independent variables from discussion at this time in order to restrict study to the gender variable. This is simplifying a complex experiment by studying the independent variables separately rather than noting how the variables interact— which is what we will study in the full factorial experiment. The graphed numbers were obtained from Table 13.2 by adding the column of average scores for the girls $(164 + 122 = 286)$ and the column of average scores for the boys $(107 + 172 = 279)$.

The procedure for computing the average of separate group averages is easy when all groups are of the same size; just add them together and divide by the number of groups. This simple computation *gives the correct answer only when all groups contain the same number of people*. When samples are not of the same size, the arithmetic becomes more complicated, so a statistics text should be consulted for the correct procedure to be used in determining the average of a group of averages. The mean for the girl group would be $286 \div 2 = 143$, and for boys the computation would be $279 \div 2 = 140$.

We can see by looking at the raw data, 143 for girls and 140 for boys, that the girls collectively did slightly better than the boys. The conclusion is illustrated graphically in Figure 13.1. The line connecting the girls' score with the boys' score is very nearly horizontal, which indicates that there was almost no change in value (i.e, almost no difference) as we go from the average score for one group of subjects

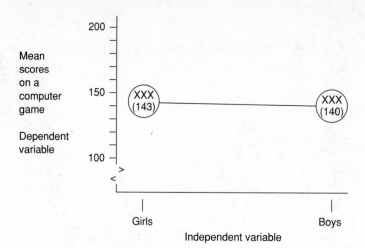

Figure 13.1
Comparison of Girls' and Boys' Scores on a Computer Game

to the average score for the other. At this point we are looking at a graphic representation of data from what is essentially a simple ex post facto experiment consisting of gender as the independent variable with two levels: boys or girls.

The standard procedure for graphic representation of these data requires that the scores derived from the dependent variable should be plotted on the vertical axis, the ordinate. In addition to fully labeling the vertical axis, the ordinate is further identified as the "dependent variable." This helps readers understand that it is the dependent variable *for all groups*. Normally "low scores," as defined by the investigator, are plotted near the bottom, and large values are plotted near the top.

The gap formed by angle brackets ⟨ ⟩ near the bottom of the ordinate was inserted to indicate that the data do not start from zero; only a limited range of scores near the top have been plotted. Graphs might be misread if attention is not specifically called to special conditions regarding them.

When a second variable is incorporated on the same graph, its structure must be altered slightly because two independent variables cannot be plotted in the same way in the same two-dimensional space. Values of the dependent variable are consistently plotted on the ordinate, and one independent variable will be plotted on the abscissa (along the horizontal line). The second independent variable is plotted in the body of the table, and parts are identified with clear labels. The graph in Figure 13.2 was drawn from data given in Table 13.2. This graph differs from the graph given in Figure 13.1 by including levels of the second independent variable in combination with the gender differences plotted in Figure 13.1.

Note how the data from Table 13.2 are represented graphically. Game scores for each level of B are plotted first as A1 variables, then the two levels of B on the A2 variable are plotted. According to both the graph and the table, we can see

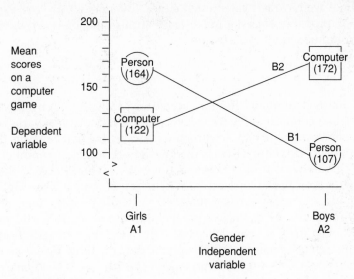

FIGURE 13.2
Girl/Boy Differences with Computer/Person Opponent

that boys playing against the computer had the highest average score. The highest average score for the girls was obtained with a person as the opponent. The mean scores for each group are given on the graph in this example to assist in understanding the concept. This information is not usually shown on the graph itself.

INTERPRETATION OF FACTORIAL DESIGN DATA

Factorial design experiments are analyzed to answer the following three questions:

Is there interaction between the two independent variables?

Is there a main effect for Factor A independent variable (gender of participants in this example)?

Is there a main effect for Factor B independent variable (computer or person opponent in this example)?

Ray and Ravizza, (1988) point out that factorial research questions should be evaluated in the order I have listed them above. "When you interpret the results of a factorial experiment, you *always interpret the interaction effects first.*" This makes sense because responses to the second two questions are in part determined by an answer to the question on interaction. ". . . if there is an interaction effect, then the main effects cannot be discussed without a qualifier."

Since we have not yet studied either "interaction" or "main effect" this explanation probably does not make sense at this time, but keep the ideas in mind as we continue with the discussion.

Interaction

Interaction is determined from an accurately drawn graph by checking whether the two lines connecting the same level of the B independent variable are parallel. The two lines on Figure 13.3 clearly are not. The line that connects the "person as the opponent" does in fact cross the line connecting the "computer as the opponent." This shows that there is interaction between the two variables. "Not parallel" does not mean the lines actually cross on the graph. They are not parallel if they would eventually cross if they were extended indefinitely. The greater the inclination to cross—i.e., the less parallel they are—the greater the interaction.

Whether lines are parallel can also be determined directly from the original scores by a simple computation. Using the data on Table 13.2 as an example, take the difference between the A1 variables: 122 – 164 = –42. Next take the difference between the A2 variables, and make sure to be consistent in your manner of taking the difference. If the B1 figure was subtracted from the B2 figure for A1, also subtract B1 from B2 for A2: 172 – 107 = 65. The two values of 65 and –42 are not equal, so it is evident there is an interaction between the two independent variables. What this means will become clearer after studying several additional examples.

Interaction in this demonstration means that *any* statement we make about the effect of gender *or* the type of competitor on a computer game performance is contingent on the value of the other. We cannot say that girls do better than boys, because it depends on whether the competitor is a computer or a person. We cannot say that people will play harder to beat a computer than they would play to beat a person, because the statement would be contingent on whether the player was a boy or a girl. This type of analysis accepts that behavior is complex. The design attempts to make sense from the complexity.

Main Effect Analysis

After interaction has been evaluated, main effect should be determined. A factorial design is a combination of (at least) two simple experiments conducted concurrently. "Main effect" looks at each of them separately by combining the two average scores at the same level for the variable being studied. Adding the scores together cancels their difference. The arithmetic for this can be most easily studied on Table 13.2.

We might first ask, "Do girls on the average react differently from boys in playing computer games, when the type of opponent is ignored?" To evaluate the main effect of gender differences, we determine whether there is a difference between the means of the two levels of the B variable. To get this value we add A1B1 and A1B2 averages: 122 + 164 = 286. Looking next at the average scores for the A2 condition, combine A2B1 and A2B2: 107 + 172 = 279. Since these samples are of the same size, we can compute their averages by dividing the sum by 2. The averages of 143 and 140 show very little difference. These are the data plotted in Figure 13.1.

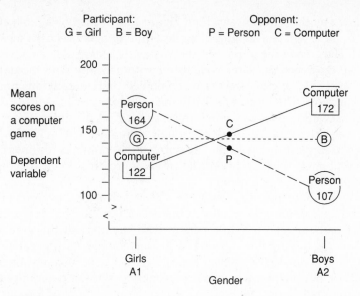

FIGURE 13.3
Factorial Design Graphic Representation (means of samples given in brackets

The general idea for determining a main effect for one independent variable requires that we ignore the factor differences in the other. This is done by combining them. "Collapsing" them is the picturesque term sometimes used. To study Main Effect A, we combine the average values for B1 and B2 for each of the A levels. To determine Main Effect B, we combine the levels of the A variable for each level of B.

The average difference can easily be determined on a graph (when all samples are of the same size) by picking a point exactly midway between the B1 and B2 scores for A1 and doing the same for A2. These midpoints can usually be estimated well enough on an accurately drawn graph.

The G and B symbols on Figure 13.3 identify the approximate average of the B values for each level of the A variable. We can see, just as we saw on Figure 13.1, that when we move from the average B score for the girls (A1) to the average B score for the boys (A2), there is only a slight change in the level of the line. A line with minimal slope graphically shows only a slight change in score value. We therefore conclude that there was no main effect for the A variable; there is no significant difference in average performance of boys compared with girls when effects of opponent type are ignored.

Main Effect B asks the question for this example, "Does the type of opponent make a difference in performance when the gender of the participant is ignored?" The principle for determining Main Effect B is the same as for A, but what we do is harder to visualize. Main Effect B is displayed by combining the A variable scores along the B lines. The two points to be compared that determine whether there is a difference between the B1 line and the B2 line are located midway along each of the lines, halfway between A1 and A2 (when samples are of equal size). These positions are shown by the letters C and P on Figure 13.3. If there is a main effect for the B variable, there will be a significant vertical difference between the mean scores of B1 and B2. The greater the difference, the greater the extent of the main effect.

We can reach the same conclusion arithmetically with the data from Table 13.2. The A1/A2 average values are combined (horizontally this time) for each of the B variables. The figures for B1 in this example are: 164 + 107 = 271. The average score would be 135.5. Combining A1B2 with A2B2 gives: 122 + 172 = 294, for an average score of 147. The 11.5-point difference (147 – 135.5 = 11.5) is large enough to suggest that "people" (remember that numbers for boys and girls have been combined) seem to be a little more aggressive when playing against the computer than against a person.

When analyzing the results of a factorial design experiment more is required than a simple statement that there is or is not interaction or that there is or is not a main effect. To help a person who has not had this course understand what we are talking about, our conclusions should be translated into English. Taking interaction first, it is clear that the gender of participants interacts with the type of competition; boys react more strongly to the computer opponent, but girls respond more to a person.

As for main effects, there is little difference between average performance for boys and girls. The fact that the computer caused higher scores for both boys and girls than did the presumed human opponent indicates a main effect for the "opponent" independent variable.

Various examples given in Figure 13.4 should be studied until the general features of factorial problems can be dealt with easily. Always check first for interaction. Lines that will not meet, no matter how far they are extended, are parallel. Example IV is the only one that shows interaction.

Second, follow the rules given earlier to determine main effect. Briefly, if there is a change in going from the combined means for one level of an independent variable to the other level (and samples are of the same size) there is a main effect for that variable. In a factorial design experiment, there are always at least two independent variables, so there is always a possibility of two main effects.

For a little practice, readers might want to make up some data that would produce an X when graphed. The data would show strong interaction but no main effects for either the A or B variable.

Here is one solution: A1B1 20, A1B2 60, A2B1 60, A2B2 20.

EXAMPLES OF FACTORIAL DESIGN EXPERIMENTS

I will not attempt to discuss the following six examples. I want to use them only to illustrate a few of the many factorial design experiments we can find in the literature.

Values shown are the number of *levels* of an independent variable. The several independent variables are separated by a × (pronounced "by") between them. A 3 × 3 factorial design is one that studied two independent variables with three levels of each. The number of research groups is determined by multiplying

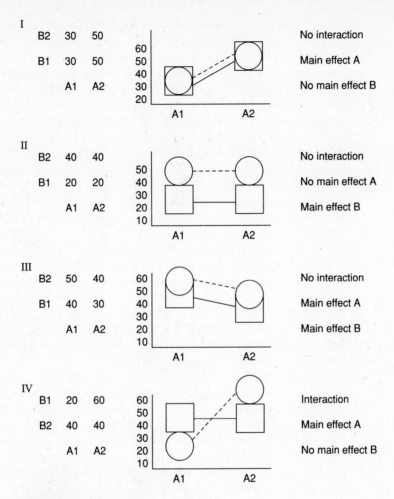

I

				No interaction
B2	30	50		
B1	30	50		Main effect A
	A1	A2		No main effect B

II

				No interaction
B2	40	40		
B1	20	20		No main effect A
	A1	A2		Main effect B

III

				No interaction
B2	50	40		
B1	40	30		Main effect A
	A1	A2		Main effect B

IV

				Interaction
B1	20	60		
B2	40	40		Main effect A
	A1	A2		No main effect B

FIGURE 13.4
Examples of Factorial Problems

all the independent variable levels together. A 3 × 3 factorial design will require 9 separate research groups of independently assigned participants. I will list the following examples in order of increasing complexity.

1. Sharkin, Mahalik, and Claiborn (1989) used a factorial design to study an effect they termed "foot-in-the-door" (FITD), which they explained as "the process by which gaining another's compliance with an initial small request increases the likelihood of compliance with a subsequent larger request." This is a 2 × 2 design in which the levels of the independent variables were: either the initial request was made or not, and the motivation level of the request was either provided or not.

2. L. L. Jacoby and C. M. Kelly (1992) used a simple factorial design to study "A Process-Dissociation Framework for Investigating Uncon-

scious Influences: Freudian Slips, Projective Tests, Subliminal Perception, and Signal Detection Theory." I am delighted to report that the factorial results were much easier to understand than the title. The dependent variable for this work was the probability of recognizing names of people as famous, as opposed to nonfamous. Subjects in respective groups studied lists of new and old famous names and nonfamous names. These were studied by subjects who were able to give the list either their full or their divided attention. People who were able to study the list with their undivided attention much more easily recognized new names as famous. People whose attention was divided during the study process were better able to correctly identify old names as famous. The graph of these data showed a strong interaction but only a slight main effect or none at all for the independent variables.

3. Gibbs, Sigal, Adams, and Grossman (1989) compared the effectiveness of hostile versus nonhostile attorneys in conjunction with the use of leading versus nonleading questions in "Cross-Examination of Expert Witness: Do Hostile Tactics Affect Impressions of a Simulated Jury?"

4. W. J. Lyddon (1989) used a 3×3 factorial design to study "the relation between a person's dominant way of knowing (rationalism, metaphorism, or empiricism) and the preference for three counseling approaches (rationlist, constructivist, and behavioral)."

5. Watkins and Terrell (1988) studied explanations for the high dropout rate of black clients assigned to white counselors. Blacks often have a lack of trust for whites, and this leads to a lowered level of counseling expectations. Black clients completed the "Cultural Mistrust Inventory" (an inventory designed to measure blacks' mistrust of whites), and the "Expectations About Counseling" questionnaire. Both the gender of the clients and the race of the counselors were studied as relevant independent variables. These produced a $2 \times 2 \times 2$ factorial design: 2 (subject sex) $\times$ 2 (subject mistrust level) $\times$ 2 (counselor race). Having more than two independent variables moves us into a third dimension, so it is not possible to make a simple graph of these results on a sheet of paper. A complex statistical analysis will be needed to determine significance of the data. (Mistrust level and its effects on counseling.)

6. Paradise and Cohl (1980) studied "The effects of counselor profanity and physical attractiveness for male and female counselors ... in a counseling analogue." This research produced three independent variables with two levels each: sex of the counselor, language of the counselor, and counselor attractiveness. The levels were: 2 (male or female) $\times$ 2 (presence or absence of profanity) $\times$ 2 (attractive or unattractive). Counselors were evaluated by 72 male and female volunteer subjects from introductory psychology classes. They were randomly assigned to the eight research groups produced by the $2 \times 2 \times 2$ research design.

PRACTICE PROBLEMS WITH FACTORIAL DESIGN

The best way to learn how to work with factorial designs is to do some problems. The following were selected to provide a challenge. After working them, check the answers in the Endnote. It is possible that a reader's solution will not agree exactly with the one given, because different people will not necessarily make the same assumptions. The general arrangement should be similar, however. These are just exercises developed for practice. Pay no attention to the meaning of the content, which might not make much sense in terms of what we know about the real world.

Instructions: Develop some data and draw a graph to illustrate each of the following ideas. Clearly label all parts of the graph; name the independent and dependent variables. Fully explain what each graph means. Do not just say that there is a main effect or that there is interaction. What the observation means has to be explained.

1. Show that whether or not a person will buy a product is a function of both the type of advertising (magazine or TV) the person has seen regarding the product and the price of the product. Assume that TV advertising is much more expensive than magazine advertising, so it must produce a greater number of purchases and/or carry a larger price to be worth the extra cost. There is a common belief that the more widely a product is advertised and the more it costs, the better it is.

2. Illustrate the hypothesis that how students study for an exam will affect their performance, but the effect will be different for bright students as compared to average ones. Grades were determined from the same multiple-choice exam for all participants. It is assumed that people who study for a multiple-choice exam and get a multiple-choice exam will do better on it than they would have done if they had studied for an essay test and then were given a multiple-choice test. It is also assumed that the difference in performance will be greater for the weaker students. People of only average ability are expected to obtain the lowest scores of all participants if they had studied for an essay exam and then received a multiple choice test. Brighter students will be expected to do better on the multiple-choice exam, no matter which exam they studied for.

3. For this problem, assume that we have data showing that neurotic people do not react to "pressure" in the same way as normal people do. Assume that normals produce the greatest output under pressure conditions and neurotics produce their maximal output in relaxed (low-pressure) conditions.

4. Following is a paraphrased abstract from a journal article. Using only the information provided, graph how you would expect the results to look.

Title: "Interaction of Achievement Cues and Facilitating Anxiety in the Achievement of Women" (McKeachie, 1969). In three studies 250—380 women psychology students, low in facilitating anxiety (FA) as measured by the Alpert-Haber AAT test, achieved better grades when taught by teachers characterized by expectations of high achievement standards than when taught by teachers not so characterized, while high FA women performed more poorly in classes taught by instructors with high standards of achievement.

5. Interpret the information from Figure 13.5.

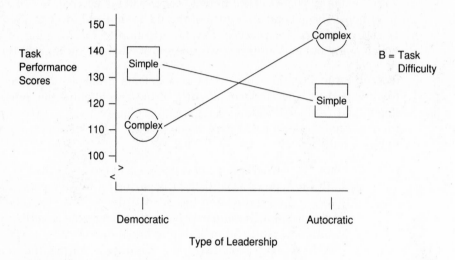

FIGURE 13.5
Leadership, Task Difficulty, and Task Performance

ENDNOTE

Answers to Problems

1.

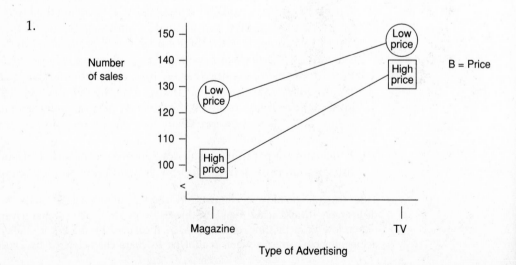

2.

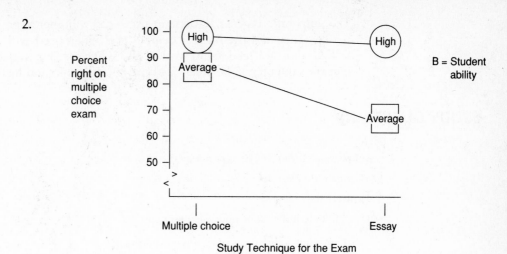

Percent right on multiple choice exam

B = Student ability

Study Technique for the Exam

3.

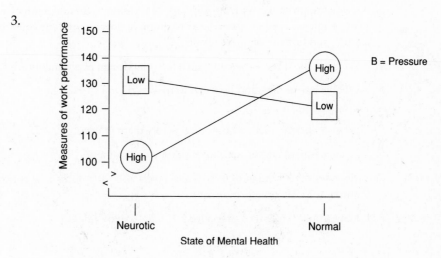

Measures of work performance

B = Pressure

State of Mental Health

4.

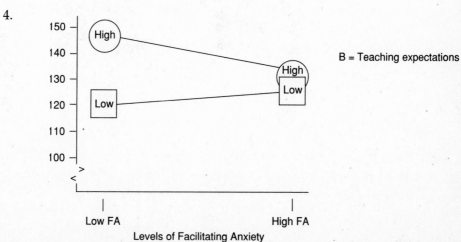

B = Teaching expectations

Levels of Facilitating Anxiety

5. The autocratic type of leadership produced a higher average level of performance and the highest overall level when used with a complex task. Democratic leadership worked best when the task was simple. This indicates interaction between the type of leadership and task difficulty.

STUDY QUESTIONS

1. What are factorial design experiments?

   When are they used?

   How are they used?

   How do they differ from simple experiments?

2. What are some advantages of factorial experiments?

3. If you are provided with appropriate data from a two-independent-variable factorial design experiment, know how to graph it, how to correctly identify and label all parts, and how to interpret results.

4. What are the three points on which factorial design experiments are analyzed?

5. What is interaction, and how is it determined?

   Explain what it means.

   Why should interaction be studied before main effects?

6. What are main effects, and how are they determined?

7. How does the number of factors and levels affect the number of research groups required for a factorial experiment?

8.D How would we draw a graph for a $2 \times 2 \times 2$ experiment?

SMALL TALK

Chapter
14

Within-Subjects Designs

Science is a continuum, and any attempt to frag-
ment it into its component parts does violence to the
whole.

    As physical measurements have steadily be-
come more elegant, definitive, and profound, it has
become obvious that all scientists are dealing with
the same basic laws. Scientists are increasingly
being required to learn one another's language in
order to remain effective. . . .

Announcement, New England Institute, Ridgefield, Conn.,
1966. Quoted in Klein (1974), p. 23.

The slightly old-fashioned title to this chapter has the stamp of history on it, and it carries an affective tone that is unmatched by any other descriptive phrase. If certain chapters can be selected as favorites, this is the one I would choose. By this point in the text some readers may have begun to feel sophisticated. Surely anyone who has mastered correlations and experimental methods already knows all that is necessary for doing research in the behavioral sciences. And a basic understanding of factorial design should more than fill the bag of basic research tools. What else is there to learn? On that point I hope this chapter produces some surprises.

    Most behavioral science research concentrates, as it should, on experimental designs that manipulate several levels of an independent variable using several groups of subjects. Since all experiments require at least two levels for an independent variable, a major task for investigators has been to ensure equivalence of all other relevant characteristics, particularly subject variables. The typical practice is to use several groups of subjects, with the hope that extraneous relevant variables will be balanced out. This chapter introduces a different approach that uses *all* levels of an independent variable with the *same* subject. A person will vary from himself or herself from time to time much less than the variations observed between groups of people. This method, when used correctly, nicely controls subject variables, and in that way it greatly increase the sensitivity of experiments. But the gains we are able to make in one area are partially canceled by the method's inherent limitations. This chapter will discuss what these limitations are and some ways of overcoming them.

I believe that every text that studies experimental methods should take a look at psychophysics, one of techniques that helped to get the science of psychology started. The nature of the material in this chapter will provide an opportunity to introduce and define the subject.

Although I did not plan it this way, the nature of the material to be studied next involves a review and an elaboration of measurement ideas studied at the beginning of the text. Some measurement arrangements are so obviously correct that there is no need to think about them—but that is where we go wrong. Readers will be surprised to discover a different element in measurement that involves judgments. The inconsistency is not apparent until the perspective is changed to show that what works in one situation will not work in others, even when they appear to be similar.

Just as the *t*-test statistic was studied with experimental designs and correlations with analyses of concomitant variation, this chapter will consider some uses for descriptive statistics, the third class of statistics usually studied in a beginning statistics class. These function to delineate several characteristics of data and are widely reported for that purpose in nearly all journal articles that involve statistical analyses. This chapter goes beyond that application to illustrate how the mean of a set of subject responses can be used as a score, which in turn is further analyzed in conjunction with responses from other subjects.

The research ideas evaluated by the single subject method are quite narrowly focused on processes that work most efficiently with repeated judgments by the same individual. Within-subjects techniques produce good results in the study of learning, operant conditioning, perception and psychophysical phenomena in general, or effects of certain drugs or other chemicals on behavior. The technique is an appropriate one for the study of physiological conditions such as fatigue, emotion, or hunger.

When special training and experience are required, as in some perception experiments, there are marked advantages in using the same subject for all the conditions. For best results, particularly when studying questions in the area of psychophysics, it is appropriate to provide extensive practice. This is necessary in order to train the human organism to become an accurate measuring instrument.

Even though we are interested in the responses of individuals, combined information from a number of different people is required to improve reliability of findings and to permit results to be generalized. If 25 subjects are involved, it is as if an investigator had run 25 separate experiments and then combined the results from all of them for a general answer to his or her research question. If judgments are involved, I would rather ask a single person, "Which do you like better, A or B?" and then combine the answers from 24 people, rather than having 12 people judge A and 12 different people judge B.

The within-S research procedures should not be confused with research that is sometimes called "S = 1" designs, which study only one subject. Nor is the within-S design meant to replace the "small N" method of research. Each is used for quite different reasons.

A PEEK AT PSYCHOPHYSICS

I think it is reasonable to argue that experimental psychology got its start with psychophysics. Over 100 years ago Gustav Fechner, who had been trained as a physicist, developed some procedures for studying perception that are still of interest and relevance today. In the early stages of his work the single subject used was himself.

In these times when there is so much new material to learn and no additional time to learn it, psychophysics no longer earns the distinctive place in the psychology curriculum it once had. When Fechner's *Elements of Psychophysics. Vol I* (1966) was finally translated and published in English (the German edition had been published in 1860) it gave Robert MacLeod (1969) an opportunity to point out how much psychologists who did not want to learn German had been missing. It took over a century to get the first volume translated,

> ... and we may have to wait a while longer for Volume II, but it should be obvious that it is better to wait a century or two rather than to learn a foreign language. In the meantime, we can in blissful innocence do all sorts of experiments and clarify all sorts of ideas without being bothered by the fact that a few generations ago the same experiments were performed with less expensive equipment and the same ideas were expressed with equal clarity. ... One of the nice things about American psychology is that each budding generation springs fresh from the parent root, saying the same old things in a fresh way, but happily unaware that they have all been said before.

I once developed plans for some new equipment that could demonstrate a moderately difficult concept in psychophysics. Some of the apparatus I wanted to use would have had to be especially designed and built, but I estimated that I could get the job done for under $5,000. It was humbling to discover that Fechner, a 100 years before, had already demonstrated the same idea using two oil lamps in a darkened room!

The study of within-S designs offers an opportunity for us to take a quick glance at "psychophysics." This area of psychological research studies ways of organizing and presenting stimuli to a single subject and then analyzes and interprets the subject's responses. Psychophysics and within-S design go nicely together, but the within-S design is not restricted to psychophysical techniques.

Psychophysics is primarily concerned with the study of thresholds. "Threshold" originally was the name given to the part of a building at the entrance to a room. The word generally identifies a transition point, a point of change from one location to another. In psychology thresholds are statistically defined "points" (actually zones) of transition from one level, or type, of a sensory perception to another. As a sound gets fainter we eventually stop hearing it. When that happens, we have crossed the sensory threshold for hearing. In a very quiet environment, if we take a sound that is so faint it cannot be heard, no matter how hard the person tries, how much must we increase its loudness before it can be heard?

Thresholds studied in this way are called "absolute thresholds." Many sensory modalities have been and are being studied by psychologists to define the transition values for being aware and not being aware of a stimulus. Examples of sensory modalities include: taste, smell, several areas of vision, several areas of hearing, and even certain aspects of touch or skin sensations. Every sensory modality has a threshold which is determined in part by the characteristics of the stimuli and in part by the sensitivity of the subject. The same general procedures are used in medicine for studying sensitivity to drugs—although I doubt that medicine knows of the psychological parentage of its methods.

Absolute thresholds are often called "limens," and nearly everyone is familiar with the concept of "subliminal perception" or "subliminal stimulation." The idea of subliminal stimulation continues to be discussed—and exploited—in popular applications. The question is, can stimuli that are below a person's thresholds of awareness (i.e. they are two weak to be perceived) nevertheless influence the person's behavior?

A publication titled *Personal Technology Times* (which claims to be "the national newspaper of personal technology") published a series of articles on "Subliminal Tapes" in the 1989, January and March issues. The first article began with this question. "Is it possible to learn, get motivated, stop smoking or lose weight by listening to audio tapes (or watching videos) which contain so-called 'subliminal affirmations?'" Apparently these tapes sell well, even though they are expensive and present only dubious evidence that they work. Advertisers make money from the belief that we might be influenced by messages we cannot consciously report having seen or heard. The point is, if a message is below your threshold of awareness, you cannot directly respond to it, but there might be a cumulative effect over numerous exposures. Many of us are deeply concerned about the possibility that "subliminal messages" might be used against the wishes of unsuspecting people. Research in the area of subliminal perception is particularly interesting, but I am sorry to say it is not relevant to our present topic of consideration.

Other psychophysical techniques are used to study a different kind of threshold called "just noticeable difference." This threshold involves comparing two stimuli that are very close together in value. The task is to determine how much one of the stimuli can be changed, by increasing or decreasing its value, before the observer becomes aware that they are then "just noticeably different." The stimuli can be two lights, two sounds, two flavors, two circles, or two of almost anything that can be presented in differing measurable amounts. How much brighter (or bigger, or smaller, greater, or less—or different) does the second one have to be in order for a subject to recognize that they are not the same? Small differences within the limits of the "jnd" threshold will not be noticed.

Manufacturers regularly use this technique to reduce the quantity of a product while keeping the price the same. If each reduction is very small, only the most astute penny counter will be aware of it. The rest of us will not realize that in effect there has been a price increase. A large change might stimulate buyer attention, but small changes made over time will largely go unnoticed.

A reader of *Consumer Reports* magazine (1988, January p. 67) sent in wrapper panels from five different rolls of Bounty towels which had been bought consecutively.

> The first lists the contents as 100 sheets, 11.05 × 11.1 inches for a total of 85 square feet. On the second wrapper the number of sheets remains at 100, but the sheets have shrunk to 11 × 11 inches, or 84 square feet in all. On succeeding wrappers, the number of sheets drops to 92 (77 square feet), 88 (73 square feet), and 84 (70 square feet).

The package price had remained the same, of course, but the price per sheet had increased. At the last change, the consumer was getting 16% fewer towels, each of which was slightly smaller.

An important variation of psychophysical research techniques involves the "theory of signal detectability," which usually goes under the acronym of "TSD." This orientation builds on old ideas of perception, but it incorporates contemporary ideas of statistical analyses. Innovative techniques often encourage imaginative applications, and that is the case here.

A modern example of how new techniques, built on old ideas, can be used to seek solutions to difficult problems was published in *Psychological Science*, "Towards an Objective Psychophysics of Pain." This article (Irwin & Whitehead, 1991) uses the concept of "Weber's law," which dates back to the first half of the 19th century. The law refers to difference thresholds as having a constant fractional magnitude to the total. This law was applied in the context of the TSD concept of receiver operating characteristic ROC. ROC curves were used to analyze subjects' perceptual judgments.

The article noted the difficulty of determining the threshold of pain. "The subject makes a measurement that cannot be contested and, in this sense, the methods are subjective." This judgmental component of pain introduces a variance that lowers, instead of improves, understanding of pain. "An experimental study of electrocutaneous stimuli showed how it is possible to interpret a traditional identification method and a category method in detection theory terms."

AN EXERCISE FOR STUDY

This approach to research will be more interesting if readers become personally involved in how it works. Please permit me to interrupt your reading long enough for you to do the following exercise. I should explain that it has been very difficult to develop a meaningful example that can be published in a book and completed by an individual using only the printed instructions. The following exercise does not entirely do the job, but it will give an idea of what is involved in research using the within-S method. It will also provide data for study and analysis, and research is always more interesting when we have our own numbers.

Instructions: On the next few pages are sets of lines for "Practice in Judging Line Lengths." Take a sheet of paper and label it "Answer Sheet." Keep it for some calculations to be done later. Number lines on the answer sheet 1 through 16. The task is to estimate in *tenths of inches* the length of various lines. One inch will be 10 (tenths of an inch); a line $1\frac{1}{2}$ inches in length will be marked as 15 (tenths of an inch). Follow your first impression. Do not go back to change a response. We are not interested in how long the lines are, we can measure that, we want to find out how long the lines appear to be. Neither are we interested in testing how good you are at judging line lengths. We are studying humans as measuring devices to help us better understand how we perceive the world around us. To score your responses the actual line lengths are given at the end of the chapter.

People who, through repeated experience with psychology, are always on the lookout for chicanery and hidden implications in every psychological experiment will be disappointed this time. There are no surprises here. The purpose of this exercise really is to assess the extent to which different people judge line lengths differently. The lines can be easily measured directly, so this is not a situation requiring human judgment to produce a measurement, although there are a great many situations in which human judgment is the only way a perception can be measured.

Readers do not normally recognize that they have just taken part in an experiment. We are so accustomed to thinking in terms of experimental conditions being applied to different groups of individuals, it does not seem logical that a true experiment can be conducted on a single person. An experiment requires the manipulation of at least two variables; this example used lines of four lengths. Instead of four different groups of people judging each of the four lines several times, which is the pattern for a typical experiment, all stimuli were shown to the same person—hence the "within-subjects" name.

The value of the method rests on the control it offers over extraneous subject variables. The same person who judged the length of Line 1 is not likely to have changed very much by the time he or she judged Line 16 only 2 minutes later. There are changes of course, and there would have been more if the presentation had not been arranged to counteract them.

ANALYZING DATA FROM PERCEPTION EXPERIMENTS

This line judgment exercise is too simplified to have value except to provide numbers for computation. We are pretending that variations in length are levels of an independent variable. This provides the structure of an experiment, but it is not of much psychological interest.

1. _____

2. _____

3. _____

4. _____

FIGURE 14.1
Practice in Judging Line Lengths

5. _____

6. _____

7. _____

8. _____

FIGURE 14.1A
Figure 14.1-continued

9.   _____

10.   _____

11.   _____

12.   _____

FIGURE 14.1B
Figure 14.1-continued

13. _____

14. _____

15. _____

16. _____

FIGURE 14.1C
Figure 14.1-continued

If a line were judged in different conditions or configurations, these would constitute the levels of the independent variable. We might compare the judgments of horizontal lines against the judgments of vertical lines of the same length. When lines are arranged to form a right triangle that does not quite touch at the corner they constitute the "H-V (horizontal-vertical) illusion," which has been studied extensively. Investigators have had to work very hard to explain why the vertical line in this configuration appears, to most people, to be longer than the horizontal line.

Data obtained from exercises such as this one are not analyzed by methods that are generally applicable to data produced in simple experimental designs. The kinds of research questions within-S designs undertake to answer do not necessarily involve the determination of significance of differences, although they could.

People who have completed the line judgment exercise should use their own data to work along with the following discussion.

Constant Error

Primarily we are studying "subject errors" in this exercise. The "error" does not carry its normal meaning of "mistake," in the sense that a person did something wrong; the response is not quite accurate perhaps, but it is not wrong. "Error" is just a name for the difference between some measured characteristic of a stimulus—length for example—and the subject's judgment.

Although this discussion emphasizes perception research, the same research principles have a wide application in the behavioral sciences. Prejudiced people, for example, might have a large constant error in their judgments of the characteristics of their fellow human beings. Some people consistently over- or underestimate how long it takes them to get ready and to go some place, so they are regularly either too early or too late. If we know their constant error, we can adjust our lives accordingly.

The "constant" in the name of this section states its case too strongly. Just as when the word is applied to the longevity of an emotion, "My love for you is constant and will last forever," the sentiment is probably stronger in the promise than in the practice. The number we want is an average of the differences between a subject's responses and the actual measured state of the stimulus. "Typical" would be a better word than "constant." The arithmetic mean, the average, is the value used to characterize the amount of divergence of a subject's responses from the measured length.

Table 14.1 provides a set of subject responses and the value of the standard being judged. These are the numbers necessary for computing constant error.

Two ways are available for computing constant error. The first one, though perhaps a shade more work, better demonstrates the meaning of the concept. In the first method we define "errors" in responding to the stimulus by computing an average of the differences between a subject's judgments and the standard. The "Difference" column in Table 14.1 lists those numbers for

Table 14.1

	CONSTANT ERROR COMPUTATION		
Subject's Responses "X"	Standard	Difference	X^2
45	40	+05	2025
35	40	−05	1225
50	40	+10	2500
50	40	+10	2500
55	40	+15	3025
41	40	+01	1681
Sum 276		+36	12,956

this example. In order to keep track of the plus or minus direction of the differences from the standard, it is necessary to be consistent. I always subtract the standard from the response. An excess of negative values produces a negative constant error, which only means that a subject made more errors in the direction of judging the stimulus to be smaller than the standard. When the average of a subject's responses is larger than the standard, the constant error is said to be positive.

The mean is obtained by dividing the algebraic sum of the difference column by the number of trials.

$36 \div 6 = 6.0$ (The constant error is 6.0.)

The alternate method is computed directly from the average of the responses by taking the difference between that figure and the standard. The difference column is not required.

276 = Sum of subject's responses
6 = Number of trials
$276 \div 6 = 46$ (the average of the subject's responses)
40 = Value of the standard stimulus
$46 - 40 = 6.0$ (the constant error).

I know several people who purposely incorporate a constant error in their lives, and perhaps readers will know such people also. I have never understood why some people purposely set their clocks or watches as much as 5 or 10 minutes fast, which makes the watches always wrong by a constant amount. They explain that if they have to leave at 8:00 and their clock shows 8:00, they know they still have 5 minutes so they do not have to rush. The rest of us know exactly the same thing when our clocks show 7:55.

Variable Error

Everyone who thinks about it will recognize that each person has a unique kind of mood variability. Some people are even-tempered; their moods do not fluctuate very much. Other people, those who have highly variable moods, can be difficult to deal with because we cannot predict accurately what their mood will be at any particular time. If we are dealing with a boss, we will ask the secretary before we go in how the boss is feeling that day.

Variability can be quickly indicated by the "range," the difference in value between the highest and lowest measurements. The range is easy to compute, but it is not very useful because its size is determined solely by the two extreme scores. It is inclined to be unstable and prone to wide fluctuations. Variability is best expressed by the standard deviation, which supplies information about the spread of scores just as the range does, but it can be used in many different ways that are not possible with the range. Unfortunately, it is not nearly so easy to calculate.

Use the following formula and the data given in Table 14.1 to compute the variability of responses. The numbers we want are those given in the X and X^2 columns. The asterisk (*) is used to indicate multiplication. It is the computer variation of the X symbol used in arithmetic for multiplication or the dot that is used in algebra. I will let "SD" stand for the standard deviation.

$$SD = \frac{\sqrt{N\Sigma X^2 - (\Sigma X)^2}}{} \qquad \Sigma X = 276 \quad \Sigma X^2 = 12{,}956 \quad (\Sigma X)^2 = 76{,}176 \quad N = 6$$

$$SD = \frac{\sqrt{6 \times 12{,}956 - 76{,}176}}{} = 6.58$$

The formula given here is one of the simpler variations of the standard deviation "raw score" computational formula. Note that I have used N in the denominator instead of $N - 1$ which it can be argued is the correct form for sample data.

Whether variability is an important or useful measure must be established by the research question being asked. Although variability can provide information that may be relevant in many areas of research, it does not generally have the practical importance that is carried by the mean.

The mean, a measure of central tendency, and the standard deviation, a measure of variability, express two different and largely unrelated characteristics of data. A person can have any combination of constant error and variable error: high constant, low variable, high constant, high variable, low or no constant error, high or low variable error. These concepts are confusing, so study the potential variations carefully. Take the time to fully understand how they describe different characteristics of data. Table 14.2 illustrates a few of these variations.

Whether constant and variable errors are said to be large or small are qualitative rather than quantitative judgments. A positive or negative constant error might be a relevant consideration for certain research hypotheses.

If you desire an average standard deviation for combined subjects you can compute one by using the average of the variances. Recall that the variance is the square of a standard deviation. The average variance can be converted to a standard deviation by taking the square root.

Table 14.2

COMPARISONS OF CONSTANT AND VARIABLE ERROR*		
Constant *Error*	Variable *Error*	
21	7.3	High constant, moderate variable error
–7	2.5	Low constant, low variable error
6	12.8	Low constant, high variable error
19	3.2	High constant, low variable error
–27	19.5	High constant, high variable error

*Assume a stimulus value of 40 units.

Reliability of Judgments

General reliability or consistency of judgments can be determined for a group of judges. This information would be used to answer a question of this sort: "How consistent are a group of judges in their evaluations of the same stimuli?" Averages of evaluations from two sets of trials for several judges are the values used with the Pearson product-moment correlation. This gives a kind of test/retest reliability. Table 14.3 illustrates the procedure.

The correlation, the reliability coefficient, is $r = .667$. This is barely large enough for significance for a one-tailed interpretation. Five pairs of scores constitute too small a sample for concluding much of anything.

Table 14.3

AN ESTIMATE OF RELIABILITY		
	Mean Scores From:	
	First Trials	*Second Trials*
Dick	8	4
Henry	1	2
Bob	2	5
Bruce	5	4
Arbie	4	1

PROGRESSIVE ERROR

Recall that when we run an experiment with the same person in all the conditions, we obtain the advantage of reducing subject variables. A person generally does not change much from one trial to another. We do, however, have to deal with a special difficulty called "progressive error." Early experience in a series of trials might affect judgments that come later. Underwood (1966, p. 32) describes it as

"... any change in behavior which occurs as a consequence of continued experience or successive trials with a given task." Assume the following sequence of letters shows the order of presentation for four levels of an independent variable, with three trials at each level.

A A A B B B C C C D D D

All the A stimuli were given first, then all the B's, C's, and D's. If the passage of time and the development of experience from the A's through D's is great enough, there could be significant changes in the judge's responses near the end of the session. A person might become tired or frustrated, impatient, or a bad case of ennui could develop. The person may gradually discover that the experiment is taking longer than he or she expected when signing up to volunteer. By the time the D variable is judged, the person is not, psychologically speaking, the same person who started. These and other gradual subject changes over time could be sufficient to confound the experiment.

Visualize a person giving these responses: The average of three trials for the A variable was 57, and 42 was the average of the D responses. (What the numbers are measuring is unimportant for this discussion.) This sequential presentation scheme makes it impossible to determine whether the difference in judgments resulted from different levels of the independent variable (which is what we are studying), or whether the judgments during the early trials had an effect on the later ones. We call any change that results from many trials over time, "progressive error." We cannot avoid subject changes that might occur over the course of an experiment. We can try, however, to arrange for subject changes and other extraneous variables to be kept *equivalent*. Extraneous influences that we cannot eliminate should be arranged so their influence will fall evenly on all levels of the independent variable.

Progressive error can be "controlled" by arranging for the values of stimuli in a perception experiment for example, to be distributed throughout the sequence so the possible changes resulting from the passage of time do not fall *differentially* on one variable more than another. The best sequence would be to present stimuli in random order within blocks. In the following sequence, the D stimulus was presented early just as frequently as A. Confounding effects of progressive error have been partialed out because stimuli are presented equally often throughout the trials.

C D A B   A D B C   B C A D

A second way of controlling progressive error takes into account that certain changes that occur with time do not occur in a linear fashion. The graph shown in Figure 14.2 is not a typical one for psychology. It is in fact very difficult to find a good psychological example to illustrate a clear linear relationship of steady improvement over time.

Learning curves often produce "plateaus," or flattened areas, when graphed. These are periods of time during which little change occurs. For many skills, early stages of practice seem to produce fairly rapid changes in performance. After the initial learning period, it takes a longer period of practice to produce an improvement. With activities that work like this, it is possible to practice subjects up to the point where relatively little change is occurring. Between the A

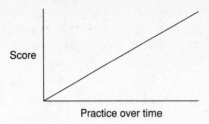

FIGURE 14.2
A Graph of Linear Change Over Time

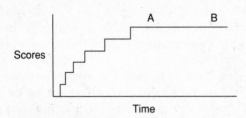

FIGURE 14.3
A Learning Curve Showing a Plateau

to B points in Figure 14.3, the effects of progressive error will be minimized. Remember that repeated trials are normal for within-S designs, so training to reach a plateau would be only a slight extension in the regular procedure.

These precautions for avoiding progressive error are necessary only with experiments involving repeated trials with the same subject. The difficulty can be avoided entirely by using separate stimuli with different subjects, but then the benefits of within-S design would be lost.

DIFFERENTIAL TRANSFER OR CARRYOVER EFFECT

The fact that all the levels of the independent variable are applied to the same subject rather than to different ones restricts the types of stimuli or conditions that can be studied. Two levels of an independent variable cannot be presented at the same time; one of them must come first. If the stimulus that comes first affects how a subject responds to the stimulus that comes second, it might be necessary to deal with *carryover effect* or *differential transfer*. Carryover effect results when a judgment of, or reaction to, one stimulus carries over and causes a change in response to another.

In a broad way, learning produces a carryover effect because the process of learning something tends to improve one's ability to learn something else. Allowances have to be made for this in designing learning experiments, but similar problems can occur in other situations.

If the task is to study judgments made in different conditions, an investigator should not have a subject first make all the X condition judgments and then make all the judgments in the Y condition. Instead of X, X, X, X, and Y, Y, Y, Y, the correct technique would be to *counterbalance*—alternate—the order within each pair. Something like the following could result: Y X, X Y, Y X, X Y. Counterbalancing means that we randomly alternate the orders of the experimental conditions. If A were given first one time, followed by B, the sequence would be counterbalanced by another sequence with B coming first and then A. Over a number of trials each level would have been presented first an equal number of times. In this way any problems that could have arisen as a result of the order of stimuli presentation would be balanced *if the conditions have approximately equal influence on each other*.

Carryover effect and differential transfer (or asymmetric transfer) have much in common to the extent that one variable affects responses to the variable that follows, but differential transfer has a stronger meaning. If A has the same effect on B as B has on the following A, we have ordinary carryover effect. If the effect of one condition—say A on B—is much greater than the effect B has on A, we have an example of differential transfer. We can taste differential transfer in this example! If the flavor of vanilla ice cream is different after we have first tasted chocolate from the taste of chocolate ice cream after we have sampled vanilla, we have differential transfer. Counterbalancing will not work if one of the conditions produces a much stronger effect than the other one does.

The problem of differential transfer makes it nearly impossible to use a within-subjects design for experiments that involve complex stimuli. If we wanted to study the effect of fear on performance, of course we could not tell our subjects that. We simply would ask them to volunteer to work math problems so that we could develop a learning curve. With that expectation in mind, many people would find it to be a fearful experience if they were sitting quietly working math problems on a table in a small room and a snake slithered out across the table from a box sitting unobtrusively to one side. (Probably a small snake would do well enough, and it need not be poisonous!) Some people might be frightened if they reached into a box to get a tissue and discovered a mouse was living there. Whenever a person is surprised, made fearful, embarrassed, or in any way uncomfortable on their first visit to help with an experiment, it is very likely indeed that the experience will be remembered. A person might not even return for a second visit. But even if the individual does return, the change in attitude is likely to affect performance. When an earlier condition might produce a lasting influence, or whenever there is any doubt about whether alternate sequences do produce the same results, within-subjects design should not be used.

SELECTION OF STIMULI INTERVALS

The material discussed next is not required very often, but it is quite important when its use is necessary. Some people will find this discussion interesting because it provides a solution for a problem beginning investigators normally do not recognize as a problem. Devising a good example to illustrate the nature of the difficulty has not been easy. With a little indulgence from the reader, the following should suffice to illustrate the points that need to be made.

This example requires people to judge the weights of four different boxes of identical appearance and size. They differ only in weight. Each of the boxes is presented individually in a pre-established order of randomized blocks. Judges lift the weights in a consistent way, estimate and report their conclusion about how much each weighs, and then another weight is presented. Reliability of judgments is achieved through the use of 24 trials, 6 trials for each box. The point of the following discussion is to determine the size of weights that should be used in this simple perception exercise.

Beginners who are assigned a project of this sort tend to select stimuli according to what seems to them to be a simple and logical procedure that produces an interval scale. Weights are an interval level measurement. The following selections are typical: 5, 10, 15, and 20 grams. A large company that supplies apparatus for psychological research projects does in fact sell weights in this sequence. Readers are encouraged to figure out, if they can, what is wrong with this selection. What arrangement would be better?

The use of increasing values in multiples of five (5, 10, 15 etc.) is not a good idea, because subjects often make their evaluations in the same units—which would tend to increase apparent accuracy. Irregular values that are not evenly spaced should produce truer results.

To comprehend the subtlety involved here, we should go back well over a 100 years to study the psychophysical concept named Weber's law—the same one that was mentioned briefly at the beginning of the chapter. Underwood (1966, pp. 30 and 47) in a slightly different context, points out that intervals along a judgment scale should not be evenly spaced, ". . . in order to accommodate a basic fact of discrimination of magnitudes, namely, that the less the magnitude of a stimulus (within limits), the better the discrimination. . . . accuracy of discrimination varies as a function of magnitude." He went on to explain that in reference to larger stimuli, "This fact, that sensitivity decreases as magnitude (of a stimulus) increases, is the basic notion of Weber's law. . . ."

Size judgments of small items, say the longest dimension of a typical textbook, are not going to be off by many inches. Judgments might range within limits of 6 to 10 inches (for an 8-inch book), but not much more. The range of judgments for a dollar bill will be even smaller, and the range for guesses about the size of a dime will be within fractions of inches. As the sizes of stimuli decrease the ranges of the errors in judgments will also decrease.

Errors in estimating the size of a room, particularly since these are judgments not often made, will be quite large. Judgments would range several feet above or below the room's actual size. Estimates of the size of a city lot, or a farm field will produce very large errors indeed.

Back to the problem of selecting weights: According to Weber's law, a progression of equal weight intervals (5, 10, 15, 20) is not correct, because accuracy of discrimination declines as the size of the stimulus increases. An arrangement that presents stimuli in progressively increasing size differences makes allowance for this.

The process of selecting the values of stimuli, such as weights in this example, is more complicated than one would expect. First, we would select a new starting value to replace the "5" that was originally proposed. We would not want a beginning value that is too small, because this would tend to limit variation in responses. A starting weight of 9 seems a reasonable choice, although other weights from 7 to 11 would work equally well.

The next decision requires the determination of suitable intervals. Adding multiples of a constant, say 5, to the first weight produces the equal intervals we do not want, (eg., 9, 14, 19, 24). Weber's law explains why this sequence would not work. At the high end, where the "magnitude of the stimulus" is larger, the errors in estimates would be sizable enough for judges to have difficulty in recognizing difference between adjacent stimuli. To compensate for this, more widely separated stimuli are necessary as their magnitudes increase.

Table 14.4 illustrates the process. Assume, for the sake of this discussion, that typical errors in judgment range between 20% above and 20% below a given value. Although the percent of error probably increases as the magnitudes of the stimuli increase, it is more convenient for this example to hold to the arbitrary 20% figure. When the computations are completed for each stimulus, the following table would result.

Numbers in brackets are proposed values of the stimuli. The two numbers connected by the line indicate a typical 20% range of errors. Stimulus values are shown at two levels to demonstrate how responses would overlap.

A well-selected sequence of stimuli forms intervals of judgment errors that are entirely separate. Note the 0.4 difference between the upper limit of the lower stimulus, 10.8, and the lower limit of the second stimulus, 11.2.

At the higher end of the scale the overlap is considerable; 16.8 is the upper limit for the stimulus value 14, which overlaps with the lower limit, 15.2 for the stimulus value 19.

The situation is worse when the low value, 19.2 for stimulus 24 is compared with the high value of 22.8 for the stimuli value of 19. This means that an object weighing 19 grams, in the judgment of these people, seems to weigh very nearly the same as a similar-appearing object that in fact weighs 24 grams. As the stimuli increase in value, there will be even greater difficulty in discriminating between them. Judges would probably be unable to tell the difference between an object weighing 44 grams and one that weighs 49 grams.

Table 14.4

ESTIMATED RESPONSE RANGE OF INCREASING STIMULUS VALUES

20% error
interval
widths

```
                        (14)                       (24)
              11.2 ——————16.8          19.2 ———————————— 28.8

          (9)                       (19)
        8.2—0.8              15.2 ———————————— 22.8

     |          |            |           |          |          |
     5         10           15          20         25         30
```

Although Weber's law was passed a long time ago, it has not been repealed, and it is still being enforced. To live within the strictures of Weber's law it is necessary to develop increasingly large intervals between the stimuli as their values increase. Ideally this would be done through research, but for this example the selections are arbitrary. Using new intervals, and keeping the ±20% error rate used previously, the data in Table 14.5 illustrate the idea of stimuli that form adequate working intervals for perception research.

A scale of stimuli having values of 9, 16, 26, and 41 might not intuitively make much sense, but from a subject's perception of them the intervals are in fact more nearly equally spaced than would have been true with 9, 14, 19, and 24. The idea of developing a judgment scale that takes into account known qualities of perception is not nearly so widely used in research as it probably should be. An illustration of the concept was made easier by using physical stimuli, but investigators in the behavioral sciences should keep the idea in mind any time they are creating a scale requiring judgments.

Referring back to the line lengths exercise used at the beginning of the chapter, we should now have a better understanding of why the line lengths do not have incremental increases in size. The actual lengths, in tenths of an inch are: 9, 14, 22, and 37.

I should also call attention to a second feature of the line demonstration. Note that the lines were presented in blocks of four, with a randomized order within the blocks. This arrangement helps to negate the effects of progressive error and to balance carryover effect. There is no reason to suspect or expect a problem of differential transfer with this demonstration, but we should always be alert to the possibility.

Table 14.5

	EQUAL-APPEARING STIMULUS INTERVALS			
Proposed stimuli	(9)	(16)	(26)	(41)
	8.2–10.8	12.8–19.2	20.8–31.2	32.6–49.4

ADVANTAGES AND DISADVANTAGES OF WITHIN-SUBJECTS DESIGN

Advantages

Within-subjects designs provide good control over subject variables, and that is their chief advantage. A person is going to be more like himself or herself from one time to another than two strangers are going to be like each other. The control of subject variables markedly improves the sensitivity of an experiment by reducing the variance between the samples. Involvement of the same person in all experimental conditions permits computation of differences with a correlated samples formula. When performance is correlated across conditions, a small difference between means is often enough to declare the results significant.

The better control over subject variables, as compared with randomly selected subjects, allows a reduction in the number of subjects required for an experiment. Fewer people have to be recruited, trained, and tested, all of which can result in significant savings.

In general, within-S works best with stimuli or conditions that can be repeated without affecting a subject. Physiological studies of all sorts work well if the condition is reversible within a short time. The method is particularly suitable for certain kinds of work in perception, especially if training can increase the reliability of judgments.

Disadvantages

Applying all experimental conditions to the same subject markedly reduces the variety of experiments that can be conducted. Any operations that cause subjects to change would have to be avoided. If conditions require an element of surprise or if a person can in any way discover information on an early trial that can be used in later trials, a subject will no longer be naive when the experiment is repeated. Different subjects would be required.

Differential transfer and carryover effects are simply variations of this fundamental idea. These difficulties can be controlled to some extent if conditions are reversible, as they must be for this method to work.

ENDNOTE

Discussion of Line-Lengths Exercise

Answers to line lengths:

1. 22	5. 9	9. 37	13. 14
2. 9	6. 22	10. 14	14. 37
3. 14	7. 37	11. 22	15. 9
4. 37	8. 14	12. 9	16. 22

Use your answers for the line lengths and compute your constant and variable error.

Compare your errors with those of other people.

How do you explain the differences?

How do you explain instances of low constant, but high variable error?

What personality correlates might you suggest to explain high constant and high variable error?

In your opinion which type of error is more important, constant or variable? Why?

STUDY QUESTIONS

1. Explain whether the line judgment exercise was or was not a true experiment.

2. What is the basic idea of a within-subject research design?

3. What is the basic idea of psychophysics?
    What is its relevance to within-subjects design?

4. What are some similarities and differences of the within-subjects design and a simple experiment?

5. What sorts of stimuli are most appropriately used with the within-S design?

6. What is constant error, and how is it determined?
    Know how to compute and explain it.

7. What is variable error, and how is it measured?
    How are standard deviations used to show its size?
    Know how to compute and interpret variable error.

8. Variable error is determined by a standard deviation which shows variability around the mean of the subject's scores or around the value of the standard score. Which? Explain.

9. Compare and contrast constant and variable error.
    How is it possible to be high on one and low on the other?

10. What is the reason for using several subjects in within-S research?

11. How are data from individual subjects combined to determine constant and variable error?

12. How is the reliability of within-S judgments determined?

13. What is progressive error?
    How is it important in within-S design?
    How might its effects be avoided?

14. Explain the ideas of differential transfer and carryover effects.

15. What is counterbalancing?
    When, how, and why is it used?
    In what circumstances will it not work?

16. What is "Weber's law," and how is it relevant to the selection of stimuli values to be used in a within-S experiment?

17. How is Weber's law of particular importance to perception studies?

18.   What are some advantages of the within-S experimental design? What are some of its disadvantages?

19.   Why does the action of independent variables have to be reversible if one is to use within-S designs for research?

20.D   Give some examples of judgments in areas other than perception which would require the stimuli to be arranged at increasingly large intervals.

SMALL TALK

PART FIVE

Putting Research to Work

Chapter
15

Organization Necessary for Research

A good way to improve the quality of scientific work is to find and point out the errors in it. A friend might be willing to do this, but an enemy is better. "An enemy is willing to devote a vast amount of time and brain power to ferreting out errors . . . and this without any compensation. The trouble is that really capable enemies are scarce, most of them are only ordinary. Another trouble with enemies is that they sometimes develop into friends and lose a good deal of their zeal."

Paraphrased from von Békésy, G. (1960). *Experiments in Hearing*. New York: McGraw-Hill.

This chapter will bring together, organize, and outline much of the material that has formed the major content of the text. Not every point to be mentioned will be relevant for every research proposal, but the general ideas are sound and each should be considered and followed whenever possible. No list of activities—and certainly not this one—is exactly right for every possible circumstance. Each time I try to explain what a beginner should do to get started in research I think of another point that definitely should have been included, and I see less-important topics that could be left out. But anyone who follows the outline should produce creditable research.

SEQUENCE OF RESEARCH PROCEDURES

1. Get a *good* testable idea.
   a. The idea should not be trivial, but beginners tend toward projects that are much too complex rather than too simple.
   b. Develop the idea into answerable questions.
2. Review the literature; find out what is already known and what has already been done with your idea.
   a. Avoid duplication of previous work, but do not overlook the importance of replication.
   b. Try to determine through an impartial analysis which studies can form a solid foundation for your work.
   c. Integrate previous observations with your ideas.
   d. Organize your thinking to identify both supporting and contradictory evidence for your idea.
3. Communicate with others working in your selected field to determine if there is similar work in progress.
4. State your ideas as propositions in the form of testable hypotheses.
   a. Follow the rules for good hypothesis development.
   b. Show the relationship of your hypothesis to broader issues of psychological understanding.
5. Identify constructs and provide meaningful operational definitions.
6. Select the research design:
   a. Naturalistic observation.
   b. Correlation, studies of relationship.
   c. Experimental designs.
      i.   Ex post facto.
      ii. Controlled conditions (laboratory experiments).
      iii. Factorial designs.
      iv. Within-S.
7. Develop a research proposal.
   a. For experimental designs, identify independent variables.
      i. You must use *at least* two.
      ii. Establish how they are to be manipulated.
   b. Identify and explain the dependent variable for each experiment.
      i. What changes in behavior will you look for?
      ii. How will you measure these changes?
   c. What potential confounding variables will you watch? How will they be controlled?
   d. What statistic(s) will you choose to analyze data?
8. How many groups of subjects will be involved?
   a. How many in each group?

     b. How will you select them?
       i.   Random methods.
       ii.   Matched, related, paired.
       iii.   Within-subject.
       iv.   Complex designs with multiple groups.

9. Complete the research; collect data.
10. Analyze data; evaluate and interpret results.
     a. Based on the statistical analysis, was the null hypothesis rejected? At what level?
     b. What decision was made about the research hypothesis?
11. Summarize and honestly state arguments that are opposed to your hypothesis as well as those that support it.
12. Now what?
     a. What old ideas have been rejected and discarded?
     b. What new ideas does the work suggest?
     c. What new research projects can be developed from the one just completed?
13. Estimate the work's internal and external validity.
     a. Assess the overall quality of the work.
     b. Did anything go wrong that should be corrected in future work?
     c. What suggestions and recommendations should you give to anyone wanting to repeat the work?
14. Organize the material and write the report.
15. Save all the data!
     Label everything carefully, and store all relevant materials so they will be available to anyone who wants to check what was done and how it was done.

All research begins with good ideas, but it is impossible to make specific recommendations about how to get them. A beginning thought or observation cannot be odd or different, unusual or peculiar, novel or rare all by itself. Observations derive their meaning from comparison with past experience. What is a brilliantly new, creative, and imaginative idea for one person might be one that is so obvious to others that it has already been tried and discarded many times over. This is why a survey of the literature is so important. Anytime I think I have a good idea I assume that someone else has also thought of it, so my job is to find out who it was and what they have done on it.

Good research is not limited to interpretation of novel events, however. The familiar, common, everyday, matter-of-fact experiences also warrant explanation; but it is hard to see the matter-of-fact as deserving of explanation. Many of us have trouble remembering the picture that has hung for years at the same place on the wall.

None of these statements offer solutions to the problem that has faced everyone who needs to write a term paper or to do work for an advanced degree: "What am I going to do for my thesis research?" The world is a very busy place these days. There are nearly always time constraints, a limited budget, and too many other matters that require attention. People who are forced into doing research do not have the time, the background of information, and sometimes not the creative ability for worthwhile projects. Research is often required of people who are not necessarily excited about doing it. Students who are required to do research for class projects or for advanced degrees know the feeling, but so do faculty members who need published research for promotion or tenure.

SELECT A STATISTIC

As the text has probably made clear, the parts that make up the research process are so integrated it is difficult to discuss one part out of the context of the others. Although the statistical evaluation comes very near the end in the sequence of research procedures, the decision about which statistic to use should have been made much earlier, at the point when the project as a whole was outlined. Inexperienced investigators have been known to collect data that cannot be analyzed with the statistic they had planned to use. The greater the number of statistics we are familiar with, the more freedom we can have in our research designs. People who know the least about statistics, research methods, and procedures are the ones most beset by the apparent and supposed limitations of standard research methods.

For the following discussion, I assume the reader is familiar with the main classes of research techniques but is a little unsure about how to select the right statistic to be used with a particular research option. If this is the case, this section is likely to be of help.

Actual selection is more difficult than the simple outline presented in the next section can suggest. Each statistic has its own set of rules. Although it might be possible to do the arithmetic for a statistic using numbers that do not satisfy the requirements applicable to it, the results will not be meaningful and cannot be interpreted. Anova (*analysis of variance*), for example, is generally applicable only to randomly selected samples, but there are exceptions. Data for correlations should be distributed broadly and symmetrically, with a range that is not attenuated. The *t*-test assumes, among other constraints, that both groups will be of approximately the same size and their population variances will be similar. Other statistics have their own restrictions, but nonparametric statistics in general are more forgiving. After a possible statistic has been chosen, it is always necessary to check standard statistics texts to be certain the selected statistic is appropriate for the proposed task, with the data that is available.

In this text we have studied three broad classes of research designs: naturalistic observation, correlation, and experimental method. Naturalistic observation by itself is not of much value for drawing definitive scientific conclusions. It works very well indeed for preliminary work that helps investigators identify hypotheses worthy of study by other methods, but its use is limited in behavioral science research because it is not helpful in situations involving multiple causation. Behavioral scientists are forced to adapt their thinking and their practice to one or the other of these two broad research categories: *experimental* or *correlational* designs.

Although parametric statistics are emphasized in the following outline, non-parametric statistics can often provide quite satisfactory alternate ways of analyzing data. They are appropriate for the lower orders of measurement, ordinal and categorical, which are commonly available in the behavioral sciences. They are quickly and easily computed with small samples, and they provide almost as much information as the parametric statistics. As I said in an earlier discussion, I think they should be more widely used.

This outline makes no pretense of being definitive. Newer statistics and those not widely known have not been included. These are old, standard formulas that are well understood, and information on them is widely available.

SUMMARIZING OUTLINE OF STATISTICS AND RESEARCH DESIGNS

Naturalistic Observation (Method of Agreement)

No inferential statistics are applicable; descriptive statistics can be used.

Correlations (Method of Concomitant Variation)

The main statistic for use with data in this area is the Pearson product-moment correlation. Correlational analyses have only a limited function in the determination of cause and effect relationships, but they are valuable—and often they are the only technique we have—for the discovery and preliminary analysis of research ideas. The Pearson r is a major statistic in psychological evaluation for determining test reliability and validity.

The Pearson correlation requires two sets of logically paired scores and interval data.

The Spearman rank correlation is a statistic that is similar in use to the Pearson, but it requires rank data.

Other Correlation Statistics

Statisticians offer research workers a number of statistics that in one way or another are appropriate for analysis of relationships: biserial, point-biserial, partial, multiple, phi or C.

Kendall's W (coefficient of concordance) is a special nonparametric statistic that is almost a research technique by itself. It is not actually a correlation, but it is a way of determining the average intercorrelation among several correlations. It is a like a complicated Spearman, also requiring ranked data.

Factor Analysis

Many factor analytic techniques are available to help identify common elements in a battery of correlational measurements. This statistic is studied in advanced courses and is generally appropriate only for advanced projects.

EXPERIMENTAL METHODS (METHOD OF DIFFERENCE)

Main Statistic: *t*-Test

The most widely used statistic for data analysis from simple two group experiments is the *t*-test.

Although the types of research questions this statistic can be used to answer are all similar, different research questions and several options for the assignment and use of subjects force investigators to select the *t*-test formula that is correct for their intended application. These include:

a. Randomly selected samples.
b. Correlated samples (paired subjects).
c. One-sample case (rarely applicable in research).

Unless subjects are matched or paired in some logical way to produce correlated samples, the typical behavioral science application uses randomly selected and randomly assigned subjects. This produces independent groups and requires the *t*-test for randomly selected samples. Samples of the same size are not necessary, but they should be close. This formula assumes that subjects have come from a population in which the *dependent measure* was normally distributed and the variances were equal. The formula is robust and works well enough even when data deviate somewhat from normality. Interval (or ratio) data are required.

Variations of Simple-Experiment Statistics

The nonparametric area offers several statistics that can make data analysis possible for lower types of measurements not appropriate for the *t*-test.

The *Mann-Whitney U* is an interesting one which evaluates significance of difference between two randomly selected samples of ordinal (but not ranked) data.

The *Wilcoxon T (matched-pairs signed-ranks test)* evaluates matched pairs of ranked data.

Statistics for Complex Experiments

Analysis of variance (ANOVA) is the statistic most widely used when investigators want to evaluate the significance of differences among several independent variables, each with at least two levels. Recall that this is the statistic recommended for analysis of factorial design experiments. A variation called the "one-way" anova is applicable to situations in which there is one independent variable with several levels. Anova can be used for two-sample experiments, but most investigators chose the *t*-test for this.

Statisticians have not been satisfied to leave things well enough alone so that beginners could have a chance to understand them! Several versions of anova are available for evaluations of data from very complex experimental designs. The "manova" variation is used for a multivariate analysis of variance, and "mancova" is the statistic to choose when you want a multivariate analysis of covariance. It sometimes seems to me that statistics are ahead of our ability to develop good enough experiments to use them.

A number of nonparametric versions of the anova statistic are available. The *Kruskal-Wallis one-way analysis of variance* is applicable when we have more than two samples, ordinal (ranked) data, and randomly selected subjects. The *Friedman two-way analysis of variance* is the one you want when you need to evaluate data from more than two samples, ordinal (but not ranked) data, and matched subjects.

The chi-square statistic is, as perceptive readers might have guessed by now, one of my favorite statistics. It is one of the oldest, and it is the most flexible one we have in its applications. Since higher orders of data can always be simplified to a lower measurement scale, it follows that chi-square can be used for any data that can at least be formed into categories. Research questions appropriate to it include evaluation of a distribution of samples presumed to have come from a population having specified characteristics, and it can compare an obtained with a theoretical distribution. It can compare two samples to determine significance of difference much as the *t*-test does, but it can also analyze data in the form of both simple and complex anova designs.

META-ANALYSIS

This is not a statistic in the same sense as those mentioned earlier. It is a set of methods for the collective analysis of many research studies and offers an alternative to the typical literature survey. Some of the work might have been well or badly done, and some of the findings might agree with or contradict the results of other work. Appropriate statistical procedures permit investigators to evaluate the amount of collective support for research hypotheses. The particular value of meta-analysis is that it can bring together reasearch findings from a number of different sources and assist in drawing conclusions from this overall perspective.

An interesting and understandable introductory discussion for this technique is given in *Science* (Mann, 1990). Rosenthal (1984) presents a full discussion of the application of this method to research in the behavioral sciences.

Earlier, in a different context, I briefly mentioned three newspaper reports about the effects of being a latchkey child and I pointed out disagreement in the findings. Anyone who wanted to do a definitive analysis of the many studies that now have been done on this topic might want to apply the technique of meta-analysis. This procedure helps a researcher to systematically evaluate and combine information from multiple research projects. It has always been necessary for investigators to analyze information from many sources. The lack of structure in the process permitted a great deal of subjectivity, which did not control bias and other errors of interpretation. Researchers often drew conclusions from an unreliable selection of available data, which itself was not always controlled for random error. Techniques of meta-analysis help investigators to integrate and quantify the results of several studies.

Even as long as 10 years ago there had been nearly three dozen contradictory studies regarding the effects of coaching on SAT scores. DerSimonian and Laird (1983) used the meta-analytic technique to evaluate these studies. Meta-analysis was ideal for this work because the studies had been conducted in different ways with widely varying subject samples and the conclusions were far from uniform. A comprehensive evaluation of research on this topic permitted the conclusion that, ". . . the data do not support a positive effect of coaching on SAT scores. . . ." There was a slight effect, however, but the authors felt its size seemed ". . . too small to be of practical importance." This work should be of particular interest to students who have or plan to resort to coaching in order to improve their performance on the SAT test.

Smith and Glass (1977) undertook a meta-analysis of the literature to evaluate the effectiveness of psychotherapy. Nearly 400 studies provided the information to be analyzed. Different types of therapy, such as client-centered or behavioral, were included. Different studies involved dissimilar types of patients, and therapeutic improvement was evaluated in many ways. Not only were the investigators able to draw a conclusion about the general effectiveness of therapy, they were able to compare and note the relative effectiveness of several specific therapeutic modes. In an area that seems to involve more subjective opinions than do other types of research, a technique that helps to organize conclusions is quite advantageous.

WRITING A RESEARCH PAPER

Anyone who has done research knows how difficult it can be to find ideas, get the research project organized, find subjects, and complete the collection of data; but for many of us, that is the easy part compared to what comes next. I refer, of course, to writing up the work.

The Publication Manual of the American Psychological Association (APA) is the accepted standard for scientific publication in psychology. This is a "must have" book for anyone who is serious about writing anything for publication, and I know instructors who insist that the APA format be followed even for class projects. I know of several additional sources of information for writing research reports, and there are probably others. Any of these might be of more practical value for beginners.

Tallent, N. (1993). *Psychological report writing.* Englewood Cliffs, NJ: Prentice Hall.

Rosnow, R.L., & Rosnow, M. (1992). *Writing papers in psychology.* Belmont, CA: Wadsworth.

Day, R.A. (1983). *How to write and publish a scientific paper.* Philadelphia: ISI Press.

Pyrczak, F., & Bruce, R.R. (1992). *Writing empirical research reports.* Los Angeles: Pyrczak Publishing.

A look at some of the chapter titles with selected subtopics will demonstrate the amount of detail with which the APA approaches its task of advising prospective writers.

INTRODUCTION TO THE *PUBLICATION MANUAL OF THE AMERICAN PSYCHOLOGICAL ASSOCIATION*

1. Content and Organization of a Manuscript
2. Expression of Ideas
   a. Writing Style
      Orderly Presentation of Ideas
      Smoothness of Expression
      Economy of Expression
      Precision and Clarity
      Strategies to Improve Writing Style
   b. Grammar
      Verbs
      Agreement of Subject and Verb
      Pronouns
      Misplaced and Dangling Modifiers
   c. Consideration of the Reader
      Guidelines for Nonsexist Language
      Avoiding Ethnic Bias
3. APA Editorial Style
   a. Punctuation
   b. Spelling
   c. Capitalization
      The contents of chapter 3 continues, listing several pages of headings with supplemental topics in all the dull detail that creative writers would as soon avoid if they could!
4. Typing Instructions and Sample Paper
5. Submitting the Manuscript and Proofreading

And so on. . . .

STRUCTURE OF A RESEARCH REPORT

The topics of most relevance to writing a term paper or research project are included in chapter 1 of the APA *Publication Manual*, "Content and Organization of a Manuscript." We should look particularly at the "Parts of the Manuscript" section, which provides a basic outline of topics included in a journal article. These are what we are interested in at this point. This form should be adequate for typical research projects, but individual instructors might suggest an alternate format or offer variations to this one. Not all sections have been used in this outline, because some (the appendix, for example) are not usually relevant to nonprofessional presentations. Short papers for a course probably would not find a use for "running heads," and tables and graphs can often be incorporated into the body of the report instead of being listed separately as required for publication.

1. Title Page

This is a separate page, on which the title is centered both left to right and top to bottom. The title is written in upper- and lowercase letters (capital and small letters) and is no longer than 15 words in length.

The title is the most important single set of words in the document, so we often expend a great deal of effort in figuring out how to briefly state what our work is about. The APA manual suggests this is what we should do:

> **Title.** A title should summarize the main idea of the paper simply and, if possible, with style.

(At the risk of being facetious, which tends to be forbidden in textbooks, I just want to briefly interrupt this discussion to point out a major objection I have with the APA manual: I have never found it is of any value to *tell* people what to do, and the *Publication Manual* contains a lot of telling. Telling someone who has studied and learned the craft of writing to write a title "simply and, . . . with style" is unnecessary. A person who knows how to write would do it anyhow, without needing to be told. Telling a person who does not write well to start writing well will not make it happen.)

The title is followed by the name(s) of the author(s) or people who have made a material contribution to the work. Names are written in upper- and lowercase letters, centered on the page. Full names are used and are listed in the order of first name, middle initial, and last name. Titles and degrees are not included.

When several authors are involved, one of them is considered the principal author; his or her name is listed first.

The institution where the work was carried out is given following the name(s). The place where the principal author can be contacted for reprints or additional information is given in a footnote at the bottom of the first page in the article. It takes the form of "Correspondence and requests for reprints should be sent to. . . ."

2. Abstract

An abstract is a brief but comprehensive summarizing statement of a paper's content. In a short paragraph the author should identify the hypothesis, tell how it was studied, and what resulted from the research. Authors generally agree that this is the most difficult part of the paper to write, so they tend to leave it for last.

I cannot overemphasize the importance of a good abstract. When we are looking for an article to read to get more information, the abstract is the only guide we have to help us decide whether or not an article is relevant to our research and whether it is likely to be worth reading. So much material seems to be available these days on almost every topic that we are forced to be selective. A good abstract can help us make the right decision about each article.

3. Introduction

The introduction begins the body of the article itself; it is not labeled because it comes first and readers will know that it is the introduction. This section answers the question, "What is the point of the study?" Present the hypotheses being considered, discuss procedures that were used to test them, show the theoretical implications of the study, and how your work ties in with earlier studies. A good introduction should give a reader ". . . a firm sense of what was done and why."

Develop the background. This section expands on the references to acknowledge relevant contributions made by others.

The introduction concludes with the study's rationale, an indication of the conclusions predicted from the hypotheses and the logic behind them.

4. Method

This section describes how the study was conducted, what was done, and how it was done. The method section is subdivided into labeled sections to more precisely identify specific features of the study.

"Who participated in the study? How many participants were there? How were they selected?" Chapter 16 of our text discusses in more detail the use of people for psychological research.

Animal studies will require more information: specific information to identify the type of animal, number of animals, sex, age, weight, and physiological condition. (Note the discussion in chapter 16 on the care and use of animals for research.)

Any complex or unusual apparatus, tests, or measuring devices should be carefully described.

Sequentially list what was done at each stage of the research. Describe special techniques used (counterbalancing, randomization). Provide all the information necessary for a reader to know exactly what you did.

5. Results

This section provides the information needed to justify why you did or did not reject your research hypothesis. Statistical conclusions should follow the guidelines given in chapter 12, "Interpreting Data." The following example illustrates some relevant points:

> When the 46 new letter strings were presented for the first time, control subjects classified 63.2% of them correctly, and amnesic patients classified 63% of them correctly. The performance of the two groups was not significantly different ($t[25] = 1.40$ $p > .1$). . . .
> (Knowlton, Ramus, & Squire, 1992)

Note the brief statement of the principal results and the presentation of the statistical conclusions. A *t*-test was the statistic chosen for data analysis. The degrees of freedom is shown in square brackets []. (The sample sizes were 14 and 13, so df for uncorrelated samples is 14 + 13 − 2 = 25). The *t*-test produced a probability greater than .1. This value is too large to reject the null hypothesis at the .05 level.

The APA recommends that authors ". . . choose the medium that presents (results) clearly and economically." "If you do use tables or figures, use as few as possible and be certain to mention them in the text." One should never use tables if the same material can be given easily in the body of the report. Authors make best use of the space available to them if they do not repeat the same data in several places.

The construction of tables requires a thorough knowledge of what important data are to be presented, the best way of presenting them, and how to make a table to achieve the most economical presentation. The "Tables" section in the APA manual includes many pages of material that must be carefully studied if tables are to be satisfactory for APA publication.

6. Discussion

For a term paper in which there is a limited discussion, this section might be combined with the preceding one and called "Results and Conclusions" or "Results and Discussion."

This is where you would make a final statement about the extent to which your experimental findings supported your research hypothesis. Explain the contribution of your research to the science of psychology and suggest how your conclusions and their theoretical implications can lead to new research in other, possibly different, areas.

7. References

The detailed information necessary for correctly writing all possible variations of references must be obtained from the APA *Publication Manual*. Styles of simple references and other detailed material one must know to create an acceptable term paper is given in the following document, which is being reproduced with kind permission from the American Psychological Society.

FOR STUDENTS . . .
A Short Course on APA Style for Psychology Students

John H. Hummel and B. Christiana Birchak University of Houston-Downtown

Papers for advanced psychology courses necessitate that students learn to identify and report information appropriately. Unfortunately, many college students at both the graduate and undergraduate levels remain unaware of the writing conventions used in different disciplines. Although English departments increasingly offer guidance in writing across the curriculum, most composition courses retain the

Modern Language Association Handbook (Gibaldi & Achteri, 1984) as the guide for preparing formal papers. Therefore, psychology students often encounter difficulties in preparing papers that conform to the *Publication Manual of the American Psychological Association* (1983).

The *Publication Manual* does not target students as its audience. Instead, it serves as a resource for professionals who desire to publish various technical manuscripts. Thus, students often blame their stylistic errors on the manual's complexity (Hummel, 1988).

The present article responds to students' complaints by condensing the specialized writing conventions associated with APA style. A handout was developed by conducting a task analysis of the requirements of the APA style as applied to student papers.

The handout is divided into three areas: typing instructions, citations used in the paper, and reference page construction. Instructions consist of a list of do's and don'ts with examples and referrals to the *Publication Manual* (1983) where appropriate. Use of standard English by students is assumed.

Typing Instructions

1. For details not specifically addressed, refer to chapter four, pp. 135–156, of the Manual.

2. Use margins of 1.5 inches (top, bottom and sides). Each page should contain no more than 25 lines of text with pica type set at 55 characters per line, and elite at 66.

3. Do not justify lines if using a word processing program.

4. End each line of text with a complete word (e.g., do not hyphenate words at the end of a sentence).

5. Double space all lines including references.

6. Number all pages starting with the title page. Page numbers are located in the upper-right corner of each page 1.5" from the top and right margins.

7. The title page should be centered and should contain: The paper's title, the author's name, and the author's affiliation.

EXAMPLE A: TERM PAPER

Training Teachers to Use
Behavior Modification
John H. Hummel
PSY 4304, Section 1721

EXAMPLE B: ARTICLE SUMMARIES/CRITIQUES

Summary of Deitz and Arrington's
"Wittgenstein's Language-games and the Call to Cognition"
John H. Hummel
PSY 4304, Section 1721

8. Term papers and data-based reports must have an abstract unless otherwise indicated by the professor. The abstract is always on a page by itself (page two of the paper). The word Abstract should be centered at the top of the page. The abstract should be 50 to 150 words in length and must be typed as one blocked (no indentation) paragraph.

9. New paragraphs should be indented five spaces from the left margin.

10. Most papers will require headings when introducing new topics. For example, the last section of a term paper should be its discussion, and would appear in the paper as follows:

DISCUSSION

Headings should be as brief as possible with the first letter of each word capitalized. (Note: The first section of a term paper, the introduction, does not have a heading.) There are five levels of headings used in APA-style manuscripts. Refer to pp. 65–68, Sections 3.28–3.30, of the APA *Publication Manual* for more detailed directions of headings.

11. Do not underline words or use single or double quotation marks to provide emphasis.

CITATIONS

1. All works cited, whether through paraphrasing or direct quoting, must be referenced in the text of the paper with one exception; if one is summarizing/critiquing a single article, paraphrasing does not have to be referenced. (Remember to paraphrase accurately.)

2. Limit your sources to published books, journals, and papers presented at conferences. Avoid citing non-copyrighted materials and materials published in newspapers and magazines (e.g., *Psychology Today*). Use of such sources may require a different method of both in-text citations and references, and one must refer to the APA *Publication Manual* for the appropriate style.

3. Obtain permission to quote when necessary. For example, APA-copyrighted works require written permission before using a total of over 500 words of another's work. Try to keep direct quotes from a single source to less than 500 words.

4. Complete quotes of 40 words or less should be incorporated within the paper's text, begun and ended with double quotation (e.g., " ") marks, and must be followed by a parenthetical reference citing the author(s), date of publication, and the page(s) where the quote is printed.

   a. The first time a work is quoted or paraphrased, all authors (if six or less) are cited in order, by their surnames in the parenthetical reference. If the work has one or two authors, cite all of them by their surnames each time the work is cited. If the work has three or more authors, cite all of them in the first parenthetical reference. Later references will parenthetically cite the first author's surname followed by the expression et al., date, and specific page number(s) if the reference is a direct quote. If the work has more than six authors, cite the primary author's surname followed by et al. and list all the authors of the work in the citation on the reference page.

EXAMPLE A: IMBEDDED TEXT REFERENCE FOR PARAPHRASING

Although many behavioral scientists feel that punishment should never be used, Deitz and Hummel (1978) offer two situations where it may be ethical to use the procedure.

EXAMPLE B: IMBEDDED TEXT REFERENCE FOR PARAPHRASING

There are two situations where punishment procedures may be warranted: When all other deceleration methods have failed or when the behavior is a clear and present danger to self or others (Deitz & Hummel, 1978).

EXAMPLE C: IMBEDDED TEXT REFERENCE FOR DIRECT QUOTES

Using punishment to decelerate behavior is problematic. In general, "Punishment should be reserved for only very serious misbehaviors and should be used only when other alternatives have been exhausted" (Deitz & Hummel, 1978, p. 81).

EXAMPLE D: IMBEDDED TEXT REFERENCE FOR DIRECT QUOTES

Using punishment to decelerate behavior is problematic. According to Deitz and Hummel (1978), "Punishment should be reserved for only very serious misbehaviors and should be used only when other alternatives have been exhausted" (p. 81).

b. Quotes of more than 40 words must be presented (a) as an indented (five spaces from the left margin) block, (b) without quotation marks, (c) followed by a parenthetical reference after the quote's final punctuation mark(s) that always cites the page(s) where the quoted materials are located in the original work.

EXAMPLE E: DIRECT QUOTE LONGER THAN 40 WORDS

Punishment is one of the most widely used procedures to decrease behavior in school settings because teachers are not familiar with other deceleration procedures, and because it works quickly and effectively.

> The decision to use punishment should be made carefully. Special consideration should be given to whether or not the procedure can be implemented properly. If implemented correctly, punishment will reduce a misbehavior faster and more efficiently than any other reductive technique. However, in many cases, once the procedure is stopped, there is a high probability that the misbehavior will return to its original level unless the child has been taught alternate, desirable behavior that can be done instead of the misbehavior.   (Deitz & Hummel, 1978, p. 96)

EXAMPLE F: DIRECT QUOTE LONGER THAN 40 WORDS

Punishment is one of the most widely used procedures to decrease behavior in school settings because teachers are not familiar with other deceleration procedures, and because it works quickly and effectively. Still, Deitz and Hummel (1978) do not advocate reliance on punishment.

> The decision to use punishment should be made carefully. Special consideration should be given to whether or not the procedure can be implemented properly. If implemented correctly, punishment will reduce a misbehavior faster and more efficiently than any other reductive technique. However, in many cases, once the procedure is stopped, there is a high probability that the misbehavior will return to its original level unless the child has been taught alternate, desirable behavior that can be done instead of the misbehavior. (p. 96)

5. Avoid quoting material that either references or quotes a second copyrighted work. If you must, follow the guidelines on p. 151, Section 4.13 of the APA *Publication Manual.*

6. Do not use ellipsis (. . .) points. These are used when one omits part of an original source (e.g., when not quoting an entire sentence). Quotes out of context can be misinterpreted. If you quote only part of a sentence, follow the directions on p. 70, Section 3.36, of the APA *Publication Manual.*

7. If possible, do not use footnotes. If you must, refer to p. 105, Section 3.83, of the APA *Publication Manual.*

CONSTRUCTING THE REFERENCE PAGES

1. The list of references is always started on a new page.

2. The word Reference should be centered at the top of the page.

3. All sources cited in the manuscript must be listed in alphabetical order on the reference page.

4. References are not bibliographies. Bibliographies refer the interested reader to additional sources for further reading that were not cited in the manuscript through paraphrasing or direct quotation, and are not used in APA-style manuscripts.

5. Each reference is typed double-spaced. All lines of a reference except for the first are indented three spaces from the left margin.

6. The general format for a book reference involves: (a) List all authors (in the order in which the names appeared on the original manuscript) by their surname followed by the initials of their first and middle name (if known); (b) the date of publication is presented in parentheses after the listing of authors, and is followed by a period; (c) the title of the book follows the publication date. The entire title is underlined and followed by a period. Only the first word of the title is capitalized with two exceptions: When proper nouns, such as a person's name, are included in that title, or when the book's complete title uses a colon. The first letter of a word following a colon is capitalized. If the book is a second or later edition, after the title, in parentheses without underlining, list the edition using the following type of abbreviations: (2nd ed.); (d) Following the book's title is publication information which includes the city where the book was published and the name of the publisher (city and publisher are separated by a colon). If the name and location of the city is not well known, the city's name may be followed by the abbreviation of the state where the city is located. Information about the publisher should be as brief as possible (avoid using Co., Inc., etc.). Table 17 (pp. 123–127) of the APA *Publication Manual* illustrates 15 variations of book references (second and later editions, edited books, corporate authors, etc.).

EXAMPLE OF A BOOK REFERENCE

Deitz, S.M., & Hummel, J.H. (1978). *Discipline in the schools: A guide to reducing misbehavior.* Englewood Cliffs, NJ: Educational Technology Publications.

7. The general format for journal references is: (a) surnames and initials for all authors, separating each with commas. Use an ampersand (&) instead of the word and before the surname of the last author; (b) list the date of publication in parentheses after the authors' names, followed by a period; (c) the article title with only the first word capitalized (again, proper nouns such as a person's name or use of a colon in the article title require additional capitalization), followed by a period; (d) title of the journal, underlined, with the first letter of each word of the title capitalized excepting prepositions (e.g., of, and, etc.), followed by a comma; (e) numeric volume number underlined (issue numbers follow the volume number in parentheses and are not underlined), followed by a comma; and (f) the inclusive range of pages where the article is published in the journal without the abbreviation pp. or the word pages.

EXAMPLE OF A JOURNAL REFERENCE

> Deitz, S.M., & Arrington, R.L. (1984). Wittgenstein's language-games and the call to cognition. *Behaviorism, 12*(2), 1–14.

8. The general format for a conference paper is: (a) author surnames and initials separated by commas in the order in which they appear on the paper, with the last author's surname preceded by an ampersand (&); (b) year and month of presentation, separated by a comma, in parentheses, followed by a period; (c) title of the paper with only the first letter of the first word of the title capitalized (exceptions include proper names and the first letter of a word following a colon), followed by a period; and (d) a short sentence naming the group to whom the paper was presented and the city and state (abbreviated) in which the meeting was held. Table 17 (pp. 129–130) of the APA *Publication Manual* illustrates four variations for referencing presentations made at conventions including symposia.

EXAMPLE OF A REFERENCE TO A PAPER

> Hummel, J.H. & Hall, J.P. (1982, May). Efficiency of handouts on the test performance of college students. Paper presented at the annual meeting of the Association for Behavior Analysis, Milwaukee, WI.

DISCUSSION

This article should help alleviate students' fears of following an unfamiliar format. It enables them to appreciate the interdisciplinary aspect of the writing task and to regard it as merely another problem to be solved. Such an approach to writing strengthens its usefulness as a learning tool. While the article is not a substitute for the APA Manual, it can be used by students (and their teachers) as an inexpensive resource by which students can more easily learn APA requirements for typing, in-text citations, and constructing the references page(s).

The authors wish to thank Samuel M. Deitz, Ph.D., Professor and Chairman, Foundations of Education Department, Georgia State University, for his editorial comments on an earlier version of this manuscript.

REFERENCES

American Psychological Association. (1983). *Publication manual of the American Psychological Association*, (3rd ed.). Washington, DC: Author.

Deitz, S.M., & Arrington, R.L. (1984). Wittgenstein's language-games and the call to cognition. *Behaviorism, 12*(2), 1–14.

Deitz, S.M., & Hummel, J.H. (1978). *Discipline in the schools: A guide to reducing misbe-havior.* Englewood Cliffs, NJ: Educational Technology Publications.

Gibaldi, J., & Achteri, W.S. (1984). *MLA handbook for writers of research papers,* (2nd ed.). New York: The Modern Language Association of America.

Hummel, J.H. (1988, May). Teaching APA style to undergraduate students. Poster presented at the annual meeting of the Association for Behavior Analysis, Philadelphia, PA.

Hummel, J.H., & Hall, J.P. (1982, May). Efficiency of handouts on the test perfor-mance of college students. Paper presented at the annual meeting of the Associa-tion for Behavior Analysis, Milwaukee, WI.

Editor's Note: The *APS Observer* does not use APA style and thus except where noted there was no attempt to ensure that the present article was consistent with it.

THE USE OF COMPUTERS IN RESEARCH

Several years ago it might have been necessary to include relatively detailed in-formation on this topic. Now that computers have become so widely used, a gen-eral discussion seems to be all that is required. The ready availability of comput-ers and software for word processing greatly simplifies technical writing—after one has learned how to use the clever writing tools they make available. Any col-lege student who has not yet learned to type would do well to take a course. Psy-chology majors should take *at least* a beginning course in the computer sciences to expedite the otherwise difficult learning required for getting started. After I have spent a great many hours figuring out how to do things with a computer, I have found that most computer tasks are fairly simple! Instructions that were presum-ably written to help me understand what I am supposed to do are usually of lim-ited help until after I have figured out the operations independently. Then when I read the instructions they make sense. I understand that many other people have the same experience.

Everyone knows that a computer, called "hardware," can, with appropriate "software," be used to do a great many more things than any one person can even think about. In their simplest form computers have a tremendous value as "word processors," and they can go way beyond that for desktop publishing. The the-saurus, the spell checker, the style checker, and the large number of miscellaneous options that help to speed along the writing job must cause one to pause and wonder: How was writing—any writing—ever done even a few years ago? After a person has started using a search program to find information with a computer, thumbing through a book to find a topic not listed in the index rapidly becomes a task too tedious to contemplate.

A major computer advantage for most us is the speed with which errors can be corrected and new copies printed. The result could be that perfect experimental reports (beautifully typed, no grammatical or spelling errors, computations correct) can be submitted to the instructor ahead of the due date!

Modern campuses have computers set up and ready to go for student use, but the software will depend on whatever program someone in charge has chosen to install on them. They will not always be readily available, particularly when they are most needed. Students who plan to work toward advanced degrees will probably conclude that a computer is as much a necessary expense of a college education as a place to sleep.

People who buy computers, other hardware devices, or software should get the opinions of the computer course instructor for the current best buys. (Certain shops can use "off the shelf" components to economically assemble a computer using an individual's specifications.) Be prepared for large differences of opinion about what to buy—the effect is much like asking a person for a recommendation on the best car. Now, a reader of this text can buy a computer much superior to the one I bought several years ago. Yours will be faster, it will have more features, your monitor and printer will be better, and the package will cost you less.

The decision about whether to buy a DOS-based computer or a Macintosh is a personal one. Most standard software is available in forms suitable for either system, so users are not so limited as they were a few years ago. There is a steady movement toward integration, so by the time this gets into print, a decision about which system to buy might not be necessary. For a discussion of supposed differences between "Mac" and "PC" users, see this chapter's endnote, "Experimental Psychology in the English Writing Class."

The selection of software for one's own computer will require study and research, because many options are available. At this writing two leading products for word processing are WordPerfect and Microsoft Word. These programs, particular in their "Windows" versions, make features available for all levels of writing through "desktop publishing," but more options are added all the time to newer versions. To take advantage of them, one needs more advanced computers and better monitors; the best buy is not necessarily the cheapest. Computer innovations occur continuously, so pick the best that you can afford—knowing that a few months after you have bought yours, you will be able to buy something better for the same money or less. Many universities have arrangements that permit students and faculty to buy computers and related products at reduced prices.

"*Manuscript Manager: APA Style*" is a special word processing program that has been approved by the APA. (The phone number for additional information is: (914) 592-7700).[1] It emphasizes features for writing in accordance with the APA format. Using it should produce a document that is correct according to APA requirements. For example, it forces main headings to be correctly capitalized and titles to be correctly underlined. References are stored in a special file that makes it possible for them to be used in several different places without having to recopy them each time. Not a big thing perhaps, but it can save time.

---

[1]Pergamon Software, Maxwell House, Fairview Park, Elmsford, NY 10523. Requires 512 K RAM, and the program is "copy protected."

These and many similar features should be handy for writing journal articles, but that is likely to be only a small part of the writing a researcher does. For me, this special program is not worth giving up all the other features I have found to be useful in regular word processing software, which any college student should be able to buy more cheaply.

A modem can be a very useful adjunct for research. It allows an investigator to contact library networks to check for availability of books and can be a great timesaver in checking a reference. The options that are available probably vary widely from one part of the country to another. Illinois has a major network that permits searching university library catalogs all over the state and an interlibrary loan system through which students and faculty can borrow the books they find. Many university libraries have connections that access libraries all over the country. Networks and loan arrangements like these are probably administered by someone at your university library.

I have found that the network of the community libraries in my area is useful for more than research needs. When anyone in my family wants to know if a particular book is available, the modem connection can give the answer very quickly—at least when the network is open and working.

Several educational bulletin boards are available, which investigators might be able to use advantageously. Someone on every campus is likely to know about one or another of these that are working at a particular time. No doubt "Internet" is the largest one; it might be of direct interest to anyone who wants to contact people with broad academic or research interests in almost any area. You will probably need to purchase of one of the several books available in the computer section of bookstores in order to get started. Many people are unable to get off the entry ramp of this huge information highway. Ordinary, dial-in computer users seem to get the best results by tying in with Internet's "special interest groups" (sig).

Many national, general-information bulletin boards are always seeking more customers, but I do not know whether any of them provide information that would be relevant to research. Some of the bigger ones I happen to know about—because I have been invited to join—include: Prodigy, America Online, Chicago Online, CompuServe, and GEnie. I have seen lists of what must be hundreds of small bulletin boards that cater to special interests. Every university campus should have a resident hacker who knows about these areas.

ENDNOTES

WHICH RESEARCH DESIGN IS BEST: CORRELATION OR EXPERIMENTATION?

Study each of the following research ideas carefully, then explain the technique that would work best to evaluate it. You will have to rephrase some statements in order to use them as formal hypotheses. In some instances the same idea can be evaluated with either a correlation or experimental design. Illustrate the method you choose, using a specific statistic. My opinions (for whatever they might be worth) are given in the last Endnote of this chapter. Readers might have alternate solutions that are at least as good as mine and possibly better. Research is a fluid endeavor which permits several ways of phrasing a problem and solving it.

1. Study the effects of the college experience on intelligence.
2. Evaluate sense of humor as a function of creative ability.
3. Determine if it is true that the richer people live in the best neighborhoods.
4. Does innate ability decline with age?
5. The problem of teenage suicides can be best explained by ____?
6. Study the effect of the full moon on behavior.
7. The value of a classroom test can be determined by correlating it with how much the person knows about the course.
8. Study the effects of hypnotic states on memory.
9. What is the effect of psychotherapy on personality?
10. Is it true that brighter people have larger brains?
11. Determine if bulls are angered by the color red more than by any other color.
12. The time, date, and place of a person's birth definitely influences personality.
13. Reading for a certain number of hours each week can improve a person's ability to write well.
14. Tape recording lectures will improve academic performance.

EXPERIMENTAL PSYCHOLOGY IN THE ENGLISH WRITING CLASS

When R. Reid and Brit Hume discussed the topic in their syndicated weekly computer article (*Chicago Tribune*, 1991, February 3), I began a search for the missing information. The headline read, "Scholar Finds Big Gap Between Mac and PC Users." Theirs was the third discussion I had seen in computer publications about an article by Marcia Peoples Halio, "Student Writing: Can the Machine Maim the Message?" (1990, January, *Academic Computing, 4*, 16–19). Her article purported to show writing differences between college students who used Macintosh computers and work by students who had done their writing on MS-DOS computers.

Reid and Hume reviewed the long-running argument between PC[2] users and those who pushed the superiority of the Mac line of computers. They noted

---

[2] PC stands for "Personal Computer." The name was originally used by IBM for its machines, but the initials are now widely used to identify any stand-alone computer that uses the DOS operating system.

that the Halio article added partisan fuel to the fire. I am not certain the authors were being sarcastic, but their selection of erudite terms that do not apply in this context suggests they might have been. The word "scholar" used earlier and "scholarly publication" and "august journal" used later are examples. Reid and Hume referred to ". . . an article in a scholarly publication called *Academic Computing.* In the pages of that august journal, Dr. Marcia Peoples Halio, an English professor at the University of Delaware, reported on a 5-year study in which she compared the written quality of student papers produced on Macintosh and MS-DOS machines." The university had both DOS and Macintosh computers available for use in the university's freshman writing class. People who chose the Mac tended to use WordWrite for software, and the DOS users chose WordPerfect.[3] Dr. Halio noticed marked differences in the type and quality of the work produced by the different computer operators.

The "Kincaid Scale" was used to evaluate the grade level of readability. DOS users averaged a grade level of 12.1, which is college level work; papers written on the Mac computers averaged less than 8th grade. DOS users were said to be more likely than Mac people to write about "serious" issues: war, pollution, and teen pregnancy. The PC users produced papers that averaged about 4 spelling errors per paper; Mac users rang up an average of 15. The general conclusion is that MS-DOS computer users also made fewer grammatical errors and got generally higher grades than did the students who used Macs.

All the writers in computer magazines who made reference to this work seemed to be having fun with their suggestions about why such a marked difference existed. It could not be, as Reid and Hume wrote, because the Mac is a harder-to-use computer than the DOS machine: "The Macintosh is a wonderful computer for word processing. Heck, almost any Mac word processing software is easier to use than the uninviting WordPerfect, the most commonly used DOS word processing program." Reid and Hume go on to conclude the difference in the work did not result from computer differences but from the different types of people who chose to use them.

> Mac users, by and large, are free spirits—artistic types, rebels, the kind of folks who don't want to be bound by stodgy old rules or plain-Jane mechanisms. It's hardly surprising that such people would eschew spelling rules or take some liberties with conventional grammar.
>   IBM people, in contrast, are no-nonsense types. They're the three-piece-suit crowd, willing and indeed eager to conform to the established ways of the world. Of course they spell the words right in their essays. Doing things right is important. . . .

Halio had suggested the difference in quality of student writing could be attributed to differences related to the computers themselves. The two computers differed in a number of ways, but the major difference was the Mac's use of a "graphical interface" rather than a "command-line interface" as on the PC. This means that the commands selected to tell the computer what to do are presented

---

[3] Contracting words like this seems to be the way computer people write.

in either of two ways: The Macintosh uses little pictures, called "icons" whereas PC users make their selection of commands from a list of English words or coded keys. The graphics system on the Mac seemed to encourage students to pay more attention to appearance and be less concerned about the content of their writing.

Anyone who has read this far in the book should be immediately alert to the possibility that there were errors in the original research. The writers in the computer publications who discussed the Halio article, all of whom had a bias tending toward approval of the PC, could not resist the opportunity to write for a quick laugh, and they were not interested in evaluating the Halio work itself. That was the area I needed information about, and it came from an unexpected source, a journal on *Computers and Composition* (1990, August, vol. 7, no. 3). Several articles in this journal addressed the topic, "Computers and Controversy" (pp. 73–107), and all of them criticized the Halio work and her conclusions. The section also included a short rejoinder from Halio.

She mentioned that her article seemed to have aroused a great deal of interest. She had received a large amount of mail, some of which was critical, but there was also heavy support for her position "from cognitive psychologists and human-computer interaction specialists." She did, however, respond to some of the criticisms of her work.

The many English writing teachers and others who published their comments about the Halio article were not shy in what they had to say. ". . . Halio's article is so seriously flawed by methodological and interpretive errors that it would probably have been dismissed had it appeared in a journal directed to an audience of professional writing teachers." Another writer states, ". . . the article is flawed by a poor experimental design and is filled with questionable logic and evidence." Her evidence was derived from 5 years of observation and was largely anecdotal. She also consulted with and got the opinions of four other faculty members who had worked with freshman writing students.

Her work was criticized in several ways. For one thing, her measurements of the finished papers were considered inadequate. To add support for her personal impressions she used programs called "Writer's Workbench" and the "Kincaid Readability Scale." Several teachers of English writing criticized these choices on the grounds that they were not appropriate for their intended purpose. We, who have studied experimental methods, would say that she had used inadequate operational definitions of the dependent variable.

Among a number of other points that were criticized was one that stood out by repetition. Subjects were not randomly assigned to the separate levels. Note, she did not do an experiment in which students were randomly assigned to one or the other computer type. The computer and its related software, of course, constituted an independent variable which differed according to type. A proper experimental design requires that subjects should be randomly assigned by the investigator to the research conditions. (And the person who does the evaluations of the finished product must not know on which machine it had been produced.) Halio's participants were free to choose whichever computer they wanted to use. "Any differences in writing may therefore reflect differences in their attitudes and backgrounds. Halio's reliance on self-selecting groups makes attributing writers' performance primarily to their writing tools virtually impossible." Another critic went on to ask, "... did students with little experience in writing on computers choose the 'friendly' Macintosh? ... The article suggests that there is something fundamentally childish about the Macintosh, its users, and their writing." Apparently a number of students see the Macintosh as a "toy," which might account for the lower level of the essays that had been written on it.

A proper experimental design requires that "subject variables" should be equivalent among all the groups prior to exposing the subjects to the independent variable. Halio's report of results were strongly criticized by the writing teachers, partly because many readers of the widely distributed original article took her opinions as fact. She was thought to be premature in publishing results that were inadequate and incomplete. They felt that she should have waited for the conclusions from "a more carefully controlled experiment," which she states is now being undertaken. One critic even went so far as to claim that both "Halio—and *Academic Computing*—have acted irresponsibly" by publishing research that was so inadequate.

I should note in conclusion that a great deal of work on psychological problems has been done by people who are not psychologists. The *Computers and Composition* journal included a number of articles that anyone interested in psychology might be interested in reading, as the following list of topics illustrates:

"Designing Research on Computer-Assisted Writing"

"Literacy Theory in the Classroom: Computers in Literature and Writing"

"Balancing Enthusiasm with Skepticism: Training Teachers in Computer Assisted Instruction"

"Leadership Dynamics of Computer-Supported Writing Groups"

"Taking Women Professors Seriously: Female Authority in the Computerized Classroom"

"Overcoming Resistance: Computers in the Computer Writing Center"

WHICH RESEARCH DESIGN IS BEST? SOME SUGGESTIONS FOR ANSWERS

Research is a complex endeavor, which frequently allows alternate solutions to the same research problem if one makes different assumptions about the research question or the nature of the data. I would have difficulty arguing in some instances that my method is necessarily the best one, but the following are my suggestions for the best statistic to use for each of the topics listed in the first Endnote of this chapter.

1. This would have to be an ex post facto design. We could compute a *t*-test between average intelligence test scores for college and noncollege graduates. This item nicely illustrates the difference between functional and causal relationships. College graduates might on the average perform better on tests than noncollege graduates, but the college attendance might not have been the "cause" of the difference.

Brighter students tend to go to college, and colleges tend to restrict admission to the brightest people. A significant *t*-test will probably not tell much of anything about what college does to improve intelligence.

2. Compute a correlation between the operational definition of sense of humor and the operational definition of creative ability.

3. Correlate a "quality of neighborhood measurement" with income.

4. We would need a better measure of "innate ability" than is provided by a typical intelligence test. Intelligence, as measured by standard tests, is at least partly dependent on culture, education, experience, health, and many other things. At first reading this might appear a simple correlational study in which both sets of data are interval. The fact is, a good answer to this question is difficult to get.

5. Suicides or attempted suicides and "normals" form categories. We could use a *t*-test to evaluate the difference between the groups on some measurement of personality, health, or environmental factor. If we form categories of observations a chi-square would be the appropriate statistic.

6. "Full moon" is a category. Define categories of behavior to be studied and use chi-square for data evaluation. This topic is one that many people continue to take seriously. (See Lieber and Sherin, 1972.) This article stimulated the publication of several articles in disagreement.

7. This is a trick question which is meant to arouse an interest in reviewing the ideas of "operational definitions of constructs." How much a person knows about the content of the course is a construct that is defined by the test.

8. Assume that participants in this experiment are either hypnotized or not hypnotized. Investigators should provide operational definitions of expected "effects." Probably use a *t*-test for correlated samples to evaluate measurements of behavior when a person is hypnotized and when he or she is not. Note how much better the within-S design works in this situation than if we had two groups of people and hypnotized one group but not the other.

9. Depending on what is measured for amounts or kind of psychotherapy and what measurements are used for "personality," this could be done with either a correlation or a *t*-test.

10. A correlation would be computed between a measure of "brightness" and an operational definition of brain size. We should hope that modern technology makes it possible to determine brain size for living people.

11. Having never known any bulls personally, I have trouble thinking of an operational definition of a bull's anger, or how it changes. The manipulation of color should involve controls of brightness as well as tint or hue. Assuming all measurements provide category data, a chi-square would be the correct statistic to use. After all that has been done the investigator would probably discover what many people already know, that bulls are color blind.

12.   Time, place, and date are category data. Personality measurement often produces interval data. I would convert this to categories and use chi-square. This is an ex post facto design.

13.   This would be done with a correlational analysis, but a *t*-test would also work if subject writing samples were categorized into good and poor to compare the difference between hours of reading.

14.   Academic performance might best be measured with test grades, which we can use as interval data. The use and nonuse of tape recorders constitute variations of the independent variable. A *t*-test would be the best choice. The way the idea is phrased suggests an ex post facto design. People who go to the trouble to tape lectures and then take the time to listen to them later probably differ in several ways from people who do not go to all this trouble. To do the experiment correctly students should be randomly assigned to, and forced to participate in, a "tape-lecture" or "do-not-tape-lecture" group. Such an arrangement borders on the ridiculous.

SMALL TALK

Chapter
16

Getting Professional

*After studying a book like this one a person's head
will be full of useless rubbish. "It comes of too much
reading. I have never set much store by books; and I
have never seen anything but trouble to come out of
learning. It unsettles a person. It complicates one's
views of life, destroys the simplicity which makes
for peace of mind and happiness."*

Paraphrased from *Scaramouche* by Sabatini. Recall that the first
chapter quotation was also from this source.

With a basic understanding of a few elementary research methods and some
simple statistical techniques well in hand, it is time to round out the presentation
by looking at what is involved in putting this knowledge to work.

Many readers will never utilize this information professionally, except as
consumers of research information. This does not mean, as it might at first seem,
that the time spent learning the material has been wasted. The emphasis psychology places on statistics and experimental methods often sets psychology majors
apart from majors in other behavioral science fields. Research methods and techniques can be usefully applied in many professions, so the additional skills provided by this course could be a general advantage in a crowded and competitive
job market.

A second group of readers will need this information for advanced studies.
A person working for an M.A, M.Sc., or Ph.D degree in psychology will almost
certainly use material discussed in this text. I hope the concepts and procedures
learned here will become so much a part of your thinking, that they will find their

way into that mental storehouse where we keep things we know but we cannot remember where we learned them.

This chapter will provide some practical information for those people who are continuing with their education in psychology. The material included here is superficial and incomplete, as it must be in the space available, but it will be adequate to call attention to several areas that some readers will find of value.

SOURCES OF ADDITIONAL INFORMATION

Good Books and Periodicals to Know

Readers who have advanced this far into the psychology major program will already be well acquainted with at least one "general psychology" text. These texts continue to be excellent sources of general information about psychology, and rereading one can be a worthwhile preparation for the GRE. If I were searching for a research topic and did not have any ideas at all to help get me started, I would look in a general psychology text for some suggestions. There are so many fine general texts and they change so frequently that no specific title recommendation can be nor needs to be made. To start, select whatever is available in your college bookstore.

For information on advanced topics of current interest the best source is the *Annual Review of Psychology*. This is published by Annual Reviews Inc., 4139 El Camino Way, Palo Alto, CA, 94306. Major university libraries will have current and past editions of this series. The *Annual Review* should not be confused with another series titled *Annual Editions*. The latter is not equivalent.

Kling and Riggs (1971) *Woodworth and Schlosberg's Experimental Psychology* is a very important reference for many topics that are not well covered—if mentioned at all—in experimental psychology texts today. This is where a person would first look for information on how to study the GSR (the Galvanic Skin Response) measurement and experiments in psychophysics, physiological reactions, sensory modalities, learning, perception, and many other areas. Be warned: This is a highly technical book that in some places requires a knowledge of physics, but if one needs this information, this is the place to start.

The local college bookstore can also be a convenient guide for books on special course topics. Take note of the books various faculty members have selected for their courses. Check with individual course instructors for their recommendations; sometimes the best book in a field might not be suitable for a course text. Usually a teacher will be pleased to recommend what he or she considers to be the important books in a particular field.

The American Psychological Association (the address will be given later) provides a list of books it publishes. A few of these are primarily for professionals, but several are likely to be of interest to undergraduate psychology majors. *Preparing for Graduate Study in Psychology: NOT for Seniors Only* might be useful. Students thinking of graduate school might be interested in *Graduate Study in Psychology and Associated Fields, 1990* (by the time this textbook is published, a more recent edition will probably be available). The APA *Publication Manual* should be in the library of every graduate student in psychology. Some psychology departments might have publications they can give or lend to interested people. *Careers in Psychology* and *Psychology and You* are pamphlets that are available quite cheaply through bulk order. *Guidelines for Ethical Conduct in the Care and Use of Animals* and *Ethical Principles of Psychologists* are two other useful pamphlets that a psychology department could order in quantity and distribute inexpensively. Anyone doing research with human subjects should study *Ethical Principles in the Conduct of Research on Human Participants,* which I will discuss later. For information on all these publications write for the booklet *APA Books for Teaching, Counseling, and Learning in Psychology.* The APA order department provides information on APA publications in the booklet *Books and Journals.* This can be obtained by writing to the address given in the section on "Professional Organizations."

Members of the APA receive two publications as part of their membership fee: the *APA Monitor* and the *American Psychologist.* The *Monitor* is the "official" newspaper of the APA and provides information on topics such as current issues, legislative developments, recent research developments, and other information on what is happening in psychology. The "State-by-State Employment Opportunity Listings" are of considerable importance for those who are looking for jobs.

The APA describes the *American Psychologist* as, "Must reading for all those who desire current knowledge of the broad and dynamic field of psychology." It is the "official journal" of the APA. In addition to publishing information about meetings, programs, and special events, it also carries scholarly articles of more topical interest than the research reports that go into the regular APA journals.

Contemporary Psychology is a monthly APA publication that is markedly different from the others, and it is a great deal more interesting than it sounds— being a publication devoted entirely to book reviews. This journal is the best way available to learn about the books that are being published in all areas of psychology and what "respected experts" think of them. People on limited budgets who have funds to buy only the best books available should make this publication regular reading. A typical review summarizes a book, compares it with other books on the same topic, if any are available, and sometimes offers a summarizing statement about the book and its relevance in certain applications. There are many shorter reviews that are helpful in calling attention to books that would otherwise be difficult to know about. Even if you are not going to buy a book, you might want to know what books are available.

I believe I should stress that APA journals are available for (nearly) every field. When enough people become interested in an area, a journal will likely become available to implement their interests. Journals for different new or developing areas seem to be added every year or so.

Professional Organizations

For over 50 years the APA was *the* professional organization for everyone interested in psychology. The APA annual convention was the place to look for jobs, to meet potential publishers of your book, and to get the latest information about psychology. Conventions made it possible to see friends who had moved to other jobs and had not been heard from for a long time. Informal meetings helped to develop important new friendships.

An APA member can become a member of any of the many "divisions" within the APA. These subgroups are frequently sources of information on special topics. General Psychology, Teaching of Psychology, Experimental, and Evaluation and Measurement are examples of divisions that interest me. A complete list of the "Psychology Divisions" was given in Chapter 2, relative to a different discussion.

Two classes of APA membership are available: associate member and member. In 1994 annual dues were as follows for members: $49 for the first year, $98 for the second, $137 for the third, $176 for the fourth, and $195 for full membership from the fifth year on. Dues for associate members are $70 for the first year and $140 for the second year and each year thereafter.[1]

Effective in the fall of 1994 the American Psychological Society had the following dues structure: Full member $110, first-year Ph.D. $65, student membership $35.

The APA offers reduced membership dues to encourage student memberships. Additional charges are levied for some division memberships, and for subscriptions to additional journals.

A few years ago, a wave of unrest within the APA swept many psychologists out of the organization. People who had a primary commitment to psychology as a scientific discipline felt that the APA no longer adequately represented their interests. They saw the APA moving in the direction of becoming a professional society, with concerns more directed toward the application of psychology to the solution of practical problems of interest primarily to clinical psychology. The very large number of clinical psychologists that had entered the APA in recent years clearly had an effect on its reorientation.

The brief discussion that follows greatly oversimplifies, and in the process distorts, the changes that are taking place in the psychology profession and the reasons for them. As a biased participant, I will nevertheless try to give a balanced account of what has happened.

In August 1988 a group of psychologists which called itself the "Assembly for Scientific and Applied Psychology (ASAP)" voted to become the "American Psychological Society," and to establish a separate organization entirely outside the APA. "The goals of APS are to advance the discipline of psychology and to preserve its scientific base; to enhance the quality of graduate education; to promote public understanding of psychological science and its applications; . . . "

The *APS Newsletter* (vol. 1, no.1) devoted a great deal of its limited space to the views of Stewart W. Cook, a distinguished psychologist and a long-time APA member. He had been actively involved in the APA at many different levels and in many different ways, but he was also active in promoting both the science and

---

[1] These figures are relevant only at the time of writing. They will, no doubt, increase over time.

the practice of psychology in the community at large. When attempts to reorganize the APA failed and the APS got started, he decided to change his allegiance.

In reviewing historical antecedents that led to the development of APS, Cook pointed out that in the early days there was no distinction between the scientific study of psychology and the study of psychology's practical applications. "No one could foresee a split between scientific and applied psychology in the sense of an applied psychology practiced without a commitment to scientific psychology." Over the years of its existence the APA had greatly increased in size and expanded in the variety of interests represented, but there seemed also to be a change "in the symbolic character of the organization" which previously had a basis in science rather than practice.

The past quarter-century's gradually increasing pressures of conflicting points of view within the APA seemed to leave no choice for many psychologists, so they resigned their memberships. This sizable group of professional people became the initial membership of the APS. The interests of the two groups overlap greatly, and many people have memberships in both, but the cleavage means that psychology no longer speaks with a unified voice.

In an address before the APS Summit on Accreditation, Stanley Schneider (Associate Director of Training at the National Institute of Mental Health) made a number of thoughtful comments that expressed ideas shared by many psychologists. After noting the long period of disintegrating ties between members' clinical practice and research orientations, he stated his opinion that, "The effects . . . are disastrous for research and for related reasons have turned out to be damaging for practice as well." Schneider felt the split in the discipline was particularly regrettable because "the *intradisciplinary* breadth of psychology should be the source of its greatest strength." The address was reported in the *APS Observer* (1992, vol. 5, no. 3, p. 12).

Anyone who wants to become actively affiliated with a professional group in psychology should consider membership in one or the other of the following organizations, or both if the combined membership fees are not too great a financial burden. You should contact both organizations for information and use the material you obtain to decide which of the two groups to join.

American Psychological Association
1200 Seventeenth Street, NW
Washington, DC 20036

American Psychological Society
Suite 1100
1010 Vermont Avenue, NW
Washington, DC 20005-4907

The APS is still new, so it is much smaller in membership than the APA and it suffers some of difficulties faced by any organization just starting out. It has grown rapidly in a very short time, and regular growth seems to be continuing.

Members of the APS receive three publications as part of their membership: *Psychological Science; Current Directions in Psychological Science;* and the *APS Ob-*

server, which contains discussion of up-to-date topics, announcements, and the "Employment Bulletin." Nonmembers can buy any of these publications.

The APS has reprinted a number of useful articles from the *APS Observer*. The current policy is to provide free single copies to individuals who request them by writing to the address given on the previous page. One of the APS articles was reprinted earlier: "A Short Course on APA Style." Other topics that are available at the present time include the following:

For undergraduate students:

"How to Apply to Graduate School"

"Writing Your Vita"

For the job seeker:

"How to Do Well in the Academic Job Interview"

For the teacher:

"How to Develop Multiple-Choice Tests"

For the article writer:

"How to Win Acceptances by Psychology Journals: 21 Tips for Better Writing"

For the grant seeker:

"Writing Successful Grant Applications"

For the textbook author:

"How to Write a Textbook, or What to Consider Before Preparing a Textbook"

Tests and Measurements

Anastasi's *Psychological Testing* is a good, standard, widely-used text for a general introduction to tests and measurements. Instructors of the testing, measurement, or evaluation courses on your campus might be able to suggest other texts that will provide similar information. Psychological testing is such an important area that anyone who is seriously interested in psychology should take a course in the subject. Testing involves a lot of statistical analyses in various forms, so a course in beginning statistics is recommended before taking the measurements course.

Psychological tests are available in several different ways. A useful test (questionnaire or checklist) can sometimes be found in the professional journals. A letter to the author will usually provide additional information that can be of value.

Before selecting one of the many tests available to qualified persons from publishers who are in the business of supplying them, a prospective user should check the standard reference book on tests, Buros *Mental Measurements Yearbook*. There are many editions of this and several specialized variations. All of them should be available in the reference section of major university libraries. The *MMY* reviews and evaluates many of the hundreds of tests that are available and provides information on test validity, reliability, ordering, and cost. A person can learn a lot by spending a few minutes thumbing through a classified list of psychology tests. It is a rare person indeed who will not be surprised at their number and diversity.

Some tests are available for use by anyone who has the money to buy them, but other tests, answer sheets, and related information can be sent only to authorized professionals. Often this means that they can only be ordered on "letterhead" stationary. Some publishers, for a small fee, sell a sort of sample test kit that includes enough information to help a potential user to evaluate whether or not the test is suitable for a particular task.

The well-known and important individual tests that are widely used in clinical practice are appropriate only for people who have studied them—usually this means in a college-level class. A few of the tests for which one needs special training include the Binet and Wechsler intelligence scales, as well as major "projective" tests such as the Rorschach and the Thematic Apperception Test (TAT). Even though the widely used Minnesota Multiphasic Personality Inventory (MMPI) has developed an interpretative foundation in computer printouts, I still believe these benefit from a human interpreter. Knowledge of testing, test development, test scoring, and test interpretation has become even more important in recent years because of the considerable concern about the use of potentially biased tests for screening and placement.

Just as there are people who practice medicine without proper training, there are people who are giving and interpreting psychological tests who are not qualified to do so. With so much controversy among highly trained practicing psychologists about tests and testing, psychology can ill afford the harm caused by nonprofessionals. Unqualified people should not perform psychological services in areas such as testing or in any other area that requires the skill and training of a professional. Measurement and evaluation must rightly remain the province of experienced specialists.

ETHICAL PRINCIPLES IN RESEARCH

Research With Human Participants

The development of a set of rules for the guidance of research with both human and animal subjects became necessary because there were abuses that concerned people felt should be controlled.

In the early days of psychological research, no one thought much about regulating experiments, so we do not have information on how much harm was done. A glance at Woodworth and Schlosberg's *Experimental Psychology* (1965)[2] shows that typical experiments or research studies from the early days of psychology were not of a nature to put "subjects at risk," to use the modern term. No harm would come to people who participated in them. Early research was heavy on learning, various aspects of perception, problem solving, and the study of

---

[2] A more recent edition of this book, by Kling and Riggs, was mentioned earlier in this chapter.

sense modalities. Nothing was done in any of these area that required subterfuge or deception. Research did not require an invasion of privacy or any threat to the psychological or physical well-being of the people who participated.

This does not mean that other experiments were not done on topics and in ways that might have been harmful to subjects. Early research was frequently under the control of a single investigator, so it was not monitored by peers; and if the results were not published, no record of the work would become public.

Psychology has now greatly broadened its interests. Research became more imaginative in the types of questions it asked, and arrangements for getting answers to them became more complex. Behavioral science in general began to study more "meaningful" aspects of behavior. This change in attention and orientation introduced a number of problems.

There were other pressures also. Psychological characteristics of human beings make them particularly vulnerable to psychological abuse. Psychological research does not usually subject participants to physical harm, but psychological effects are complex and not always easy to identify. A psychologist studying the effects of frustration on children would need to frustrate at least a few of them in some way. Although a simple form of frustrations might be used, such as not giving a prize to a child who did not complete a jig-saw puzzle in the time allowed, the effect might be much more important and therefore more troubling to some children than to others.

Adult participants typically try to do well on psychological tasks. When they appear to be performing inadequately, they may reasonably feel embarrassment in the presence of the person who is running the experiment—no matter how impersonally he or she has performed the job.

Psychologists cannot easily discover how harmful an experience is likely to be to a particular participant. Aggression is a very important subject for study, but it is difficult to know how to go about observing it. Should psychologists do experiments that might arouse subjects to violent action? How about studies of sexual behavior?

Psychology gradually became more daring in the ideas it was willing to evaluate experimentally. "Effects of Erotic Stimuli on Male Aggression Toward Females" (Donnerstein & Barrett, 1978) is one title I happen to have on hand. In the same journal containing this article was another one which studied aggression in a different way: "Aggression-Inhibiting Influence of Sexual Humor" (Baron, 1978).

Still a third article introduced a topic that is not often studied in a college psychology laboratory situation: "Sex differences in response to erotica? Love versus lust (Fisher & Byrne, 1978). Articles of this sort call attention to several interesting research problems. How does an experimenter measure sexual response (arousal)? How can one create a "natural" situation while controlling extraneous variables? Do subjects who volunteer for research of this sort adequately represent human behavior in general? To what extent can results be generalized? In terms of the topic under discussion here, how could an investigator decide, *before beginning the research*, if there might be a lasting psychological effect on participants?

Malamuth, Heim, and Feshbach (1980), in their article, "Sexual Responsiveness of College Students to Rape Depictions: Inhibitory and Disinhibitory Effects, reported experiments designed to help us understand how enactments of sexual assault might inhibit or disinhibit sexual responsiveness of male and female college students. My discussion here does not question the importance of research of this sort. The concern is with any effects this research might have for contributing to participants' antisocial behavior: Are some people harmed—might some people be harmed—by involvement in this research? If psychology is to do research in these and other important areas, we must become very clever indeed to develop techniques that will tell us what we need to know but without harm to participants.

Following publication of the Malamuth et al. article, there was a discussion in the same journal about the ethical issues inherent in this research. Sherif (1980) raised several points to which Malamuth, Feshback, and Heim responded.

Psychological research with human participants involves their feelings, attitudes, fears, assumptions, biases, and thoughts. These all become a part of the research itself. Participants, while trying to be helpful, often do whatever it is they think is expected of them. Recall the discussion of "demand characteristics" earlier in the text.

Deception in the form of withholding information or providing false information is an undesirable but common and accepted practice in behavioral research. Experimentation that requires shading or hiding the truth, or which might produce discomfort for participants presents a set of conflicting responsibilities. A participant has a right to be informed of what is to be done, how it is to be done, what the effects (if any) there are likely to be, and to have all questions about the project answered. But the nature and objectives of a particular research project sometimes impose restrictions on the amount of information that can be supplied. An investigator must decide whether the expected advancement of psychological knowledge is balanced by the inherent dishonesty.

In every instance the participant has a right to be treated fairly and not to be exploited. The variety and complexity of research make it impossible to provide an all-purpose consent form, but the general rules for the development of one will be clear enough after studying the published list of APA ethical principles.

It is not likely that research in psychology will cause physical injury to a participant, but psychological discomfort is another matter. Being called on in class can be an uncomfortable experience for some people. Involvement in a therapy group can sometimes make more direct psychotherapy necessary; even concern over a low score in a learning experiment might produce a temporary depression. If anything has caused uneasiness to a participant, the person in charge of the project has the responsibility to deal with it.

When it has not been possible to provide a full disclosure of information to participants at the beginning of an experiment, it is very important to provide full information as soon as possible after the project has been completed; this procedure is mandated by the APA. The "debriefing" might involve nothing more important than explaining the "real" reason for the project and disclosing why the initial deception seemed necessary. People who give up their time to participate in research have a right to know what the investigator was trying to find out. In some instances they might even be entitled to have copies of the results. Experiments that have made a participant feel uncomfortable require the investigator to devote special attention in the debriefing session to the alleviation of any remaining unpleasant feelings and to resolve any lingering irritations.

Rubin (1973) has argued that psychologists should devote more of their attention to designing "honest experiments." There are often ways of reorganizing research so there is no necessity for subterfuge. Cozby's (1993) experimental psychology text includes a chapter on "Ethical Concerns." In it he mentions several alternatives to deception that should be considered before undertaking research involving deceit. "Role-playing" was the first alternative listed. "Simulation" is a variation of role-playing that "involves simulation of a real-world situation."

And of course, "honest experiments" should be tried. Deception might not be necessary at all, and a better experiment would result if participants were fully informed of the research objectives. Rubin (1973 and 1985) is a useful reference on designing honest experiments. See also Smith and Richardson (1983 and 1985) and note the comments and replies between them.

The number of people doing research and the varieties of research questions that are studied today have made it necessary for sponsoring institutions to undertake active supervision and control of research done under their authority. Many universities and other organizations have established "institutional review boards" (IRBs). Shaughnessy and Zechmeister (1985, p. 411) have pointed out that a movement toward the establishment of IRBs had begun before the enactment of the National Research Act of 1974. Research with human participants was considered such an important area that many institutions had already established review committees (see Gray, Cooke, & Tannenbaum, 1978). Federal regulations imposed very specific requirements on the makeup and duties of these committees (see *Federal Register*, 1975, March 13).

From time to time faculty members at colleges and universities might receive a memo like this one.

To: The University Community
From: The Provost
Re: Committee for the Protection of Human Subjects

The U.S. Department of Health and Human Services, in accordance with Public Law 93-348, calls for the creation within all institutions engaged in research involving human subjects of an institutional review board for the protection of human subjects.

This memo, which I received, then went on to explain the committee and to list the names of the representatives of our university community who had been selected to serve on it. Even though research has been approved by an official review board, the final responsibility for treatment of subjects and for the general work of the research stays with the authorized person.

The right of "informed consent" is a fundamental one for prospective participants in research. When there is no possibility of harm to the participant the agreement will probably be simple and informal, but the "responsibilities and obligations" of both the experimenter and participant should always be clear in advance.

A great deal of the research that is likely to be done by readers of this text will make such small demands on participants that an informed consent agreement will be a simple routine. When one moves outside the formal structure of "laboratory research" to observe behavior as it occurs naturally, there is no possibility of obtaining informed consent from the people who will make up the research sample. (Recall that the study of people in "real-life situations" restricts an experiment's internal validity but greatly enhances the possibility of generalizing results.)

One must have ample justification for research that requires invasion of privacy. Suppose the topic is cheating. An investigator can probably arrange a situation in which students could, if they were inclined to do so, cheat in some way. If the students were in the investigator's class, one must seriously question the ethics of the research. An instructor might be able to use the results to identify which students were inclined to cheat—information that could work to their disadvantage throughout the course. Even if the instructor did not know the results of the experiment, students involved in the research could be affected by the belief that the instructor had identified them and might use the information.

Faculty evaluation is a way of life at many universities. Some instructors have stated that they believe a student's evaluation of an instructor is in large part determined by the grade. "It's easy to get a good evaluation; just give high grades," is the simplistic statement sometimes heard. Holmes (1972) devised an experiment in which students were misled in order to discover the effect of grades on faculty evaluation.

He tried to assess how students "graded" a college teacher who gave them the grade they expected to get, compared to students who were given a lower grade. Participants were students whose early work in a class had led them to believe they were to receive either an A or B grade. Half of these students were given the grade they expected to receive and the other half received a grade that was one point lower than they expected. The hypothesis was that students who received the grade they expected would grade the instructor fairly; those who did not would not. This brief explanation greatly oversimplifies the project, so a statement of results cannot be given without many reservations. Suffice it to say that there were differences, but it is not at all clear what they mean in the context of the original idea. The experiment itself is not our concern here. We are interested in the effect this research could have on students who were given incorrect grades. Grades are important, and it is a serious matter for a person to feel that he or she has been cheated by the teacher. The open, trusting interaction many teachers encourage in their classrooms is strongly challenged by an instructor's dishonesty.

The topic of criminal behavior is an important one for psychology and for society, but how can psychologists study it without violating their own code of ethics? What is the investigator's responsibility to the people whose privacy will be violated, and what is the responsibility owed to society? These are serious questions that are not easily answered.

One piece of research stands out above nearly all others because of the ethical principles it seems to violate, *Tearoom Trade: Impersonal Sex in Public Places*

(Humphreys, 1970). This book excited a lot of controversy. In the late 1960s the investigator studied the behavior of homosexuals in public restrooms located in parks; these were called "tearooms" by those who used them for sexual contacts. By tracing license numbers the investigator was able to obtain a great deal of information about many of the men he had seen engage in homosexual activities. Humphreys felt the large amount of important information he obtained was worth the invasion of privacy required by his method of research. In 1975 he published a revised and enlarged edition of his book, to include a reconsideration of the ethical issues.

Ethical Principles of Psychologists (an APA Publication)

Anyone who plans to do research in psychology should first consult the APA publication *Ethical Principles of Psychologists* (APA, 1981).[3] The preamble summarizes the document's objectives.

> Psychologists respect the dignity and worth of the individual and strive for the preservation and protection of fundamental human rights. They are committed to increasing knowledge of human behavior and of people's understanding of themselves and others and to the utilization of such knowledge for the promotion of human welfare. While pursuing these objectives, they make every effort to protect the welfare of those who seek their services and of the research participants that may be the object of study. They use their skills only for purposes consistent with these values and do not knowingly permit their misuse by others. While demanding freedom of inquiry and communication for themselves, psychologists accept the responsibility this freedom requires; competence, objectivity in the application of skills, and concern for the best interests of clients, colleagues, student, research participants, and society. In the pursuit of these ideals, psychologists subscribe to principles in the following areas: 1. responsibility, 2. competence, 3. moral and legal standards, 4. public statements, 5. confidentiality, 6. welfare of the consumer, 7. professional relationships, 8. assessment techniques, 9. research with human participants, and 10. care and use of animals.
>
> Acceptance of membership in the American Psychological Association commits the member to adherence to these principles.

A fully developed treatment of Principle No. 9 is available from the APA in a special 76-page publication: *Ethical Principles in the Conduct of Research with Human Participants*. The following simplified statement of the major points should be adequate to introduce the topic.

a. An investigator is responsible for determining whether a research proposal is ethical. The rights of human participants must be protected.

b. The investigator must determine if a subject will be placed "at risk," so that adequate arrangements for protecting the subject can be devised.

---

[3] Copyright 1981 by the American Psychological Association. Reprinted by permission. This publication can be obtained from The Administrative Offices for Ethics, American Psychological Association, 1200 Seventeenth St., NW, Washington, DC 20036.

c. An investigator is also responsible for the ethical treatment of participants by other people who are working with him or her on the project.

d. The investigator must establish a "clear and fair agreement" with possible participants. This should clarify the obligations and responsibilities of each. All "promises and commitments" in the agreement must be honored. An investigator who obtains an "informed consent" agreement from a possible subject must fully explain all aspects of the research. If the nature of the research does not permit full disclosure, a special responsibility is incurred by the investigator to ensure that "the welfare and dignity" of those taking part in the research will be protected.

e. The investigator is responsible for determining whether the "prospective scientific, educational, or applied value" of the research justifies the use of deception or whether alternate procedures are available that would make duplicity unnecessary. After such an experiment it is necessary for the investigator to provide a full disclosure as soon as possible.

f. The right of prospective subjects to decline to participate and the right to withdraw at any time must be respected by the investigator.

g. The investigator must inform prospective subjects if there is a possibility that the research might cause "mental or physical discomfort, harm, and danger." A participant should be informed about how the investigator can be contacted "within a reasonable time period following participation should stress, potential harm, or related questions or concerns arise."

h. As soon as possible following data analysis participants should be informed of the results, and any lingering doubts or questions about the research should be removed or answered.

i. If a participant has suffered "undesirable consequences" as a result of the experiment, it is the responsibility of the research person to detect them so their short- or long-term effects can be ameliorated.

j. All information obtained about a subject during the course of research must remain confidential unless there is mutual agreement about the release of the information.

Research With Animals

When one mentions psychological research to a person outside the field, a common reaction from many listeners seems to be that psychologists are doing something with white rats. A lot of certain types of research does include white rats, but psychologists have also studied primates (of all species), dogs, cats, and birds. Even planaria and earth worms have found a place in psychological research and possibly other creatures I cannot personally identify! Altogether, one might estimate that animal research probably makes up no more than 10% of the published articles in psychology journals, but that is enough to arouse the attention of animal-rights activists. Psychologists who subscribe to the ethical principles of the APA will never cause unnecessary pain or suffering or mistreat animals under their care. In general, it is probably true that animals used in psychological research are better looked after than many dogs and cats that are kept as pets. (For a not uncommon example, consider the pets that unthinking owners leave locked in cars on hot days while they shop. I am saddened to say that it is not unusual to see dogs tied with short leashes in hot, sunny places and without water.)

In recent years, well-financed animal rights activists have become militant in their objections to any research with animals. They have gone much further than just holding up a sign at an annual APA meeting: "Death to Experimental Psychologists!" Some of the more aggressive believers in animal rights have fought the use of animals in research by destroying research facilities and research documents; they have released research animals and in other ways attempted to frustrate research that uses animals.

The *APS Observer* (a publication of the American Psychological Society) reports in the 1990, March issue (vol. 3, no. 2) on the law to protect the interests of scientists who use animals for research. "Dedicated scientists conducting human animal research must not continue to be subjected to crimes perpetrated by those who consider themselves outside the law," was the opinion expressed by Senator Howel Heflin (D-AL) shortly before the Senate unanimously passed the Heflin bill. The *Animal Research Facilities Protection Act of 1989, S.727*, an amendment to the "Animal Welfare Act," would make it a federal crime to break into research facilities, steal laboratory animals, or destroy data or equipment. The bill will require payment of costs for loss or damage as well as restitution for costs of repeating experiments made necessary as a result of outside interference. Legislative work in this area is continuing.

The APA provides guidance on animal care in the document, *Guidelines for Ethical Conduct in the Care and Use of Animals.* It can be obtained free from the APA. Note that this is an expansion of Proposition 10 mentioned in *Ethical Principles of Psychologists.*

The Public Health Service has published a document which controls treatment of animals (PHS Policy on Humane Care and Use of Laboratory Animals, IV B, 1986). The regulating federal laws require every institution that uses animals for research to establish a committee to supervise animal research. The Institutional Animal Care and Use Committee (IACUC) is the group charged with this task at my institution. Its members make unannounced visits at least twice a year to check on the care and treatment of animals that are used in the biology and psychology departments, the only two departments that have animals.

In addition, research facilities are registered with the U.S. Department of Agriculture. Representatives from this body are responsible for making "unannounced inspections" between the hours of 7:00 A.M. and 7:00 P.M. on Monday through Friday. "According to Federal Regulations you must provide access to your facility for the purpose of inspecting your animal records, your animals, and your animal facility. Failure to do so is a violation of the Code of Federal

Regulation (9CFR 2.126)." That statement is in a letter from the "Inspection Service" of the USDA.

New standards for treatment of animals used in research have been established by the Department of Agriculture (DOA), and they are to be enforced by the DOA Animal and Plant Health Inspection Service. The new standards were published in the *Federal Register*, 1991, February 15. They were scheduled for primary implementation on March 18, 1991, but no later than August 14, 1991, which gave research personnel time to develop plans for satisfying the new requirements.

There is probably no substitute for the use of animals in some types of research, so it is important to treat them well and use as few animals as necessary to accomplish one's scientific objectives. According to some observers the animal rights activists have gone too far in their desire to entirely abolish research with animals. Neil Miller's interesting and important article (1985) has identified many ways in which research with animals has improved the well-being of both animals and humans.

OTHER AREAS OF ETHICAL CONCERN FOR PROFESSIONALS

In addition to the ethical treatment of human and animal subjects in research, there are two other important areas of ethical concern. The first of the following two short sections will look briefly at honesty in research, and the second will examine a general problem caused by psychologists, teachers, and people in authority who use their position to gain a special advantage from a person under their supervision.

Fraud and Falsification of Results

The search for truth is the foundation for scientific work. For scientists, it is unthinkable that it should be necessary to include a comment about the topic of research fraud in a beginning text. Unfortunately for science, a few instances of discovered fraud have made it necessary to discuss the topic. The discussion of "Fraud and 'sloppy science'" in "The Chronicle of Higher Education" (1989, February 22) is one of several interesting presentations that can be found in nonprofessional publications. The 1991, August 26 issue of *Time* magazine used "Science Under Siege" as its lead article. In it the authors called attention to several instances of "frauds and embarrassments" in the scientific community and some widely publicized scientific failures. Research in psychology escaped criticism. Most of the highly publicized cases of suspected fraud have been in the biomedical field and physics, but psychology has not entirely escaped.

Psychology's most famous case by far involved Sir Cyril Burt, at the University of London, in what has become known as the "Burt affair." Leo Kamin (1974) is the investigator who discovered ambiguities in Burt's research that suggested fraud, and he is a major source of information about it, but see also Hearnshaw

(1979). Burt's apparent fraud has been discussed at length in many different places both in the professional literature and in the popular press.

In reviewing some of Professor Burt's twin-study data, Kamin discovered that repeated samples produced identical correlational results—something that would be exceedingly unlikely by chance. An expanded investigation failed to discover two of Burt's "co-workers" who had been listed as having worked on the project. Many writers concluded that these and other elements in Burt's work were difficult to explain except by concluding that Burt had deliberately falsified his data.

Difficulty of explanation does not constitute proof, however, and 10 years after publication of Hearnshaw's book, J. B. Joynson arrived at entirely different conclusions in his book titled simply, *The Burt Affair*. In 1991 R. Flecher approached the topic in a different way with *Science, Ideology and the Media: The Cyril Burt Scandal*. Both writers presented evidence that markedly altered the Kamin and Hearnshaw interpretations. Green (1992) undertook a reevaluation of the evidence against Burt, "Exposé or Smear? The Burt Affair," and also concluded that Burt had been unfairly treated, partly as a result of "politicial enthusiasms." These recent reevaluations seem to have gone a long way toward removing Burt's name from the list of those who have committed scientific fraud.

Abuse of Authoritarian Positions

Teachers, administrators, psychotherapists, and supervisors all have a special responsibility not to use the inherent authority of their position in order to extract special advantages from people in a subordinate relationship. A teacher might, by suggestion and innuendo, make it difficult for students not to volunteer for research projects. In a different, more extreme and possibly less common situation, a senior investigator might strongly suggest to a subordinate what he or she expects the results to show. The subordinate person may not deliberately falsify data to make the research turn out in the expected direction, but knowing what results are desired could cause things to happen that would produce the same result.

Other areas of abuse do not directly involve research, but they are of particular importance to psychology. Clinical psychologists, psychotherapists, counselors, teachers, all of us who work closely with other people, have a special responsibility not to use our positions of trust in order to take advantage of others. There are many stories, anecdotes, and other more solid evidence to show that this rule of conduct is not infrequently violated in the sense of male therapists taking sexual advantage of female patients. This topic is typically discussed at length in courses that teach psychotherapy, so it will not be developed here.

The number of teachers who are sexually involved with their students might be surprising. Pope, Levenson, and Schover (1979) were not the first to identify the problem, but their study on "Sexual Intimacy in Psychology Training" called attention to it. They surveyed members of the APA Psychotherapy Division and received completed questionnaires from 481 people. It was discovered that "10%

of the respondents reported sexual contact as students with their educators; 13% reported entering sexual relationships as educators with their students."

The women's movement has encouraged women to discuss more openly the problems of sexual harassment, which they had previously tried to solve by themselves in silence. Evidence accumulates to show that many female students are subjected to sexual and other forms of harassment from their male instructors. "The lecherous professor is a standard figure at most colleges, as much a part of the campus scene as ivy-covered brick or the statue of the founder," read the opening sentence in a *Time* article: "Fighting Lechery on Campus" (1980, February 4, p. 84). These days, women students are finding support in fighting back against educators and other people in authority who use their positions for sexual or other favors. The power teachers have to give grades, to approve theses, or to write letters of recommendation can seriously affect a student's chances for professional advancement. Unethical exploitation exists whenever a faculty person threatens to withhold or alter some condition of a student's academic work. The authority a faculty member has over a student can be considered exploitation, even if the student agrees to participate.

CONCLUDING COMMENTS

Anyone who has studied the material in this text has probably learned quite a lot about the general principles for conducting research. That is the easy part.

The attitudes, the points of view, the critical thinking that precedes the design and implementation of research, the creativity that is necessary for one person to see further into the subject than anyone else has done—these cannot be taught, or if they can, I confess that I do not know how to do it.

A person cannot appreciate, until he or she has become actively involved in research, what research is really like. First there are worries and concerns about getting a good idea. These are followed by excitement (and relief) when an idea is found. Then the worry begins again. What will be measured? How can I control extraneous variables? Where can I get subjects? How can I manipulate the independent variable? What data will I have, and how can I analyze them according to my research design? How will I measure the outcome?

At some point there will be the frustration and tedium of collecting data. Feelings of incompetence can creep in to cause a researcher to question his or her ability. Will I find out anything at all worthwhile? Was this whole project a waste of time? Why did I make it so complicated? Now that it is halfway through I can see a dozen things I should have done to make it better.

After the work is finished and handed in for evaluation comes the worrying delay as the researcher waits for a response. Will it be accepted? What will the editors have to say? Eventually we have to face the reality that other people will read—and criticize—our work. Those are a few of the feelings this book has not been able to talk about.

Perhaps a lot of human suffering would be saved by fewer people doing research. Why do people get involved in research anyhow? The first level, for many readers, is over. Term papers and research projects add substance and reality to the otherwise dry reading of a textbook. Doing research is the best way there is to pull the parts together. Even for people who will never do research again, the experience is useful to the extent that it helps them to appreciate what is involved in the research process.

Theses provide a way for various advanced-degree candidates to demonstrate they know how to do research and have therefore fulfilled some of the research requirements that are an important part of many degree programs. This research component emphasizes the importance of research to the science of psychology, but the learning that takes place while we do research should also help us to become better judges and critics of others' research.

In the future we can try to develop experimental ideas to control extraneous variables more adequately. Psychologists must continue to work toward the improvement of measurement techniques; good research is based on good measurement. Faster computers, more adaptable software, and easier programming techniques should help investigators to use computers in more ingenious ways not limited to data analysis. But in the end computers can never substitute for good thinking and creative ideas.

My own orientation toward science has been very broadly based. I have always acted as if knowledge of the world is a large well-integrated pot of stew, in which everything is all mixed up. It has never made sense to me that a person would deliberately choose to study one area of science to the almost total exclusion of the others. The more broadly I study, the greater is my amazement at how much important material I would have missed had I narrowed my selection. My own experience causes me to believe that research in psychology will increasingly require investigators to have a working understanding of scientific concepts normally studied in other disciplines. We cannot use principles, ideas, or even equipment, if we do not know they exist—but all of this will not necessarily improve our research. For that to happen we need people with brilliantly creative imaginations.

We should continue to hope that a very clever person will one day provide us with better methods for data analysis. Reliance on statistics can be reduced a little by tighter research designs, but the behavioral sciences also need different techniques. The chapter on data analysis tried to suggest that profound conclusions derived from observations declared to be "significant at the point-oh-five level" are, by definition, almost guaranteed to be wrong some of the time. We need a firmer base for interpreting research results.

If there is one observation that I can share that will summarize what I feel about research in psychology, this is it: Everyone I talk to seems to know more about human behavior and the reasons for it than I do. Newspapers, books, magazines, TV, radio, colleagues, friends and family, my students, and everyone I meet at social gatherings—all seem to be better able than I am to explain behavior. They quickly and easily explain almost any behavior, usually with a reference to a childhood experience, in a way that is both simple and to the point. They have no doubts; their judgments are not clouded by ambiguities. From their point of view, there is no possibility that an alternate explanation might be the true one.

Just as everyone else does, I speculate about behavior and I wonder about possible cause and effect relationships. But there is a major difference between the way I do it and the approach of many other people. All of my explanations are only tentative, because I never know what important concept I might have overlooked. The history of science has taught me that we should never hold an idea too strongly. Someday, somehow, someone is likely to make today's quite sensible idea look foolish.

I once bought a plant from a woman in a garden center and asked her a question about it. She apologized for not knowing the answer by saying, "I'm sorry, but I am the stupidest person in the world about that plant." She was not, of course, because she was aware of her lack of knowledge and admitted it. Really stupid people do not know they do not know. I was better off with her not answering than I would have been had she answered my question incorrectly.

Much more than I was able to suggest in this book, my classes emphasize a critical analysis of psychological research. Reviewers of my preliminary work have rightly pointed out that a beginning text is not the place for criticism. Most of us who have traditional educational backgrounds do not easily learn that science does not so quickly advance by identifying what we think is right as it does by dropping what is wrong. Psychology professionals who take research seriously understand this. A skeptical, "show me your evidence so we can evaluate it" attitude is the one that offers the most promise. That has been the underlying theme of much of my material.

I have observed teachers of psychology courses—both those who are experienced and those who are just beginning—submit course outlines that appear to suggest that the instructor has identified a finished and completed set of principles. "Learn these things," they seem to say, "and you will know psychology." I have been able only to hint at the attitude that no research technique is perfect and no belief has so much foundation in fact that it should not be questioned. A healthy self-criticism is what we need to buttress the thin walls of scientific structure this book has been able to provide.

Thank you for sticking with me to the end. I hope that you will think the time spent was worthwhile and that what you have learned will one day be useful.

SMALL TALK

Appendix

Journal Article Evaluation

Now is the time to bring together many of the ideas that were covered in the text. Testing a reader's ability to plan, carry out, and write the results of an experiment is not possible, but a reasonable alternative is available. For every research project undertaken an investigator will read and evaluate many books and articles written by others. Professional people will frequently consult the literature in their areas for information on what is happening.

I was surprised to discover, when I began to study journal articles, that they occasionally contain mistakes. A wrong statistic will be used, or it will be used incorrectly. A flaw in the design will cause a conservative reader to question whether the reported conclusions are justified. The following study is presented to give readers an opportunity to test their skills for the evaluation of articles from the professional literature. Think of this exercise as a final exam.

The following article has been selected for evaluation because it is about a topic that people often find interesting and it contains a number of errors that informed and attentive readers should be able to identify. Each reading of it uncovers new ones. This article also has the additional advantages of being short and uncomplicated.

The "Marathon Group" movement at one time aroused a great deal of interest in psychology. Chasing after fads is no less common in psychology than it is in other sciences. When someone hits on a new idea or a different way of handling an old one, a large amount of interest drives it for a few years. Then it becomes a page—or perhaps just a paragraph—in history. Young people sometimes cannot understand why an older person (who has lived through several cycles) does not get excited about some new activity that promises to change the foundations of psychology forever.

The article has been edited somewhat by eliminating references. The many that were listed were important for publication, but leaving them out has improved readability. Some sentences had to be slightly rewritten to make sense after the references were dropped. Lines have been numbered to make it easier to direct attention to specific locations.

Begin the study of a journal article by reading the abstract printed as an indented paragraph at the very beginning. This summarizing overview of the article can provide helpful guidance in working one's way through a complicated paper.

Although the approved sequence of topics in a journal article seems logical, it does not follow the way I think about research. A typical article begins with an introduction, which usually takes the form of a historical review in which many references are listed. This establishes a background for the current research and shows the author has done his or her homework in the library before developing a topic. At this point in the article we know only what we have read in the abstract, so we do not yet fully understand and can only speculate about the hypotheses that were tested. The historical summary tells what was done in the past relevant to the topic to be discussed later in the paper—whatever it is.

Next, the "Methods" section explains what was done. It is usually necessary for readers to formulate for themselves tentative hypotheses they believe the article will eventually address.

The "Subjects" section tells how participants were selected. In this article there is also an "Instrument" section, which explains the test that was used as the dependent variable. The discussion gave a little information on what it was supposed to measure and why the authors thought it was a valid measure of the specified constructs.

A "Procedures" section expands on the nature of what was actually done in the research; and the last two sections, "Results" and "Discussion" are self-evident. All articles published in professional journals include a list of references, as did this one. These were irrelevant to my purpose, so I have not included them.

In reading the article it is useful to identify the main research elements.

First: State the research hypotheses being evaluated.

Second: Identify the type of the research structure: experimental or correlational.

Third: Identify the independent variable.

Fourth: Identify the dependent variable. If it is a test, consider whether it seems to be an appropriate operational definition of the construct(s).

Fifth: Study the results section to determine if the null hypothesis was rejected. Draw a conclusion about the research hypothesis.

Sixth: Carefully study all the technical details to see if you can find anything a critical investigator might question. A good place to start is the area that includes the statistical evaluations. In this article, look carefully at the tables. Explain why the "Difference Between Correlated Means" was computed for Table 1, and the "Difference Between Uncorrelated Means" was computed for Table 2.

Seventh: Use the discussion section to help evaluate the article. What mistakes were made? What worthwhile objective was accomplished? Explain how the data should have been analyzed according to the method recommended in this text.

Note that this article is an example of applied rather than theoretical research. The authors simply tried out a technique to assess the extent to which it was able to change scores on a particular measurement instrument.

A useful way for dealing with this assignment would be to write out all the points mentioned above and then look at my summary at the end. Readers who jump ahead to see what I have done will have lost the challenge of testing themselves.

ARTICLE

MARATHON GROUP: FACILITATOR OF PERSONAL GROWTH?

James F. Guinan and Melvin L. Foulds, Bowling Green State University

The present study is a report of changes on the scales of the Personal Orientation Inventory (POI), a measure of positive mental health, following a weekend marathon group experience. Pretest and posttest results indicated significant changes in the mean scores of an experimental group on the following scales: Inner-Direction, Exis-
5   tentiality, Feeling Reactivity, Spontaneity, Self-Acceptance, Acceptance of Aggression, Capacity for Intimate Contact. There were no significant changes for a control group. Differences were found between those who volunteered for the group experience and those from the same population who volunteered "to be in an experiment." The results were discussed with reference to a number of hypotheses that are in need
10   of testing.

Since Bach and Stoller first introduced Marathon Group Dynamics, the use of marathon group experiences has become frequently publicized but infrequently studied. While authors seem to be uniformly positive about the effectiveness of marathon groups, a review of the literature indicates no published experimental or
15   quantitative studies of the impact of time-extended group experiences. Bach stated, "The Marathon Group encounter has been found—after the first three years of practice and research—to be the most direct, the most efficient, and the most economical antidote to alienation, meaningless, fragmentation, and other hazards of mental health in our time." Such an assertion is strong and, when made without the support
20   of empirical research, unjustified.

Of particular interest is the implication that marathon groups are meaningful antidotes to the hazards of mental health. This suggests that such experiences would prove fruitful to "normal," relatively healthy, growth-seeking persons who desire to be more integrated and to relate with others more authentically and trans-
25   parently. Should a group of individuals who seem to be functioning reasonably well engage in a marathon experience? It can be hypothesized that one effect would be to induce changes in the direction of increased positive mental health and personal growth. The present investigation represents an effort to test this hypothesis.

30   **METHODS**

Subjects

The experimental group consisted of 10 college students (6 males and 4 females, ranging from freshmen to seniors) who volunteered to participate in a marathon "growth group" during the academic year 1967–1968. For comparison purposes, an

35   equal number of students was selected for a non-treatment group controlled for sex, age, and college class.

INSTRUMENT

The Personal Orientation Inventory (POI), a measure of positive mental health or self-actualization used as an index of change or personal growth. This inventory is a
40   reasonably valid and reliable measure of psychological well-being or positive mental health. The POI consists of 150 two-choice paired-opposite statements of values, and scores are reported for 12 scales which assess personality characteristics commonly associated with positive mental health or self-actualization.

In other studies this instrument has been demonstrated to show a relationship
45   between one or more of its scale scores and effects of therapy, the effects of group experiences and such personality characteristics as psychopathy, family background, academic achievement, and teaching ability.

PROCEDURE

The experimenters appeared before several psychology classes and invited students
50   to participate in a weekend "growth group" to be held at the university counseling center. The structure and goals of the group were briefly explained, and the fact that the group was designed for "normal, relatively healthy" persons was stressed. The size of the group was limited to the first 12 volunteers. Two of the 12 subjects did not remain for the entire group experience, however, and these were withdrawn from
55   the experimental group. The remaining 10 subjects made up the experimental group. The control group consisted of 10 students from psychology classes who volunteered when asked to participate in an experiment.

The experimenters served as group leaders during the marathon which met for a total of 30 hours during the course of the weekend. Both experimenters are experi-
60   enced psychotherapists with an experiential-gestalt orientation. The content of the group experience itself was similar to many therapy sessions with the exception that participants were urged to "keep to the here and now" and concentrate on the persons and relationships that existed within the group itself. Upon occasion a group or individual "exercise" (e.g., fantasy exploration, role playing, non-verbal communication)
65   was suggested to deal with a specific issue or experience. The subjects were administered the pretest immediately before beginning of the group experience on Friday evening. Actual meeting times were from 7:00 PM Friday to 1:30 AM Saturday, from 10:00 AM Saturday to 1:30 AM Sunday, and from 12:00 noon to 8:00 PM Sunday. The subjects responded to the posttest on the following Tuesday.

70   After the data were obtained, responses were scored and tabulated. Group mean scores and one-tailed t-tests of significance of difference between means for each of the 12 POI scales for each group were then calculated.

RESULTS

Pretest and posttest mean scores for the 12 POI scales for both the experimental and
75   control groups are presented in Table 1. The data disclose that all 12 mean scores of the experimental group changed in a positive direction, and there were significant changes ($p < .05$) in mean scores on 7 of the 12 scales. None of the mean scores for the control group changed significantly.

Experimental subjects appeared to change significantly in a positive direc-
80   tion on the scales of the POI which purport to assess the following personality characteristics: (a) feelings or attitudes of personal freedom, independence, and in-

Appendix Table 1

PRETEST AND POSTTEST PERSONAL ORIENTATION INVENTORY SCALE MEANS AND STANDARD DEVIATIONS FOR EXPERIMENTAL AND CONTROL GROUPS; DIFFERENCES BETWEEN CORRELATED MEANS

Personal Orientation Inventory Scale	Experimental Group						Control Group				
	Pretest		Posttest		t		Pretest		Posttest		t
	M	SD	M	SD			M	SD	M	SD	
Time competence (Tc)	13.9	3.31	14.7	2.96	1.10		16.9	2.43	17.4	2.57	.83
Inner-direction (I)	75.1	5.37	86.5	3.93	5.12***		83.0	2.45	84.9	2.69	1.77
Self-actualizing values (SAV)	18.2	4.42	19.5	3.04	1.54		19.2	3.12	19.4	3.01	.51
Existentiality (Ex)	18.7	6.01	22.8	5.32	3.95**		19.8	4.38	20.1	4.68	.45
Feeling reactivity (Fr)	13.7	3.57	17.0	3.68	3.97**		16.2	2.96	15.5	3.08	.80
Spontaniety (S)	10.2	3.02	12.1	2.92	3.35**		13.2	2.04	12.8	2.19	1.00
Self-regard (Sr)	9.8	3.34	10.7	3.19	1.20		12.2	.75	12.4	1.11	.38
Self-acceptance (Sa)	13.0	3.87	16.0	3.92	4.50***		16.7	2.79	17.4	3.41	.93
View of the nature of man (Nc)	11.9	2.21	12.0	2.05	.19		11.7	2.23	12.1	2.26	.80
Synergy (Sy)	6.4	1.62	6.8	1.25	.77		7.3	1.42	7.2	1.47	.56
Acceptance of aggression (A)	14.4	2.61	16.0	3.35	2.18*		16.3	2.53	17.1	2.74	1.14
Capacity for intimate contact (C)	15.6	4.78	19.4	3.04	3.84***		18.5	3.04	18.3	2.23	.25

*$p < .05$.
**$p < .01$.
***$p < .001$.

ternal direction based upon inner motivations rather than upon external expectations and influences (I); (*b*) flexibility in the application of values and reduced compulsivity and dogmatism as well as increased ability to situationally or existentially react without blind or rigid adherence to principles (Ex); (*c*) awareness of and sensitivity to one's own needs and feelings (*Fr*); (*d*) ability to express feelings in spontaneous action, to be on the outside what one is on the inside (S); (*e*) acceptance of one's self in spite of weaknesses or deficiencies (Sa); (*f*) ability to accept one's natural aggressiveness (A); (*g*) ability to develop intimate and meaningful relationships with other human beings which are unencumbered by expectations and obligations, to develop "I-Thou" relationships in the here and now (C).

Table 2 reveals significant differences between the pretest mean scores of the experimental and control groups on a number of POI scales (Tc, I, S, Sr, Sa, and C). The two groups differed significantly on only the Tc scale with regard to posttests, however. Because of these observed differences between the two groups, the experimental group pretest mean scores were compared with mean scores for a sample of 2,607 entering college freshmen included in normative data supplied by Shostrom to determine if the experimental group was composed of relatively "normal" persons. This comparison yielded positive results.

Appendix Table 2

PERSONAL ORIENTATION INVENTORY SCALE MEANS AND STANDARD DEVIATIONS FOR EXPERIMENTAL AND CONTROL GROUPS AT PRETEST AND POSTTEST; DIFFERENCES BETWEEN CORRELATED MEANS

Personal Orientation Inventory Scale	Pretest					Posttest				
	Experimental		Control		*t*	Experimental		Control		*t*
	M	SD	M	SD		M	SD	M	SD	
Time competence (Tc)	13.9	3.31	16.9	2.43	2.19*	14.7	2.96	17.4	2.57	2.06*
Inner-direction (I)	75.1	5.37	83.0	2.45	2.04*	86.5	3.93	84.9	2.67	1.01
Self-actualizing values (SAV)	18.2	4.42	19.2	3.12	.55	19.5	3.04	19.4	3.01	.07
Existentiality (Ex)	18.7	6.01	19.8	4.38	.44	22.8	5.32	20.1	4.68	1.14
Feeling reactivity (Fr)	13.7	3.51	16.2	2.96	1.61	17.0	3.68	15.5	3.08	.93
Spontaniety (S)	10.2	3.02	13.2	2.04	2.47*	12.1	2.92	12.8	2.19	.56
Self-regard (Sr)	9.8	3.34	12.2	.749	2.05*	10.7	3.19	12.4	1.11	1.51
Self-acceptance (Sa)	13.0	3.87	16.7	2.79	2.32*	16.0	3.92	17.4	3.41	.81
View of the nature of man (Nc)	11.9	2.21	11.7	2.23	.19	12.0	2.05	12.1	2.26	.10
Synergy (Sy)	6.4	1.62	7.3	1.42	1.25	6.8	1.25	7.2	1.47	.63
Acceptance of aggression (A)	14.4	2.61	16.3	2.53	1.56	16.0	3.35	17.1	2.74	.76
Capacity for intimate contact (C)	15.6	4.78	18.5	3.04	2.54*	19.4	3.04	18.3	2.23	.87

*$p < .05$.

DISCUSSION

100   This study was designed to investigate whether a group of relatively "normal" college students would produce changes on a personality inventory assessing positive mental health or self-actualization following a 30-hour weekend marathon group experience. Results disclose that posttest experimental group mean scores were higher than pretest scores on each of the 12 POI scales and that changes were statis-
105 tically significant on 7 of the 12 scales. Since higher scores on the POI are representative of "healthier" personal functioning, it would appear that the marathon group was a highly fruitful and growth inducing experience for the participants. The short period of time between pretesting and posttesting and the absence of change in a control group strongly suggests that observed changes were probably the effects of
110 the marathon group experience. These findings suggest that marathon groups may be a productive method of fostering increased levels of personal growth and interpersonal functioning.

    The observed differences between the pretest mean scores of the experimental and control groups are of interest. Since all subjects were volunteers from similar
115 classroom situations, it can be hypothesized that students who volunteer for personal growth experiences seem to live more in the past or future than in the present, to be more other-directed and less spontaneous, to have lower self-regard and self-

acceptance, and to have greater difficulty establishing intimate interpersonal relationships than do those students who volunteer to be in an experiment. This hypothesis is
120   in need of further verification because of the small number of subjects included in the
present study. This finding may have important implications for research investigators, for it suggests that students who volunteer for experiments without the promise
of rewards may not be representative samples of college students in general. This also
implies that the task being volunteered for has a selective effect on those who volun-
125   teer. Caution must be urged in interpreting the present findings. While changes did
occur, the precise causes of these changes remain open to speculation. In order to
increase confidence in the findings, replication of the present study (perhaps with a
larger sample) would be advisable. Also, in further investigations both the experimental and control groups should consist of students who volunteer for a marathon
130   group but who are randomly assigned to treatment or nontreatment groups so that
the control group consists of more similarly motivated subjects. Another approach
would be to select a control group which consists of students who volunteer for a
marathon group and who are matched with experimental subjects for level of positive
mental health (POI scale scores) as well as sex, age, and college class. Either type of
135   control group would be more adequate than the one in the present investigation.

Several questions arise as a result of this study. What specific personality
types would be most likely to benefit (or be most vulnerable to harm) from a
marathon experience? What are the long-term effects of a marathon group, for
example, do people who change quickly in a positive direction lose some of their
140   positive gain over a period of time? Are there changes which seem to occur that
have negative effects on the person? What are the effects of differential treatment
(orientations or techniques of group leaders) on outcomes of marathon group
experiences? Additional research is required to answer these questions.

The structure of a marathon provides an excellent opportunity to observe and
145   measure the impact of a therapeutic experience, and future studies may shed light on
the process of change in those persons who are in groups and on the process of
psychotherapy in general.

REFERENCES

This section of the article included 25 references.

EVALUATION OF MARATHON GROUPS ARTICLE

The following discussion will not cover all the points that could be mentioned in
the article. To include everything, even if I could, would obviate your fun in making discoveries for yourself.

The purpose of the experiment was to determine the effects of a marathon
weekend on mental health. The authors wanted to determine if a marathon weekend can be a "meaningful antidote to the hazards of mental health." They tried to
determine if the experience "would prove fruitful to the 'normal,' relatively
healthy, growth-seeking persons who desire to be more integrated and to relate
with others more authentically and transparently." I have not seen operational

definitions of those terms, so I cannot comment on them. This is not my area, so I really do not know what they are talking about.

Independent Variable: Growth group experience.

Levels: Participated in a growth group; did not participate in a growth group.

Dependent Variable: "Personal growth" mentioned in the title was the construct studied. It was defined by scores on the Personal Orientation Inventory.

Subjects: "Experimental group" consisted of 10 college students who volunteered for a marathon weekend. Originally 12 people volunteered, but 2 dropped out. In such a small group, could the loss of 17 percent of the original subjects have been a confounding factor through differential elimination?

Comparison group was an equal number of students "controlled for sex, age, and college class." I presume this means that if a female sophomore of 19 years of age were in the marathon group, a person with similar characteristics would be included in the other group as a control. Question, are these relevant variables for this experiment?

Form of the Experiment: Two groups were used in a before/after design.

Data Analysis: Table 1 used a one-tailed t-test to evaluate mean differences between pretest and posttest scores for each group. The correlated samples formula was used to compare two measurements for the same subjects.

Table 2 used a one-tailed t-test formula for unrelated samples to compare pretest scores for the two groups and posttest scores for the two groups. Different people were compared for mean differences on the same measurements.

Was the one-tailed interpretation the correct one? How would the results have been affected if a two-tailed test had been used?

Discussion: People who volunteer to participate in an experiment are probably not random samples of the general population being studied. Participation in this experiment involved a significant time investment that many students would have used for study or recreation. People who chose to use their time in this way clearly had motivations not shared by many other students. Several prettest score differences suggested the "experimental" and "control" group people were not equivalent. The "experimental" group was not "reasonably normal" according to my interpretation of the pretest scores.

The authors conclude ". . . the absence of change in a control group strongly suggests that observed changes were probably the effects of the marathon group experience." The pretest scores for the nonmarathon people were already within normal limits, so according to my thinking no change was expected.

General Questions and Comments: Are college students the best choice of subjects for answering the questions posed in this study?

How should the data from this experiment have been analyzed according to the your knowledge of the pretest/posttest design?

How should one deal with a test battery that produces multiple measurements? Of the 12 possible scores in this experiment, only 7 changed for the marathon weekend group between the pretest and the posttest. Why was there not a change in all 12 scores? Was a change expected? If not, why include the measurement? I think it is important in an experiment to discuss expected changes that did not occur.

In fairness, we should note that with such small samples differences would need to be fairly large to be statistically significant.

We should recall also that when data are analyzed with multiple *t*-tests the number of statistically significant differences will be increased.

In addition to the test scores, I would be interested in behavioral observations of how the behavior of the marathon weekend people changed.

How did the people themselves feel they had changed? What did they think of the happening?

How long did the effects of the marathon experience last?

Several places in the article the authors used the expression "It can be hypothesized . . . " I am not interested in what "can" be done. I want to know what *was* done, and why.

SMALL TALK

References

Allport, G. W. (1937). *Personality, a psychological interpretation*. London: Constable.

Anastasi, A. (1988). *Psychological testing*. New York: Macmillan.

Anderson, L. P. & Rehm, L. P. (1984). The relationship between strategies of coping and perception of pain in three chronic pain groups. *Journal of Clinical Psychology, 40*, 1170–1177.

Andrews, T. G. (1943). A factorial analysis of responses to the comic as a study in personality. *Journal of General Psychology, 17*, 209–224.

Badia, P. Haber, A. & Runyon, R. P. (1970). *Research Problems in Psychology*. Reading, MA: Addison-Wesley.

Bakan, D. (1967, April–June). Psychology's research crisis. *Illinois Psychologist: Newsletter of the Illinois Psychological Assn.*

Barker, R. G., Kounin, J. S., & Wright, H. F. (1943). *Child behavior and development*. New York: McGraw-Hill.

Baron, R. A. (1978). Aggression-inhibiting influence of sexual humor. *Journal of Personality and Social Psychology, 36*, 189–197.

Bartz, A. E. (1988). *Basic statistical concepts* (3rd ed.). New York: Macmillan.

Berkowitz, L. (1964). The effects of observing violence. *Scientific American, 210*, 35–41.

Bettelheim, B. *The uses of enchantment: The meaning and importance of fairy tales*. New York: Knopf.

Bok, S. (1974). The ethics of giving placebos. *Scientific American, 231*, 17–23.

Bridgman, P. W. (1961). *The logic of modern physics*. New York: Macmillan. (Original work published 1927)

Buckhout, R. (1974). Eyewitness testimony. *Scientific American, 231*, 23–31.

Byrne, D. (1966). *An introduction to personality: A research approach*. Englewood Cliffs, NJ: Prentice-Hall.

Campbell, D. T. (1957). Factors relevant to the validity of experiments in social settings. *Psychological Bulletin, 54*, 297–312.

Campbell, D. T., & Fiske, D. W. (1959). Convergent and discriminant validation by multitrait-multimethod matrix. *Psychological Bulletin, 56*, 81–105.

Campbell, D. T., & Stanley, J. C. (1963). *Experimental and quasi-experimental designs for research*. Chicago: Rand McNally.

Cartwright, D., Jenkins, J. L, Chavez, R., & Peckar, H. (1983). Studies in imagery and identity. *Journal of Personality and Social Psychology, 44*, 376–384.

Cattel, R. B., & Luborsky, L. B. (1947). Personality factors in response to humor. *Journal of Abnormal and Social Psychology, 42,* 402–421.

Cavanaugh, J. C., & Park, D. C. (1993, December 3). The graying of America: An aging revolution in need of a national research agenda [Special issue], *APS Observer.*

Clarke, A. M., & Clarke, A. D. B. (Eds.). (1976). *Early experience: Myth and evidence.* New York: Free Press.

Cohen, D. B. (1978). Dark hair and light eyes in female college students: A potential biologic marker for liability in psychopathology. *Journal of Abnormal Psychology, 87,* 455–458.

Cohen, M. R., & Nagel, E. (1934). *An introduction to logic and scientific method.* London: Routledge & Kegan Paul.

Conrad, E., & Maul, T. (1981). *Introduction to experimental psychology.* New York: Wiley.

Cozby, P. C. (1993). *Methods in behavioral research.* Mountain View, CA: Mayfield.

Craig, J. R., & Metze, L. P. (1979). *Methods of psychological research.* New York: Saunders.

Cronbach, L. J. (1970). *Essentials of psychological testing* (3rd ed.). New York: Harper & Row.

Cronbach, L. J. (1984). *Essentials of psychological testing* (4th ed.). New York: Harper & Row.

Dawber, T. R., Kannel, W. B., & Lyel, L. P. (1963). An approach to longitudinal studies in a community: The Framingham study. *Annals of the New York Academy of Science, 107,* 539–556.

Day, R. A. (1993). *How to write and publish a scientific paper.* Philadelphia: ISI Press.

DeKruif, P. (1953). *Microbe hunters.* New York: Harcourt, Brace, & World.

DerSimonian, R., & Laird, N. M. (1983). Evaluating the effect of coaching on SAT Scores: A meta-analysis. *Harvard Educational Review, 53,* 1–15.

Donnerstein, E., & Barrett, G. (1978). Effects of erotic stimuli on male aggression toward females. *Journal of Personality and Social Psychology, 36,* 180–188.

Dotterer, R. H. (1924). *Beginners logic.* New York: Macmillan.

Dubos, R. (1960). *Pasteur and modern science.* Garden City, N.Y.: Anchor Books.

Dunham, P. J. (1988) *Research methods in psychology.* New York: Harper & Row.

Eastman, P. (1988, July/August). Life after menopause 'liberating' women say. *AARP News Bulletin, 29,* p. 465.

Ekman, P., & Davidson, R. J. (1993). Voluntary smiling changes regional brain activity. *Psychological Science, 4,* 342–345.

Eron, L. D., Huesmann, L. R., Lefkowitz, M. M., & Walder, L. D. (1972). Does television violence cause aggression? *American Psychologist, 27,* 253–263.

Estes, W. K. (1972). Reinforcement in human behavior. *American Scientist, 60,* 723–729.

Ewen, R. B. (1969). The GRE psychology test as an unobtrusive measure of motivation. *The Journal of Applied Psychology, 53,* 383–387.

Eysenck, H. J. (1943). An experimental analysis of five tests of "appreciation of humour." *Educational Psychology Measurement, 3,* 191–214.

Eysenck, H. J. (1960). *Uses and abuses of psychology.* Harmondsworth, Middlesex, Eng.: Penguin.

Fagan, J. F. III (1992). Intelligence: A theoretical viewpoint. *Current Directions in Psychological Science, 1,* 82–86.

Fechner, G. (1966). *Elements of psychophysics* (Vol.I). New York: Holt, Rinehart & Winston.

Feynman, R. P. (1983). *The art of finding things out.* "Nova" TV series #1002. WGBH Boston, MA.

Feynman, R. P. (1986). *Surely you're joking Mr. Feynman.* New York: Bantam.

Feynman, R. P., & Leighton, R. (1988). *What do you care what other people think?* New York: W. W. Norton.

Fischhoff, B. (1975). Hindsight ≠ foresight: The effect of outcome knowledge on judgment under uncertainty. *Journal of Experimental Psychology: Human Perception and Performance, 1,* 288–299.

Fisher, E. H. (1989). Gender bias in therapy? An analysis of patient and therapist causal explanations. *Psychotherapy, 26,* 389–401.

Fisher, W. A., & Byrne, D. (1978). Sex differences in response to erotica? Love versus lust. *Journal of Personality and Social Psychology, 36,* 117–125.

Flecher, R. (1991). *Science, ideology, and the media: The Cyril Burt scandal.* New Brunswick, NJ: Transaction Publishers.

Forer, L. K. (1976). *The birth factor.* New York: David McKay.

Fossey, D. (1983). *Gorillas in the mist.* New York: Houghton Mifflin.

Freedman, J. L. (1984). Effect of television violence on aggression. *Psychological Bulletin, 96,* 227–246.

Freedman, J. L. (1986). Television violence and aggression: A rejoinder. *Psychological Bulletin, 100,* 372–378.

Freud, S. (1938). Psychopathology of everyday life. In A. A. Brill (Ed.), *The basic writings of Sigmund Freud* (A. A. Brill, Trans.). New York: Modern Library. (Original work published 1904)

Freud, S. (1938). Wit and its relation to the unconscious. In A. A. Brill (Ed.), *The basic writings of Sigmund Freud* (A. A. Brill, Trans.). New York: Modern Library.

Friedrich-Cofer, L., & Huston, A. C. (1986). Television violence and aggression: The debate continues. *Psychological Bulletin, 100,* 364–371.

Gaito, J. (1970). Non-parametric methods in psychological research. In E. F. Heermann & L. A. Braskamp (Eds.), *Readings in statistics for the behavioral sciences.* Englewood Cliffs, N.J.: Prentice Hall.

Galston, A. W. (1974). *Bios,* March, 18–23.

Gibbs, M. S., Sigal, J., Adams, B., & Grossman, B. (1989). Cross-examination of expert witness: Do hostile tactics affect impressions of a stimulated jury? *Behavioral Sciences and the Law, 7,* 275–281.

Goldman, F. (1948). Breastfeeding and character-formation. *Journal of Personality, 17,* 83–103.

Goldman-Eisler, F. (1951). The problem of "orality" and of its origin in early childhood. *Journal of Mental Science, 97,* 765–782.

Gray, B. H., Cooke, R. A., & Tannenbaum, A. S. (1978). Research involving human subjects: The performance of institutional review boards is assessed in this empirical study. *Science, 201,* 1094–1101.

Green, B. F. (1992). Exposé or smear? The Burt affair. *Psychological Science, 3,* 328–331.

Guilford, J. P. (1954). *Psychometric methods.* New York: McGraw-Hill.

Guilford, J. P., & Fruchter, B. (1973). *Fundamental statistics in psychology and education* (5th. ed.). New York: McGraw-Hill.

Guinan, J. F., & Foulds, M. L. (1970). Marathon group: Facilitator of personal growth? *Journal of Counseling Psychology, 17,* 145–149.

Haggard, H. W. (1946). *Devils, drugs, and doctors.* New York: Pocket Books, Harper & Row.

Hall, G. S. (1897). The psychology of tickling, laughing, and the comic. *American Journal of Psychology, 9,* 10–41.

Haney, C. W., Banks, C., & Zimbardo, P. G. (1973). Interpersonal dynamics in a simulated prison. *International Journal of Criminology and Penology, 1,* 69–97.

Harlow, H. F. (1958). The nature of love. *American Psychologist, 13,* 673–685.

Harlow, H. F., & Harlow, M. K. (1965). The affectional systems. In A. M. Schrier, H. F. Harlow, & F. Stollnitz, (Eds.), *Behavior of nonhuman primates* (Vol. 2). New York: Academic Press.

Harlow, H. F., & Suomi, S. J. (1970). Nature of love—simplified. *American Psychologist, 25,* 161–168.

Harlow, H. F., & Zimmermann, R. R. (1959). Affectional responses in the infant monkey. *Science, 130,* 421–432.

Hawking, S. (1988). *A brief history of time.* New York: Bantam Books.

Hayes, H. T. P. (1990). *The dark romance of Dian Fossey.* New York: Simon & Schuster.

Hearnshaw, L. S. (1979). *Cyril Burt, psychologist.* Ithaca, NY: Cornell University Press.

Hogben, L. (1958). *Statistical theory.* New York: W. W. Norton.

Hollander, E. P. (1992). The essential interdependence of leadership and followership. *Current Directions in Psychological Science, 1,* 71–75.

Holmes, D. S. (1972). Effects of grades and disconfirmed grade expectancies on students' evaluations of their instructor. *Journal of Educational Psychology, 63,* 130–133.

Holmes, T. H., & Rahe, R. H. (1967). The social readjustment rating scale. *Journal of Psychosomatic Research, 11,* 213–218.

Hostetler, A. J. (1987, May). Fraud inquiry revives doubt: Can science police itself? *APA Monitor,* 1–12.

Huff, D. (1954). *How to lie with statistics.* New York: W. W. Norton.

Humphrey, N., & McManus, C. (1973, 23 August). Status and the left cheek. *New Scientist,* 437–439. (See also for letters: 1973, *6 September,* p. 581.)

Humphreys, L. (1970). *Tearoom trade: Impersonal sex in public places.* Chicago: Aldine.

Irwin, R. J., & Whitehead, P. R. (1991). Towards an objective psychophysics of pain. *Psychological Science, 2,* 230–235.

Jacoby, L. L., & Kelly, C. M. (1992). A process-dissociation framework for investigating unconscious influences: Freudian slips, projective tests, subliminal perception, and signal detection theory. *Current Directions in Psychological Sciences, 1,* 175–179.

Jenkins, C. D., Rosenman, R. H., & Friedman, M. (1967). Development of an objective psychological test for the determination of the coronary-prone behavior pattern in employed men. *Journal of Chronic Diseases, 20,* 371–379.

Joynson, J. B. (1989). *The Burt Affair.* London: Routledge.

Kahneman, D., Fredrickson, B. L., Schreiber, C. A., & Redelmeier, D. A. (1993). When more pain is preferred to less: Adding a better end. *Psychological Science, 4,* 401–405.

Kamin, L. G. (1974). *The science and politics of IQ.* New York: Wiley.

Keeton, W. T. (1974, December). The mystery of pigeon homing. *Scientific American*, pp. 96–107.

Kent, D. (1990). A conversation with Lynn Cooper. *APS Observer, 3*(1), 9–11.

Kerlinger, F. N. (1973). *Foundations of behavioral research* (2nd ed.). New York: Holt, Rinehart & Winston.

Kimble, G. A. (1978). *How to use (and misuse) statistics.* Englewood Cliffs, NJ: Prentice-Hall.

Kintz, B. L., Delprato, D. J., Mettee, D. R., Persons, C. E., & Schappe, R. H. (1965). The experimenter effect. *Psychological Bulletin, 63,* 223–232.

Kipling, R. (1978). *Just so stories.* New York: Weathervane Books. (Originally published 1902)

Kirk, R. E. (1968). *Experimental design.* Belmont, CA: Brooks/Cole.

Klein, A. K. (1987). The relationship of temperament scores to the way young adults adapt to change. *Journal of Psychology, 121* (12), 119–135.

Kling, J. W., & Riggs, L. A. (1971). *Woodworth and Schlosberg's experimental psychology* (3rd ed.). New York: Holt, Rinehart & Winston.

Knowlton, B. K., Ramus, S. J., & Squire, L. R. (1992). Intact artificial grammar learning in amnesia. *Psychological Science, 3,* 172–179.

Kuhn, T. S. (1970). *The structure of scientific revolution* (2nd ed.). Chicago: University of Chicago Press.

Landy, F, Rosenberg, B. G. & Sutton-Smith, B. (1969). The effect of limited father absence on cognitive development. *Child Development, 40,* 941–944.

Leahey, T. H., & Harris, R. J. (1989). *Human learning* (2nd ed.). Englewood Cliffs, NJ: Prentice-Hall.

Leary, M. R., & Altmaier, E. M. (1980). Type I error in counseling research: A plea for multivariate analysis. *Journal of Counseling Psychology, 27,* 611–615.

Leeper, R. W. (1943). *Lewin's topological and vector psychology.* Eugene: University of Oregon Press.

Lehrman, D. S. (1971). Behavioral science, engineering, and poetry. In E. Tobach, L. R. Aronson, & E. Shaw, (Eds.). *The biopsychology of development.* New York: Academic Press.

Leo, John. (1984, March 19). Sex, death, and Red Riding Hood. *Time*, p. 68.

Lewin, K. (1935). *A dynamic theory of personality.* New York: McGraw-Hill.

Lieber, A. L., & Sherin, C. R. (1972). Homicides and the lunar cycle: Toward a theory of lunar influence on human emotional disturbance. *American Journal of Psychiatry, 129*(1), 101–106.

Lindzey, G., & Aronson, E. (Eds.). (1968). *The handbook of social psychology* (Vol. 2.) Reading, MA: Addison-Wesley.

Little, W. W., Wilson, W. H., & Moore, W. E. (1955). *Applied logic.* Boston: Houghton Mifflin.

Loftus, E. F., & Fries, J. F. (1979). Informed consent may be hazardous to your health. *Science, 204,* 11.

Lyddon, W. J. (1989). Personal epistemology and preference for counseling. *Journal of Counseling Psychology, 36,* 423–429.

MacFarlane, G. (1984). *Alexander Fleming: The man and the myth.* Cambridge, MA: Harvard University Press.

Mackowiak, A. Wasserman, S. S. & Levine, M. M. (1992). A critical appraisal of 98.6 F, the upper limit of normal body temperature, and other legacies of Carl Reinhold August Wunderlich. *JAMA, 268,* 1578–80.

MacLeod, R. B. (1969). Psychology classics in translation. *Contemporary Psychology, 14,* 374–375.

Madigan, J. (1985). Comparable worth judgments: A measurement properties analysis. *Journal of Applied Psychology, 70,* 137–147.

Mahoney, M. J. (1978). Experimental methods and outcome evaluation. *Journal of Consulting and Clinical Psychology, 46,* 670–671.

Malamuth, N. H., Heim, M., & Feshbach, S. (1980). Sexual responsiveness of college students to rape depictions: Inhibitory and disinhibitory effects. *Journal of Personality and Social Psychology, 38,* 399–408.

Malamuth, N. H., Heim, M., & Feshbach, S. (1980). Ethical issues and exposure to rape stimuli: A reply to Sherif. *Journal of Personality and Social Psychology, 38,* 409–412.

Mann, C. (1990). Meta-analysis in the breech. *Science. 249.* 476–480.

May, C. P., Hasher, L., & Stoltzfus, E. R. (1993). Optimal time of day and the magnitude of age differences in memory. *Psychological Science, 4,* 326–330.

May, R. B., & Hunter, M. A. (1988). Interpreting students' interpretations of research. *Teaching of Psychology, 15,* 156–158.

McKeachie, W. J. (1969). Interaction of achievement cues and facilitating anxiety in the achievement of women. *Journal of Applied Psychology, 53* (2, pt. 1), 147–148.

McLeod, R. B (1969). Psychological classics in translation. *Contemporary Psychology, 14,* 374–375.

McNemar, Q. (1946). Opinion-attitude methodology. *Psychological Bulletin, 43,* 289–374.

McNemar, Q. (1969). *Psychological statistics* (4th ed). New York: Wiley.

Medawar, P. (1984). *The limits of science.* Oxford: Oxford University Press.

Messer, S. C., Wuensch, K. L., & Diamond, J. M. (1989). *Journal of Genetic Psychology, 150,* 301–309.

Milgram, S. (1974). *Obedience to authority: An experimental view.* New York: Harper & Row.

Miller, D. B. (1977, March). Roles of naturalistic observation in comparative psychology. *American Psychologist,* 211–219.

Miller, N. E. (1985). The value of behavioral research with animals. *American Psychologist, 40,* 423–440.

Montgomery, S. (1991). *Walking with the great apes.* Boston: Houghton Mifflin.

Mook, D. G. (1983). In defense of external invalidity. *American Psychologist, 38,* 379–387.

Moser, P. K., & vander Nat, A. (1987). *Human knowledge.* New York: Oxford University Press.

Motley, M. T. (1987). What I meant to say. *Psychology Today, 21*(2), 26–28.

Murray, T. S. (1975). *New Scientist,* 27 February, 493.

Nagel, E. (Ed.). (1950). *John Stuart Mill's philosophy of scientific method.* New York: Hafner.

Newton-Smith, W. H. (1981). *The rationality of science.* Boston: Routledge & Kegan Paul.

Norwood, R. (1985). *Women who love too much: When you keep wishing and hoping he'll change.* Los Angeles: J. P. Tarcher.

Nunnally, J. C., Jr. (1970). *Introduction to psychological measurement.* New York: McGraw-Hill.

Nunnally, J. C. (1978). *Psychometric methods.* New York: McGraw-Hill.

Oakes, W. (1972). External validity and the use of real people as subjects. *American Psychologist, 27,* 959–962.

Omwake, L. (1942). Humor in the making. *Journal of Social Psychology, 15,* 265–279.

Orne, M. T. (1959, September). *The demand characteristics of an experimental design and their implications.* Paper read at the meeting of the American Psychological Association, Cincinnati.

Orne, M. T. (1962). On the social psychology of the psychological experiment: With particular reference to demand characteristics and their implications. *American Psychologist, 17,* 776–783.

Orne, M. T. (1969). Demand characteristics and the concept of quasi-controls. In R. Rosenthal & R. L. Rosnow (Eds.). *Artifact in behavioral research.* New York: Academic Press.

Ortega, D. F., & Pipal, J. E. (1984). Challenge seeking and type A coronary-prone behavior pattern. *Journal of Personality and Social Psychology, 46,* 1328–1334.

Padilla, M. L., & Landreth, G. L. (1989). Latchkey children: A review of the literature. *Child Welfare, 68,* 445–454.

Paradise, L. V., & Cohl, B. (1980). Effects of profane language and physical attractiveness on perceptions of counseling behavior. *Journal of Counseling Psychology, 27,* 620–624.

Paulos, J. A. (1990). *Innumeracy: Mathematical illiteracy and its consequences.* New York: Vintage Books (a division of Random House).

Phillips, D. P., & Smith, D. G. (1990). Postponement of death until symbolically meaningful occasions. *JAMA, 263,* 1947–1951.

Pierce, A. H. (1908). The subconscious again. *Journal of Philosophy, Psychology, Scientific Method, 68,* 3–12.

Pope, K. S., Levenson, H., & Schover, L. R. (1979). Sexual intimacy in psychology training. *American Psychologist, 34,* 682–689.

Popper, K. R. (1961). *The logic of scientific discovery.* New York: Basic Books.

Popper, K. R. (1979). *Objective knowledge: An evolutionary approach.* Oxford: Clarendon Press.

Press, S. J. (1978). Size of police force versus crime. In J. M. Tanur (Ed.). *Statistics: Guide to the unknown.* San Francisco: Holden-Day.

Pyrczak, F., & Bruce, R. R. (1992). *Writing empirical research reports.* Los Angeles: Pyrczak Publishing.

Ray, W. J., & Ravizza, R. (1988). *Methods toward a science of behavior and experience.* Belmont, CA: Wadsworth.

Ree, M. J., & Earles, J. A. (1992). Intelligence is the best predictor of job performance. *Current Directions in Psychological Science, 1,* 86–89.

Remick, H. (1981). The comparable worth controversy. *Public Personnel Management Journal, 10*(4), 371–383.

Roberts, R. M. (1989). *Serendipity, accidental dicoveries in science.* New York: Wiley.

Rodman, H., Pratto, D. J., & Nelson, R. S. (1985). Child care arrangements and children's functioning: A comparison of self-care and adult-care children. *Developmental-Psychology, 21*, 413–418.

Rosenberg, M. J. (1969). The conditions and consequences of evaluation apprehension. In R. Rosenthal, & R. L. Rosnow, (Eds.). *Artifact in behavioral research.* New York: Academic Press.

Rosenman, R. H. (1978). History and definition of the type A coronary-prone behavior pattern. In T. M. Dembroski, S. M. Weiss, J. L., Shields, S. G. Haynes, & M. Feinleib, (Eds.). *Coronary prone behavior* (55–69). New York: Springer Verlag.

Rosenthal, R. (1965). The volunteer subject. *Human Relations, 18*, 389–406.

Rosenthal, R. (1976). *Experimenter effects in behavioral research.* New York: Irvington.

Rosenthal, R. (1984). *Meta-analytic procedures for social research.* Beverly Hills, CA: Sage Publications.

Rosenthal, R., & Fode, K. L. (1963). The effect of experimenter bias on the performance of the albino rat. *Behavioral Science, 8*, 183–189.

Rosenthal, R., & Rosnow, R. L. (1969). The volunteer subject. In R. Rosenthal & R. L. Rosnow (Eds.). *Artifact in behavioral research.* New York: Academic Press.

Rosenthal, R., & Rosnow, R. L. (1975). *The volunteer subject.* New York: Wiley.

Rosnow, R. L., & Rosnow, M. (1992). *Writing papers in psychology.* Belmont, CA: Wadsworth.

Rozeboom, W. W. (1960). The fallacy of the null-hypothesis significance test. *Psychological Bulletin, 57*, 416–428.

Rubenstein, J. (1975). *The study of psychology.* Guilford, CT: Dushkin.

Rubin, Z. (1973). Designing honest experiments. *American Psychologist, 28*, 445–448.

Rubin, Z. (1985). Deceiving ourselves about deception: Comment on Smith and Richardson's "Amelioration of deception and harm in psychological research." *Journal of Personality and Social Psychology, 48*, 252–253.

Ruby, L. (1960). *Logic: An introduction.* New York: Lippincott.

Runyon, R. P., & Haber, A. (1984). *Fundamentals of behavioral statistics (5th ed.).* New York: Addison-Wesley.

Runyon, R. P., & Haber, A. (1988). *Fundamentals of behavioral statistics* (6th ed.). New York: Random House.

Sagie, A., Larson, M. G., & Levy, D. (1993). The natural history of borderline isolated systolic hypertension. *The New England Journal of Medicine, 329*, 1912–1917.

Seligman, M. L. P., Nolen-Hoeksema, S., Thornton, N., & Thornton, K. M. (1990). Explanatory style as a mechanism of disappointing athletic performance. *Psychological Science, 1*, 143–146.

Senter, R. J. (1969). *Analysis of data.* Glenview, IL: Scott, Foresman.

Sharif, M. (1956). Experiments in group conflict. *Scientific American, 195*, 54–58.

Sharkin, B. S., Mahalik, J. R., & Claiborn, C. D. (1989). Application of the foot-in-the-door effect to counseling. *Journal of Counseling Psychology, 36*, 248–251.

Shaughnessy, J. J., & Zechmeister, E. B. (1985). *Research methods in psychology.* New York: Knopf.

Sheldon, W. H. (1942). *The varieties of temperament*. New York: Harper & Row.

Sheldon, W. H., Stevens, S. S., & Tucker, W. B. (1940). *The varieties of human physique*. New York: Harper & Row.

Sheridan, C. L. (1976). *Fundamentals of experimental psychology* (2nd ed.). New York: Holt, Rinehart & Winston (p. 21).

Sherif, C. W. (1980). Comment on ethical issues in Malamuth, Heim, and Feshback's "Sexual responsiveness of college students to rape depictions: Inhibitory and disinhibitory effects." *Journal of Personality and Social Psychology, 38*, 409–412.

Siegel, S. (1956). *Nonparametric statistics for the behavioral sciences*. New York: McGraw-Hill.

Siegel, S., & Castellan, N. J., Jr. (1988). *Nonparametric statistics for the behavioral sciences* (2nd.ed.). New York: McGraw-Hill.

Skolnick, A. (1978). The myth of the vulnerable child. *Psychology Today, 11*, 56–65.

Smith, M. L., & Glass, G. V. (1977). Meta-analysis of psychotherapy outcome studies. *American Psychologist, 32*, 752–760.

Smith, S. S., & Richardson, D. (1983). Amelioration of harm in psychological research: The important role of debriefing. *Journal of Personality and Social Psychology, 44*, 1075–1082.

Smith, S. S., & Richardson, D. (1985). Deceiving ourselves about deception: A reply to Rubin. *Journal of Personality and Social Psychology, 48*, 254–255.

Stevens, S. S. (1951). *Handbook of experimental psychology*. New York: Wiley.

Tallent, N. (1993). *Psychological report writing*. Englewood Cliffs, NJ: Prentice-Hall.

Thompson, L. A., Detterman, D. A., & Plomin, R. (1991). Associations between cognitive abilities and scholastic achievement: Genetic overlap but environmental differences. *American Psychological Society, 2*, 158–165.

Thorndike, E. L. (1965). *Animal intelligence*. New York: Hafner Press. (Original work published 1911)

Thorndike, R. L., & Hagen, E. (1969). *Measurement and evaluation in psychology and education* (3rd ed.). New York: Wiley.

Thurstone, L. L. (1935). *The vectors of the mind; Multiple-factor analysis for the isolation of primary traits*. Chicago: University of Chicago Press.

Tolman, E. C., Hall, E. C., & Bretnall, E. P. (1932). A disproof of the law of effect and a substitution of the laws of emphasis, motivation, and disruption. *Journal of Experimental Psychology, 15*, 601–614.

Tompkins, P., & Bird, C. (1973). *The secret life of plants*. New York: Harper & Row.

Turner, C. W., Hesse, B. W., & Peterson-Lewis, S. (1986). Naturalistic studies of the long-term effects of television violence. *Journal of Social Issues, 42*, 51–73.

Underwood, B. J. (1966). *Experimental psychology* (2nd ed.). New York: Appleton-Century-Crofts.

Underwood, B. J., & Shaughnessy, J. J. (1975). *Experimentation in psychology*. New York: Wiley.

Van Lawick-Goodall, J. (1968, May). Tool-using bird: The Egyptian vulture. *National Geographic*, 631–640.

de Waal, F. (1989). *Peacemaking among primates*. Cambridge, MA: Harvard University Press.

Watkins, C. E., & Terrell, F. (1988). Mistrust level and its effects on counseling expectations in black client/white counselor relationships: An analogue study. *Journal of Counseling Psychology, 35,* 194–197.

Weber, S. J., & Cook, T. D. (1972). Subject effects in laboratory research: An examination of subject roles, demand characteristics, and valid inference. *Psychological Bulletin, 77,* 273–295.

Wertheimer, M. (1970). *A brief history of psychology.* New York: Holt, Rinehart & Winston.

Wolpert, L., & Richards, A. (1988). *A passion for science.* New York: Oxford University Press.

Woodworth, R. S., & Schlosberg, H. (1954). *Experimental psychology* (Rev. ed.). New York: Holt, Rinehart & Winston.

Wright, H. F. (1943). The effect of barriers upon strength of motivation. In R. B. Barker, J. S. Kounin, & H. F. Wright. *Child behavior and development* (379–396). New York: McGraw-Hill.

Wyler, A. R., Masuda, M., & Holmes, T. H. (1971). Magnitude of life events and seriousness of illness. *Psychosomatic Medicine, 33,* 115–122.

Yarnold, J. K., & Berkley, M. H. (1954). An analysis of the Cattell-Luborsky humor test into homogeneous scales. *Journal of Abnormal and Social Psychology, 49,* 543–546.

Subject Index

A priori knowledge, 25
Absolute thresholds, 300
Abuse of authoritarian positions, 366–67
Accuracy of predictions, 175, 177–79
Agreement, method of, 132–35, 194. *See also* Naturalistic observation
Alternate hypotheses, 168, 263
American Journal of Nursing, 106
American Psychological Association. *See* APA
American Psychological Society (APS), 128, 354–56
American Psychologist, 353
Analysis of variance (ANOVA), 328–29
Animal Research Facilities Protection Act of 1989, 364
Animals
    captive versus field studies and, 124–25
    field work with, 120–24
    research with, 353, 363–65
Annual Review of Psychology, 352
ANOVA (analysis of variance), 328–29
Antecedent, historical, 202
APA (American Psychological Association), 234, 353–55, 359, 362, 364
    divisions of, 38, 39
    Publication Manual of, 330–40, 353

publications of. *See* specific journals
Standards for Educational and Psychological Testing of, 82
APA Monitor, 105, 353
APS (American Psychological Society), 128, 354–56
APS Newsletter, 354
APS Observer, 355, 356, 364
Aspartame, 210–11
Assembly for Scientific and Applied Psychology, 354
Assignment
    procedures for, and random selection, 220–21
    random, 202
    sequential, 222–23, 241
Asymmetric transfer, 312–13
Attributes, measurement of, 203
Attributional Style Questionnaire (ASQ), 77
Authority
    abuse of, 366–67
    appeal to, 13–16
    obedience to, 131

Behavior
    "after the fact" explanations of, 6–7
    cause and effect problems and, 33–34
    complexity of, 5–6
    constructs and, 73–76
    familiar sayings and, 11–12

idiographic orientation and, 29
naturalistic observation of, 120–35
necessary and sufficient conditions and, 34–36
nomothetic orientation and, 29
personal observation of, 7–10
reasoning by analogy and, 11–12
reliance on opinion of authorities and, 13–16
Beliefs, 24–25
Biserial correlations, 158
Block randomization, 223–24
"Burt affair," 365–66

Careers in Psychology, 353
Carryover effect, 312–13
Categorical syllogisms, 49–50, 52–53
Category(ies)
    developed, 95–96
    from higher orders of measurement, 96–97
    logically ordered, 96
    scales, 94–97
Causal relationships, 36
Cause and effect relationship, 32–33, 140, 180–83, 195
Children
    in latchkey situations, 203–4
    and violence on TV, 183–85

Author Index